Robert W. McChesney is the Gutgsell Endowed Professor in the Department of Communication at the University of Illinois at Urbana-Champaign. He is the author of some two dozen books on media and political economy, including *Digital Disconnect*, *Communication Revolution*, and the award-winning *Rich Media, Poor Democracy*; a co-author, with John Nichols, of *Tragedy and Farce*; a co-editor, with Ben Scott, of *Our Unfree Press*, and, with Victor Pickard, of *Will the Last Reporter Please Turn Out the Lights* (all published by The New Press). McChesney and Nichols are also the co-authors of the award-winning *Dollarocracy: How the Money and Media Election Complex Is Destroying America*. McChesney's work has been translated into thirty-one languages. He lives in Champaign, Illinois, and Madison, Wisconsin.

ALSO BY ROBERT W. MCCHESNEY

Dollarocracy (with John Nichols)

The Endless Crisis (with John Bellamy Foster)

The Death and Life of American Journalism (with John Nichols)

Our Media, Not Theirs (with John Nichols)

Communication Revolution

The Political Economy of Media

Tragedy and Farce (with John Nichols)

The Problem of the Media

Rich Media, Poor Democracy

The Global Media (with Edward S. Herman)

Corporate Media and the Threat to Democracy

Telecommunications, Mass Media, and Democracy

EDITED VOLUMES

Will the Last Reporter Please Turn Out the Lights (with Victor Pickard)

The Future of Media (with Russell Newman and Ben Scott)

Our Unfree Press (with Ben Scott)

Capitalism and the Information Age
(with Ellen Meiksins Wood and John Bellamy Foster)

Ruthless Criticism (with William Solomon)

DIGITAL DISCONNECT

HOW CAPITALISM IS TURNING THE INTERNET AGAINST DEMOCRACY

Robert W. McChesney

NEW YORK
LONDON

First published in the United States by The New Press, New York, 2013
This paperback edition published by The New Press, 2014
Distributed by Perseus Distribution

ISBN 978-1-62097-031-7 (paperback)

LIBRARY OF CONGRESS CATALOGING-IN-PUBLICATION DATA
McChesney, Robert Waterman, 1952–
Digital disconnect : how capitalism is turning the Internet against democracy /
Robert W. McChesney.
p. cm.
Includes bibliographical references and index.
ISBN 978-1-59558-867-8 (hardcover)
ISBN 978-1-59558-891-3 (e-book)
1. Internet—Political aspects. 2. Capitalism. 3. Democracy. I. Title.
HM851.M393 2013
302.23'1—dc23

2012035748

The New Press publishes books that promote and enrich public discussion and understanding of the issues vital to our democracy and to a more equitable world. These books are made possible by the enthusiasm of our readers; the support of a committed group of donors, large and small; the collaboration of our many partners in the independent media and the not-for-profit sector; booksellers, who often hand-sell New Press books; librarians; and above all by our authors.

www.thenewpress.com

Composition by dix!
This book was set in Electra

Printed in the United States of America

2 4 6 8 10 9 7 5 3 1

CONTENTS

LIST OF ILLUSTRATIONS

PREFACE

When I was young, in the late 1960s and early 1970s, I was attracted to the political left, like many of my generation. If I may generalize, this sizable cohort, though not an entire generation, was deeply concerned with economic and social inequality and corruption in American society. We were appalled by its brain-dead commercialism and rampant militarism. Many of us thought that existing capitalism really was a dying system that had no future: it needlessly permitted grotesque poverty and was antithetical to democratic values and practices. We were also decidedly optimistic; we thought we had the winds of history behind us. With the arrogance of youth, we thought we had figured it all out and there would be no turning back.

What does it say about our times that most contemporary observers now look at that period as the high point of American capitalism, when it was hitting on all cylinders? Many people today, and certainly most young people, would give anything to have an economy like American capitalism in 1972. Inequality was narrowing and barely existed by contemporary standards, good-paying jobs were plentiful, the infrastructure was the envy of the world, and governance was downright benign compared to modern corruption. There was a place for young people in the economy. There was hope, something that is awfully hard to muster nowadays.

That paradox prompts this book, which attempts to connect the digital revolution—arguably the most extraordinary and important development of the past half century—to the overriding crises of our times.

I began writing this book twenty years ago, in 1992. I was putting the finishing touches on my first book and was about to put it in the mail when I read a review of George Gilder's *Life After Television* in the *Financial Times*. Gilder argued that the Internet was in the process of eliminating broadcasting as we knew it. The Internet would also eliminate all traditional concerns about media monopoly and commercialism and terminate the need for policy making. Just let the market do its thing and witness the greatest democratic communication revolution ever. Because my first book dealt with the policy battles that led to the entrenchment of commercial broadcasting in the United States, I felt compelled to add an endnote concerning Gilder's argument. It was the first time I had seen the case for the Internet as a revolutionary medium put so concretely and provocatively. So I pasted a note to the end of the book moments before I sent it away.

Since that moment, the Internet has turned media and communication upside down and inside out. It has been a major factor in my research. I have also taught classes on the Internet, and have continually updated my notes. What I lecture on today has few elements of my 2005 lectures, which had little from 1999. Between 1995 and 2011, I wrote a half-dozen major journal articles or book chapters about the Internet, each based on considerable research. I always knew that I wanted to write a book on the subject, but the time never seemed right. In all but the last of the six pieces, I wrote with an acknowledgment that matters were changing so quickly and were so unpredictable that my analysis might soon be dated or need serious revision. Grasping the Internet was like trying to shoot a moving target in a windstorm.

The last piece was "The Internet's Unholy Marriage to Capitalism," *Monthly Review*, vol. 62, no. 10 (March 2011), which I co-authored with John Bellamy Foster. While writing this article it struck me that matters had crystallized enough online that it was possible to make sense of where the Internet was at and the range of options for where it is going. Certain digital institutions and practices were now sufficiently entrenched that they were not going anywhere soon. The feedback to the piece was positive. It was clear Foster and I had struck a nerve.

For that reason, I decided to write this book. I also had an overarching argument to provide the thread for the book. I believe the current understanding of the Internet and its potential that informs popular writing is deeply flawed. This is especially important because there are a series of crucial policy fights in the next decade that will determine where the Internet—and, by extension, our society—are going to go, possibly for generations.

My core argument is that most assessments of the Internet fail to ground it in political economy; they fail to understand the importance of capitalism in shaping and, for lack of a better term, domesticating the Internet. When capitalism is mentioned, it is usually as the "free market," which is taken as a benevolent given, almost a synonym for democracy. The conventional discussion of capitalism often degenerates into a bunch of clichés and is only loosely related to the capitalism that really exists.

Now that capitalism is in the midst of a global crisis with no apparent end and the state of democratic governance, in the United States at least, is appalling, it seems high time to take a more critical look at the relationship of the Internet to capitalism and both of them to democracy. Everywhere in the world, there is the sort of political upheaval that comes only a few times in a century, and everywhere capitalism is in the hot seat and the Internet is directly involved in the struggles. The Internet's development is intricately connected to the political economy's development. That is the point of this book.

The 2011 piece with Foster provides a framework for chapters 4 and 5, although those chapters are based on subsequent research. Those are the chapters that assess the way capitalism has shaped the Internet specifically. The discussion of political economy draws from research I have done with Foster over the past few years, which is developed explicitly in our 2012 book, *The Endless Crisis* (Monthly Review Press).

I concentrate almost exclusively upon the United States. It is my own country and the one I know best. I would be hesitant to write with much authority about any other nations or regions. At the same time, nearly all the issues I raise in this book are global and apply in varying degrees worldwide. Moreover, many of the most important policy battles over the Internet are international or transnational in character. The U.S. digital future will be determined in global fora as well as in Washington, D.C., and other domestic locations.

I could not have written this book without the assistance of a number of people. The aforementioned John Bellamy Foster, Inger Stole, Ben Scott, Dan Schiller, and Victor Pickard read the entire book and gave me detailed criticism. Jeff Cohen and Matt Rothschild also read the entire book and did superb editing. Patrick Barrett, Michael Perelman, Rodney Benson, Sascha Meinrath, James Losey, and Josh Stearns each read portions of the book. These friends gave the book a "hard" read and dispensed with niceties to really get after the book's weaknesses. I am a fortunate person to have such loyal and talented friends. I hope I can return the favor someday, though it will be hard to do so. I dread to think where this book would be without their criticism. Of course, I am responsible for what ended up in the book and for any errors.

R. Jamil Jonna is responsible for the tables and charts in the book. Most of these were compiled by Jamil specifically for the book. He worked tirelessly to make sure the charts were as close to perfect as possible.

John Nichols talked at length with me about the material in the book, and our conversations helped me crystallize my thinking. His influence can be felt throughout. Some of the material in chapter 6 on journalism is derived, and at times taken directly, from recent work I have done with John, including *The Death and Life of American Journalism* (Nation Books, 2010).

John Bellamy Foster has been my intellectual and political brother for forty years. He poured himself into this book as if he were the author. The only thing that exceeds his knowledge and his wisdom is his generosity.

Marc Favreau of The New Press was encouraging about this project from the first moment we discussed it. The press's staff is heroically professional. I want to thank Sarah Fan, Kianoosh Hashemzadeh, and Gary Stimeling in particular. Gary did a masterful copyediting job with fastidiousness, enthusiasm, intelligence, and humor. It is an honor to be a New Press author. I hope and trust it will be an honor I will have again in the future.

My colleagues in the Department of Communication at the University of Illinois at Urbana-Champaign are invariably supportive of my research—especially my chair, Dave Tewksbury—and for that I am grateful. The university's support for my research made this book possible.

The people at Free Press (Freepress.net)—Craig Aaron, Derek Turner, Tim Karr, Joe Torres, Yesenia "Jessy" Perez, Kimberly Longey, Matt Wood, and Josh Stearns—have been a wealth of information, analysis, and support. Doing this book made me appreciate far more than ever what an important organization Free Press is.

A number of other people helped me on specific points or in some other capacity. They include: Heather Brooke, Paul Buhle, Pedro Caban, Sundiata Cha-Jua, Vivek Chibber, Matt Crain, James Curran, Ryan Ellis, Natalie Fenton, Tom Ferguson, Des Freedman, James K. Galbraith, Peter Hart, Matthew Hindman, Amy Holland, Hannah Holleman, Janine Jackson, Paul Krugman, Rebecca MacKinnon, Fred Magdoff, John Mage, Greg Mitchell, Evgeny Morozov, John Naughton, Eric Newton, Molly Niesen, Rich Potter, Einar Scalloppsen, Travers Scott, Norman Stockwell, and Kristina Williams.

This book is for Lucy and Amy, and Inger, always and forever.

And it is for young people everywhere, especially in my beloved America. If there is any conclusion to be drawn from what follows, any takeaway from the digital revolution, it is the heightened importance—indeed the necessity—of the famous slogan from May 1968: Be realistic, demand the impossible!

Madison, Wisconsin
September 2012

DIGITAL DISCONNECT

1

What Is the Elephant in the Digital Room?

Any history of the past three decades will give prominent, if not preeminent, attention to the emergence of the Internet and the broader digital revolution. In the second decade of the twenty-first century, signs point to its being a globally defining feature of human civilization going forward, until it eventually becomes so natural, so much a part of the social central nervous system, as to defy recognition as something new or distinct to our being, like speech itself.

To some extent, the revolution can be chronicled in the sheer amount of information being generated and shared. In 1989, which seems like a century ago, Richard Saul Wurman wrote of "information anxiety" created by overload because there were a thousand books published every day worldwide and nearly ten thousand periodicals then being published in the United States.[1] Google's Eric Schmidt estimates that if one digitally recorded all extant human cultural artifacts and information created from the dawn of time until 2003, one would need 5 billion gigabytes of storage space. By 2010 people created that much data every two days.[2] By 2012 the amount of video being uploaded to YouTube had *doubled* since 2010, to the equivalent of 180,000 feature-length movies per week.[3] Put another way, in less than a week, YouTube generates more content than all the films and television programs Hollywood has produced in its entire history.

Another way to grasp the digital revolution is by the amount of time people immerse themselves in media. An extensive 2009 study found that most Americans, regardless of their age, spend *at least* eight and a half hours per day looking at a television, computer screen, or mobile phone screen, frequently using two or three screens simultaneously.[4] Another 2009 study, by the Global Information Industry Center, determined that the average

American consumes "information" for 11.4 hours per day, up from 7.4 hours in 1980.[5] A 2011 study of twenty thousand schoolchildren throughout Massachusetts determined that 20 percent of third graders had cell phones and over 90 percent were going online. Forty percent of fifth graders and nearly 85 percent of middle schoolers had cell phones, generally smartphones with Internet access.[6] The Internet has long since stopped being optional.

In the United States, Europe, and much of the rest of the world, one need not have a teenage child to understand that "social networks have become ubiquitous, necessary, and addictive."[7] To the students I teach, life without mobile Internet access is unthinkable. When I describe my college years in the early 1970s, they have trouble grasping how people managed to communicate, how anything could get done, how limited the options seemed to be, how life could even be led. It would be akin to my great-grandparents from 1860 Nova Scotia or eastern Kentucky returning to describe their youth to me when I was growing up in suburban Cleveland in the 1960s. "For society as a whole the Net has become the communication and information medium of choice," Nicholas Carr writes. "The scope of its use is unprecedented, even by the standards of the mass media of the twentieth century. The scope of its influence is equally broad."[8]

Consider this: in 1995 the Internet had 10 million users, still disproportionately at U.S. universities, and it was all the rage. By 2011 the Internet had 2 billion users and was growing by leaps and bounds. By 2020 another 3 *billion* people will be online. In Africa, mobile telephone penetration has gone from 2 percent in 2000 to 28 percent in 2009 to an expected 70 percent in 2013.[9] By 2020, according to IMS Research, there will be roughly 22 billion devices connected to the Internet and communicating online.[10] By 2012 three quarters of the world population already had access to a mobile phone.[11] "Mobile communication," a 2012 World Bank report stated, "has arguably had a bigger impact on humankind in a shorter period than any other invention in human history."[12]

This only begins to convey the extent of the changes being wrought. The Internet is the culmination of nearly two centuries of electronic developments in communication, from the telegraph, photography, telephony, and recording to cinema, radio, television, and finally satellites and computers. The Internet itself has already experienced several lifetimes in the course of two decades, from Usenet days to the World Wide Web and AOL and then broadband followed by Google and now wi-fi, iPads, smartphones, and social media. As Ben Scott puts it, we are in a "triple paradigm shift," wherein personal communication, mass media, and market information have been subsumed within the new order so that the distinctions are becoming passé.[13] The economy has adapted to the Internet and is now populated by digital industries, with colossal firms that mostly did not exist when most Americans were born. The Internet has seemingly colonized and transformed everything in its path.

Even more astonishing, this is just the beginning. Eventually, at least in theory, all humans could be connected to one another at speeds approaching the speed of light, able to send and receive all manner of communication with instant access to the entirety of human culture. Moreover, the "interface among human beings, objects, and the infosphere," Pamela Lund writes, "is becoming intuitive, less cumbersome."[14] We are entering terra incognita as machines change our basic understanding of what it means to be a human. Even now, the nature of such a world defies our comprehension.

Despite the difficult-to-imagine twists and turns in the future, the Internet has extensively crystallized. With the Internet enmeshed in the fabric of nearly every aspect of life, with giant firms attempting to dominate it (and our politics), and with a series of crucial policy issues emerging that will be central to its development, we seem to have reached a base camp of sorts. From the firmer ground of this base camp we can look back to where we came from and look ahead to where we might be going. We are in a position, in some respects for the first time, to make sense of the Internet experience and highlight the cutting-edge issues it poses for society. We are also in a position to better understand the decisions that society can make about what type of Internet we will have and, accordingly, what type of humans we will be and will not be in future generations.

The purpose of this book is to contribute to that conversation. Because of the enormity of the digital revolution, I make no pretense of providing a comprehensive or general theory. Instead the point is to ask a series of questions about the Internet and begin to offer answers. The first and most important question is this: in view of the Internet's magnitude, complexity, exponential growth, and unpredictable gyrations, how can we even begin to make sense of what is taking place?

We have mountains of scholarly examinations, in the finest American social science tradition, of discretely defined problems concerning the Internet, but they focus primarily on micro-issues, like how specific sets of people use digital communication for specific types of purposes. This research tends to studiously avoid making any larger claims about the broad role of the Internet in society. It tends to ignore institutional matters and questions of structure. It takes the world as it is, accepts it, and assesses it on those terms. This research is necessary and can have considerable value—I cite some of it herein—but it is not asking the central questions, so it is not set up to produce the answers we need.

For the big questions, the way to start is by reviewing the body of work produced by public intellectuals and scholars from a wide range of disciplines that has assessed the Internet over the past two decades, attempting to locate it in a broad historical perspective. Going back to the early 1990s—from George Gilder's *Life after Television* and Nicholas Negroponte's *Being Digital* to Clifford Stoll's *Silicon Snake Oil* and Lawrence Lessig's *Code and Other Laws of Cyberspace*, numerous writers have provided their assessment of the digital revolution. As one might expect, some of this material ages well, and some of it now seems ridiculous. The amount has increased, perhaps exponentially, in the past decade, becoming a veritable publishing genre. In view of how the Internet affects nearly every aspect of our lives, that is to be expected.

Even if the work does not always stand the test of time, and if some of it may seem superficial, it is of tremendous importance. These efforts by public intellectuals to make sense of the digital revolution, more than anything else, define how Americans—including scholars, concerned citizens, activists, journalists, and policy makers—view the Internet and lay out what many of the relevant issues are. It is a discussion I wish to join.

Robin Mansell has analyzed this Internet literature as falling into two broad camps, the "celebrants" and the "skeptics." Both camps continue to thrive, though the context and issues have changed. Some observers have been in both camps; there is no Berlin Wall dividing the two sides. It is a schema that captures two distinct frames of mind as much as two distinct sets of individuals, although there are some individuals who fall squarely, even defiantly, in one of the two camps.

I have been influenced by both celebrants and skeptics but believe each position is ultimately unsatisfactory and puts us on a dead-end street. I propose in this book a means to take the best of what each side has to offer and make it part of a far more serious discussion with real political implications. Beyond its self-evident importance, there is immense and revolutionary potential implicit in the Internet. My overriding concern has been and remains that this tremendous democratic potential—some of which has been realized—can be and has been undermined, leading to a world, at worst, where one could logically wish the computer had never been invented.

The Celebrants

Because the celebrants are the loudest and most publicized Internet observers, it is probably best to allow them the opening argument. In the illuminating 2012 book *Misunderstanding the Internet*, James Curran summarizes the first tidal wave of Internet celebrants: "In the 1990s," he writes,

> leading experts, politicians, public officials, business leaders and journalists predicted that the internet would transform the world. The internet would revolutionise, we were told, the organisation of business, and lead to a surge of prosperity. It would inaugurate a new era of cultural democracy in which the sovereign users—later dubbed "prosumers"—would call the shots, and old media leviathans would decay and die. It would rejuvenate democracy—in some versions by enabling direct e-government through popular referenda. All over the world, the weak and marginal would be empowered, leading to the fall of autocrats and the reordering of power relations. More generally, the global medium of the internet would shrink the universe, promote dialogue between nations, and foster global understanding. In brief, the internet would be an unstoppable force: like the invention of print and gunpowder, it would change society permanently and irrevocably.

And, of course, changing "the world beyond all recognition" permanently and irrevocably for *the better.* As Curran puts it, at the heart of most of these claims was what he terms "Internet-centrism, a belief that the internet is the alpha and omega of technologies, an agency that overrides all obstacles, and has the power to determine outcomes."[15] Or as Mansell puts it, "innovations in digital technologies, including the virtual spaces on the Internet, are accorded near-mystical qualities."[16]

The early celebrants generated a wave of resistance from the skeptics as few of their predictions materialized and as problems emerged—including the economic crash of 2000–2001 following the high-tech bubble—that seemed to provide daunting obstacles to reaching the digital promised land. Nevertheless, the continued expansion of the Internet, especially Google search, the blogosphere, wikis, broadband, smartphones, and social media, has rejuvenated the celebrants and has spawned a number of successful careers explaining the genius of cyberspace and the glorious world it is in the process of creating.

No one has celebrated and championed the revolutionary Internet in recent years more furiously than Clay Shirky, who is somewhat of a digital Johnny Appleseed. In his 2010 *Cognitive Surplus*, Shirky writes that with the new digital media, "the kind of participation we're seeing today, in a relative handful of examples, is going to spread everywhere and to become the backbone of assumptions about how our culture should work." The young generation "will just assume that media includes the possibilities of consuming, producing, and sharing side by side, and that those possibilities are open to everyone." Moreover, and this is where the revolution really kicks in, "the wiring of humanity lets us treat free time as a shared global resource, and lets us design new kinds of participation and sharing that take advantage of that resource." It is this "cognitive surplus" that holds the potential for previously unimaginable collaboration that will radically transform and improve our lives.[17] Henry Jenkins makes a similar argument, extolling the mushrooming "collective intelligence," when, because of the Internet, "we pool our resources and combine our skills."[18]

Physicist and quantum computing expert Michael Nielsen argues in 2012's *Reinventing Discovery* that the mass collaboration generated by the Internet is in the process of revolutionizing science by increasing scale and cognitive diversity. "Online tools are transforming the way scientists make discoveries," leading to a big shift in the relationship of science to society. Now countless citizens can also participate and the potential is endless and endlessly exciting. "Will we one day see," he asks, "Nobel Prizes won by huge collaborations dominated by amateurs?" Nielsen concedes this revolution in "how knowledge is constructed" faces some speed bumps—not the least of which comes from commercial interests' desire to patent everything—but the general trajectory is irreversible.[19]

In his 2011 *The Penguin and the Leviathan*, Yochai Benkler sees the Internet as driving a fundamental shift in human nature, one very much for the better:

> All around us we see people cooperating and working in collaboration, doing the right thing, behaving fairly, acting generously, caring about their group or team, and trying to behave like decent people who reciprocate kindness with kindness. Nowhere has this fact been more obvious than online, where Wikipedia and open-source software have been so successful. Tux, the Linux Penguin, is beginning to nibble away at the grim view of humanity that breathed life into Thomas Hobbes's Leviathan.[20]

These developments are so powerful, they have even brought a pronounced skeptic back toward the celebrant fold. Cass Sunstein once wrote of "information cocoons" and how the Internet would make it possible for people to avoid or ignore much of humanity, with dire implications for public life.[21] With his 2006 *Infotopia*, Sunstein turned—heralding "the development of cumulative knowledge" online, "producing an astonishing range of new goods and activities." With wikis, with "respect to the aggregation of information, we are in the first stages of a revolution."[22]

"Enabled by the Internet and social media," Simon Mainwaring writes in 2011's *We First*, "we are connecting with each other across geographic, cultural, and language barriers, reawakening our innate capacity for empathy and allowing ourselves to derive great satisfaction from social contributions as well as our self-interested endeavors." He continues: "We have entered an amazing and exciting era in human history. We are fast acquiring the knowledge and technology to meet the challenges of poverty, malnutrition, child mortality, and the myriad social ills that blight our planet."[23]

In his 2011 *Public Parts*, Jeff Jarvis captures the political implications of a wired society now typified by unprecedented "publicness," with the Internet as a supercharged public sphere. "Publicness is an emblem of epochal change. It is profoundly disruptive. Publicness threatens institutions whose power is invested in the control of information and audience." He continues:

> Publicness is a sign of our empowerment at their expense. Dictators and politicians, media moguls and marketers try to tell us what to think and say. But now, in a truly public society, they must listen to what we say, whether we're using Twitter to complain about a product or Facebook to organize a protest. If they are to prosper, these institutions must

> learn to deal with us at eye-level, with respect for us as individuals, and for the power we can wield as groups—as publics.[24]

In sum, the celebrants reaffirm one of the most important original arguments from the 1990s, that the Internet will be a force for democracy and good worldwide, ending monopolies of information and centralized control over communication. In 2009 Manuel Castells chronicled the many cases worldwide in which insurgent popular forces had successfully used the Internet to advance democratic politics.[25] Celebrants like Peter H. Diamandis and Steven Kotler cite the 2009 Swedish government report that concluded increasing access to digital communication in the developing world encouraged "economic development, poverty reduction and democratization—including freedom of speech, the free flow of information and the promotion of human rights."[26]

The 2011 revolutions in Tunisia and Egypt and protests worldwide are offered as clinching evidence, exhibits A and B through Z. "Social media and technology," Pamela Lund concludes, "give you more power than ever before to create the world you want."[27] Though some celebrants express concern that bureaucrats or monopolists might muck it up a bit, the general sense is that these genies are supercharged and cannot be put back in the bottle. "The tipping point is upon us. The unprecedented power of the emerging social media is helping people connect online and in the streets to push the entire world over the edge of change," veteran journalist and filmmaker Rory O'Connor notes. "Watch out, Big Media, Big Business, and Big Government—here come our friends, our followers, and our future!"[28] As Jarvis puts it, "Resistance is futile."[29] It is difficult to read these books and not look to the sky and thank one's lucky star for having been put on the planet at this unprecedented glorious moment in history.

The Skeptics

The skeptics directly counter some of what the celebrants say, but to a certain extent the two sides are talking past each other. Shaheed Nick Mohammed, in his 2012 *The (Dis)information Age*, takes dead aim at the notion that the Internet is spawning greater levels of knowledge, "the notion that these technologies and their popular modes of usage necessarily lead to a more informed public." He notes that the Internet works as much or more to promote ignorance as knowledge; hence survey research demonstrates little if any improvement in the knowledge levels of Americans between 1989 and 2007.[30] Mark Bauerlein develops this point, noting that study after study confirms that young people today constitute "the dumbest generation," shockingly ignorant of civics, history, geography, science, literature, the works. To Bauerlein, the emergence of digital media is the main culprit in this sudden transformation. "Dwelling in a world of puerile banter and coarse images," they "are actively cut off" from world realities like no other generation.[31]

Jaron Lanier, considered the father of virtual reality technology, also questioned the idea that the Internet is a knowledge factory in 2010's *You Are Not a Gadget*. In summarily dismissing Shirky, he notes:

> Some of my colleagues think a million, or perhaps a billion, fragmentary insults will eventually yield wisdom that surpasses that of any well-thought-out essay, so long as sophisticated secret algorithms recombine the fragments. I disagree. A trope from the early days of computer science comes to mind: garbage in, garbage out.

After describing Shirky's idea of cognitive surplus at length, Lanier responds, "So how many seconds of salvaged erstwhile television time would need to be harnessed to replicate the achievements of, say, Albert Einstein? It seems to me that even if we could network all the potential aliens in the galaxy—quadrillions of them, perhaps—and get each of them to contribute some seconds to a physics wiki, we would not replicate the achievements of even one mediocre physicist, much less a great one."[32]

In his 2011 book, *The Filter Bubble*, Eli Pariser argues that because of the way Google and social media have evolved, Internet users are increasingly and mostly unknowingly led into a personalized world that reinforces their known preferences. This "filter bubble" each of us resides in undermines the common ground needed for community and democratic politics; it also eliminates " 'meaning threats,' the confusing, unsettling occurrences that fuel our desire to understand and acquire new ideas." Pariser invokes research on scientific discovery showing that serendipity is necessary for creativity and that "blind discovery is a necessary condition for scientific revolution." The research demonstrates that the filter-bubble environment will likely make discovery less likely: "The Einsteins and Copernicuses and

Pasteurs of the world often have no idea what they are looking for. The biggest breakthroughs are sometimes the ones we least expect."[33]

Lanier extends the argument to all creativity on the Internet and observes that the most discernible effect of the Internet on artists has been to make it ever more difficult for them to support themselves, with dire consequences for art and culture. "Creative people—the new peasants—come to resemble animals converging on shrinking oases of old media in a depleted desert."[34]

Rebecca MacKinnon in her 2012 *Consent of the Networked* and Evgeny Morozov in his 2011 *The Net Delusion* each reject the idea that the Internet will necessarily lead to democratic political revolutions worldwide. They point out that the bad guys—who are in power—have the ability and resources to regulate, manipulate, and use digital communication just as much as, if not more than, those out of power. MacKinnon documents, for example, how the Chinese government is able to let the Internet provide what it needs for economic purposes while providing layers of regulation and subtle censorship that render it mostly impotent as a democratic organizing force.[35] She also documents how private corporations, as well as governments both authoritarian and democratic, participate in this shrinking of Internet freedom. Resistance to the Internet apparently is *not* futile.[36]

This realization leads to a familiar refrain among skeptics: that technology is as capable of being destructive as it is progressive. Virginia Eubanks, in her 2011 *Digital Dead End*, notes that "many of us in the United States have engaged in a massive, collective, consensual hallucination about the power of technology, particularly information technology (IT), to 'level the playing field,' create broad-based economic and social equality, and nurture transparency and accountability in democratic governance."[37] Even in the United States, skeptical scholars have chronicled how the Internet routinely generates bogus information, violates people's privacy and civil rights, and facilitates various forms of harassment.[38] Viktor Mayer-Schönberger writes about how people can never escape their pasts in the Internet era, and something very important to being human is being lost.[39]

This harks back to the first wave of skepticism by people like Clifford Stoll. In 1999's *High-Tech Heretic*, Stoll emphasized that the Internet isolated people, made them addicted, and probably created more unhappiness and dissatisfaction with life than anything else.[40] Sexuality is one area to which skeptics can point. The explosion in online pornography has created an "orgasmatron" effect, as an increasing number of people get their sexual satisfaction via the Internet.[41] The writer Russell Banks acknowledges this phenomenon in the title of his 2011 novel, *Lost Memory of Skin*, which "refers to the way real flesh has been supplanted by the virtual kind."[42]

Skeptics argue that the emergence of Facebook and other social media, ironically enough, correlates with a marked increase in loneliness. An AARP study showed that the rate of loneliness in Americans over forty-five has nearly doubled in just the last decade. "Within this world of instant and absolute communication," Stephen Marche writes, "we have never been more detached from one another, or lonelier." Scholars term this the Internet paradox. "Our omnipresent new technologies lure us toward increasingly superficial connections," Marche writes, "at exactly the same moment they make avoiding the mess of human interaction easier." And the evidence is in: "loneliness makes us miserable," leading to all sorts of health-related problems.[43] Psychologist Larry Rosen argues that Internet addiction and/or obsession contributes to a wide-range of mental health problems.[44]

Psychologist Sherry Turkle notes that people "seem increasingly drawn to technologies that provide the illusion of companionship without the demands of a relationship." She writes of the "flight from conversation," as people find it increasingly difficult to talk with each other. "Many people tell me they hope that as Siri, the digital assistant on Apple's iPhone, becomes more advanced, 'she' will be more and more like a best friend—one who will listen when others won't." Turkle concludes, "Even when they are with friends, partners, children, everyone is on their own devices."[45]

The idea that the Internet is transforming people unwittingly in ways that may be less than desirable is best developed in *The Shallows* by Nicholas Carr. While acknowledging all the benefits of the Internet, and his own addiction to it, Carr argues that the advantages "come at a price," specifically by reshaping the way our brains work. Carr draws from the recent surge in brain science research demonstrating that brains are "massively plastic" and can be changed dramatically by their environment and how they are used and not used. Carr argues that research demonstrates that with the rise of the Web and the decline in traditional reading, humans are losing their "linear thought process."[46] The Internet's "cacophony of stimuli short-circuits both conscious and unconscious thought, preventing our minds from thinking either deeply or creatively." People substitute skimming for reading, and "off-load" their memory to computers. The consequences are disastrous. Carr invokes William James, who declared that "the art of remembering is the art of thinking."[47]

The concerns resonate even with people like Arianna Huffington, one of the great champions of the Internet as the basis of new media and democratization. "All these new social tools can help us bear witness more powerfully," she acknowledged in a blistering 2012 attack on the inanity of the exuberant self-congratulation of social media, "or they can help us be distracted more obsessively."[48] Skeptics like Carr and Lanier fear deeply that the Internet is re-creating people in technology's image, flattening our intelligence and lessening our creativity. In short, they worry that we are losing what was once thought of as our humanity. It is a world where the past, warts and all, looks more attractive than the future.

What Elephant?

Reviewing these two sets of critiques, one feels like a person who has one foot in an ice bucket and the other in boiling water. There is no immediately apparent intellectually honest way to split the difference and say, "On balance, I feel fine." Although there is much to learn from both sides, both have their weaknesses. The celebrants mostly tap into an untethered love of some combination of technology, gadgetry, markets, utopianism, progress, and individualism that is quintessentially American and downright intoxicating; you get the benefits of a revolution without the messy politics. This may explain why it is so widely embraced in the mainstream culture and can be regarded as the dominant mode of thought about the Internet.

The skeptics provide a dash of realism and raise important deep-seated concerns, but like the original skeptics in ancient Greece, their values are unclear and they generally offer no credible alternative course. John Naughton characterizes the skeptics as contrarians who provide dissent to the dominant groupthink.[49] The skeptics provide plaintive wails, basically footnotes to the celebrants' defining narrative. In this sense, they are almost necessary to legitimize the celebrants and make the dominant view appear the result of extended debate. The skeptics can have the ironic effect of ending further examination, not encouraging it. And in this supporting role, some skeptics can be prone to playing the role of curmudgeon and bending the stick too far to make their point.

Both camps, with a few exceptions, have a single, deep, and often fatal flaw that severely compromises the value of their work. That flaw, simply put, is ignorance about really existing capitalism and an underappreciation of how capitalism dominates social life. Celebrants and skeptics lack a political economic context. The work tends to take capitalism for granted as part of the background scenery and elevate technology to ride roughshod over history.[50] Both camps miss the way capitalism defines our times and sets the terms for understanding not only the Internet, but most everything else of a social nature, including politics, in our society.

Political economy—an understanding of capitalism and its relationship to democracy—can provide a rudder as we make sense of the Internet. To the extent that both celebrants and skeptics consider capitalism, they often do so in almost mythical form. It is high time to recognize the elephant in the room.

Political economy should be the organizing principle for evaluating the digital revolution for numerous reasons. The ways capitalism works and does not work determine the role the Internet might play in society. The profit motive, commercialism, public relations, marketing, and advertising—all defining features of contemporary corporate capitalism—are foundational to any assessment of how the Internet has developed and is likely to develop. Any attempt to make sense of democracy divorced from its relationship to capitalism is dubious. Despite all of the routine assumptions equating capitalism—or its euphemism, free markets—with democracy, they remain distinct undertakings with very strong tensions that can boil over into direct conflict.

The most striking tension, the one that has been an issue between property systems and self-government from the beginning of the republic, indeed since classical Athens, has been the conflict between rich and poor caused by the inequality generated by the economy, which can undermine the political equality upon which democracy is premised. "If income, wealth, and economic position are also political resources, and if they are distributed unequally, then how can citizens be political equals," the Yale political scientist Robert Dahl asked. "And if citizens cannot be political equals, how is democracy to exist?"[51]

The now widely acknowledged massive increase in economic inequality in the United States over the past three decades poses an existential threat to the possibility of self-government and eventually to many of the freedoms most Americans take for granted. The scholarly research demonstrates that the poor and even middle class have virtually no influence over their elected representatives. Not so for the wealthy.[52] The ability of wealthy interests to play an outsized role in American elections is merely one manifestation of a long process. Any big-picture assessment of the Internet that disregards the very real and immediate threat of inequality to self-governance and freedom is going to be flawed from the get-go.[53]

Inequality promotes a thoroughgoing corruption of the governing process as wealthy special interests come to dominate, forcing the system to maintain and even increase their privileges further. As celebrants and skeptics alike acknowledge, there are several core policy issues that will influence or determine the course of digital communication. If the governing system is in the tank for special interests, it is going to directly affect the shape of the Internet. But without an understanding of capitalism's dynamics, most celebrants and skeptics have undermined their ability to provide much more than bland generalizations and hand-wringing.

To be clear, few if any of the Internet observers I have cited are apologists for existing capitalism; many envision a world in which the excesses and problems of capitalism are eliminated, if not capitalism itself. Many celebrants, in particular, extol the Internet because it is allowing for a more cooperative and humane economy and society, and considering the growth of *Wikipedia* and other cooperative efforts, the basis for the argument is not purely hypothetical.

But it is not historical or credible. Untethered from a historical or empirical understanding of capitalism, celebrants tend to have a decidedly utopian notion of political economy. "The entire system of free market capitalism, as it is practiced in the United States and in many Western nations," Simon Mainwaring writes,

> is leading us further and further down the wrong path, toward a world dominated by narrow self-interest, greed, corporatism, and insensitivity to the greater good of humanity and to the planet itself. Short-term thinking and the single-minded pursuit of profit are increasingly subverting an economic system that otherwise has the capacity to benefit everyone.

He concludes that because of social media, "we can transform the role of the private sector, including both corporations and consumers, to build a better world."[54]

The problem is that celebrants often believe digital technology has superpowers over political economy. "What I found," Yochai Benkler writes, "was that the Internet has allowed social, nonmarket behavior to move from the periphery of the industrial economy to the very core of the global, networked economy."[55] "We are talking about deep changes in the structure and modus operandi of the corporation and our economy," Don Tapscott and Anthony D. Williams write, "based on new competitive principles such as openness, peering, sharing, and acting globally." And the good news is, "smart companies are encouraging, rather than fighting, the heaving growth of online communities."[56] Jeff Jarvis sees corporations evolving into effectively democratic institutions—"radically public companies"—with control in the hands of employees, consumers, and other stakeholders.[57] Rachel Botsman and Roo Rogers characterize this epoch as a time "when we took a leap and re-created a sustainable system built to serve basic human needs—in particular, the needs for community, individual identity, recognition, and meaningful activity—rooted in age-old market principles and collaborative behaviors. Indeed, it will be referred to as a revolution, so to speak, when society, faced with grave challenges, started to make a seismic shift from an unfettered zeal for individual getting and spending toward a rediscovery of collective good."[58]

"Business is rising to the challenge" of social media, Mainwaring tells us. "Top-down hierarchical organizing principles rooted in fear are being superseded by organic, distributed, and free-flowing structures. Leading-edge companies are integrating values into their business strategies and embracing their role as enduring custodians of community and planetary well-being."[59]

Wow! Wouldn't all our lives be blissful, were this the case! We could head off to a beach with our laptops, iPods, Kindles, and smartphones—not to mention a daiquiri and a bag of potato chips—and live happily ever after. There is only one problem: there is precious little proof that capitalism as a system is moving in this direction. To be more precise, there is none. The system is in a fairly significant crisis, and there is not a scintilla of evidence that it is in the process of bursting through to a new digital Age of Aquarius. Certainly the Internet is changing capitalism in significant ways, and it may well assist those who wish to reform or replace it in the political arena; but it is not making capitalism become, in effect, for lack of a better term, a green, democratic socialist utopia. I argue in what follows that it cannot do so.

I think when celebrants incorporate political economy into their analysis, they do not become skeptics and certainly not cynics, but they do become much more aware of the importance of politics. They need not abandon their vision of digital promise; they simply have to accommodate that vision to the political economic world in which they actually live. Likewise, when the most militant skeptics engage with political economy, their powerlessness and defeatism can be trumped by a better appreciation for what human agency can accomplish via technology. In this way, the ice water and boiling water can be merged, producing a comfortable outcome.

Why Is Capitalism the Third Rail of Internet Scholarship?

What accounts for the persistent reluctance, even refusal, of Internet observers to engage in political economy and make a no-holds-barred assessment of really existing capitalism? To be accurate, it is not only Internet observers like Cass Sunstein who see markets and democracy as two sides of the free-society coin.[60] This is the case throughout the social sciences and the punditry, from liberal to conservative. It includes much of the respectable left, which sees its role as humanizing capitalism, not questioning it.

The core problem is that observers confuse the market, which exists to some degree in all modern societies, including Maoist China, with capitalism, or the market *system*, which has an overriding logic with powerful implications. The quasi-mythical competitive "free market" provides an overpowering metaphor for a free and efficient economy, but it has little to do with real-world capitalism. As Charles E. Lindblom put it, conventional wisdom continually "stumbles" and is incapable of grasping capitalism as a system, "because the market's dazzling benefits half blind it to the defects."[61] To be intentionally provocative, the "genius of the free market" to which all are expected to pay homage has as much to do with really existing capitalism as paeans to the workers' paradise did to really existing communism in the old Soviet Union.

What gives the notion of the "free market" such a sacred position in our society, such that even those who study capitalism as a whole feel obliged to swear fealty to the existing economic structure as the ante to admission?

Consider a superb economist like the University of Cambridge's Ha-Joon Chang—who is sharply critical of "the 'truths' peddled by free-market ideologues" that "are based on lazy assumptions and blinkered visions." Chang emphasizes his unwavering belief that capitalism is the best possible economic system before launching his devastating and often brilliant critique of a "global economy" that "lies in tatters."[62] Why is this loyalty oath necessary? What purpose does it serve?

Moreover, this is a problem limited to the analysis of contemporary capitalism. A scholar studying the Soviet Union would never discount the monopoly of economic and political power held by the Communist Party and the state and then focus on other matters. The political economy would be central to any credible analysis, or the scholar would be dismissed as a charlatan. The same is true of any academic study of any ancient civilization.

This gets to probably the best explanation: whenever scholars examine their own society, it is generally taboo to challenge the prerogatives and privileges of those who stand atop it and benefit from the status quo, even in political democracies. This may be nearly as true of the United States as it was of the old Soviet Union. And there is little doubt that in the United States, real power is with those who have the most money. Now of course the contemporary United States is not a police state and does not have gulags, but it has a variety of powerful material and cultural inducements to encourage a hands-off policy toward capitalism. A ritualized chant to the genius of the free market is a good place to start.

To some extent this internalization of capitalism can be explained by the dismal record of those one-party communist regimes, which were proclaimed by their supporters and their enemies as the only possible alternative to capitalism. If they were the only possible alternative, scholars committed to democracy understandably had no desire to open that proverbial door. Stick with capitalism, regardless of any faults, and thank your lucky stars! But that narrow "capitalism or communism" choice never made much sense, as the same political left that criticized capitalism was responsible for an outsized portion of the political liberties, voting rights, and social programs of advanced democracy. Likewise, those who benefited from and promoted capitalism tended to be either agnostic about these democratic advances or resistant to them. Moreover, much of the left opposed left-wing dictatorships and developed some of the strongest critiques of them on democratic grounds.

At any rate, because mainstream scholarship simply accepted capitalism as the same as democracy and the only possible economic system, scholarship that emphasized political economy was left to those who were by definition radicals, which increased its likelihood of being stigmatized as "ideological" and "unscientific." The rational play for a scholar who wished to change the system for the better in the here and now was to pledge allegiance to it, hoping to get taken seriously by those with power and thereby be effective. The motivation to take the loyalty oath was based on a realistic assessment of the political lay of the land as well as a desire to do good.

In stable times when the political economic system is working adequately, presupposing the status quo as a benevolent given would be an intellectual problem, but it would be understandable. However, when the political economy is in crisis, as it is in the United States and much of the world today, this presupposition moves from benign neglect to irresponsibility, from scholarship to propaganda. This is doubly true when one is discussing a social phenomenon of such sweeping importance as the Internet.

Internet scholars need not become anticapitalist. To the contrary, in my view it is a reasonable position to think that capitalism, and especially markets, have some, perhaps many, virtues that will be present in a good society. But I think it is a similarly reasonable position to think that a good society will have progressive taxation, widespread free trade unions, high-quality mass transit, universal free health care, guaranteed employment, and high-quality universal public education. Yet all of these points are debatable if not controversial among American scholars and pundits. There is no valid reason why American scholars should bow down to capitalism in general and corporate power specifically.

In the end, this is not a left-right issue. Some of the finest public intellectuals of the past century who ruthlessly criticized capitalism and its relationship to democracy were also advocates of capitalism as well as political conservatives. The most famous was Joseph Schumpeter, but the tradition lives on. Kevin Phillips wrote a series of thoughtful books in this vein over the past two-plus decades. In 2009 and 2010, renowned conservative Richard Posner wrote two stellar books precisely on the crisis of capitalism and the problem of self-government. Honest inquiry is not monopolized by any political ideology.[63] Indeed, only a handful of liberals, like John Kenneth Galbraith, have been up to the task of providing an unvarnished view of capitalism's deep flaws, without necessarily rejecting it.[64] If capitalism is as great as its defenders claim, it can survive and even prosper by being subjected to criticism, examination, and open debate. And if it cannot triumph after a round in the hot seat, this becomes a conversation that was long overdue.

Preview

In this book I will make the case that political economy holds a key to understanding the Internet. Political economy does not provide all the answers to all the questions, but it provides valuable and indispensable context and insight for the most important questions. The celebrants and skeptics alike—as well as the majority of Internet social scientists—have produced much of value as we ponder the fate of the Internet. Political economy does not obviate that work; it elevates and empowers it.

I am not the only person who has made this argument. Dan Schiller, Michael Perelman, James Curran, Vincent Mosco, Graham Murdock, and Luis Suarez-Villa, among others, have all contributed to the cause, but to date little of our work has had much success in penetrating the mainstream debate.[65] Through a grounding in political economy and capitalism, scholars and citizens can make much better sense of why the Internet is the way it is and what the real options are. Political economy is the necessary missing ingredient to take the debate from parlor chitchat to serious social critique.

Chapters 2 and 3 set up the explicit analysis of the Internet that comes in the subsequent chapters, although at numerous points I bring the Internet directly into the discussion. In chapter 2 I introduce elements of political economy. I debunk the mythological notion of free markets—the "catechism"—and provide what I believe is a more accurate understanding of capitalism. My aim is to introduce those elements necessary for the critique of the relationship of capitalism to political democracy that follows. In particular, I assess how capitalism affects inequality, concentrated economic power, and economic growth. Political democracy is threatened when the first two factors are large and growing and the third is small and stagnant.

I argue that the nation Americans generally regard as the epitome of what is possible for self-government, the present-day United States, is actually a rather weak democracy once one sees it in the light of capitalism. If scholars want to make big claims about how the digital revolution is fundamentally invigorating democracy, they must start from a stronger foundation. Moreover, capitalism is not a magical merry-go-round that continually improves people's material well-being. The evidence points in one direction: for the visible future, capitalism in the United States is marked by increasing stagnation, the likes of which have not been seen for eight decades, which translates into declining incomes, austerity, ever increasing inequality, and a lower quality of life. History suggests that this is not a political economy compatible with a high level of democracy. Something has to give.

In chapter 3, I introduce the subfield of the political economy of communication, or the PEC. If the standard free-market model is of only marginal analytical value for understanding bricks-and-mortar capitalism, it is useless for understanding how markets operate regarding information, commercial entertainment, and journalism. The same is true for the Internet. The discussion shows how, and with what effects, all these markets diverge at their very creation from the free-market norm. It pays particular attention to the relationship of communication to capitalism and to democracy. Students of PEC are centrally concerned with technology, advertising, and public relations, and most important, they have a singular devotion to studying communications policies and the policy-making process. The entire tradition is germane to making sense of the digital revolution and finding workable solutions to its problems.

In chapters 4 and 5, I turn to the relationship of really existing capitalism to the Internet. Much of the Internet literature, celebrant and skeptic alike, accepts that the Internet and capitalism have been and will be bound together in a natural and necessary relationship. I will provide an alternative view, one that elevates the many disharmonies between the two. Indeed, at several places in recent history, the tensions between the possibilities of the technology and the needs and desires of commercial interests have crescendoed, leading to ferocious policy debates.

In chapter 4, I review the Internet's 1990s transition from noncommercial oasis to capitalist hot spot. I assess how the "dinosaur" firms in telecommunications and media, which were generally considered to be facing extinction, have fared. In chapter 5, I examine the rise of a handful of gigantic monopolistic firms to dominance of the Internet alongside the telecommunication giants. I chronicle how advertising has flooded the Internet in a manner quite unlike the way it operated in "old media." It has led to a degree of surveillance of nearly all Americans far beyond anything remotely possible only a decade ago. The chapter concludes with an examination of the relationship between the Internet giants and the military and national security agencies of the U.S. government; it seems to be a marriage made in heaven, with dire implications for liberty and democracy.

In chapter 6, I examine the state of journalism in the digital age. Way back in the 1990s, the emerging digital era was often referred to as the information age. The assumption was that there would be a wealth of quality information readily available to citizens such that they could exert effective control over their lives and make politics appreciably more democratic. This was arguably the most powerful and attractive claim for the Internet. It is an issue of first-order importance, because a credible political information system is the foundation of effective self-governance. It is mandatory if there are going to be effective democratic solutions to the social problems of our times.

Journalism is the main way modern societies produce and disseminate political information, and it is of singular importance in democracies. Much has been made of how the Internet has destroyed the commercial news media business model. With no sense of irony, the same people argue that the Internet will combine with free markets to magically re-create a new, different, and superior news media system sometime in the future. I assess and reject those claims. Moreover, there is general naïveté about the quality of journalism, even in its "golden age." Drawing from the PEC tradition, I provide an alternative way to understand journalism and its importance to a free society. I provide the actual history of journalism in the United States and other democratic nations as the basis for my argument that journalism is a public good and if it is to thrive, it will require resources and institutions, and that will mean large public investments.

Throughout the book, in virtually every chapter, I touch on specific Internet and communication policies and debates. In the conclusion, chapter 7, I consider them as a whole and ask what it will take to get these core policies out of the hands of self-interested corporations (and the politicians they own) so the broader population might participate. For this central political question, I draw on my work as a scholar and as the co-founder of Free Press, the media reform group.

I then turn to the implied questions: can the Internet be a democratic force without making any changes in the broader political economy? What sort of revolution is this, anyway? I argue that the United States and the world are not merely in political economic turmoil, but that we are witnessing the emergence of broad social movements for democratic renewal, reform, and revolution. Even the United States, long regarded as a political laggard, is seeing a generational shift politically, although the bankruptcy and corruption of its political system is masking this phenomenon. At the center of political debate will be economics: what sort of economy can best promote democratic values and structures and self-governance while nurturing the environment? And at the center of *everything* will be the Internet. The democratization of the Internet is integrally related to the democratization of the political economy. They rise and fall together.

2

Does Capitalism Equal Democracy?

Capitalism is a society where individuals freely come together in the marketplace to buy and sell products, including their labor. It is a free exchange; there is no coercion. Markets guarantee that supply and demand determine prices, which accurately reflect their products' value. Businesses emerge to better serve market demand for products, and profits are the reward successful businesses get for meeting those demands. Competition for profits among businesses guarantees the most efficient production, ensures that the economy will generate products and services that people actually want, and encourages technological innovation; hence the standard of living will continually increase. Those who become rich deserve it because they have earned their fortune in the marketplace; those who are poor have incentive to produce more for the market so they too can become wealthy. Their economic fate is in their hands, because it is a free society.

Capitalism has always been incipient in humanity, but it was only with the democratic revolutions that government was put in a cage and freedom and entrepreneurship flowered. This is the only democratic way to run an economy; any other system invariably involves the government or some other force, no matter how well intended, telling people and businesses what they should do, rather than letting people and businesses decide for themselves in the market. A market is the closest thing to an infallible institution that humans have created or discovered, and only in unusual circumstances are there any justifications for interfering with it. Capitalism, unlike free markets, may not be flawless, but its problems can and must be addressed within the system. Digital technology can be an important factor in improving capitalism.[1]

That is pretty close to the official catechism of the United States. Some people may believe the government needs to play a larger role than others, to iron out problems and make capitalism work better for everyone, but virtually all agree that capitalism is the optimum regulator in most areas of the economy, that the profit system works, and that it is in everyone's interest to encourage something as close to that system as possible. It is the American way, and the doctrine underlies most of the thinking about the Internet.[2]

This catechism has elements that ring true, and hurricane-force ideological winds spread it, but it is mostly useless as a way to understand real-world capitalism. It is also striking that a nation as devoted to capitalism as the United States has such half-baked ideas about it.

The catechism not only presents a flawed understanding of really existing capitalism, but also makes it synonymous with democracy, which is charged mostly with protecting and promoting the functioning of the private economy. In the conventional wisdom, it is impossible to imagine a democratic society with political freedom that does not have a capitalist economy. This view does grave injustice to the actual democratic tradition, which is quite distinct from and often antagonistic to that of capitalism. This conventional wisdom obscures the nature of politics in the United States and prevents the expansion of democracy. The key to a better appreciation of the democratic dilemma in our times is taking understanding of capitalism beyond the catechism.

That is my goal in this chapter. I draw from the tradition of political economy to debunk the catechism and provide what I regard as a more accurate picture. I highlight a number of key themes in the political economic literature that touch on major issues with regard to the development of capitalism, especially as to its implications for democracy. In particular, capitalism tends to promote inequality, monopoly, hypercommercialism, and stagnation, all of which are corrosive to political democracy. The first three factors contribute to depoliticization, whereby those without means are alienated from the political process. I also address whether the emergence of the Internet mitigates (or will realistically mitigate) these antidemocratic factors generated by the capitalist economy. Obviously I am making broad generalizations that in a more detailed study would demand all sorts of elaboration and qualification, but for my purposes this level of abstraction is appropriate for the task, and similar to what other Internet observers provide.

As you may have already guessed, the short answer to the chapter title's question is no. The long answer follows.

Foundations of Capitalism

The relevant history begins roughly eight to ten thousand years ago with the invention of agriculture and the domestication of large mammals. Then, for the first time, humans were able to generate a regular surplus, producing more than was necessary to keep everyone alive. For the previous fifty to two hundred millennia humans had existed in nomadic hunting-gathering tribes. These were effectively classless societies, and only in rare instances were they able to generate a regular surplus. Now with agriculture, food output soared, people settled down, populations increased, and a small number of people were freed from daily toil, living off the labor of others.[3] From this elite sprang chieftains, religious leaders, soldiers, and eventually empires. Human population increased from 5 million to 50 million between 8000 and 3000 BCE, then increased to 100 million by 1000 BCE.[4]

Human societies subsequently assumed a variety of forms, but before modern capitalism, one thing was true of all but those that remained unacquainted with agriculture: the surplus tended to be small, controlled by a feudal or landed elite, and the vast majority of people toiled and lived at subsistence level. Elites battled over the existing surplus—anthropologists sometimes refer to this as an era of kleptocracy—often starting a war in which one kingdom conquered another and put the population in some form of servitude to produce surplus for the new rulers. Starting from a world that had been largely egalitarian for fifty thousand years, humanity established slavery and intense class divisions over a few thousand years as agriculture spread. No wonder Jared Diamond has written that for the quality of life of much of humanity, agriculture arguably was a significant step in the wrong direction.[5] Ironically, it was the price of civilization.

Markets existed in these precapitalist societies to varying degrees. They tended to be for lending or for merchants, and they were peripheral. The bulk of the surplus remained tied to agriculture. Surplus was generated to be consumed, and there was no particular incentive to increase its size. Capitalism emerged between 1500 and 1850 in a transition from feudalism through mercantilism to full-throttle industrial capitalism, marked by a radical transformation: surplus became something different from the amount society produced above the necessities of survival. Surplus now took the form of capital, money invested to generate profit. When it makes profit, it is then invested again for more profit, and on and on and on to infinity and beyond. Unlike any previous economic system, that is the entire point of the system, and its logic pretty much forces participants to comply. No longer a static entity based on gouging peasants for goods to be consumed by elites, the productive surplus in capitalism is seen as being saved and invested, not consumed, even when it *is* consumed by the wealthy.

The kicker is when peasants leave the countryside and come to cities where they need to sell their labor to survive. This was the beginning of industrial capitalism, first in England, then in Western Europe and the United States, and thereafter all over the planet. (Most of the planet was on the receiving end of imperialism, a defining part of capitalism's history.) Under capitalism the surplus is constantly growing, unlike all previous societies, and how the surplus is generated and distributed becomes the portfolio of political economy. The greatest empirical claim on behalf of capitalism is that it increases the surplus, wealth, and incomes dramatically, in a previously unimaginable manner. The debate over its merits emerges when one looks at the cost of generating growth in such a manner and at the way the surplus is allocated and deployed.

By all accounts, capitalism was a radical shift from precapitalist economies, even those with relatively developed markets in trade and credit, and it has proven to be a dynamic economic system that seemingly remakes the world nearly every generation. The United States is a very different nation in 2013 than it was in 1913 or 1813; the differences in, say, France or Japan or Afghanistan from 813 to 913 to 1013 were far smaller, even allowing for wars and plagues. Historians like Ellen Meiksins Wood make convincing arguments that capitalism was not inevitable where it first appeared—humanity in northwestern Europe might have found another route out of feudalism—and it needed a distinct set of historical circumstances to solidify.[6] But once capitalism became established, it followed a distinct logic that locked it in place and created powerful pressure for other countries to modernize or suffer being economically and militarily dominated by the few industrialized countries.

Under capitalism those at the top are capitalists. They earn their money not by selling their labor to others but by generating profits and income from their capital. Unlike feudalism or other precapitalist societies, their position is not secure; there are no guarantees that they will make profits, and if they fail, they face a fate some might consider worse than death: they have to work for someone else. Capitalists are in a Hobbesian war against all other capitalists to seize profits and protect their turf. This dynamic drives the system and defines it.

The percentage of people in any given economy who are capitalists—able to live securely and very comfortably off their capital without having to sell their labor power and with significant ownership of the means of production and finance—is quite small. Karl Marx and Friedrich Engels depicted nineteenth-century England as a society in which 10 percent of the population owned the means of production.[7] Today we talk about society being owned by the 1 percent, and even that figure is too high. In fact, as capitalist nations get wealthier, there is no marked increase in the percentage of the population that is capitalist, but there is often an increase in the standard of living for the workforce, including a well-paid upper-middle professional class.

Capitalism is not feudalism, so theoretically anyone can get rich, and anyone who's rich can become poor. Of course, those at the top generally stay there, and those below the top almost always remain there, but the system is the most fluid and dynamic class society in history, although that is a bit like saying someone is the best ice hockey player in Sri Lanka. As the *Wall Street Journal* noted in 2005, "A substantial body of research finds that [in the United States] at least 45 percent of parents' advantage in income is passed along to their children, and perhaps as much as 60 percent. . . . It's not only how much money your parents have that matters [in determining your class position]—even your great-great-grandfather's wealth might give you a noticeable edge today."[8]

This limited economic mobility provides some context to address one of the arguments of the Internet's celebrants, that social media and new technologies are generating a new type of warm and fuzzy capitalist and a new type of business organization. Gone are the bad old days of Ebenezer Scrooge, John D. Rockefeller, Mr. Potter, Exxon, Goldman Sachs, and Walmart. In their place are Richard Branson, Steve Jobs, and hacky-sack-playing CEOs at Google and Facebook. "The high-tech revolution created an entirely new breed of technophilanthropists who are using their fortunes to solve global, abundance-related problems," Peter Diamandis and Steven Kotler write.[9] These new emblems of capital are cool people, community minded and ecofriendly. Short-term profits and all the trappings of bad capitalism are soon to be in history's rearview mirror. The good guys are going to win.

Everything we know about capitalism suggests that this is poppycock. Bill

Gates and Warren Buffett may give billions to charity, just as the Ford Foundation has for decades donated huge sums to nonprofit and noncommercial endeavors. But the wealth-generating part of the operation—e.g., Microsoft in Gates's case—is hard at work trying to maximize profit by any means necessary. It lives in fear of Google, Facebook, Apple, and Amazon and knows any slipup may lead to an opening that will undermine its ability to generate maximum profits. This fear is as old as capitalism itself. There are today and have been for generations plenty of cool artists and bons vivants who have made or inherited vast fortunes. It seems they have not a care in the world, but you can be sure that somewhere their capital is being ruthlessly managed to maximize return. These rich kids give a cut of the action to someone else who manages the money so they can enjoy the privileges of being fabulously wealthy. But their capital is at war to grow or it faces death.

It is true that with the advent of the Internet many of the successful giants—Apple and Google come to mind—were begun by idealists who may have been uncertain whether they really wanted to be old-fashioned capitalists. The system in short order has whipped them into shape. Any qualms about privacy, commercialism, avoiding taxes, or paying low wages to Third World factory workers were quickly forgotten. It is not that the managers are particularly bad and greedy people—indeed their individual moral makeup is mostly irrelevant—but rather that the system sharply rewards some types of behavior and penalizes other types of behavior so that people either get with the program and internalize the necessary values or they fail. Capitalism has an unforgiving logic: if you play, you have to play to win. Successful capitalists and managers tend to internalize the necessary values and rarely even notice it as an issue. This is not an antibusiness critique; it has been made most forcefully by Milton Friedman as his main defense of the system.

There is little evidence that today's capitalists are more charitable or socially conscious than yesterday's. For every Richard Branson or Ted Turner, there are a bushel of billionaires like David and Charles Koch and even more cento-millionaires, quite content with the status quo and keen to maintain it for self-evident reasons. Turner has complained that too many of his fellow billionaires are a bunch of cheapskates when it comes to philanthropy. People with vast fortunes, including high-tech impresarios, tend to acquire considerable hubris. Recent research indicates that upper-class people are less likely to feel compassion toward others and much more likely to feel that their greed is justified by their station in life.[10] "Wealth gives rise to a me-first mentality," as the psychologist Dacher Keltner puts it, and the greed it rationalizes "undermines moral behavior."[11] PayPal's billionaire co-founder Peter Thiel, for example, gives significant amounts to nonprofit groups, but much of that money goes to push his pro-business right-wing political agenda.[12] And when corporations enter the public sphere, even high-tech ones, it is to advance their commercial interests directly or indirectly. Our society looks the way it does in the United States to no small extent because this is how they wish it to.

There may be good arguments that the Internet is altering capitalism and revitalizing democracy, but the existence of a new class of warm and fuzzy *netrepreneurs* is not one of them. In the first place, it is questionable enough that billionaires should have so much discretionary power over the planet's surplus; there is no great amount of evidence that now that they are so cool, they have become remarkably selfless and visionary and are providing better public services than democratic governments might have provided if they had access to the same resources.

Labor and Inequality

Although capitalism constantly turns the world upside down because of its dynamic nature, it also has a few characteristics that are true of it at *all* times, which emerge inexorably out of the pursuit of profit. At all times capitalists want to maximize their possible return and minimize the risk that they might lose their investment. There is no available evidence suggesting these factors will disappear in the digital age; in fact, as much as anything, they shape it and define it.

First, class and inequality are built into the system's DNA. It's not just that only a small percentage of the population, even in the wealthiest capitalist nations, can be capitalists. It's that the system of making profits is predicated upon paying labor as little as possible.[13] If some hippie capitalist decides to pay workers more than she has to, her competition will pounce on her—not to mention her shareholders and/or heirs—and she will likely become a hippie ex-capitalist. Economics shows that firms hire workers as long as they generate revenue greater than their cost. The lower the cost, the larger the profit. For self-evident reasons, the class basis of wealth is not loudly advertised by capitalism's champions.[14]

It is for this reason that under capitalism it is always a struggle to establish labor unions so workers can have leverage to claim a larger share of the pie. Likewise, it is for this reason that most capitalists not only oppose unions but use their political muscle to support politicians and laws that will make organizing unions more difficult, if not impossible.[15]

One of the great stories of the past generation in the United States, overlapping the digital revolution, has been the collapse of organized labor, the stagnation of wages, and the massive increase in economic inequality. During these times the rich have prospered and everyone else has floundered. Joseph Stiglitz states that the field of economics has provided no credible justification for anything remotely close to America's staggering inequality.[16] Pundits and politicians tell us that increasing inequality is a function of a new information economy that rewards skilled workers—a necessary consequence of an innovative and dynamic economy. Scholars like James Galbraith, as well as Jacob Hacker and Paul Pierson, systematically demolish this rationalization. Galbraith's research emphasizes the importance of the growth of the financial sector and debt, which created massive inequality over the past three decades.[17] This growth required government policies and support.[18] Hacker and Pierson establish that the skewing of American incomes was due primarily to major policy changes, especially pro-billionaire revisions in the tax code and business regulations, as well as the weakening of organized labor. These changes occurred primarily for one reason: business organized brilliantly and came to dominate Washington more thoroughly beginning in the late 1970s.[19]

As a result, it has been all but impossible to launch successful private-sector unions since then, even when evidence suggests workers would very much like union representation. Around 11 percent of American workers are in unions today—only 6 percent in the private sector—whereas 35 percent were union members in the 1950s.[20] (Public-sector unions have fared better because governments cannot engage in the same union-busting activities as corporations, though there has been a recent political drive to eliminate public-sector unions.[21]) This has directly enhanced inequality, as a 2011 study in the *American Sociological Review* demonstrated, because unions are a significant force for raising the wages not only of union workers, but of all workers in the labor market. Unions also tend to promote more wage equality among workers.[22] The result: in 1980, the wages of production and non-supervisory workers in manufacturing accounted for 35 percent of the value added, around where the percentage had been since the 1950s; by 2011, the workers' slice had been reduced to 17 percent.[23] The loss of private-sector unions has enhanced inequality indirectly, too, because unions are the one organized institution that has the resources and strength to be a political and policy adversary to corporations and the wealthy. It is labor that has led fights for public education, health care, public pensions, and the like. As Seymour Martin Lipset and Noah Meltz observed in a classic comparative study, "support for unions is associated with social democratic strength."[24] Some indication of the changing role (and power) of organized labor is shown in chart 1. Strikes barely exist any longer in the United States, at least compared to fifty years ago.

The downward pressure on wages was also encouraged by new trade policies that made it easier for U.S. firms to "offshore" manufacturing jobs to extremely low-wage locales. Between 1980 and 2007, the global labor force, according to the International Labor Organization (ILO), grew from 1.9 billion to 3.1 billion, a rise of 63 percent—with 73 percent of the labor force located in the developing world and 40 percent in China and India. Stephen

Chart 1. Number of work stoppages involving 1,000 or more workers

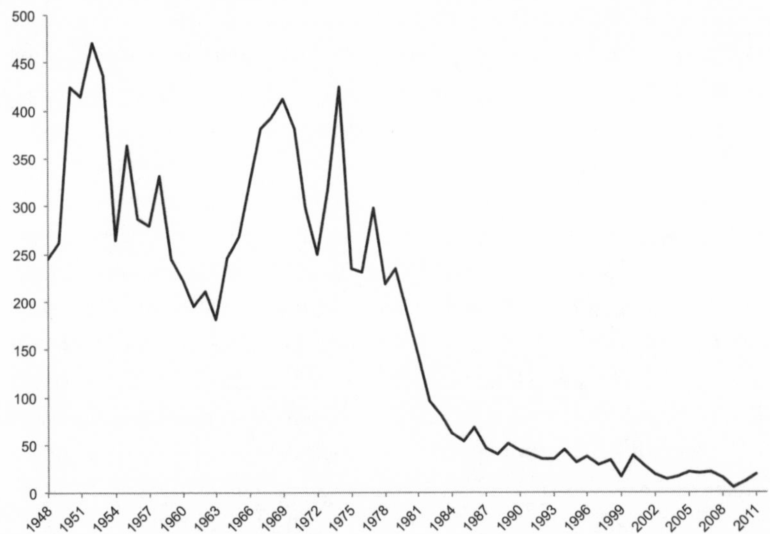

Source: U.S. Bureau of Labor Statistics, "No. of Work Stoppages Idling 1,000 Workers or More Beginning in Period" (WSU100), bls.gov.

Roach of Morgan Stanley dubbed this "global labor arbitrage," i.e., the system of economic rewards derived from exploiting the international wage hierarchy, which resulted in outsize returns for corporations and investors. Research demonstrates that the pool of untapped labor in the world is so enormous that the downward pressure on wages will almost certainly remain powerful for many more decades, even assuming high global growth rates for capitalism.[25]

Internet-related industries have led in offshoring manufacturing jobs, primarily to low-wage locales like China. In 2012 Apple, for example, is the largest U.S. corporation in market value, but employs, by generous count, only around sixty thousand people in the United States. When General Motors was the largest U.S. firm, it employed nearly ten times as many Americans. Instead, Apple indirectly employs some seven hundred thousand people outside the United States.[26] A 2012 *New York Times* in-depth report on working conditions in the factories that produce Apple products in China described conditions that made the age of Dickens look like a workers' paradise: seven-day workweeks, excessive overtime, crowded dorms, dangerous working conditions, no effective unions or protection, and a small fraction of the wages a worker in the West would expect for the same labor.[27] Apple defended itself by noting that all its competitors engage in the same practices, therefore no one can afford to leave China. So much for the idea that hippie capitalists can override the logic of the system. In addition, offshoring and the threat of more offshoring put tremendous downward pressure on wages and working conditions for jobs that remain in the United States (and other advanced countries).

What can only be termed a class struggle is clearly depicted by the results. From 1945 to 1975, as worker productivity increased in the United States, wages increased proportionately. Since the late 1970s, worker productivity has continued to increase, but almost all the newly produced income has gone into capital. Workers have received virtually none of it. As Robert Reich put it after crunching fresh government productivity data in March 2012, "The share of the gains going to everyone else in the form of wages and salaries has been shrinking. It's now the smallest since the government began keeping track in 1947."[28] A Wall Street executive noted that 93 percent of the increase in personal income in the United States in 2010—$288 billion—went to those with annual incomes over $350,000.[29] Charts 2, 3, and 4 give some sense of the growing inequality.

Chart 2. Income share of the bottom 99.5 percent

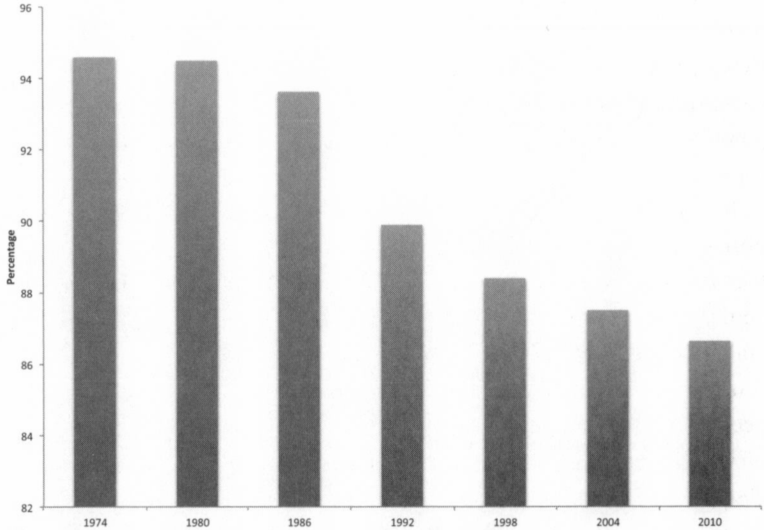

Source: Thomas Piketty and Emmanuel Saez, "Income and Wage Inequality in the United States 1913–2002," in Anthony B. Atkinson and Thomas Piketty, eds., *Top Incomes over the Twentieth Century: A Contrast Between Continental European and English-Speaking Countries* (New York: Oxford University Press, 2007), ch. 5. Excludes capital gains as negligible.

Business is well aware of how income and wealth have been radically reshaped over the past few decades. In a confidential 2006 memo, Citigroup said America had become a modern-day plutonomy, where "economic growth is powered by and largely consumed by the wealthy few." In 2011, a special report by *Advertising Age* concluded, "Mass affluence is over," saying that the top 10 percent of American households is where Madison Avenue needs to devote its attention because it now accounts for nearly half of all consumer spending, and a disproportionate share of that spending comes from the top 10 percent's upper reaches.[30] "Simply put," sums up *Advertising Age*'s David Hirschman, "a small plutocracy of wealthy elites drives a larger and larger share of total consumer spending and has outsize purchasing influence—particularly in categories such as technology, financial services, travel, automotive, apparel, and personal care."[31]

At the other end of the spectrum, the 2010 census determined that 48 percent of Americans are either poor or "low-income."[32] The much-vaunted youth market of eighteen- to thirty-four-year-olds—the 70 million

Chart 3. Income share of the top 1 percent

Source: Ibid. Includes capital gains.

Chart 4. Labor productivity and labor compensation

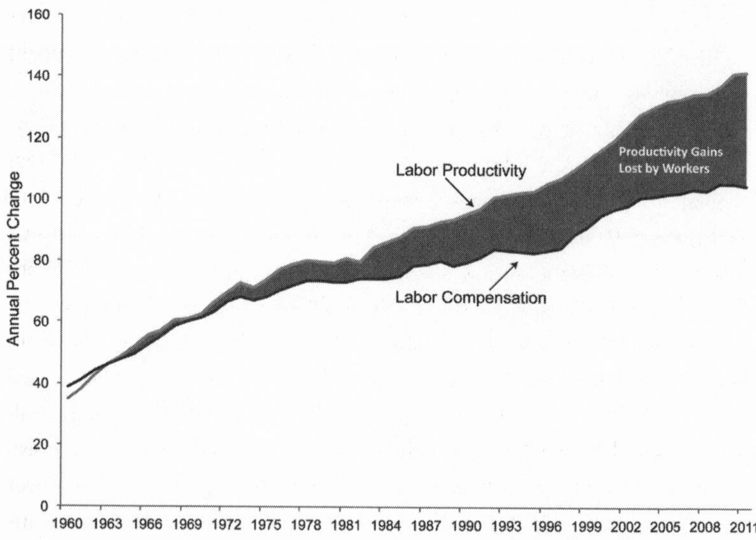

Source: U.S. Bureau of Labor Statistics, "Labor Productivity (Output Per Hour)" (PRS85006091) and "Real Hourly Compensation" (PRS85006151), Nonfarm Business, bls.gov.

emerging "middle-class" Americans who've long been the dream target for corporations—has lost much of its allure. By 2009 the percentage of eighteen- to twenty-four-year-olds with employment was 54 percent, the lowest since the government began keeping records in 1948. Households led by people under thirty-five had 68 percent less inflation-adjusted wealth in 2009 than such households in 1984. Marketers had long thought, one ad agency executive said in 2012, that "we're going to have a wonderful time selling to them," but that door has seemingly been "slammed in their face."[33]

Economists have long used the Gini index, or Gini coefficient, to measure inequality within nations, with a score of zero being perfect economic equality (everyone getting the same income) and a score of one being perfect economic inequality (one person getting all the income in the nation). In 2009, the most recent calculation available, the Gini coefficient for the United States was 0.47, a 20 percent rise in income disparity over the past forty years, according to the U.S. Census Bureau. Germany (0.27), Italy (0.32), Ireland (0.29), and Sweden (0.23) give some sense of where European nations are in calculations determined between 2005 and 2009. America has become a global outlier in terms of economic equality among the wealthy nations. "We now have a Gini index similar to the Philippines and Mexico—you'd never have imagined that," says Phyllis Jackson, Procter & Gamble's vice president of consumer market knowledge for North America. "I don't think we've typically thought about America as a country with big income gaps to this extent."[34]

American economic inequality is the direst threat to effective democracy, which is premised upon political equality. Timothy Noah calls it the Great Divergence in his illuminating 2012 book of that title. He concludes from his research that there is consensus among most experts about the existence of economic inequality and, increasingly, its causes.[35] It is difficult to reconcile such extreme inequality with anything but a superficial democracy.

Ironically the one issue that best demonstrates that may be inequality itself. Michael Norton of Harvard Business School and Dan Ariely of Duke created a survey to determine what Americans considered a desirable level of inequality in society. They looked at wealth, rather than income; wealth refers basically to one's capital and savings, so it is the measure of real economic power in a capitalist society. When Ariely and Norton asked thousands of Americans to give their ideal wealth distribution, they described, on average, a nation where the wealth distribution looks not like that of the United States but of

Sweden, only more so—the wealthiest quintile would control just 32 percent of the wealth, the poorest just over 10 percent. In the present-day United States, the top quintile has 84 percent of the wealth, and the poorest has 0.1 percent of the wealth. Even 90 percent of the respondents who voted for George W. Bush in 2004 opted for Swedish wealth distribution. "People dramatically underestimated the extent of wealth inequality in the U.S.," says Ariely. "And they wanted it to be even more equal" than Sweden's.[36] Yet despite these values, wealth and income inequality is effectively off the table in American politics—an absolute nonstarter—except for periodic rhetorical flourishes by Democrats when elections draw near. What proposals do get a hearing, like the so-called Buffett rule in 2012—which would have applied a minimum income tax of 30 percent to people making more than a million dollars a year—would have been dream legislation for the U.S. Chamber of Commerce in 1965, when the minimum rate for the rich was about 67 percent. Such has been the corruption of American politics since then.

But the problem of economic inequality goes even wider and deeper. A mountain of research has been generated in the past decade on the consequences of growing inequality for the health of American society—or any nation, for that matter. Richard Wilkinson and Kate Pickett's *The Spirit Level* has earned justifiable acclaim for its documentation of how increasing inequality—far more than simply the actual amount of wealth in the elites of society—damages almost every measure of well-being, from life expectancy and mental health to violence and human happiness. This is largely true for the very rich, ironically enough, as well as the poor. People and cultures thrive in more egalitarian societies.[37] The Internet may not be responsible for growing inequality, except to the extent that it may be connected to the financialization of the economy, but the digital revolution has done nothing notable to ameliorate the situation.

Monopoly

The second destructive factor built into capitalism is its tendency toward monopoly. On the one hand, successful firms get larger and larger over time, so it requires much more capital for newcomers to enter their markets and attempt to seize some of their profits. Larger firms have distinct advantages of scale over smaller firms, and they come to rule the roost. By the twentieth century, the local owner-operator of capitalist lore, common to the nineteenth century, was replaced by the large national and multinational corporation as the dominant unit in the economy. The owners buy and sell shares in the stock market, while the management is professional and distinct, overseeing a vast bureaucracy and competing in several different product categories. When new industries emerge, as with the Internet, they often go through a manic start-up phase until crystallizing in this manner.

But it is much more than that, as observers beginning with Adam Smith understood. A capitalist's chance of success is greatly enhanced if she faces less competition. The notion of competitive free markets in the catechism—wherein a firm will lose any superprofits it earns because new competitors will enter the field and increase output, leading to lower prices and lower profits—may be great for economics textbooks and for consumers, but it is a nightmare for any sane capitalist. The dream scenario is to go to market and discover you are the only one selling a product for which there is demand. Then you can set the price, not have it determined for you. This greatly reduces risk and increases profits. That is why so many of the great fortunes have been built on a foundation of near monopoly. "The real key to success" in a capitalist economy, Joseph Stiglitz writes, "is to make sure there won't ever be competition for a long enough time that one can make a monopoly killing in the meanwhile."[38]

Pure monopoly, in which one firm sells 100 percent of a product and can scare away or crush any prospective competition, almost never exists. Instead, capitalism tends to evolve into what is called monopolistic competition, or oligopoly. These are markets where a handful of firms dominate output or sales in the industry and have such market power that they can set the price at which their product sells. The key to an oligopoly is that it is very difficult for newcomers to enter the market, no matter how profitable it may be, because of the size and power of the existing players. Under oligopoly there is strong disincentive to engage in price warfare to expand one's market share, because all the main players are large enough to survive a price war, and all it would do is shrink the size of the industry revenue pie that the firms are fighting over. Indeed, the price in an oligopolistic industry will tend to gravitate toward what it would be in a pure monopoly, so the contenders are fighting for slices of the largest possible revenue pie.[39]

At first blush, this is a pretty accurate picture of the commanding heights of the U.S. economy in the twentieth and twenty-first centuries. In few areas

Chart 5. Number and percentage of concentrated U.S. manufacturing industries

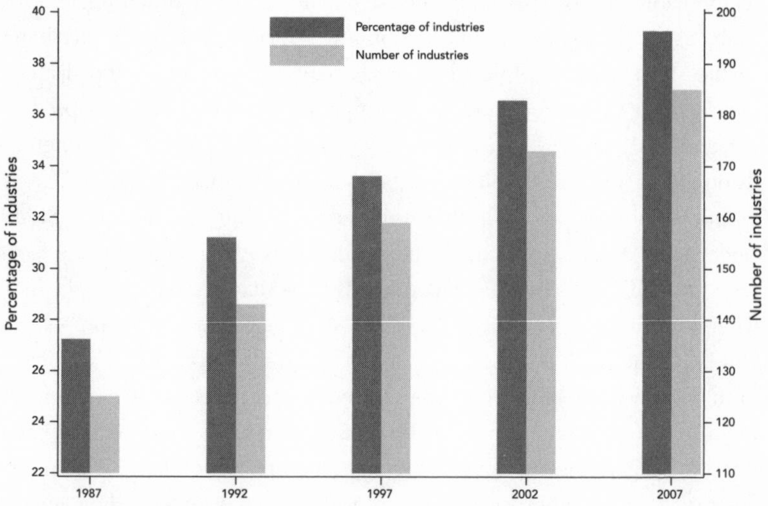

Source: Census of Manufactures, "Shipments Share of 4, 8, 20, & 50 Largest Companies in each SIC: 1992–1997," and Economic Census of 1997, 2002, and 2007, American FactFinder (U.S. Census Bureau), census.gov (accessed February 2011).

have the claims about the Internet been greater than that it would empower consumers, break down barriers to entry, and create much greater market competition in traditional industries and online. Although some industries have been turned upside down, as a rule the digital era has seen a continued, arguably accelerating, rate of monopoly in the economy. One measure for this is demonstrated by industry concentration ratios, meaning the percentage of sales controlled by a small number of firms.[40] Chart 5 shows that both the number and percent of manufacturing industries (for example, automobile production) that have a four-firm concentration ratio of 50 percent or more have risen dramatically since the mid-1980s, the digital era. More and more industries in the manufacturing sector of the economy are tight oligopolistic or quasi-monopolistic markets characterized by a substantial degree of monopoly. And if anything, the trend is accelerating.

Concentration is also proceeding apace in most other sectors of the economy, such as retail trade, transportation, information, and finance. In 1995 the assets of the six largest bank holding companies (JP Morgan Chase, Bank of America, Citigroup, Wells Fargo, Goldman Sachs, and Morgan

Stanley—some of which had somewhat different names at that time) had assets equal to 17 percent of U.S. gross domestic product (GDP). By the end of 2006, this total had risen to 55 percent, and by the third quarter of 2010, to 64 percent.[41] In retail, the top fifty firms went from 22.4 percent of all retail sales in 1992 to 33.3 percent in 2007.

The inexorable emergence of monopoly undermines the case for the genius of free markets and has been a highly sensitive issue in economic circles for nearly a century. By 2012 Stiglitz wrote how "some of the most important innovations in business in the last three decades have centered not on making the economy more efficient but on how better to ensure monopoly power."[42] Friedrich Hayek once insisted, "The price system will fulfill [its] function only if competition prevails, that is, if the individual producer has to adapt himself to price changes and cannot control them."[43] Warren Buffett provided a real-world description of the economy in 2011: "The single most important decision in evaluating a business is pricing power. If you've got the power to raise prices without losing business to a competitor, you've got a very good business. And if you have to have a prayer session before raising the price by 10 percent, then you've got a terrible business." For Buffett it is all about monopoly power, not management. "If you own the only newspaper in town, up until the last five years or so, you had pricing power and you didn't have to go to the office" and worry about management issues.[44]

The consequences for mainstream economics are disastrous if the price mechanism and market competition are removed as the main regulatory mechanisms. The economy will be inefficient and unfair. In general, economists have punted on this issue rather than face up to the reality of Buffett's world and the implications of Hayek's concern.[45]

As important and revealing as concentration ratios for industries are, they are of more limited value today than in the past in getting at the full range of monopoly power of the giant corporation. This is because the typical giant firm operates not in just one industry but is a conglomerate, operating in numerous industries. Hence the best way to get an overall picture of the trend toward economic concentration that takes into account the multi-industry nature of the typical giant firm is to look at some measure of aggregate concentration, e.g., the economic status of the two hundred largest firms compared to all firms in the economy.[46]

To put the top two hundred firms in perspective, in 2000 there were 5.5 million corporations, 2 million partnerships, 17.7 million nonfarm sole proprietorships, and 1.8 million farm sole proprietorships in the U.S. economy.[47] Chart 6 shows the revenue of the top two hundred U.S. corporations as a percentage of total business revenue in the economy as a whole since 1950. The revenue of the top two hundred corporations has risen substantially, from around 21 percent of total business revenue in 1950 to about 32 percent in 2009.[48]

The prevalence of oligopoly—or in more popular parlance, corporate power—undermines the case for the marriage of capitalism to democracy. The core argument, made beautifully by Milton Friedman, is that the genius of capitalism for democracy is that it is the one system that separates control over the economy from control over the government. That diffusion of

Chart 6. Revenue of the top 200 U.S. corporations as a percent of total business revenue

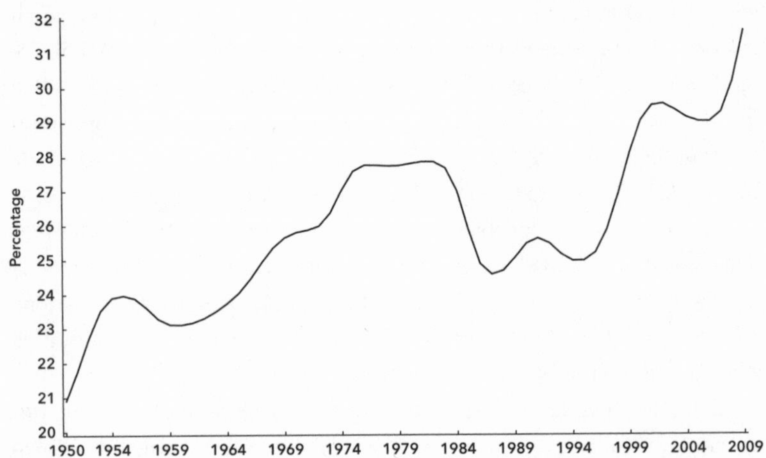

Source: Data for the top two hundred corporations were extracted from McGraw-Hill's subsidiary Standard & Poor's division Capital IQ's Compustat.com summary "Fundamentals Annual" (accessed Feb. 15, 2011). Total revenue was taken from "Statistics of Income" (SOI) "Corporate Income Tax Returns" Division, Internal Revenue Service, Washington, D.C., 1950–2008. "Total revenues" (REVT in Compustat) and the line item "total receipts" (from the SOI) are equivalent. Since the Compustat North America data set contains only conglomerate-level data for foreign companies operating in the United States; all foreign companies (i.e., those not incorporated in the United States) were dropped from the sample. The data points, which were smoothed using a robust linear smoother, approximate five-year moving averages. Compustat data were extracted via Wharton Research Data Services (WRDS). WRDS was used in preparing this article. This service and the data available thereon constitute valuable intellectual property and trade secrets of WRDS and/or its third-party suppliers.

power creates the space that protects individual freedom, he argued. Even if the government does not like someone, as Friedman pointed out, it cannot prevent that person from gainful employment in the private sector. The crucial element in his analysis is that the private sector is competitive, open, and fluid, and no entrenched monopolies exist to distort the system.[49]

With the rise of giant monopolistic corporations, that separation is compromised. Governance tends to become corrupt; successful politicians and policies are determined by powerful corporate interests. The state and capital effectively merge, with the state geared to the interests of wealth. There are political debates, but the most important ones are when different corporations or sectors are battling each other. During the twentieth century, political scientists posited that labor unions and other organizations representing nonwealthy people could provide a structural balance to offset corporate power and make the governing system responsive to popular concerns. This idea was sometimes called pluralism and probably is a good explanation for many of the progressive victories from the 1930s to the 1970s. Today, with the demise of labor and the ever increasing size and power of corporations, that theory explains why the notion of pluralistic democracy is in such a deep crisis. In 2012, *The Economist* forecast a wave of corporate mergers and increasing consolidation of monopoly market power.[50] There are few reasons to think that is a positive development for democratic governance.[51]

The ideology of any social order eventually accepts and trumpets the existing system; the prevalence of monopoly is no longer possible to ignore, so it is celebrated by the troubadours of the status quo. "The future of the country," David Brooks concluded in 2012, "will probably be determined by how well Americans can succeed at being monopolists."[52] "Don't you see?" former U.S. Treasury secretary Robert Rubin answered when asked if the big banks, the most controversial of modern megacorporations, should be broken up. "Too big to fail isn't a problem with the system. It *is* the system."[53]

Advertising

There is one important development for media, communication, and the Internet that is triggered to a significant extent by the growth of monopoly in the economy: advertising. Modern commercial advertising is not a function of competitive markets, profitable ones into which new businesses can easily enter, increase output, lower prices, and help the consumer live happily ever after. Such markets tend to have relatively little advertising, because producers can sell all that they produce at the market price, over which they have little or no control. This is why the largely local and competitive U.S. economy prior to the late nineteenth century had little advertising by the standards of the past one hundred years.

Modern persuasion advertising blossomed as a function of less competitive markets where a handful of firms dominate output or sales. Advertising emerges front and center as a major way to increase or protect market share without engaging in destructive profit-damaging price competition. It represents a dramatic change in how capitalism operates, taking it that much further from the catechism. As Paul A. Baran and Paul M. Sweezy put it in 1964:

> The purpose of [the corporate] sales effort is no longer merely to promote the sales of commodities the function of which is to satisfy human needs prevailing at any given time. The purpose of his sales effort is to *create* wants which will generate the demand for [the] product. The monopolistic producer is thus not only in a position to manipulate the price and the volume of his output, he can also adapt the physical properties of his product to the requirements. . . . The sales effort, in other words, develops from an auxiliary of the production process into an integral, and indeed decisively important part of it. What can be sold is no longer what is produced; on the contrary, what is produced is what it is possible to sell. In such a setting the molding of human wants and the designing of products to satisfy them cease to be a result of the objectified forces of the market and become the outcome of a conscious manipulative effort on the part of a relatively small number of monopolistic corporations.[54]

Advertising became a fully mature industry by the 1920s, accounting for around 2 percent of GDP, at which level it remains to this day.

Advertising, due to its content, has always been a controversial undertaking, one that can make the marketplace seem more absurd than efficient. Under conditions of oligopoly, firms tend to produce similar products and sell them at similar prices. Therefore advertising that emphasizes price and product information can be ineffectual, if not counterproductive. (That type of price and product information advertising can be found in more competitive retail markets, or in classified advertising.) An ad campaign based on *"Hey, buy our soft drink because it costs the same and tastes the same as our competitor"* probably won't lead to awards, a promotion, or a long career. Firms exert inordinate effort to create brands that are perceived as different from competitors', and advertising is crucial in creating the aura surrounding these brands. To be fair, there are occasionally meaningful differences between products, and ad agencies generally welcome the opportunity to promote such a product.

But that is rarely the case. The legendary adman Rosser Reeves was reputed to have repeated the same presentation for years for newly hired copywriters at his Ted Bates advertising agency in the 1960s. He would hold up two identical shiny silver dollars, one in each hand, and would tell his audience in effect: "Never forget that your job is very simple. It is to make people think the silver dollar in my left hand is much more desirable than the silver dollar in my right hand."[55] Reeves was an advocate of such deceptive advertising stratagems as presenting as new and unique what was actually old and ordinary in a given product. Moreover, much of the product differentiation built into a brand is superficial and not truly related to usefulness, but it provides grist for an ad campaign. "Since most brands are basically not that different," William Greider writes, "advertising's fantasies provide as good a reason as any to choose one brand over another."[56]

Take a look at endless beer ads, soap ads, oil company ads, or ads for countless other products to see the inanity of much advertising. Pabst beer, for example, simultaneously markets itself as a downscale working-class brew, an ironically cool brew for urban hipsters, and as a champagne substitute and signifier of conspicuous consumption in China. "The same beverage means very different things to different people," as Eli Pariser puts it.[57] Likewise, advertising tends to be expert at playing upon emotions and using fear as a motivational weapon. Television advertising, in particular, uses cultural cues to communicate fairly complex messages in fewer than thirty seconds, exploiting stereotypes and cultural references to pack a lot of meaning into a few fleeting moments. It uses visuals in such a way that if one only reads the text or listens to the words, one will miss the heart of what is being communicated.[58] As more than one critic has emphasized, a recurring theme in much advertising (especially aimed at women) is that you have a problem and the product is the solution.[59] This is not a "radical" critique of advertising per se;

it grows from mainstream microeconomic theory. It is "obvious" that "many ads provide essentially no information," University of Chicago economists Gary S. Becker and Kevin M. Murphy wrote in 1993. "Rather, they entertain, create favorable associations between sexual allure and the products advertised, instill discomfort in people not consuming products popular with athletes, beauties, and other elites, and in other ways induce people to want the products."[60]

The nature of oligopolistic advertising leads to two paradoxes. First, the more alike the products are and the more similar the prices, the more the firms must advertise to convince people they are different. Becker and Murphy note the irony that many of the most heavily advertised products "surely usually convey very little information."[61] The second paradox of advertising is that the more firms advertise to distinguish themselves from their competition, the more commercial clutter there is in the media and culture. As a result, firms are forced to increase their advertising even more to get through the clutter and reach the public.[62] If there is anything close to an iron law in advertising, it is this: repetition works; the more exposure to a brand's advertising the better. This follows from the conclusion drawn from social science research: people are more inclined to believe what they have heard before.[63] It doesn't guarantee success, but it increases the odds considerably.

Put all together, these forces spread advertising constantly into every available nook, cranny, and crevice of society in order to sell their products. Advertising is the advance army of capitalism.[64] Although there is considerable debate about how effective any particular ad or ad campaign may be, there is no doubt that advertising as a whole is a dominant cultural force in the United States.[65] Advertising is, as Mark Crispin Miller once put it, the most sophisticated system of applied propaganda in the world.[66]

Traditional economics, enmeshed in its free-market models, has paid little attention to advertising and has traditionally regarded it as wasteful, a sign of monopoly. In 1960 the Swiss free-market apostle Wilhelm Ropke launched a famous attack on "soulless" advertising that was laying waste to the genius of capitalism.[67] The best defense of modern advertising is that it stimulates consumer demand and keeps the corporate capitalist economy functioning.[68] If one does not regard corporate capitalism as mandatory regardless of the costs, the case for advertising weakens.

One of the initial claims for the Internet, which will be discussed in chapters 4 and 5, was that it would eliminate advertising by providing easy access to legitimate consumer information that would make commercial propaganda look ridiculous. It was one of the loudest claims about how the Internet would radically improve our lives and culture, at least for those not enthralled by commercialism. Correspondingly, the problem of how to make the Internet advertising friendly bewildered and obsessed Madison Avenue for much of the 1990s. In some respects, this conflict was a test of what values would drive the course of the Internet.

I will not keep you in suspense. Advertising won, and the hypercommercialization of our culture proceeds swiftly. Corporations cynically use "cause-related marketing," linking their brands to some socially worthy project, to "tug at consumer heartstrings."[69] Inger Stole notes the irony that the same corporations that have battled successfully to denude the public sector of the resources it needs to tackle social problems turn around and offer to address the same problems as part of marketing campaigns, with dubious outcomes that do only one thing for certain: commercialize public life.[70] Michael J. Sandel documents the spread of commercialism and argues that arresting and reversing its growth is a fundamental need if the United States is to have a credible civic culture and a functional democracy.[71]

Advertising devotes considerable resources to linking brands to people's emotions and deep wiring. Its function, writes Yale's Robert E. Lane, "is to increase people's dissatisfaction with any current state of affairs."[72] The key is to gain the "irrational edge."[73] "We are encouraged to act on impulse and fantasy instead of reason," the economist Jeffrey Sachs wrote in 2011 in a discussion of advertising's power.

> We need to understand that the difficulty of maintaining our balance in a media-rich economy is even greater than we might have supposed even ten or fifteen years ago. The advances in modern neurobiology and psychology have revealed a level of human vulnerability that would have surprised even Freud and Bernays. . . . Within one generation, Americans have displayed a shocking array of addictive behaviors (smoking, overeating, TV watching, gambling, shopping, borrowing, and much more) and loss of self-control. These unhealthy behaviors surely have reached a macro-economic scale and raise deep questions about our well-being in an era of relentless advertising and excess.

Sachs developed a commercialism index to judge the advanced nations on how commercialized their media and cultures were and then compare that judgment to measurements of overall public well-being and the common good. The correlation was strong: nations that were the most commercialized also had the sharpest signs of being societies with disorderly public and civic life. The United States topped the list as most commercialized and most socially backward.[74]

One can only imagine what sort of incredible society we might live in if the same resources and talent that go to commercial indoctrination went to education in the arts and sciences, liberal values, and critical thinking. Would self-government be on stronger footing then? The point is not that the firms that advertise are morally bankrupt; rather it is a reflection of an economic system that makes such expenditures mandatory, regardless of their cultural impact.

Technology and Growth

For readers of a book about the digital revolution, the third and final characteristic to be found in capitalist economies at all levels is no surprise: it is the endless drive to develop new technologies. Capitalists have tremendous incentive to use technology to increase productivity and gain an advantage over their competition. If a firm fails to do so and its competition beats it to the punch, the firm could be in trouble. Hence technological change is built right into the system and always will be. To make a comparison to precapitalist times, there has arguably been more technological change in the world in the week before you read these words than there was in any randomly selected century before 1700.

Technology also points up how distasteful the free-market catechism is to actual capitalists. In the catechism, a firm that innovates gets to make superprofits for a brief period, but then every other firm copies the product, new firms enter the fray, and the firm loses its profit advantage. What fun is that? (To some extent, patents allow firms to keep a monopoly advantage for a certain period of time, but not all innovations can be protected by patents. I turn to this problem in chapters 4 and 5.) The best protection for a firm's technological innovation is being in an oligopoly. Then the firms can increase productivity and lower costs, but the price of the product need not fall. The increased net revenues go into the pockets of the firms, and maybe some might go to the workers if they have a union.

Technology is central to growth, and growth is central to capitalism. It is one economic system that delivers serious increases in output over time, to some extent because the system requires economic growth to survive. When a capitalist economy stops growing or shrinks for even a brief period, it is in a recession. If shrinkage continues for any length of time, it's in a depression. This is an existential question for a capitalist economy. As with the individual firm, the mantra for the system is Grow or Die.

That is easier said than done.

Capitalists invest only if they think there is a reasonable chance that they can make a profit; otherwise it is better to keep the capital out of circulation rather than risk losing it. However, what is rational for an individual capitalist is irrational for the system as a whole. If a number of capitalists withdraw, they undermine demand for all products, and soon more capitalists suspend investment. This is a recession, and it is a part of a business cycle that has always existed under capitalism. Of course, recessions end when conditions change—inventories run down, wages fall, bad debt is cleared off the books—and generally turn into booms.

Even at the business cycle's peak, as contemporary Americans know well, it will not necessarily gravitate to full employment. Instead, as John Maynard Keynes posited in his *General Theory*, the logical resting spot for an advanced capitalist economy may be with significant unemployment and unused capacity. The business cycle may "peak" with millions unemployed and incomes in decline.[75] A major conclusion of Keynesian economics was the need for an increased role of the government in the economy. If private investment was not forthcoming, the government could borrow (or use taxation to get) capital lying fallow, spend it, stimulate the economy, and thereby provide markets to stimulate private investment.

This approach worked for many decades, such that the initial 1930s concern about stagnation was put on the back burner. Since the 1930s, the number-one job of the government has been to prevent depressions and foster a growing economy, and all political careers are judged by that one issue more than any other. Of course there are any number of areas where governments could spend to stimulate the economy. Left to Lord Keynes or to me—or, I suspect, most people in an open debate—the spending would have gone to schools, public transit, health care, parks, and the like. In the

United States, however, the one area of government spending that has proven to have no powerful enemies in the business or political class, and many strong allies there, is military spending. Beginning in the 1940s, it became a massive component of the American economy.[76] In 2012 it accounted for a trillion dollars annually in the federal budget when all the various wars, intelligence budgets, interest payments, and other expenses were added up, and it is a sacred cow.[77] How much it continues to stimulate the economy is a matter of debate; that it did so for decades is not controversial.[78]

By the 1970s, the Keynesian policy solutions to stagnation were less effective, and the system slipped into a decade of slump and readjustment. A crucial factor that kept the economy afloat since the 1980s was the massive increase in debt. Now that option has been played out, and the United States, by most accounts, is looking at growth for the next decade at rates lower than any decade since the Great Depression.[79]

Some economists and historians argue that major new technologies like the railroad and the automobile played a crucial role in stimulating investment and propelling the economy for decades to growth rates higher than

Chart 7. Real U.S. GDP growth

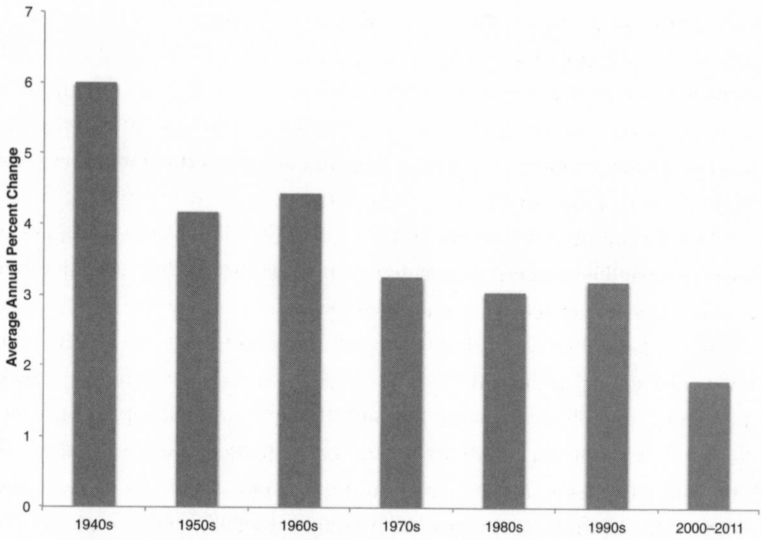

Source: Bureau of Economic Analysis, "Percent Change from Preceding Period in Real Gross Domestic Product," Table 1.1.1, bea.gov.

they would have been otherwise. One of the great political economic questions concerning the Internet has been whether it would do this too. This hope was the basis for the commotion over the New Economy in the 1990s. On the one hand, the commanding heights of corporate capitalism today are digital. Investment has flooded the Internet and information technology. On the other hand, the evidence that this is translating into any sort of economic growth surge to date is underwhelming.

Stagnation is here, and that is bad news for most people. The evidence also suggests that the greater the degree of inequality in the economy, the greater the likelihood of slower economic growth and stagnation. History suggests that we may be entering tumultuous times.[80] When capitalist economies stagnate, they put severe pressure on democratic states and society as a whole. As Paul Krugman notes, "it would be foolish to minimize the dangers a prolonged slump poses to democratic values and institutions."[81] After much suffering, this can lead to periods of significant reform and renewal or to periods of reaction, even barbarism.

Government and Markets

Perhaps the most striking blind spot in the catechism is the manner in which it treats the government, or what academics like to call the state. In the catechism, the state plays no particularly important role in the economy and is generally hostile to the market and profit making. The state is on the sidelines while the private sector produces wealth, and then the state is tempted to gunk up the process with taxation and regulation.

On the contrary, government took an active role in the economy long before the Great Depression. In fact, government has been foundational in the creation of a market economy and making the profit system possible. Beyond setting up laws to protect private property and investment, controlling currency, and setting tariffs and the terms of trade, the government has played the central role of coordinating the building of the nation's infrastructure. This includes both transportation and communication—roads, canals, railroads, postal systems, the telegraph, and much more. The complexity and extent of such infrastructure projects preclude private interests from accomplishing them without heavy coordination and support by the state. Alfred DuPont Chandler Jr., arguably the greatest American business historian, credits the creation of the modern transportation and communication infrastructure in the nineteenth century as the primary development that led to the creation of modern corporate capitalism as we know it.[82]

The task of providing an infrastructure for the market economy has grown in the past century—now including bridges, water systems, sewage and waste systems, dams, airports, and public utilities that form the backbone of economic activity. Increasingly, Americans understand that the Internet and broadband access are necessary parts of our infrastructure, as so much of our economic activity has shifted online.

What governments do will determine not just whether a society has a capitalist economy, but also what type of capitalism a society will have. It is true that in any capitalist society there is going to be powerful pressure to open up areas that can be profitably exploited by capital, regardless of the social costs. After all, capitalists—by definition, given their economic power—exercise inordinate political power. But it is not a given that all areas will be subjected to the market. Indeed, many areas in nature and human existence cannot be so subjected without destroying the fabric of life itself, and large portions of capitalist societies have historically been and remain largely outside the capital accumulation process. One could think of religion, education, romance, elections, research, and national defense as examples, although capital is pressing to colonize those where it can. Few, if any, religious conservatives have considered the implications of the family possibly being the most anticapitalist institution in history, even though the most successful families operate by the communist maxim, "From each according to his ability, to each according to his need."[83]

Many important political debates in a capitalist society are concerned with determining where the pursuit of profit will be allowed to rule and where it will not. At their most rational and most humane, capitalist societies tend to preserve large noncommercial sectors, including health care and old-age pensions, that are highly profitable when turned over to commercial interests. At the very least, the more democratic a capitalist society is, the more likely it is for there to be credible public debates on these matters.

Over the years, economists have generated a few concepts or tools to understand flaws in markets and thereby define a proper role for the state to address these problems and strengthen the capitalist economy. These are all of central importance for understanding media and the Internet. One such area is what economists call *externalities*. These are the costs and benefits of market transactions that are not borne by the buyer or seller. Pollution, or overall environmental degradation, is the classic negative externality. Neither the purchaser of automobiles nor the producer of automobiles has had to factor the immense environmental cost of automobiles into the price of the product, so the market cannot address pollution. Society pays these costs because they are external to the market. As a rule, markets are considered to be inefficient and inappropriate if there are large negative externalities or potentially large and valuable *positive* externalities the market has no interest in generating.[84]

Government spending is often used in areas where it can generate large positive externalities or where it will prevent or minimize negative developments. Public education is a classic case. Good public schools will lead to a more educated society with a higher standard of living and a more developed culture. This benefits everyone, even people who do not have children in public schools. The loss of the positive externality would produce consequences no one would want: lower economic growth, more crime, social insecurity, and the like.[85] It is why people support public education and why many of the founders of our nation put such emphasis upon it.

Advertising, as Sachs points out, has large negative externalities that are not being addressed. Journalism is chock-full of powerful externalities. Tremendous journalism that informs and engages people leads to more efficient and effective governance, a healthier economy, and a vibrant culture. All our lives will be fuller and richer. It will benefit everyone, even people who elect not to consume journalism directly. Likewise, if the market downgrades and corrupts journalism, it will produce an ignorant citizenry with resultant corruption and misery. We will all suffer as a result. This is the scenario unfolding at present. Understanding journalism as having important externalities does not tell us what specific policy or policies to employ, but it tells us how to think constructively about the policy-making process.

A related and arguably more important concept from economics is the notion of *public goods*. It refers to materials or benefits that cannot be effectively excluded from use by consumers who do not "pay" for them and can be used by one person without reducing their availability to another.[86] National defense and anti-epidemic public health services are generally offered as examples of public goods. We need to be defended, and we need to have measures taken to prevent pandemics, but it is impossible for individuals to purchase these, despite their importance. Moreover, few would pay for national defense voluntarily if someone else will do so; they would prefer to get the "free ride" by living in the same country. No one wants to be a chump. So no business can produce and sell this good. Either we all have it, or no one has it. It is something society needs, but the market cannot produce it in sufficient quantity or quality. It requires collective action.

The more a good or service has public-good attributes, the more there is a need for the government to play a role in creating policies to encourage production of that good and to share the expense equitably. That does not mean that there is not a role for commercial players and market forces, but the government plays quarterback, or the game never gets moving. It is a matter for policy deliberation and debate. Also, as Diane Ravitch astutely chronicles, the experience with education reform in the United States has demonstrated over the past two decades that innately unprofitable public goods like education do not lend themselves to "market discipline." If they did, they would have been profitable operations in the first place.[87] Subjecting a public good like education to commercial logic is generally disastrous, though for those steeped in the catechism, this can be a difficult point to grasp.

Public-good theory is valuable in several ways for understanding media and the Internet. Over-the-air broadcasting as it has been practiced is a public good. Whether three or 300 million people watch a program does not change the cost of producing that program or affect the satisfaction of individual viewers. There is no incentive to produce programs, because no one will pay you for them when they can watch them for free. Most nations solved this problem by using public money to create broadcasting content available to all. In the United States, advertising emerged as the means to support content and make broadcasting viable.

The Internet, too, has strong attributes of a public good, and has undermined the "private good" attributes of old media. Internet service providers obviously can exclude people, but the actual content—the value, the ideas—can be shared with no loss of value for the consumer. It is also extremely inexpensive and easy to share material. Sharing is built into the culture and practices of the Web and has made it difficult for the subscription model to be effective. It explains much of the problem the film and music industries are having with the Internet, as well as firms that produce journalism. Even if advertising is going to subsidize media content on the Internet as it did for broadcasting—a big if that I turn to in chapters 5 and 6—it may do so with such large negative externalities that we may wish to limit it. In any case, we are in a situation where we may learn from public-good theory.

For economic activities that are public goods and/or that have powerful positive externalities, it can be difficult, even impossible, for people to use the marketplace to express their desires for the good or service. How does one demonstrate in the marketplace that one wants national defense or public health? What goods do you buy? It cannot be done. Sometimes people want to have goods and are willing to pay for them even if they do not ever plan to use them. The market strikes out there too. Research with working-class Americans demonstrates that a large number of them want public broadcasting and are willing to pay taxes to support it even if they do not plan to watch it themselves.[88] They want it for their children or just to know there is somewhere to turn for noncommercial programming. It is therefore a popular use of government funds.[89] I suspect the same thing is and will be true of journalism. Even people who do not regularly consume journalism like the idea that it exists, that people are reporting on government, economics, and the news of the day. They would be willing to pay to see that journalism thrives even if they, for whatever reason, do not themselves plan to partake of it.

Revisiting the Relationship of Capitalism to Democracy

With this foundation, let's turn to the relationship of economics to politics and look at the American experience. The catechism provides a more accurate picture of the American economy in the first half of the nineteenth century, at least in the Northern states, than it does of more recent times. It is revealing, then, to see how the relationship of the economy to the government and political system has changed since the catechism went from some semblance of reality to being mostly mythology. The key to effective democracy has always been clear. "Democracy [is] when the indigent, and not the men of property, are the rulers," Aristotle observed in his *Politics*. "If liberty and equality . . . are chiefly to be found in democracy, they will be best attained when all persons alike share in the government to the utmost."[90]

Notice that Aristotle was writing about democracy and republics some two millennia before anyone had ever uttered the term *capitalism* or understood it as an economic system. Notice, too, that Aristotle emphasizes the tension between democracy and property. It was always understood this way prior to capitalism; democracy was all about empowering men without property, and inegalitarian property ownership was democracy's mortal enemy. As democracy emerged in the United States and elsewhere, it was rare that wealthy property owners led the fight for its expansion; they were sometimes dragged along kicking and screaming. Many of the champions of American democracy and civil liberties—from Tom Paine and Eugene Debs to Martin Luther King Jr.—tended to be people on the left of their political spectrums, detested by many of those with property.

The founders of the republic and the people who fought for freedom from Britain included elements that were unsympathetic to the idea of democracy, and it is not hard to locate slaveholders and hypocrites among the most prominent. That being said, it is striking how truly revolutionary the American Revolution was. The people who rose up did so inspired by the words of Thomas Paine, and the commitment to egalitarian politics was astonishing for the time. The historian Gordon S. Wood said it was as radical in the late eighteenth century as Marxism would be in the nineteenth century.[91] Equality meant more than formal political or legal equality, Noah Webster remarked in 1787. It required "a general and tolerably equal distribution of landed property" and therefore genuine economic autonomy.[92] Such a political economy would render severe inequality, corruption, and tyranny far less likely and be most likely to promote liberty and popular, effective self-government. A localized, competitive, and mostly one-class market economy was the foundation of Jefferson's and Paine's conceptions of an ideal democratic political economy, and Lincoln's as well.

Slavery and feudalism by their very nature are inhospitable to anything remotely close to democracy. The emerging market economy in the United States in the early nineteenth century, specifically the Northern states, was far more conducive to egalitarian politics, for property ownership was spread widely and a large portion of the workforce was self-employed as farmers, mechanics, tradesmen, or merchants. As modern capitalism developed, corporations replaced the small-scale entrepreneurs, employed a large propertyless working class, and generated massive fortunes unimaginable in earlier times, undermining the political economy most conducive to American democracy. Inequality mushroomed, poverty deepened, and there was tremendous incentive for commercial interests to use their power, at times illicitly, to have the government advance their interests at the expense of the balance of the citizenry. This process began to grow in the middle third of the nineteenth century during the great industrial revolution, and it exploded in the decades after the Civil War, the infamous Gilded Age.

The rise of great fortunes and the attendant political influence of big business horrified Lincoln. His first State of the Union Address in December 1861—arguably the most important speech of his political career to that point—was given as the Civil War had begun and the Union was in a fight for its survival. The eyes of the nation, even the world, were upon him. Lincoln understandably dedicated most of the address to a discussion of the war and its importance. Then, astonishingly, he sounded the alarm about a problem far from the battlefield: "In my present position I could scarcely be justified were I to omit raising a warning voice against this approach of returning despotism." The despotism that so concerned Lincoln was "the effort to place capital on an equal footing with, if not above, labor in the structure of government." Lincoln elaborated on the notion: "Labor is prior to and independent of capital. Capital is only the fruit of labor, and could never have existed if labor had not first existed. Labor is the superior of capital, and deserves much the higher consideration." In particular, it was imperative that the wealthy not be permitted to have undue influence over the government.

> No men living are more worthy to be trusted than those who toil up from poverty; none less inclined to take or touch aught which they have not honestly earned. Let them beware of surrendering a political power which they already possess, and which if surrendered will surely be used to close the door of advancement against such as they and to fix new disabilities and burdens upon them till all of liberty shall be lost.[93]

It did not take long for Lincoln's warning to look prescient. In 1887 the retired nineteenth president of the United States, Rutherford B. Hayes, observed,

> . . . it is time for the public to hear that the giant evil and danger in this country, the danger which transcends all others, is the vast wealth owned or controlled by a few persons. Money is power. In Congress, in state legislatures, in city councils, in the courts, in the political

> conventions, in the press, in the pulpit, in the circles of the educated and the talented, its influence is growing greater and greater. Excessive wealth in the hands of the few means extreme poverty, ignorance, vice, and wretchedness as the lot of the many.

Recalling Lincoln's stirring defense in the Gettysburg Address of the Civil War's appalling carnage as only justifiable if it protected democracy, Hayes wrote, "This is a government of the people, by the people, and for the people no longer. It is a government by the corporations, of the corporations, and for the corporations."[94] Paul Buhle, a leading historian of the American left, states that it was in this period, the 1880s, that capitalism was arguably most threatened by a popular uprising.[95] Future Supreme Court Justice Louis Brandeis captured a growing attitude: "We may have democracy, or we may have wealth concentrated in the hands of a few, but we can't have both."[96]

It is worth noting that in addition to inequality, some of the framers understood one other phenomenon as a contributor to inequality and cancerous for self-government: militarism. This has been a concern since ancient Greece and Rome. James Madison thought it arguably the single gravest threat to the republic—one reason why the Constitution has such strict rules to be followed before the nation can go to war and strict prohibition on military involvement domestically. As he put it,

> Of all the enemies of true liberty, war is, perhaps, the most to be dreaded, because it comprises and develops the germ of every other. War is the parent of armies; from these proceed debts and taxes; and armies, and debts, and taxes are the known instruments for bringing the many under the domination of the few. In war, too, the discretionary power of the Executive is extended; its influence in dealing out offices, honors and emoluments is multiplied; and all the means of seducing the minds, are added to those of subduing the force, of the people. The same malignant aspect in republicanism may be traced in the inequality of fortunes, and the opportunities of fraud, growing out of a state of war, and in the degeneracy of manner and of morals, engendered in both. No nation can preserve its freedom in the midst of continual warfare.[97]

More prescient or brilliant words have rarely been written. By the second half of the twentieth century, the United States became the leading military power in the world, and by the beginning of the twenty-first century, the most dominant military power in world history. Militarism also produces a great dilemma for modern journalism and has meant that the military played a far larger role in the development and management of the Internet than is generally recognized. I return to these issues in chapter 5.

Corporate Capitalism and Weak Democracy

The democratic state always has the potential to implement policies that benefit the whole population at the expense of those owning large amounts of property. This was a central concern of many of the republic's founders, who feared that those fighting the revolution might get too carried away with the idea of democracy. Although Benjamin Franklin and Thomas Paine forcefully advocated universal male suffrage, theirs was a minority position. "They who have no voice nor vote in the electing of representatives," Franklin observed, "do not enjoy liberty, but are absolutely enslaved to those who have votes."[98] Even for white males, Madison feared and opposed universal suffrage, while John Adams was downright hostile to it. If men without property could vote, Adams stated, "an immediate revolution would ensue."[99] John Jay, the first chief justice, was hardly outside the mainstream when he stated, "Those who own the country ought to govern it."[100] Some of the greatest political fights in American history have been over extending the franchise. The threat to property and the emerging corporate order became more pressing with the advent of universal adult suffrage, in the northern United States by the third decade of the twentieth century and in the South with the passage of the Voting Rights Act of 1965.

This threat has generally been contained, though many of the most progressive government programs in the past century, from the right to organize unions to Social Security and Medicare, came about when those without property organized to force the state to accede to their wishes. Much of the stuff of politics in the United States ultimately resolves to this calculus.

Why, despite seeming to have the numbers on their side, haven't popular forces been more successful in the United States historically, and why are they an abject failure in more recent times? Why were the 1880s the high-water mark for resistance to capitalism? Above I highlighted the crucial role organized labor plays in advancing popular politics. To some extent the question becomes in part, why has organized labor been incapable of being more effective politically?

The answers to these questions could consume many volumes, and there has been no small amount of scholarship on them. For our purposes, two points are important. First, precisely when the corporate political economy consolidated a century ago, there emerged the institution of public relations. PR is a complex matter. On the one hand, as Alex Carey points out, PR addresses the fundamental political problem of the times: how can concentrated wealth protect its privileges in a political world where the vast majority of eligible voters have strong interests in policies that may attack or even eliminate the prerogatives of the wealthy? In this sense PR serves the role of banging out a strong drumbeat extolling the virtues of business and capitalism and denigrating labor and government social programs. As Carey put it, the point of PR was "to take the risk out of democracy" for those who owned the country.[101]

However, public relations explicitly implemented along these lines—by trade associations like the U.S. Chamber of Commerce and the National Association of Manufacturers—is only a smidgen of the PR output. The lion's share of PR funds are spent for specific political/commercial purposes. PR is produced by those who are lobbying the government and need to massage public opinion, to the extent public opinion might influence the regulation and policies the special interest wants (or does not want) from the government. Anyone can do it, including labor and nonprofit groups, but the big money comes from corporations and corporate trade associations that have a lot at stake in how the government treats them.[102] This PR generally reinforces the themes Carey outlines: business good, markets good, government bad, labor very bad. Sometimes PR is a component of a traditional advertising campaign, where the goal is the sale of the company's products.

There is one other crucial component of public relations: it takes advantage of the conventions of professional journalism so that PR comes to provide the basis for a significant percentage of the "news" stories. One of the reasons the amount of PR is less appreciated than, say, advertising, is that PR tends to be much more effective if it is done surreptitiously. If the ten greatest PR campaigns of all time are widely recognized by the public, then they probably do not belong on the list of the ten greatest PR campaigns of all times.[103] The opposite is the case, obviously, with the ten greatest advertising campaigns of all time.

The combination of public relations and advertising has made our times the golden age of insincere communication, or you can insert the barnyard epithet of your choice. It promotes the view that one says what needs to be said to get what one wants. The truth is whatever you can get people to believe. It is a toxic environment for democracy, and it fans the flames of cynicism.

It therefore contributes to a second development in the past century: the increase in depoliticization. Americans simply are less interested in politics, at least if most measures, including voter turnout, are consulted. Depoliticization is not necessarily seen as a bad thing by society's leaders; it is implicitly understood that if a disproportionate percentage of lower-income people do not get involved in politics, the wealthy benefit. In 1975, an elite business-intellectual group, the Trilateral Commission, released a report titled *The Crisis of Democracy*, which concluded that "the effective operation of a democratic political system usually requires some measure of apathy and noninvolvement on the part of some individuals and groups."[104] Paul Weyrich, founder of the Heritage Foundation and one of the great organizers of the corporate right since the 1970s, put it bluntly in a 1980 speech to conservative activists: "I don't want everybody to vote . . . our leverage in the elections quite candidly goes up as the voting populace goes down."[105]

In recent times, voting turnouts range from 15 to 60 percent of voting-age adults, depending upon the location and the election. If the figure gets near or over 60 percent, people start doing backflips about how tuned in to democracy people are getting. In the late nineteenth century, for comparison's sake, 78.5 percent of eligible voters participated in presidential elections, 84 percent if one excludes the South. In 1896, for example, arguably the most sharply defined election in American history because of the brief Populist takeover of the Democratic Party's national ticket under William Jennings Bryan, a whopping 95 percent of Michigan's eligible voters went to the polls.[106] Even more striking is which sectors of society have stopped voting: it is disproportionately poor people. Nor is this a recent development. V.O. Key's trailblazing research in the 1950s demonstrated the class bias in voting turnout—rich people often voted at nearly twice the rate of poor people—in the first half of the twentieth century.[107] Charts 8 and 9 provide graphic detail, breaking the adult population into six roughly equal groups by income levels.

As far back as the 1970s, research by scholars like Walter Dean Burnham

Chart 8. Voter turnout by income in presidential elections

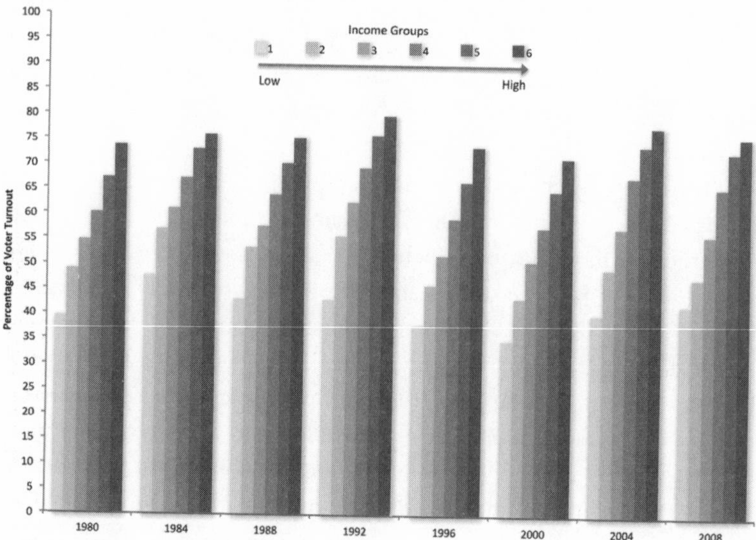

Source: U.S. Census Bureau, "Reported Voting and Registration of Family Members, by Age and Family Income," various years; and Robert Sahr, "Inflation Conversion Factors," Oregon State University, 2011, oregonstate.edu/cla/polisci/sahr/sahr (accessed Sept. 1, 2011). The number of income groups reported by the Census Bureau has changed from year to year and does not take inflation into account. The census data are also not reported in percentiles, so the proportion of the total voting-age population represented by each income group varies considerably. To get a consistent number of groups over the time periods listed, as well as to attain a more equal population distribution, the income categories for certain years were collapsed as indicated in Chart 8 (below). The average income in constant 2008 dollars for the income categories (1–6) thereby derived from Census Bureau data is also reported in Chart 9.

lent credence to the notion that if Americans of all income levels voted at the same rate as most northern European nations, the nation would be electing governments with greater sympathy to social democratic policies and to the left of anything the United States had ever seen.[108] Research demonstrates that Americans have not moved to the right on a battery of core political issues since the 1970s; indeed, they may be more progressive.[109] James K. Galbraith's research shows that as economic inequality increases, voter turnout among the poor and working class tends to decrease.[110]

C.B. Macpherson was among the first to grasp how a duopolistic party system in a modern capitalist society like the United States will tend to provide a "competition between elites," which "formulate the issues."[111] The basics

Chart 9. Voter turnout by income in interim elections

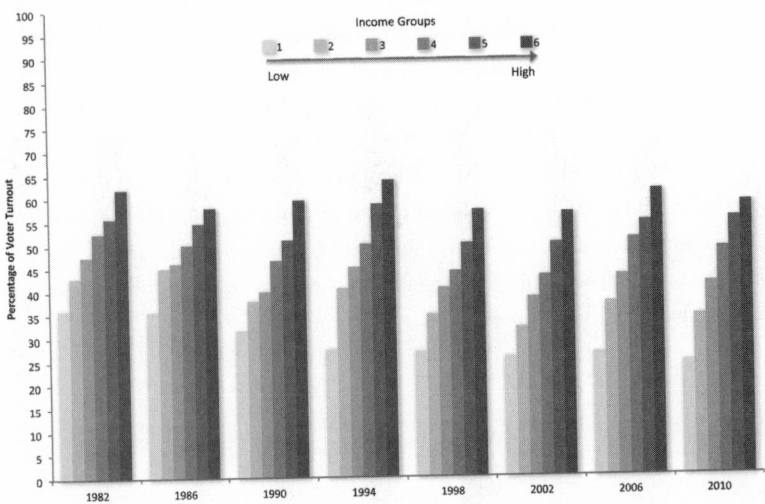

Source: Ibid.

of the political economy are agreed upon by the two parties and are off the table for public debate or discussion. In Macpherson's view, the two-party system was ideal for the production of citizen apathy and depoliticization—especially among those at the bottom end of the economic spectrum—and the maintenance of elite rule. As extraordinary recent research by Martin Gilens as well as by Kay Lehman Schlozman, Sidney Verba, and Henry E. Brady demonstrates, the widespread apathy among the poor, working class, and middle class has a rational foundation: the evidence is clear that they have virtually no influence over politicians and policies compared to corporations and the wealthy.[112]

The catechism has nothing to say about the caliber of American democracy, depoliticization, or public relations, Nor do most of the people who write exegeses about the Internet. They take the existing state of affairs as the natural order of things and as "democracy." Anything else, apparently, is pie-in-the-sky stuff and not part of grown-up conversations. The bar has been set so low that most Americans have only a hollowed-out notion of democracy: the act of voting for politicians you know little or nothing about, who probably will ignore you to the extent you are one of the few who has any idea what the key issues are. We are a long way from the vision of Paine or Franklin or Lincoln. Thomas Jefferson made the same case, arguing that merely voting for representatives was far from sufficient. "Every day," he wrote, a citizen must be a "participator in the government of affairs."[113]

If the Internet is worth its salt, if it is to achieve the promise of its most euphoric celebrants and assuage the concerns of its most troubled skeptics, it has to be a force for raising the tide of democracy. That means it must help arrest the forces that promote inequality, monopoly, hypercommercialism, corruption, depoliticization, and stagnation. To do so would put the Internet in the crosshairs of really existing capitalism. That is the conflict I examine in the balance of this book.

3

How Can the Political Economy of Communication Help Us Understand the Internet?

While the catechism presents a superficial and misleading picture of capitalism and condones a weak democracy, the commercial media system in the United States supplements this with its own catechism. It goes something like this:

Commercial media compete with each other to satisfy audience demands. Competition forces commercial media to comply, or else a competitor will steal their market and force them out of business. As a result, the system "gives the people what they want." As for journalism, it too has the threat of competition to keep the firms in line. But there commercial pressures can be a problem, so the most important development is the rise of independent professional reporters committed to unbiased, objective news. The key to the success of both the entertainment and journalism components of the media system is that they be competitive and part of the private sector, not controlled by the government. If there is anything that is beyond debate, it is that government involvement with media is dangerous and should be avoided at all costs. A free press is the key to a free society, and the free market is the foundation of a free press and a healthy democratic culture.

As with the broader catechism from chapter 2, this vision of a free media system is pretty much accepted by most observers and is then adapted to digital technology. Although this vision of a free press has some accurate and attractive components, it is dubious for effective understanding and action with regard to the Internet or all media. As valuable as political economy is for shedding light on capitalism and on the relationship of capitalism to democracy, it cannot provide in its traditional form the basis for more than a cursory critique of this notion of a free media system. Fortunately, there is a subfield of political economy—the political economy of communication (PEC)—that is ideally suited to address most of the central issues surrounding the digital revolution in considerable detail.[1]

The PEC brings communication into the picture alongside capitalism and democracy. It evaluates media and communication systems by determining how they affect political and social power in society and whether they are, on balance, forces for or against democracy and successful self-government. This critical or explicit normative basis distinguishes it from related fields like media economics or media law. Those fields, like mainstream economics, take the United States as it is, for better or worse, and regard themselves as neutral regarding the status quo, so they give little critical thought to the system as a whole. This neutrality generally resolves into a tacit acceptance of the status quo and the existing power structure as the appropriate one for a free society.

The PEC has two general lines of inquiry. First, it examines the institutions, subsidies, market structures, firms, support mechanisms, and labor practices that define a media or communication system. The way media markets actually operate has little in common with the free-market catechism, so bromides about competition and the invisible hand are of mostly ideological value. The PEC strives to provide a more accurate understanding of media markets and the true role of the government. It examines how these structural and institutional factors shape the content of media and how communication systems function in society. Political economists of communication take a keen interest in evaluating the caliber of journalism produced by the commercial news media system.

Second, the PEC emphasizes the foundational role of government policies in establishing media systems, even commercial profit-driven systems. The PEC studies and assesses how communication policies have been debated and determined, and it has a strong historical component looking at how media policies and systems were created in the past. Communication policy debates are the nucleus of the atom, and if media systems are to be reformed or changed, this is where one must go.

Both elements of the PEC, in my view, provide an indispensible way to understand how the Internet has developed, what the great issues have been and are, and what options remain before us. The PEC cannot provide all the answers to all the questions, but it can at least contribute a useful context to provide a basis for answers to most of them.

The ABCs of the PEC

The place to start is to understand media as a problem for society. By *problem* I mean its first definition in *Merriam-Webster's Collegiate Dictionary*: "a question raised for inquiry, consideration, or solution." The media, in this sense, are a political problem, and an unavoidable one at that. Media systems of one sort or another are going to exist, and they do not fall from the sky. The policies, structures, subsidies, and institutions that are created to control, direct, and regulate the media will be responsible for the logic and nature of the media system. Understood this way, the manner in which a society decides *how* to structure the media system, how it elects to solve the problem of the media, becomes of paramount importance. These policy debates will often determine the contours and values of the media system that then produces the content of media that are visible to all.[2]

The problem of the media exists in all societies, regardless of their structure. A society does not approach the problem with a blank page; the range of options is influenced by the political economic structure, cultural traditions, and the available communication technologies, among other things. In dictatorships and authoritarian regimes, the problem is solved by those in power, with the transparent goal of generating a media system that supports their domination of the nation and minimizes the possibility of effective opposition. The direct link between control over the media and control over the society is self-evident. In formally democratic societies, too, the same tension exists between those who hold power and those who do not, but the battle assumes different forms. Media are at the center of struggles for power and control in any society, and this is arguably even more often the case in democratic nations, where the issue is more up for grabs.

The PEC is oriented toward solving the problem of the media in a way that produces a media system most conducive to democratic values. There is no one answer to this problem, and the more study, debate, and experimentation, the better the answers will be. Due to circumstances, the PEC tends to highlight the problems associated with the dominant commercial media system. Raymond Williams, the great Welsh scholar, pioneered discussions about the necessity of reforming media systems as part of building a more just, humane, and democratic society. His trailblazing work in the 1960s and early 1970s made the replacement of commercial media systems and structures a central part of the modern democratic political project. As early as 1962, in a pamphlet for the Fabian Society, Williams argued that creating nonprofit and noncommercial media structures was a necessary part of modern democracy.[3] That Williams was considered among the most important scholars of communication in the English-speaking world only elevated the importance of his claims and concerns.

In my view, the most influential concept that has guided the PEC is the notion of the public sphere. The term is drawn from the work of the German scholar Jürgen Habermas, who argued that a crucial factor in the democratic revolutions of modern times has been the emergence of an independent realm, a public sphere, a commons, where citizens could meet to discuss and debate politics as equals free of government scrutiny or interference.[4] The media have come to assume the role of the public sphere in the United States (and elsewhere). The logic of the public-sphere argument is to emphasize the importance of having a media system independent of both the state and the dominant corporate economic institutions. This insight has transcended much of the left's difficulty in being critical of the government in principle and the conventional refusal to contemplate the core problems brought on by corporate control and advertising. The public-sphere reasoning rejects the notion that our two choices are Rupert Murdoch or Joseph Stalin. For a generation it has provided a democratic road map and blasted open a way of thinking about a third way—an independent nonprofit and/or small-business sector—as the necessary democratic media system. As with public-good theory, it does not tell which policies to employ, but it provides a valuable framework for thinking about appropriate policy making.[5]

Policies are crucial to establishing media systems, and governments have the capacity to change policies and media systems, but they do so only on rare historical occasions. Indeed, it is so rare that most people understandably do not realize that the right to change these policies and systems even exists. What accounts for that? This is where critical junctures are important.

The idea of critical junctures helps explain how social change works: there are rare, brief periods in which dramatic changes are debated and enacted drawing from a broad palette of options, followed by long periods in which structural or institutional change is slow and difficult.[6] "Critical junctures are *rare* events in the development of an institution," as Giovanni Capoccia and R. Daniel Kelemen put it; "the normal state of an institution is either one of stability or one of constrained, adaptive change."[7] During a critical juncture, which usually lasts no more than one or two decades, the range of options for society is much greater than it is otherwise. Ideas that were once verboten or unthinkable are suddenly on the table. The decisions made during such a period establish institutions and rules that put society on a course that will be difficult to change for decades or generations.

This notion of critical junctures is increasingly accepted in history and the social sciences. It has proven valuable for thinking broadly about society-wide fundamental social change, and also as a way to understand fundamental change within a specific sector, like media and communication. Most of our major institutions in media are the result of such critical junctures; once one has passed, the existing media regime is on stable ground, and its legitimacy and permanence are largely unquestioned. In times like those, communication policy debates tend to support the dominant institutions and attract little public awareness or participation.

Critical junctures in media and communication tend to occur when two or all three of the following conditions hold:

- There is a revolutionary new communication technology that undermines the existing system;
- The content of the media system, especially the journalism, is increasingly discredited or seen as illegitimate; and/or
- There is a major political crisis—severe social disequilibrium—in which the existing order is no longer working, dominant institutions are increasingly challenged, and there are major movements for social reform.

In the past century, critical junctures in American media and communication occurred three times: in the Progressive Era (1890s–1920s), when journalism was in deep crisis and the overall political system was in turmoil; in the 1930s, when the emergence of radio broadcasting occurred at the same time as public antipathy to commercialism rose against the backdrop of the Depression; and in the 1960s and early 1970s, when popular social movements in the United States provoked radical critiques of the media as part of a broader social and political critique.[8]

The result of the critical juncture in the Progressive Era was the emergence of professional journalism. The result of the critical juncture in the 1930s was the model of loosely regulated commercial broadcasting, which provided the model for subsequent electronic media technologies like FM radio and terrestrial, cable, and satellite television. The result of the 1960s and 1970s critical juncture was less sweeping for communication, although a number of reforms were enacted. In many respects the issues raised then were never resolved, buried by the pro-corporate epoch that followed.

Today we are in the midst of another profound critical juncture for communication. Two of the conditions are already in place: the digital revolution is overturning all existing media industries and business models, and journalism is at its lowest ebb since the Progressive Era. The third condition—the overall stability of the political and social system—is the last domino to fall.

It remains to be seen whether the people will engage with the structural crises our society is facing or leave matters to elites. In the critical juncture of the 1960s and early 1970s, for example, elites were concerned by a "crisis of democracy." This "crisis" was created by previously suppressed, apathetic, passive, and marginalized elements of the population—minorities, students, women—becoming politically engaged and making demands upon the system.[9] The Occupy movement and mass demonstrations of 2011 provide glimmers of popular political activism not seen for many decades; if this is the start of something big, we truly are entering a full-throttle critical juncture, and what the country will look like when we get to the other side is impossible to predict.

Technology

As the discussion of critical junctures suggests, communication technology plays an enormous role in the political economy of communication. To some extent this role is self-evident, as many media are defined by their technology, be it the printing press, the radio, or the television. So when new technologies emerge, so do new media. But it goes much deeper than that. In some ways, the field can be better understood as political economy *and* communication. The PEC is *not* just about making a structural analysis of communication systems and policy debates, as important as those are. Its practitioners also analyze how communication defines social existence and shapes human development. A study of communication can provide keen insights into our historical development. Communication affects political economy as much as political economy affects communication. When both are put in the hopper as codependent variables, things get interesting. This is precisely the intellectual cocktail we need in order to address the Internet and the digital revolution.

Here the importance of technology for communication—what are called "intellectual technologies"—is paramount. The Canadian political economist Harold Innis pioneered work that emphasized the "biases" of communication distinct from its political economic utilization, or, better yet, in combination with the political economic uses. In the mid-twentieth century, he wrote long studies on the importance of communication in shaping the course of human history.[10] Innis argued that modes of communication and communication technologies were of central importance in understanding human development and that they had profound intrinsic biases. Marshall McLuhan was an acolyte of Innis, though this Canadian English professor altered Innis's arguments. McLuhan is best known for his notion that the "medium is the message," that the nature of media content derives from the structure and technology of the medium. The dominant media technology defines a society, he said, changing the very way we think and the way that human societies operate.[11] His work was very influential on innumerable thinkers, including Neil Postman, who argued that television had an innate bias toward superficiality.[12]

"Every intellectual technology," as Nicholas Carr puts it, "embodies an intellectual ethic, a set of assumptions about how the human mind works or should work." These technologies "have the greatest and most lasting power over what and how we think."[13] Without a political economic context, this approach can smack of media technological determinism, but with the PEC this approach highlights that media technologies have significant impact, an extra-large helping of what sociologists term "relative autonomy."[14] Innis did not only focus upon the importance of communication technologies; he was also a sharp critic of corporate media and media commercialization.[15] The same was true of Postman, who termed the United States a technopoly, "a system in which technology of every kind is cheerfully granted sovereignty over social institutions and national life, and becomes self-justifying, self-perpetuating, and omnipresent." "The core of technopoly," Postman wrote, "is a vast industry with license to use all available symbols to further the interests of commerce, by devouring the psyches of consumers."[16]

For an example of this fusion, Nicholas Carr makes a strong critique of the Internet's effect on how our brains function, discussed in chapter 1. Likewise, Eli Pariser expresses concerns about how the Internet is producing "bubbles" that keep us in a world that constantly reinforces our known interests and reduces empathy, creativity, and critical thought. In both cases, aspects of the technology that seem most disastrous to Carr and Pariser are enhanced or driven by commercial imperatives. As Carr puts it, Google is "quite literally, in the business of distraction."[17] Indeed, the criticism of out-of-control technology is in large part a critique of out-of-control commercialism.[18] The loneliness, alienation, and unhappiness sometimes ascribed to the Internet are also associated with a marketplace gone wild.[19] They are very closely linked in modern America.

Because so much of the debate surrounding the digital revolution comes down to how this technology is not only revolutionizing society but possibly changing the very nature of human beings, it is appropriate to begin considering the digital communication revolution in the broad sweep of human development. The question is not whether the Internet's impact has equaled or passed that of the telegraph or radio or television. The question is much grander: Is the digital revolution going to qualify as the fourth great communication transformation in human history. I use the term *transformation* to indicate a communication revolution of such stunning magnitude that it alters the way our species develops. These great communication transformations are always accompanied by dramatic changes in the material conditions and structures of humanity in our political economy.

The first great transformation was the emergence of speech and language. Although there is some genetic basis for language, it did not emerge overnight as a result of one or two mutations.[20] Some scholars place its development a mere fifty thousand to sixty thousand years ago. Some, perhaps many, anthropologists believe that it was this emergence of language that permitted a small band of hominids to avoid possible extinction and to branch out from one corner of Africa across the planet in a geological nanosecond.[21] The acquisition of language helped develop human brains and made more-advanced toolmaking possible. The eventual development of agriculture—which permitted the accumulation of surplus and then civilization and history—would not have been remotely possible without language.[22] So the first communication transformation was a big deal. In many ways, it defined our species; it created us. As Aristotle and the ancient Greeks understood, we are the "talking animal."

The second great communication transformation was writing, which came many thousands of years after agriculture, only around five thousand years ago. Writing was not a "natural" development; many fairly advanced societies never had it, and there was never anything close to the diversity found in human languages.[23] Even today all the world's written languages come from three or four basic systems. Writing was driven in growing empires by the need to record information because of surpluses generated by agriculture, and those that did not have writing faced real limits to their expansion or survival. Indeed, empires with writing had a decided advantage over nonwriting societies and tended to crush and absorb them. As for the benefits of writing for humanity, Claude Lévi-Strauss writes that "the immediate consequence of the emergence of writing was the enslavement of vast numbers of people."[24] Innis, too, was skeptical about writing's emergence; he lamented the loss of oral cultures.

Writing also had enormous unanticipated consequences, with much of what we regard as our cultural heritage the direct and indirect result. Without writing, for example, it is impossible to imagine the human brain being capable of generating the scientific, philosophical, and artistic accomplishments that define us. The development of the phonetic alphabet was decisive. Its origins can be traced to the Phoenicians before 1000 BCE, and the Greeks definitely had it by around 750 BCE and had advanced it. Alphabets are "energy efficient" in that "considerably less of the brain is activated in reading words from phonetic letters than in interpreting logograms or other pictorial symbols."[25] Shortly thereafter, classical Athens blossomed in a manner that some still consider the high point of human civilization. Athens is nothing if not a tribute to the written word, although Innis thought its unique genius was as much due to the fact that the oral tradition was still strong and co-existed with writing in a manner that would never be the case again.

The third great communication transformation, the printing press, is better understood among scholars, as it has been the subject of considerable analysis and debate.[26] Before the printing press made reading, writing, and literacy widespread, the vocabulary of the English language, for example, was limited to a few thousands words. After the printing press, it expanded upward to a million words. "As language expanded," Carr writes, "consciousness deepened."[27] The printing press made possible the radical reconstruction of all major institutions, most immediately religion. It is difficult to imagine political democracy, the scientific revolution, or much of an industrial economy without the printing press and mass literacy. By no means did the printing press generate modern democracy and industrial capitalism on its own, but it was a precondition for either to exist.[28]

Whether this current critical juncture develops into the fourth great communication transformation may not be settled until we are all long gone. To some, the jury has already returned. "With the exception of alphabets and number systems, the Net may well be the single most powerful mind-altering technology that has ever come into general use," Carr writes. "At the very least, it's the most powerful that has come along since the book."[29] John Naughton cautions us that this communication revolution has only just begun, and if history is any guide, we really have little idea how it will eventually turn out.[30] We do know for certain that the interplay of digital communication with political economy will determine its trajectory and strongly shape its ultimate role in human development.

In the meantime, the United States, like other nations and transnational bodies, faces myriad communication policy issues affecting digital communication that are often about technological choices. Technologies reinforce the status quo once a communication regime is put in place. Technologies are "path dependent," meaning that once they are in place with a certain technological standard, it is very difficult and expensive to replace them unless there is a major technological revolution, even if they have considerable flaws. We still live with the limitations of the QWERTY keyboard, to take one example, though the rationale for that system disappeared generations ago.[31] Likewise, communication technologies invariably have unintended consequences—the more significant the technology, the greater the unintended consequences. Both of these features point to the need for as careful and thoughtful an approach to communication policy making as possible. As Philip N. Howard puts it, "technology design can actually involve political strategy and be part of a nation's 'constitutional moment.'"[32]

The Commercial Media Entertainment System

The Internet and digital technology encompass all communication. By most accounts, they have disrupted the business models of existing communication industries and forced media firms to rejigger their operations. These are some of the greatest concerns brought on by the Internet, and they are precisely where the PEC can be of value. Beyond simply figuring out a way to give consumers better deals or help firms figure out how to be more profitable, it can help us go large, to think about what type of cultural system digital technology makes possible. Let's start by looking at the commercial entertainment sector.

The United States has a vibrant commercial entertainment media industry. It mushroomed into a key part of the U.S. economy and culture in the twentieth century with the advent of films, recorded music, radio, and television. American popular commercial culture has its share of critics, but most of them hold to the view that if there are problems, they are due to the audience, which demands questionable content. After all, if people demanded great culture, it would be in the interests of the firms to give the people what they want. If the free market works anywhere, for better or for worse, it is certainly in the realm of entertainment. At least, that's the theory.

Commercial media do generate some exceptional material and serve the needs of many Americans. In many ways, the output of commercial media is quintessentially American and has become the way we understand our cultural heritage. The PEC cannot and does not say much about aesthetics or the nature of content, nor does it analyze the way audiences deal with media content. The PEC does look at structural and institutional factors and assess what types of pressures exist that will shape the content.[33] The catechism asserts that commercial media "give the people what they want," that the audience barks out orders and media firms race to satisfy them in a direct and unambiguous relationship. The consumer is king. The PEC examines these claims.

Right away, the catechism washes up against the rocks. Media content industries tend to be oligopolistic, with only a few firms dominating production in each sector. Moreover, in the past two generations, the largest media corporations have become conglomerates, meaning they tend to have major market shares in several different media markets, such as motion pictures, television, recorded music, and magazines.[34] A small handful of gigantic firms control film production, network television, cable TV systems and channels, publishing, and music recording. It is not simply the standard tendency toward market concentration in capitalism; it has to do with the nature of entertainment media markets. In such markets, the "first-copy" costs—say, of producing a film—are enormous, long before a penny of revenue is earned. This is a very high-risk industry. On the other hand, the marginal costs of serving additional customers after the first are rock-bottom, so blockbusters can be extremely profitable. Having size and being a conglomerate is the smartest way for firms to manage risk.[35]

Consequently, instead of consumer sovereignty, there is producer sovereignty. The media firms have a great deal of power over what they produce and do not produce. They may give the people what they want, but only within the range that is most profitable for them: This tends to be a narrower range than one would find in a competitive market. That's why media consolidation has been a central concern of the PEC. Concentrated control over culture (and journalism) instantly raises red flags in liberal democratic theory, for good reason.

The catechism also assumes that media firms and creative talent are conjoined and march in lockstep to high profits and high incomes. This elides a tension that has been present for centuries: art done purely for profit tends to be of dubious artistic value. Artists need compensation to be able to do their work, may need to have a sense of the audience in their minds, and may desire and embrace public acclaim. But if the commercialism overrides the art, the art—to invoke Howard Stern, who rejected using marketing surveys to determine the content of his radio program—will most likely suck. The conflict between creative talent and commercial pressures recurs often. If it didn't, Rupert Murdoch and the other media CEOs could simply write and direct films themselves or indiscriminately hire people to do so at much lower wages.

Monopoly aggravates the tension: If creative people are dissatisfied, their options are not great in an oligopolistic market, especially when all the players ape each other. This is why media firms and creative talent tend to have such a complicated and often antagonistic relationship. As a rule, the best stuff comes when it has as little corporate interference as possible, and that goes against the logic of a system in which firms make risky investments.

The corporate instinct is to re-create what worked yesterday. Let some other chump take a chance—and if it pans out, imitate away.

Moreover, in the conglomerate era, the projects that get green-lighted are often those that lend themselves to prequels, sequels, spin-offs, adaptation to other media, toys, videogames, merchandising, and licensing income. Tim Wu compared the ten most expensive Hollywood films of the 1960s and 1970s to the ten most expensive Hollywood films of the 2000s. The earlier films were all stand-alone properties that rose and fell on their box office; the 1970s were indeed a golden age for American cinema by most critical accounts. The more recent blockbuster budgets were all spent on films that had all sorts of additional revenue streams built in, to the point that the actual quality of the film itself seemed to be far less a concern for ultimate profitability.[36] When one studies the industrial production of culture in Hollywood, it is almost bewildering that anything good can be done once a project runs the gauntlet of a corporate bureaucracy.[37]

The notion that the system invariably "gives the people what they want" further unravels when advertising is added to the equation. Advertising is of particular importance because it has provided much of the revenue that has supported entertainment media for the past eighty years. That support has been one of the main defenses of advertising's otherwise questionable contribution to society. Advertising creates distinct pressures to appeal to certain types of audiences—generally more affluent—and to avoid certain types of themes. It can strongly influence the nature of media content, mostly for the worse.[38] Those entertainment sectors, like most of radio and television, which depend upon advertising for the lion's share of their revenues, are all about giving the advertisers what they want, and that is often different from what people want. They are effectively branches of the advertising industry.

Moreover, internal industry surveys show that most people want much less advertising in their media and would even be willing to pay more to have less commercialism.[39] But this is rarely a profitable option, so it is not one people can routinely vote for in the marketplace. The commercial marketplace cannot be used effectively to reject commercialism. For all the talk about how the system "gives the people what they want," it also gives people a truckload of uninvited material they desperately wish to avoid.

So audience demands for entertainment are filtered through the commercial requirements of media conglomerates and advertisers. The market research that these firms do is less about determining what audiences want than what is the cheapest, safest, and most profitable way to reach target audiences. Audience demands that do not fit the commercial needs are likely to go unmet.

The catechism assumes that popular demand for programming is exogenous, that it springs from some other world and is divinely democratic. But what people are exposed to significantly shapes what they will demand. To adapt Say's law: supply creates demand. Media firms have no incentive to upgrade the tastes of the audience; they take the market as they find it. One could argue that through commercialism they degrade it. It is generally nonprofit institutions and noncommercial environments that are tasked with exposing people to culture they would not experience otherwise. It was marginalized communities that produced the great breakthroughs in popular music—from jazz and rock to reggae and hip-hop—not the R&D office in a media conglomerate. It is when young people are exposed to—and educated in—literature, musical traditions, and the panoply of filmed entertainment that they develop broader tastes. It was once thought that the Internet would provide a massive treasure chest of culture that would dramatically expand any individual's horizon. As Eli Pariser argues in *The Filter Bubble* and I discuss in chapter 5, cyberspace is becoming less a frontier where citizens are like explorers on a glorious adventure than a cul-de-sac where advertising-driven cues keep people in their little individualized bubble, making it unlikely for serendipity to occur.

The primary education of Americans today appears to be in commercial values.[40] Consider the education provided in the children's market, which has exploded in the past generation. It goes way beyond just selling products *to* children; a majority of people use brands remembered from childhood, and children influence their parents' purchases, too.[41] Hence children under three years old—a market that barely existed forty years ago—are now a $20 billion annual market for advertisers. By three months old, 40 percent of infants watch screen media regularly; by two years, 90 percent do. By her third birthday, the average American child recognizes one hundred brand logos. The typical child is exposed to forty thousand screen ads per year. Children know the names of more branded characters than of real animals. By her tenth birthday, the average American child knows three hundred to four hundred brands. Research shows over and over that preschoolers will overwhelmingly think advertised products, branded products, are superior even when the actual contents are identical.[42]

In short, for all its problems in teaching other subjects, the United States is leading the pack in commercial indoctrination. The massive wave of advertising to children is considered a contributing factor in the epidemic of juvenile obesity, the growth of attention-deficit disorders, and other psychological issues, as well as the rampant sexualization of girls at ever-younger ages.[43] In 2010, Alex Bogusky, who was named *Adweek*'s Creative Director of the Decade in 2009 and called "the Elvis of advertising," announced he was quitting the industry, in part to protest marketers "spending billions to influence our innocent and defenseless offspring." Bogusky termed advertising to children a "destructive" practice with no "redeeming value."[44] "There can be no keener revelation of a society's soul," Nelson Mandela once stated, "than the way it treats its children."[45] It is difficult to study the commercial marination of children's brains and not regard it as child abuse.[46]

Free Market in Action?

The fatal flaw in the catechism is the notion that the commercial entertainment media system is based upon a free market. It is profit driven, to be sure, but that is a different matter. One need only start with the value of the monopoly licenses that are given free to commercial radio and TV stations, or spectrum to satellite television, or monopoly cable TV franchises. One recent estimate by Federal Communications Commission (FCC) staffers of the market value of the publicly owned spectrum today—some of which is given to commercial broadcasters at no charge—is around $500 billion.[47] When one considers all the wealth created from the free gift of spectrum to broadcasters since the 1920s, all the empires built upon it, the total transfer is certainly well into the hundreds of billions of dollars. Or consider the massive empires that firms like Comcast built with government-granted monopoly licenses for cable television systems. Economists acknowledge that these companies earn "rent"—i.e., superprofits—from the monopoly franchises. (Much of the policy-making process is an effort by communities to get something in return for these rents.) These old media subsidies remain of concern in the digital era. As chapter 4 chronicles, these firms are using their monopoly franchises and spectrum allocations to lock in a piece of the action online.

There are numerous other important direct and indirect subsidies that the government provides commercial media, and I have documented them elsewhere.[48] Two are of particular importance. First, advertising is condoned and encouraged by government policies and regulations. Allowing businesses to write off their advertising expenditures as a business expense on their tax returns not only costs the government tens of billions annually in revenues, but also encourages ever greater commercialism in our culture. By performing only lax regulation of advertising content, even as permitted by the law, the floodgates to commercialism are kept wide open. In addition, federal, state, and local governments themselves spend billions annually in advertising, which in effect is money that bankrolls commercial media.

Second, and by far the most important for entertainment media, is copyright. Media products have *always* been a fundamental problem for capitalist economics, going back to the advent of the book. Without direct government intervention, the marketplace would barely exist as we have come to know it. The problem is that a person's use of information, unlike tangible goods and services, does not prohibit others from using it. (In economic terms, it is nonrivalrous and nonexclusionary.) For tangible products, the type that fills economics textbooks, one person's use of a product or service precludes another person from using the same product or service. Two people cannot eat the same hamburger or simultaneously drive the same automobile. More of the product or service needs to be produced to satisfy additional demand. Not so with information. "If you have an apple and I have an apple and we exchange apples, then you and I will still each have one apple," George Bernard Shaw allegedly once said, "but if you have an idea and I have an idea and we exchange these ideas, then each of us will have two ideas."[49]

Stephen King doesn't need to write an individual copy of his novels for every single reader. Likewise, whether two hundred or 200 million people read one of his books would not detract from any one reader's experience of it. What this meant for book publishing was that anyone who purchased a book could then print additional copies and sell them. There would be free market competition, and the price of the book would come tumbling down to the marginal cost of publishing a copy, *exactly where it should be in a competitive market*. But authors would receive compensation only for those copies of the book they personally published or authorized, and competition would force them to lower the price to where their compensation was zero. Consumers might get cheap books, great for a democratic culture, but authors would not receive enough compensation to make it worth their while to write books. The market fails. The problem with nonrivalrous resources is not allocating consumption; rather, it is encouraging production.

This was apparent long before modern capitalism. It was the basis for copyright laws, so important that their principle is inscribed in the U.S. Constitution. Authors received temporary monopoly rights to control who could publish their books in order to make certain they received sufficient compensation. The trick was to encourage production without creating dangerous monopolies over information. Thomas Jefferson only reluctantly agreed to copyright, detesting it as a government-created monopoly that was effectively a tax on knowledge. The Constitution states explicitly that copyright licenses cannot be permanent, and their initial length was fourteen years.[50]

In the early republic, authors or publishers had to specifically apply for copyright to get such protection; only 556 of the 13,000 books published in the 1790s were covered. Only American authors were eligible, which pained Charles Dickens to no end. But Dickens kept on writing, fortunately, able to build up a fine income on his British sales. He also made a good living giving speaking tours in the United States, where his inexpensive books made him wildly popular.

When new media technologies developed and powerful media corporations emerged in the twentieth century, they were able to get Congress to make copyright automatic and to dramatically extend the length and scope of copyright protection—or to put it in plain English, government monopoly protection licenses. This has been a godsend to their bottom lines—indeed, to the very existence of their industries—but at a high cost to consumers and artists wishing to use material that can remain copyright protected for well over one hundred years. The copyright for this book, for example, will last for 70 years *after* my death. (What is the thinking? That I would not write a book if it were covered by copyright only for 20 or 30 or 50 years after my death?) A corporate copyright, as for a film, lasts 95 years after it is published or 120 years after its creation, whatever come first. The numbers are almost meaningless, because copyright terms invariably get extended before they expire.[51] We have, in effect, permanent copyright on the installment plan, and nothing produced since the 1920s has been added to the public domain. Copyright long ago lost its connection to promoting the interests of authors or creative artists so they might have short-term monopoly control over their work—just long enough for them to theoretically make enough money to make more culture.[52]

Today copyright has become a huge market in which control over copyrights is frequently unconnected to the actual persons who created the original work—and the terms for copyright are extended after the fact, which makes no sense at all. Copyright is now something entirely different: it protects corporate monopoly rights over culture and provides much of the profits to media conglomerates. *They could not exist without it.*[53] Copyright has become a major policy encouraging the wholesale privatization of our common culture.[54] It is also an enormous annual indirect subsidy for copyright holders, mostly large media corporations, by the public, in the form of severely inflated prices both for consumers and for cultural producers wishing access to material. No one knows the exact amount of "rent" these monopoly privileges confer upon copyright holders, because there is no accounting for this category. But the handful of lawsuits over the spoils of copyright suggests it is enormous, probably running into the tens of billions annually. It was for this reason that Milton Friedman regarded copyright as an anticompetitive mechanism, and he generally opposed the various extensions it received in the twentieth century.[55]

Scholars term this history the paradox of copyright. A policy meant to encourage creativity and cultural output has become a primary weapon to prevent the same. The media conglomerates routinely take public-domain material, like *Cinderella*, and make a fortune using it—because it was produced before copyright began to be routinely extended. But no future artists will be able to do the same to their creations without the conglomerate's permission (and usually a generous payoff).

Consider, for example, Bob Dylan. His first six albums of original material from the early to mid-1960s—*The Freewheelin' Bob Dylan* through *Blonde on Blonde*—are some of the greatest, most iconic albums in American history. Many of them rank on any list of the top fifty or hundred popular music albums of all time, and a couple of them are usually in the top ten. If I had a dollar for every time I listened to one of the songs on those albums I could retire comfortably. Yet when a Library of Congress musicologist studied the first seventy songs Dylan composed and recorded, he documented that "about two-thirds of Dylan's melodies from that period were lifted directly from the Anglo- and African-American traditional repertory." Dylan admitted that was his approach to songwriting. Because those songs were unprotected by copyright, Dylan was able to do what he did, and we are very fortunate that Dylan was not prohibited from producing his great songs. The catch is that today no one could do to Bob Dylan what Dylan did to the folk canon without making far greater alterations to the melodies than Dylan did, because those melodies will be protected by copyright for a very long time.[56] For that reason, we are all the poorer.

In this light, the existential threat posed by the Internet to the commercial media system becomes clear: Now digital content could be spread instantly, at no charge, all over the world with the push of a button. The marginal cost of reproducing material was zero, nothing, nada. By free-market economics, that was its legitimate price. Once sufficient broadband existed, music, movies, books, TV shows—everything!—would be out there in cyberspace accessible to anyone for free. Copyright enforcement would be helpless in the face of all-powerful digital technology.

To make matters worse from the capitalist perspective, advertising, which had been the way commercial interests had been able to convert the public good of over-the-air broadcasting into a lucrative industry, was likewise imperiled by the Internet. Who would ever voluntarily watch an ad on their computer, not to mention allow herself to be carpet-bombed with ads? On the Internet, media corporations could no longer hold people prisoner. "We are talking about a field," one commercial website producer lamented in 1997, "where it's not even clear who should pay whom."[57]

This led in the 1990s to an initial deluge of euphoria from those who found the corporate media status quo unsatisfactory. "The world has suddenly developed a printing press for every person on the planet," Henry Jenkins enthused.[58] The media conglomerates, in their wheeling and dealing, were simply engaging in the "rearrangement of deck chairs on the *Titanic*," as Grateful Dead lyricist John Perry Barlow of the Electronic Freedom Foundation famously put it. The infinitude of websites and the ability of anyone to go toe to toe with Rupert Murdoch was their death knell: "I think they are, in their present manifestations, goners."[59] Scarcity, a requirement for capitalist markets, no longer existed! There was no longer any need for the PEC; the digital revolution was ending scarcity and making communication ubiquitous, free, participatory, and wonderfully empowering and democratic. We can have a generation of potential Bob Dylans able to draw from, and be inspired by, all the fruits of human culture.

Of course, it has not developed quite that way. The giant media firms have not disappeared, nor has the Internet eliminated television and Hollywood. Marketing is a mandatory core institution of contemporary capitalism; the $300 billion spent annually on advertising and sales promotion was not about to go gentle into that good night when John Perry Barlow fired up his bong and showed it the door. These are extremely powerful institutions with tremendous political and economic power; they have flexed it mightily and with great effect. But their world was being turned upside down, and the emergence of social media only underscored their dilemma. "At the end of this first decade of the twenty-first century, the line between media producers and consumers has blurred," Michael Mandiberg writes, "and the unidirectional broadcast has partially fragmented into many different kinds of multidirectional conversations."[60]

This blurring and fragmentation pointed to an even more fundamental problem. No matter how much havoc the digital revolution might wreak upon commercial media business models, the Internet offered no solution at all to the core problem of funding and organizing media content. If a shrinking number of people could make a living producing content, what sort of culture would society produce? The online logic seemed as much pre-surplus as post-scarcity, as much Dark Ages as Age of Enlightenment. In short, the need for the PEC, the need to develop effective systems and policies, was and is more important than ever.

Journalism

I separate news media from the rest of commercial media (entertainment) for three reasons. First, journalism has developed out of a somewhat different tradition than entertainment: from the beginning of the republic, it has been a key part of the governing system and has been understood that way. Largely in recent decades, when media conglomeration merged the ownership of news media with that of entertainment media, especially in broadcast and cable TV news, the distinction between news media and entertainment media has been blurred, if not obliterated.

Second, even in the catechism, market criteria cannot to be used to evaluate the quality of journalism. Commercialism has been a key factor in journalism since the beginning of the republic and has grown in importance, but it has never been embraced as entirely legitimate. Indeed, the pure pursuit of profit has generally produced sensationalism, corruption, and crisis for the news media. It has also meant that control over political information has been placed in the hands of a small number of very wealthy people. Normative assessments of journalism use different criteria, so the tension between the capitalist basis of news media and the information requirements of self-government is a central issue in the PEC critique of the news media.

Third, although broadcast news gets the generous subsidy of monopoly spectrum licenses and all news media benefit from the advertising subsidy, the news media get little benefit from copyright, because their product tends to become quickly dated. Hence the single most important subsidy for commercial entertainment media is of minimal value to news media. If journalism is in crisis due to the Internet and/or commercial pressures, it will likely require a specific set of policies devoted to it, because the economics are different.

There is considerable consensus in democratic theory and among journalism scholars about what a healthy journalism should entail:[61]

1. It must provide a rigorous account of people who are in power and people who wish to be in power in the government, corporate, and nonprofit sectors.
2. It must have a plausible method to separate truth from lies or at least to prevent liars from being unaccountable and leading nations into catastrophes—particularly wars, economic crises, and communal discord.
3. It must regard the information needs of all people as legitimate. If there is a bias in the amount and tenor of coverage, it should be toward those with the least economic and political power, for they are the ones who most need information to participate effectively. Those atop the system will generally get from their own sources the information they need to rule the roost.
4. It must produce a wide range of informed opinions on the most important issues of our times. Research demonstrates that this is a crucial factor for encouraging informed citizen involvement in politics.[62] Such journalism addresses not only the transitory concerns of the moment,

> but also challenges that loom on the horizon. It must translate important scientific issues accurately into lay language. These issues cannot be determined primarily by what people in power are talking about. Journalism must provide the nation's early warning system, so problems can be anticipated, studied, debated, and addressed before they grow to crisis proportions.

It is not possible that all media outlets can or should provide all these services to their communities; that would be impractical. It is necessary, however, that the media system as a whole makes such journalism a realistic expectation for the citizenry. There should be a basic understanding of the commons—the social world—that all people share, so that all people can effectively participate in the political and electoral processes of self-governance. A free press is measured by how well it meets these criteria for giving citizens the information they need to keep their freedoms and rights.

There is more. Great journalism, as Ben Bagdikian put it, requires great institutions. Like any complex undertaking, a division of labor is required to achieve success: Copy editors, fact checkers, and proofreaders are needed, in addition to reporters and assigning editors. Great journalism also requires institutional muscle to stand up to governments and corporate power—institutions that people in power not only respect, but fear. Effective journalism requires competition, so that if one newsroom misses a story, it will be caught by someone else. It requires people being paid to cover stories they would not cover if they were doing journalism on a voluntary basis. In short, to have democratic journalism requires material resources, which have to come from somewhere and need to be organized on an institutional basis. It also must be an open system, so anyone can engage in the practice without needing a license, credentials, or approval from on high.

Of course, journalism is not the only provider of political information or stimulant for informed debate and participation. Political information also comes from schools, art, academic research, entertainment media, and conversations with friends and family. But all of those other avenues are much more effective and valuable if they rest atop a strong journalism and support that journalism. A basic weakness of the catechism is the superficial understanding of journalism's history and evolution. Defenders of the catechism and Internet celebrants tend to fail to appreciate how far twentieth-century American journalism has strayed from reaching these ideals. Hence reconstructing the journalism system under digital auspices begins on a suspect foundation.

In the first century of the republic, journalism was marked by a ubiquitous and highly partisan press that tended to have a wide range of viewpoints, including a crucial abolitionist press. The mostly unknown feature of this period, which I return to in chapter 6, is that this system was based on extraordinarily large public subsidies; it was anything but a testament to the free market. As advertising increasingly supported newspapers and publishing became a source of growing profitability, the subsidies decreased in importance. For much of the final third of the nineteenth century, the news media system tended to be quite competitive in economic terms. Large cities often had over a dozen competing daily newspapers; papers came and went, and nearly every newspaper was owned by a single publisher who also was the editor or had a strong say in the editorial direction.[63]

But capitalism imposed its logic. In some cases profit-hungry publishers found that sensationalism, what came to be called yellow journalism, was a lucrative course. Bribery of journalists, showing favoritism toward advertisers, and many other unethical practices were common. Most important, by the 1890s newspaper markets began to shift from competitive to oligopolistic, even monopolistic. Although revenues and population continued to increase sharply, the overall number of newspapers began to stagnate and then fall. "The stronger papers are becoming stronger and the weaker papers are having a hard time to exist," one newspaper executive observed in 1902.[64] Newspapers began to serve a larger and larger portion of their community's population—with much less fear of new competition than had been the case—and had considerable power as a result.

Moreover, the great newspaper chains of Pulitzer, Hearst, and Scripps were being formed almost overnight. The new publishing giants no longer had any need to be closely tied to political parties; in fact, as local newspapers grew more monopolistic, partisanship could antagonize part of the market and undermine their commercial prospects. Yet many publishers continued to use their now monopolistic power to advocate for their political viewpoints, which were generally conservative, probusiness, and antilabor.[65] The great progressive Robert La Follette devoted a chapter of his 1920 book on political philosophy to the crisis of the press. "Money power," he wrote, "controls the newspaper press . . . wherever news items bear in any way upon the control of government by business, the news is colored."[66]

By the first two decades of the twentieth century, this bias became a major crisis for American journalism. The news business was under constant attack for venality and duplicity. As even the publisher of the Scripps-owned *Detroit News* acknowledged in private in 1913, the corrosive influence of commercial ownership and the pursuit of profit were such that the rational democratic solution would be to set up municipal ownership of newspapers with popular election of the editors.[67] In view of the explicitly political nature of newspapers in American history, this was not as absurd a notion as it may appear today. Scripps, always the most working-class dedicated of the major chains and realizing how commercialism undermined the integrity of the news, even launched an ad-less daily newspaper in Chicago in 1911.[68]

Reconciling a monopolistic commercial news media with the journalism requirements of a political democracy is difficult. In many wealthier European nations, the solution came in the form of strong partisan and occasionally public subsidies to support journalism dedicated to working-class and labor interests, as well as the creation of independent public broadcasting. In Latin America, news media often have been the private preserve of wealthy families with strongly conservative politics and no interest in political democracy if their probusiness candidates do not win. They seldom care to expand the power or privileges of the great mass of poor people in their nations. Efforts by popularly elected socialist or populist governments to generate a news media that is not abjectly hostile to their policies—or, in the governments' claims, to have elements representing the interests of the majority—understandably have met with charges of censorship.[69] But even those who defend the Latin American media chieftains acknowledge they are often a dubious sort, and that their dominance is no democratic solution to a very real problem.[70]

In the United States, the solution to the problem was self-regulation by the newspaper industry, in the form of professional journalism. This embodied the revolutionary idea that the owner and the editor could be separated and that the political views of the owner (and advertisers) would not be reflected in the nature of the journalism, except on the editorial page.

This was a 180-degree shift from the entire history of American journalism, which was founded on the notion of an explicitly partisan and highly competitive press. Now, news would be determined and produced by trained professionals, and the news would be objective, nonpartisan, factually accurate, and unbiased. Whether there were ten newspapers in a community or only one or two would be mostly irrelevant, because trained journalists—like mathematicians addressing an algebra problem—would all come up with the same news reports. As press magnate Edward Scripps explained, once readers "did not care what the editor's views were . . . when it came to news one paper was as good as a dozen."[71] There were no schools of journalism in the United States (or the world, for that matter) in 1900. By the 1920s all the major journalism schools had been established, and by 1923 the American Society of Newspaper Editors had been formed and had established a professional code for editors and reporters to follow.

There is nothing inevitable or natural about the *type* of professional journalism that emerged in the United States in the last century. The professional news values that came to dominate in this country were contested; the journalists' union, the Newspaper Guild, in the 1930s unsuccessfully attempted to foster a nonpartisan journalism far more critical of all people in power. It argued journalism should be the agent of people outside of power—to "comfort the afflicted and afflict the comfortable," as humorist Finley Peter Dunne put it. The guild regarded journalism as a third force independent of both government and big business and wanted to prohibit publishers from having any control over the content of the news. As the leading history of the formation of the guild reports, "The idea that the Guild could rebalance the power struggle between public and publisher through a new kind of stewardship of freedom of the press became a core tenet of their mission as an organization."[72] This institutionalized independence remains a compelling vision of journalism, worthy of being a portion of a good news system, and it is still practiced today by some of our best journalists.

This way of practicing journalism was anathema to most publishers, however, who wanted no part of aggressive reporting on their fellow business owners or the politicians they routinely worked with and relied upon for their success. They also were never going to sign away their direct control over the newsroom; editors and reporters had their autonomy strictly at the owners' discretion. The resulting level of professionalism was to the owners' liking, for the most part, and more conducive to their commercial and political needs. It was also porous, so commercial factors could influence the values that led to story selection and advertising could influence the nature and content of news coverage.[73]

The core problem with professional journalism as it crystallized was that it relied far too heavily upon official sources as the appropriate agenda setters for news and as the deciders as to the range of legitimate debate in our political culture. There is considerable irony in this development. Consider Walter Lippmann, generally regarded as the leading advocate of professionalism and a ferocious critic of the bankrupt quality of journalism in 1910s America. In two brilliant essays written in 1919 and 1920, Lippmann argued that the main justification for, and requirement of, professionalism in journalism was that it provide a trained group of independent nonpartisan reporters who could successfully, systematically, and rigorously debunk government (and implicitly, corporate) spin, not regurgitate it.[74]

This reliance upon official sources—people in power—as setting the legitimate agenda and range of debate removed some of the controversy from the news, and it made the news less expensive to produce. It didn't cost much to have reporters repeat what the mighty said. Thus the news had an establishment tone. Reporters had to be careful about antagonizing those in power, upon whom they depended for "access" to their stories.[75] Chris Hedges, the former *New York Times* Pulitzer Prize–winning reporter, describes the reliance on official sources this way: "It is a dirty quid pro quo. The media get access to the elite as long as the media faithfully report what the elite wants reported. The moment that quid pro quo breaks down, reporters—real reporters—are cast into the wilderness and denied access."[76]

This fundamental limitation of professional journalism does not manifest itself in the coverage of those issues where there is rich and pronounced debate between or within leading elements of the dominant political parties. Then journalists have generous space in which to maneuver, and professional standards can work to assure a measure of factual accuracy, balance, and credibility. There tend to be slightly fewer problems in robust political eras, like the Sixties, when mass political movements demand the attention, respect, and fear of the powerful.

The real problem with professional journalism becomes evident when political elites do not debate an issue but march in virtual lockstep. In such a case, professional journalism is at best ineffectual and at worst propagandistic. This has often been the case in U.S. foreign policy, where both parties are beholden to an enormous global military complex and accept the exclusive right of the United States to invade countries when it suits U.S. interests.[77] In matters of war and foreign policy, journalists who question the basic assumptions and policy objectives and attempt to raise issues no one in the leadership of either party wishes to debate are considered "ideological" and "unprofessional." This has a powerful disciplinary effect upon journalists.[78]

So it was that, even in the glory days of Sixties journalism, our news media helped lead us into the Vietnam War, despite the fact that dubious claims from the government—e.g., the Gulf of Tonkin hoax—could in many cases have been easily challenged and exposed. "The process of brain-washing the public starts with off-the-record briefings for newspapermen," I.F. Stone wrote at the time. Two great dissident Democratic senators, Alaska's Ernest Gruening and Oregon's Wayne Morse, broke with both their own party and the Republicans to warn against imperial endeavors in places such as Vietnam. Their perspective, which history has shown to be accurate, was marginalized in mainstream news media. The press, Stone observed, had "dropped an Iron Curtain weeks ago on the antiwar speeches of Morse and Gruening."[79] Morse recognized that the lack of critical coverage and debate in the news media was undermining popular participation in foreign policy. "The American people need to be warned before it is too late about the threat which is arising as a result of monopolistic practices [in newspaper ownership]."[80]

Journalism schools lament these lapses in retrospect, but the situation never improves; such is the gravitational pull of the professional code toward the consensus of those in power in matters of war and peace. The 2003 invasion of Iraq—based upon entirely fictitious "weapons of mass destruction"—was one of the darkest episodes in American journalism history. It had astronomical, almost unimaginable, human and economic costs. In his 2012 book, *The Operators*, foreign correspondent Michael Hastings, who spent considerable time in the company of General Stanley McChrystal and his staff, wrote about how military officials gloated in private at "how massively they were manipulating the press," including the most prestigious correspondents.[81] In March 2012, Glenn Greenwald critiqued National Public Radio's hallowed coverage, in particular a report on Iran in which the correspondent

> gathers a couple of current and former government officials (with an agreeable establishment think-tank expert thrown in the mix), uncritically airs what they say, and then repeats it herself. This is what establishment-serving journalists in Washington mean when they boast

> that they, but not their critics, engage in so-called "real reporting"; it means: *calling up Serious People in Washington and uncritically repeating what they say.*[82]

It seems the only time elite journalists exhibit rage is when their practices are exposed. "The unwritten rule" for journalists is a simple one, Hastings wrote. "You weren't supposed to write honestly about people in power. Especially those the media deemed untouchable."[83]

Another weakness built into professional journalism as it developed in the United States was that it opened the door to an enormous public relations industry that was eager to provide reporters with material on their clients. Press releases and packets came packaged to meet the requirements of professional journalism, often produced by former journalists. The point of PR is to get the client's message in the news so that it looks like legitimate news. The best PR is that which is never recognized for what it is. Although reporters generally understood the dubious nature of PR and never embraced it, they had to use it to get their work done. Publishers tended to appreciate PR because it lowered the costs of production. The dirty secret of journalism is that a significant percentage of our news stories, in the 40 to 50 percent range, even at the most prestigious newspapers in the glory days of the 1970s, was based upon press releases. Even then, a surprising amount of the time, these press releases were only loosely investigated before publication.[84]

The high-water mark for professional journalism was the late 1960s and early 1970s. Even at its best, however, it tended to take the context and excitement out of politics, turning it into a dry and sometimes incoherent spectator sport. Unlike the partisan journalism of the nation's first century, it tended to promote depoliticization and apathy as much as participation. Christopher Lasch characterized one of the limitations of American-style professional journalism: "What democracy requires is vigorous public debate, not information. Of course, it needs information too, but the kind of information it needs can be generated only by debate. We do not know what we need to know until we ask the right questions, and we can identify the right questions only by subjecting our own ideas about the world to the test of public controversy."[85]

Since the early 1980s, commercial pressure has eroded much of the autonomy that professional journalism afforded newsrooms and that had provided the basis for the best work done over the past fifty years. It has led to a softening of standards such that stories about sex scandals and celebrities have become more legitimate because they make commercial sense: they are inexpensive to cover, they attract audiences, and they give the illusion of controversy without ever threatening anyone in power.

The emergence of the Internet has done much more damage to news media than it has done to entertainment media. The entire area is disintegrating, as I chronicle in chapter 6. Most of the discussion of this issue, however, has been vacuous because of the lack of a political economic critique of journalism. Professionalism has tended to be regarded as the natural American or democratic system of journalism, the organic result of profit-driven media firms, which were doing a bang-up job until the digital revolution rained on their parade. Imprisoned by this bogus schema, commentators have been incapable of addressing what is arguably the single most important communication issue of our time: creating a system of journalism in the digital era sufficient for credible self-government.

Policy Making

Ultimately the nature of entertainment media, journalism, and the Internet depend on policy making. As digital communication comes to engulf all traditional media, all of telephony, and much of commerce and social life, the stakes are enormous. Here the PEC has important lessons. As a rule, policies will be made by elites and self-interested commercial interests, unless there is organized popular intervention. In the United States today, there is considerable cynicism about democratic governance, such that many people have abandoned hope that anyone but powerful commercial interests have a say.

The cynicism is well founded. The metaphor that best captures American communication policy making is the famous Havana patio scene in *The Godfather II*, in which Michael Corleone, Hyman Roth, and other American gangsters are dividing up Cuba among themselves during the Batista dictatorship. They each take a slice of Hyman Roth's birthday cake—appropriately shaped like Cuba—to demonstrate their piece of the action. After divvying up the spoils, Hyman Roth states how great it is to be in Cuba, with a friendly government that knows how to work with "private enterprise." That is pretty much how communication policy making has been conducted in the United States. Monopoly broadcast licenses, copyright extensions, and tax subsidies are doled out all the time, but the public has no idea what is going on. Like Michael Corleone and Hyman Roth, extremely powerful lobbyists battle it out with each other—in this case to get cushy deals from the FCC and the relevant congressional committees—whose members and top staffers often move to private industry to cash in after their stint in "public service."

Above all else, the FCC has been dedicated to making the dominant firms bigger and more profitable. Congress, too, is under the thumb of big money. The one thing the big firms all agree upon is that it is their system and the public has no role to play in the policy-making process. And because the news media—generally owned by beneficiaries of the secretive system—almost never cover this story in the general news, 99 percent of the public has no idea what is going on. The best way to describe the role of the public in communication policy deliberations is this: *If you're not at the negotiating table, you're what's being served.*

An example of corrupt policy making is the "debate" over copyright in the U.S. Congress. It has been entirely one-sided, and for the past three decades, copyright terms have been extended several times, *for material that had already been produced.* Why? The powerful media corporations and interests that own most copyrights spent $1.3 billion on public relations and lobbying Congress on this issue from 1998 to 2010. The proponents of protecting the public domain and fair use—librarians, educators, and the like—have spent $1 million in the same period. That is a 1,300-to-1 ratio.[86] Furthermore, few Americans have any awareness of the issue except through the news media, so their exposure to it is largely via extravagant corporate PR scare campaigns against "piracy."

Is it any wonder that few members of Congress even understand there is an issue to debate? Giving the copyright industries what they want is basically beyond debate; the specific ways Congress can expand and protect the domain of copyright holders is what is under review. Hence the gargantuan lobbying expenses. Congress is creating enormous profits for these industries by extending, expanding, and enforcing monopoly rights. The only time copyright industries seem to face opposition is when they square off against other corporate lobbies that want access to copyright-protected material in their operations. Such was the case in the 2011–12 debate over the Stop Online Piracy Act (SOPA), when Google joined an avalanche of public opposition to battle the unprecedented extension of government policing power desired by the copyright lobby. In that rare instance, the pro-copyright forces were unable to get their dream legislation passed.

But cynicism must be avoided, as it feeds pessimism and depoliticization, and becomes self-fulfilling. It is also wrong. In fact, American history is rich with popular involvement with communication policy making, and many of the most democratic aspects of our systems were due to popular political pressure. Most of these moments of popular participation were during critical junctures, when the stakes were higher and the range of possible outcomes greater. During the nineteenth century, abolitionists and populists fought to keep postage low on periodicals, and they were successful to the point that these publications were able to survive and sometimes thrive. It was popular pressure that helped force universal service and common carriage on the AT&T telephone monopoly. Popular pressure in the Progressive Era pushed newspapers to lessen explicitly right-wing journalism.[87] What public interest regulation of commercial broadcasting and advertising exists came from grassroots popular organizing efforts in the 1930s and 1940s.[88] The social movements of the 1960s and 1970s were able to increase minority media ownership, establish community radio stations, and create public-access TV channels.[89] And that is just a partial list.

As we are now arguably in the mother of all critical junctures, it is worth noting that there has been an attendant burst of organized popular media-policy activism. Beginning in the 1990s, the burgeoning political economic critique of commercial news media generated by people like Edward S. Herman, Noam Chomsky, and Ben Bagdikian and organizations like Fairness & Accuracy In Reporting (FAIR) spawned a generation of activists who saw changing media as a necessary part of creating a more just and humane world. The emergence of the Internet fueled this desire, both as a means to that end and because of the great concern that citizens needed to organize to prevent commercial interests from doing to the Internet what they had done to U.S. broadcasting.[90] As I have been a participant in this movement, I can report that its very existence is predicated upon the work done in the PEC.

Specifically, I co-founded the public interest group Free Press with John Nichols and Josh Silver late in 2002. The idea behind Free Press was simple: to get democratic media policies, we need to have informed and organized public participation in communication policy making. We needed to generate popular awareness of the issues and organize it as a political force. While we lobbied on the issues at play in Washington, our goal had to be to expand the range of debate and options beyond what was countenanced inside the corporation-dominated Beltway culture. We could not continue the practice of just taking the "lesser-of-two-evils" side in intracorporate scrums about who would get the biggest slice of the media pie. We needed to have one foot in the future and one foot in the present, and our goal had to be to convince all organized popular groups that media reform had to become a central issue for them. Unless we could do so, our chances of success, of real structural reform, were slim.

On the one hand, Free Press has been a striking success. In conjunction with its partners, it has organized or participated in major successful campaigns around a range of issues, including diverse media ownership, stopping fake news, protecting public and community broadcasting, preventing harassment of independent journalists covering political demonstrations, making TV stations disclose online who is paying for political ads, establishing low-power community radio stations, and preserving what there is of Net neutrality. The group counts around five hundred thousand active members and has thirty-five full-time staff members. It has become a force in Washington and has played a key role in helping draft public interest regulations. Perhaps the highest recognition is the extent to which corporate communication firms have gone to attack it. Glenn Beck and the coin-operated right-wing PR firms have regarded Free Press as a major threat to the republic, because it challenges AT&T's monopoly power.[91]

At the same time, the Free Press experience demonstrates how far we have to go and how little time we have. It has been too isolated from other organized popular groups that still fail to understand the importance of media policy making. Too often, it is forced to operate inside the Beltway's parameters, so it must continually evince a commitment to "free-market competition," even when that is an unworkable option—or else be cast into the wilderness. It must spend too much time fighting defensive battles, getting caught up in the game of picking sides in intracorporate squabbles, because that is where the action is. This makes it doubly difficult to galvanize popular interest, as the issues seem wonky and the stakes seem low: no matter the outcome, corporations still win.

The fact that both the Democratic Party and the Republican Party are effectively owned by communication corporations highlights the difficulty for any populist group in Washington. As a veteran activist put it, whichever party is in power mostly determines "whether AT&T overtly or covertly writes the laws."[92] Nowhere is the corruption and bankruptcy of the political system more apparent. The lack of a broader political base is smothering Free Press and the media reform movement. It is like trying to grow plants in the richest Iowa topsoil without sunlight.

Presently in the coming decade there will be a series of policy debates that will be crucial for the fate of the Internet. "What happens in the next ten years," Heather Brooke wrote in 2011's *The Revolution Will Be Digitised*, "is going to define the future of democracy for the next century and beyond."[93] That, in a nutshell, defines a critical juncture. Left to the usual suspects, who will embrace and brandish the catechism, the Internet will be put to the service of capital, with dubious or disastrous consequences. Armed with the insights of the political economy of communication, we can take a hard look at the marriage of capitalism and the Internet and the resulting crisis of communication and democracy in the digital era. There are alternative paths leading to a much brighter future.

4

The Internet and Capitalism I: Where Dinosaurs Roam?

With the foundation provided in chapters 2 and 3, we can turn specifically to an evaluation of the relationship of the Internet to capitalism. We can also reconsider the promise of the Internet, as understood by its most fervent advocates in the late 1980s and early 1990s; these accounts were almost uniformly optimistic, for legitimate reasons. With all information available to everyone at the speed of light and impervious to censorship, all existing institutions were going to be changed for the better. There was going to be a worldwide two-way flow, or multiflow, a democratization of communication unthinkable before then. Corporations could no longer bamboozle consumers and crush upstart competitors; governments and militaries could no longer operate in secrecy with a kept press spouting propaganda; students from the poorest and most remote areas would have access to educational resources once restricted to the elite. In short, people would have unprecedented tools and power. Not only would there be information equality and uninhibited instant communication among all people everywhere, but also there would be access to a treasure trove of uncensored knowledge that only years earlier would have been unthinkable even for the world's most powerful ruler or richest billionaire. Genuine democracy would become a realistic outcome for the bulk of humanity for the first time in history. Inequality, exploitation, corruption, tyranny, and militarism were soon to be dealt their mightiest blow.

That seems like ten centuries ago. For all of the digital revolution's accomplishments, it has failed to deliver on much of the promise that was once seen as inherent in the technology. The Internet was expected to provide more competitive markets, accountable businesses, open government, an end to corruption, and decreasing inequality—or to put it baldly, increased human happiness. It has been a disappointment. If the Internet actually has improved the world over the past twenty years as much as its champions once predicted, I dread to think where the world would be if it had never existed.

To some extent, the gap between the vision of utopians and reality can be explained by their failure to appreciate fully that the Internet would be in direct conflict with hierarchical capitalist powers. James Curran argues that capitalism shaped the Internet far more than vice versa, that if the Internet were to remain a public service institution, it would likely stay on the margins. But leaving the analysis at that point barely scratches the surface of what has taken place and is taking place today.

The tremendous promise of the digital revolution has been compromised by capitalist appropriation and development of the Internet. In the great conflict between openness and a closed system of corporate profitability, the forces of capital have triumphed whenever an issue mattered to them. The Internet has been subjected to the capital-accumulation process, which has a clear logic of its own, inimical to much of the democratic potential of digital communication. What seemed to be an increasingly open public sphere, removed from the world of commodity exchange, seems to be morphing into a private sphere of increasingly closed, proprietary, even monopolistic markets. The extent of this capitalist colonization of the Internet has not been as obtrusive as it might have been, because the vast reaches of cyberspace have continued to permit noncommercial utilization, although increasingly on the margins.

In this chapter I assess how capitalism conquered the Internet—an institution that was singularly noncommercial, even anticommercial, for its first two decades—in the 1990s and what the consequences have been subsequently. By capitalism I mean the really existing capitalism of large corporations, monopolistic markets, advertising, public relations, and close, collegial, important, necessary, and often corrupt relationships with the government and the military. I do not mean the fairy-tale catechism of American politicians and pundits: heroic upstart little-guy entrepreneurs battling in competitive free markets while the deadbeat government is on the sidelines screwing up the job-creating private sector with a lot of birdbrain liberal regulations. I review how specific real-world powerful giant corporations in telecommunications and media have responded to the Internet's existential challenge to their modus operandi. Could these dinosaurs survive?

Once the Internet was largely turned over to capitalists to make as much money as possible, the overriding questions became: What's the killer app? What firms will emerge that will be the new Standard Oils and GMs? In chapter 5 I continue the analysis, assessing the new digital corporate giants that have come forth, looking at why and how they tower over not only the Internet but the whole economy. The key question for most of these new giants has been: where will the money come from to make this a viable market? The answer is advertising. I look at how the Internet has been converted into an advertising-based medium and what that portends for media, not to mention traditional liberal and democratic values. Throughout chapter 5, the crucial role of government policies and subsidies in creating and extending the commercial system will be foregrounded. The chapter concludes with a discussion of how the military and national security interests in the United States play an increasingly prominent role in Internet regulation and governance, in a largely copacetic manner with the corporate giants.

In many respects, chapters 4 and 5 provide an argument against the capitalist development of the Internet, though not necessarily capitalism per se. I draw from a wide body of research on telecommunications, copyright, monopoly, microeconomics, civil liberties, privacy, and advertising that has been produced by respected scholars and writers, the vast majority of whom would be regarded as sympathetic to the market system. Indeed, some of the critique has been generated by libertarians and self-described conservatives. Much of the contemporary data I rely upon comes from the business and trade press and from investment analysts. That being said, when viewed as a whole, the critique herein does invite fundamental questions about the overall capitalist system itself, which are taken up in chapter 7, the conclusion.

So Who Invented the Internet?

During the 2000 presidential campaign, Democratic candidate and vice president Al Gore was repeatedly ridiculed for allegedly claiming that he "invented" the Internet. The conventional response was along the lines of "how could any government bureaucrat think that he could have anything to do with something as entrepreneurial and genius-inspired as the

Internet?" Republican candidate George W. Bush lampooned Gore: "If he was so smart, how come all the Internet addresses start with W?"[1] Of course, the charge against Gore was false but became an urban legend.[2] His actual claim was merely that as a member of Congress he had played a key role in channeling funds to support the development of what would become the Internet.[3] The person often regarded as the father of the Internet defended Gore, with little effect: "VP Gore was the first or surely among the first of the members of Congress to become a strong supporter of advanced networking while he served as Senator," Vint Cerf stated. "While it is not accurate to say that VP Gore invented the Internet, he has played a powerful role in policy terms that has supported its continued growth and application, for which we should be thankful."[4]

This episode demonstrated how quickly the true history of the Internet had been swallowed up in collective amnesia and replaced by the mythology of the free market.[5] In fact, the entire realm of digital communication was developed through government-subsidized-and-directed research during the post–World War II decades, often by the military and leading research universities. Had the matter been left to the private sector, the Internet may never have come into existence.

The story has been told many times, but certain aspects bear repeating. When computer scientist Paul Baran (not the economist Paul A. Baran mentioned elsewhere) imagined a decentralized network in the early 1960s, the telephone monopoly AT&T scoffed at his idea, telling him "he didn't know how communications worked."[6] The Internet was designed as an "open and designable technology" through which scientists could contribute easily in a nonhierarchical environment. It was unlike the closed systems of corporate telecommunication, in which private control over the bottleneck, what Tim Wu has called the master switch, was the basis for profitability.[7] The Internet predecessor, ARPAnet, under Cerf and Robert Kahn, was designed with no central control so that the system would be neutral or dumb, leaving the power to develop specific applications to people on the edges, who could participate as they wished.[8] This "decentralized control meant all machines on the network were, more or less, peers. No one computer was in charge."[9] Corporations accordingly had little interest in the Internet during its formative decades. IBM declined to even make a bid to provide subnet computers in 1968, saying the venture was not sufficiently profitable.[10] In 1972 the government famously offered to let AT&T take control of ARPAnet—i.e., the Internet—and the monopolist declined "on the grounds that it would be unprofitable."[11]

The Internet's origins teach two important lessons. First, basic research of the kind that generates innovations like the Internet is a public good, and private sector firms have little incentive to produce it. Without the pressure to generate returns, as Cerf observed, government-based research has "the ability to sustain research for long periods of time."[12] Moreover, corporate research labs "rarely if ever invest in fundamental technology that will likely undermine the economic dominance they currently enjoy."[13] In corporate-think, the proper role of the government goes like this: make the massive initial investments and take all the risk. Then, if and when profitable applications become apparent, let commercial interests move in and rake in the chips, soon followed by shamelessly denouncing government taxation and regulation as interference with the productive work of the private sector. Another approach would accept that government investment in research is desirable and necessary, but argue that the public, through the government, deserves to get the same sort of deal for *its* investment from commercial interests that private investors would expect if they had bankrolled all the initial research and development and assumed all the risk when the risk was greatest.[14] This return for the public is what was effectively being negotiated (and given away) in the 1990s when the Internet was turned over to the private sector.

Second, the Internet experience highlights the utterly central role that military spending has played in bankrolling technology (and economic development) in the United States since the 1940s. By one study, since 1945 fully one third of U.S. research professors have been supported by national security agencies.[15] "Across the spectrum of high-technology industries," Nathan Newman writes, "the single overwhelming factor correlating with the rise of technology firms in any region is the level of defense spending."[16] This is particularly true for communication. The U.S. Air Force, for example, did the research in the early 1960s that provided the basis for the personal computer and the mouse.[17] Likewise, the basic architecture of computer design, advances in time-sharing minicomputers, and most of networking technology were the result of military spending and "massive government support."[18] As John Hanke, an Internet CEO and one of the creators of Google Earth, put it, "The whole history of Silicon Valley is tied up pretty closely with the military." Google Earth specifically would not exist unless the military had been "willing to pay millions of dollars per user to make it possible." "We've come to the point," Peter Nowak writes, "where it's almost impossible to separate any American-made technology from the American military."[19] Nor is this ancient history. In 2012 *Wired* magazine's Chris Anderson provided a cover story describing the extraordinary potential benefits of drone warfare for communication and society: "This new generation of cheap, small drones is essentially a fleet of flying smartphones," he enthused.[20] Military spending on research and development is such a central part of American capitalism that it is almost impossible to imagine the system existing without it.

The total amount of the federal subsidy of the Internet is impossible to determine with precision. As Sascha Meinrath, a leading policy expert at the New America Foundation, puts it, calculating the amount of the historical federal subsidy of the Internet "depends on how one parses government spending—it's fairly modest in terms of direct cash outlays. But once one takes into account rights of way access that were donated and the whole research agenda (through the Defense Advanced Research Projects Agency, the National Science Foundation, etc.), it's pretty substantial. And if you include the costs of the wireless subsidies, tax breaks (e.g., no sales taxes on online purchases), etc., it's well into the hundreds of billions range."[21] Meinrath does not even include the immense amount of volunteer labor that provided a "continuous stream of free software to improve its functionality."[22] For context, even a conservative take on Meinrath's estimate puts the federal investment in the Internet at least ten times greater than the cost of the Manhattan Project, allowing for inflation.[23]

The issue is not only public subsidies with no return on investments. It's also about a public ethos. The early Internet was not only noncommercial, it was anticommercial. Computers were regarded by many of the 1960s and '70s generation as harbingers of egalitarianism and cooperation, not competition and profits. Apple's Steve Wozniak recalls that everyone at his 1970s computer club "envisioned computers as a benefit to humanity—a tool that would lead to social justice."[24] Salvador Allende's democratic socialist government in Chile in the early 1970s devoted considerable resources to computing, in the belief that it could provide efficient economics without the injustice and irrationality of capitalism.[25] By the 1970s and 1980s, the computer professionals and students who comprised the Internet community "deliberately cultivated an open, non-hierarchical culture that imposed few restrictions on how the network could be used."[26] Rebecca MacKinnon calls this the digital commons, which would provide the foundation for all subsequent commercial applications.[27] The hacker culture that emerged in that period was typified by its commitment to information being free and available, hostility to centralized authority and secrecy, and the joy of learning and knowledge.[28]

Nothing enraged the Internet community more than advertising and commercialism. Prior to the early 1990s, the National Science Foundation Network (NSFNet), the immediate forerunner of the Internet, explicitly limited the network to noncommercial uses. The first commercial e-mail message, which gained considerable attention, was sent in April 1994 to every board in the massive Usenet system, which held the noncommercial Internet culture near and dear to its heart.[29] The sender of that e-mail was flamed by countless Usenet users, meaning that they clogged the advertiser's inbox with contemptuous messages demanding that the sales pitch be removed and such conduct never be repeated. This internal policing by Internet users was based on the assumption that commercialism and an honest, democratic public sphere do not mix. Advertising already saturated the balance of the mass media; it wasn't as if people couldn't find enough commercials. The Internet was to be the one place where citizens could seek refuge and escape the incessant sales pitch.

This contempt for digital commercialism was well understood in the business community. In 1993 the trade publication *Advertising Age* lamented how the Internet is encased in a culture "which is loathe [*sic*] to advertising."[30] Marketers feared that their efforts to use the Web would be greeted by a tidal wave of flaming from "a cyberspace community peopled by academics and intellectuals" who regarded a commercialized Internet as "advertising hell."[31] As late as 1998, Google founders Larry Page and Sergey Brin rejected the idea that their search engine should be supported by advertising. "We expect that advertising funded search engines will be inherently biased towards the advertisers and away from the needs of consumers," they wrote. "The better the search engine is, the fewer advertisements will be needed by the consumer to find what they want."[32] The Internet was expected, as Madison Avenue feared deeply, to make advertising irrelevant and obsolete.

As the Internet grew, it gradually attracted the interests of commercial concerns keen to see how they might capitalize upon it. Perhaps the first skirmish came with e-mail, which was created in 1972 by a hacker to piggyback on the file transfer protocol. With the support of ARPAnet, e-mail soon surpassed all other forms of computer resource sharing.[33] It was the first "killer app." By the end of the decade, the U.S. Postal Service proposed the creation of an electronic mail service that it would administer, at first for business customers who expressed an interest, and then to others as the system developed. Even then, postal analysts argued that "the Postal Service must enter and participate vigorously in an electronic mail system if it is to survive." Perhaps a decade earlier, this might have flown, but during the Reagan administration, business opposition from firms like AT&T was sufficient to quash the proposal.[34] Had the Postal Service been successful, it might have put the Internet on a rather different trajectory as a decidedly nonprofit public service medium.[35] By 1982 Cerf left the government and was working for the telecommunication company MCI, where he put together the first commercial e-mail system. When the MCI e-mail system was formally attached to the Internet in 1989, the commercial Internet was born.[36]

Another commercial application of the Internet was the wave of online computer services—proprietary networks like America Online, CompuServe, and Prodigy—that provided "walled gardens" where the services controlled the content. These services enjoyed brief success, but they all failed after the emergence of the World Wide Web in the 1990s provided for free an infinitely greater amount of material than these services provided for a fee.[37] AOL managed to survive and prosper by providing dial-up Internet access, rather than a walled-off system, in the prebroadband era of the late 1990s.

The single greatest concern in the Internet community during this period was the growth of patents and efforts by commercial interests to make proprietary what had once been open and free. As commercial interests were seen taking an increasing interest in the Internet, there was, as James Curran has documented, a "revolt of the nerds"—led by people like Richard Stallman and Linus Torvalds—which launched the open-software movement in the 1980s.[38] Much of the noncommercial institutional presence on the Internet today can be attributed to this movement and its progeny. When Tim Berners-Lee created the World Wide Web in 1990, he said it would have been "unthinkable" to patent it or ask for fees. The point of the Internet was "sharing for the common good." That was about to change. As the market exploded in the 1990s, patents became the rage. The use of patents to create unnecessary and dangerous monopolies rather than as incentives for research, as Berners-Lee put it, became a "very serious problem." By 1999 he wondered openly if the Internet was becoming a "technical dream or a legal nightmare."[39]

During the 1990s, the Internet was transformed from a public service to a distinct, even preeminent, capitalist sector. The Internet was formally privatized in 1994–95 when the NSFNet turned the backbone of the Internet over to the private sector. Thereafter market forces were to determine its course. The transition culminated a good six years of mostly secret high-level deliberations involving government and the private sector. Compared to the political debate that surrounded the emergence of radio broadcasting in the 1930s or the uprising against Western Union's telegraph monopoly in the late nineteenth century, there was nary a trace of popular discussion about whether this privatization and commercialization was appropriate and what its implications might be. Press coverage was nonexistent, so the general public did not have a clue; the media watch group Project Censored ranked the privatization of the Internet as the fourth most censored story of 1995. The number-one most censored story was that of the deliberations leading up to what would become the Telecommunications Act of 1996.[40]

Why was there no organized or coherent opposition? In view of the dominant noncommercial ethos that had driven the Internet and had been one of its most attractive features before 1995, the lack of opposition is striking. In my view, there were four crucial factors that account for the uncontested triumph of a privatized Internet.

First, the point emphasized in chapter 3 came into play: the policy-making process throughout the 1990s (and beyond) was dominated by large corporations and their trade associations. The traditional pattern was for the government to develop new communication technologies and then turn them over to capitalists once they could make profits. What little debate there was concerned what (generally minor) public interest obligations would be attached to the gift. Press coverage was restricted to the business press, so the general public had virtually no idea what was taking place. Politicians in both parties benefited by relations with the massive incumbents, who basically owned the board in Washington, D.C., and the state capitals. Due to the imbalance of power in these negotiations, the benefits invariably redounded to private interests. The Internet posed a distinct existential challenge to numerous superpowerful corporations and industries, as well as almost unimaginable promise to them and other businesses. They were not about to disappear quietly for the good of humanity and allow a fair, widespread public discussion on how best to deploy digital technologies to enhance democracy, the economy, and quality of life.

Second, there was no single policy or coherent set of policies that determined the nature of the Internet. The implications of the 1994–95 privatization were not at all clear. Numerous crucial policy changes and technological advances would be required to get the Internet to where it is in 2013, none of which could have been anticipated in the 1990s. There were numerous institutions, industries, and government agencies that had a role in how the Internet would develop, and none was all-powerful. It was very difficult to get a handle on it. The threat that the Internet would be taken over by Big Brother or Rupert Murdoch seemed remote. For activists concerned about what to do to protect the public interest and prevent corporate domination online, it was difficult to get a sense of what policies were going to be effective. If this was a critical juncture—and many in the 1990s understood it as exactly that—it was not at all clear what the exact issues and alternatives were. Plenty of room existed in the infinite digital realm for everyone to "do their thing," so it seemed that commercial and noncommercial users could easily co-exist. The only clear policy concern was to prevent explicit government censorship of Internet speech, as exemplified by the Communications Decency Act of 1996, which was almost immediately ruled unconstitutional.

There was also an element of arrogance among hackers, who tended to believe that no matter what the corporate guys cooked up, they would be able to circumvent it. The revolutionary nature of the technology could trump the monopolizing force of the market. This might help explain the 1990s alliance of sorts forged between some prominent counterculture types who embraced the Internet, like Stewart Brand, John Perry Barlow, and Esther Dyson, with free-market ideologues and techno-enthusiasts, like George Gilder and Newt Gingrich.[41]

Third, even in the context of a corporation-dominated polity, the political culture of the 1990s was close to an all-time high for procapitalist sentiment and close to an all-time low for notions of public service or regulation. The notions of public goods and regulation in the public interest were suspect, if not ridiculed. The digital revolution exploded at precisely the moment that what is commonly known as neoliberalism was in ascendance, its flowery rhetoric concerning "free markets" most redolent. The dynamism of technological revolution imbued the power-grab of corporations with the patina of moral rectitude, virtue, and public service. The core opinion was that businesses should *always* be permitted to develop any area where profits could be found and that this was the most efficient use of resources for an economy.[42] Digital technology supercharged the free-market mantra as it undermined the case for regulation of oligopolistic and monopolistic industries. New technologies created new competition, the argument went, and let the market work its magic.

Conversely, anything smacking of the left was suspect. Democrats, with a renewed commitment to free enterprise, were running full-speed away from the term *liberal*. They could do so with impunity because their base would be unlikely to vote Republican. President Clinton proclaimed, "The era of big government is over." Anything interfering with capitalist expansion was seen as bad economics and ideologically loaded, advanced by a deadbeat "special interest" group that could not cut the mustard in the world of free-market competition and so sought protection from the corrupt netherworld of government regulation and bureaucracy.[43] This credo led to the drive for deregulation throughout the economy and for the privatization of many once public-sector activities. The Clinton administration and Republicans were in sync when it came to the Internet: As Clinton and Gore put it in their 1997 *Framework for Global Electronic Commerce*, the first principle was that "the private sector should lead." Electronic commerce "over the Internet should be facilitated on a global basis." Matthew Crain's trailblazing dissertation research on this period demonstrates that the Clinton administration worked extensively, quietly, and harmoniously with private industry on all policy matters related to the Internet, while incipient public interest concerns about privacy and advertising were marginalized. When controversial issues emerged, the preferred solution was industry self-regulation.[44]

The symbolic coup de grâce for the public interest came in the bipartisan 1996 Telecommunications Act. This bill dealt with the Internet only indirectly, and was mostly the result of a turf war between the regional Bell monopolies (the "Baby Bells") and the long-distance carriers. Derek Turner of Free Press argues, in fact, that a careful reading of the act reveals that it included several measures that could have spawned more competition and advanced the public interest in the digital realm. The real tragedy was that Congress washed its hands of fundamental policy making at this point, ending the possibility of meaningful public involvement. Matters were turned over to endless court challenges of public interest provisions in the law brought by the corporate players, and to the Federal Communications Commission (FCC), which in the dark of night had little compunction about serving the needs of large corporate interests as they looked to exploit the Internet. "Before the ink was even dry on the 1996 Act," Turner writes, "the powerful media and telecommunications giants and their army of overpaid lobbyists went straight to work obstructing and undermining the competition the new law was intended to create. By the dawn of the twenty-first century, what they could not get overturned in the courts was gladly undone by a new FCC staffed and led by the same lobbyists."[45]

In public pronouncements that accompanied the 1996 Telecommunications Act, this addition to communication law was premised on the notion that traditional concerns with "natural monopoly" in telecommunications and concentrated markets in media were rendered moot by the Internet, which would unleash so much new competition that there was no longer any justification for regulation. The propaganda was so thick, no one stopped to ask why huge monopolistic firms would be lobbying for deregulation if it would leave them facing increased competition and therefore reduced profits.

The biggest lie of deregulation was that these were markets that the government could exit, allowing market competition to work its magic. On the contrary, all the communication markets—including telephone, cable and satellite TV, broadcasting, motion pictures, and recorded music—were created or decisively shaped by the government and based on government monopoly licenses or privileges. Deregulation did not remove the government or the importance of policy making by one iota. In every area of importance, the government still played a central role. What deregulation did was remove or severely lessen the idea of government action in the public interest. The point of government regulation, pure and simple, became to help firms maximize their profits, and that was the new public interest. Deregulation in communication meant, in effect, "re-regulation strictly to serve the largest corporate interests." "If the present trend is not comprehensively interrupted," Dan Schiller perceptively wrote in 1999, "the extent to which cyberspace becomes a commercial consumer medium will be very largely determined by profit-seeking companies themselves."[46] This reregulation let companies locate the most profitable uses and then build policies to support those activities.

There was a fourth factor that undermined opposition or even debate despite this blatant pandering to a handful of corporations. The Internet bubble of the late 1990s made policies promoting the commercial development of cyberspace seem not only appropriate, but brilliant. After a difficult recession in the early 1990s following a scary crash in 1987, the Internet-inspired New Economy seemed to be the solution to the growth problems of capitalism. The late 1990s were a giddy moment, and the U.S. news media could barely contain themselves with their enthusiasm for the happy couple. Capitalism and the Internet seemed a marriage made in heaven.[47] The emerging CEOs were the conquering heroes of the time, visionary seers, world-historical geniuses, and men of action, fully deserving of their rewards. "I think Bill Gates has the right to make $50 billion," Harvard's Henry Louis Gates Jr. stated in 1998, "if he's smart enough to figure all that stuff out."[48] Where the hell did Al Gore get off thinking he deserved credit for the work of these titans?

Although the policy battles were won decisively by capital, it is important to acknowledge that there remained plenty of space for people to use the Internet as they wished, so this was not a case like radio broadcasting, wherein the system was turned over to a small number of commercial interests as a monopoly. There has been a tremendous burst of nonprofit and noncommercial Internet sites and free or open software and applications—Yochai Benkler puts the number in the thousands—that have become a central part of the digital realm as experienced by many online.[49] *Wikipedia* is the most striking example. As John Naughton puts it, amateurs "have created what is effectively the greatest reference work the world has yet produced."[50] *Wikipedia* founder Jimmy Wales understood from the outset that it could not be credible and successful if it was commercial, and *Wikipedia* still has a stance toward advertising that conjures up the Net's salad days.[51]

At their best, these noncommercial cooperative ventures hark back to what Internet celebrants have most extolled about the technology's virtues and potential.[52] The most prominent of these developments have found a niche that sits comfortably with the dominant commercial players. As Rebecca MacKinnon puts it, "Open-source software is not inherently anti-business," and many of the giants like Google use it where it helps them.[53] "Many businesses built on top of open source," notes James Losey of the New America Foundation, "such as Apple building its OSX on top of Unix."[54] Google and *Wikipedia*, as Siva Vaidhyanathan writes, have such a strong synergy—*Wikipedia* ranks near the top of most Google searches—that "it's unlikely any reference source would unseat Wikipedia."[55] This cooperative sector is important for the corporate players too, because it brings legitimacy to the commercial Internet as something more than a digital ATM for billionaires. When Mark Zuckerberg prepared the initial public offering for Facebook in 2012, he wrote to potential investors that Facebook "was not originally created to be a company." Instead, "it was built to accomplish a social mission—to make the world more open and connected."[56]

Internet Service Providers: From Monopoly to Cartel?

Two of the industries most immediately threatened by the Internet were the telephone and the cable television industries. For many generations the giant telephone and, to a lesser extent, cable TV firms had been the recipients of enormous indirect government subsidies through their government monopoly franchises. Almost all of them operated with local monopolies. Although often unpopular with consumers, they were arguably the most extraordinary lobbying force in the nation, as their survival depended on government authorization and support.

The great challenge for these industries was to survive the digital revolution. It seemed to be only a matter of time until the Internet provided all sorts of voice communication and access to all sorts of audiovisual entertainment at virtually no cost, making both of these industries superfluous or at least far smaller and less profitable. They were able to meet the challenge through their unrivaled political muscle not only in Washington, but in state and municipal governments as well. Their great leverage was due to the fact that, thanks to government-created monopolies, they controlled the wires necessary for Internet access, at least until a more sophisticated, wireless system could be constructed. The telephone companies had lent their wires to Internet transmission, and in the 1990s, they—soon followed by the cable companies—realized that the wires were their future, and a lucrative one at that. But there were crucial political victories that needed to be won first, and it was not at all clear that they would win them.

The first threat to these firms was the new competition that was going to arrive with the ownership deregulation inscribed in the Telecommunications Act of 1996. There were roughly a dozen major telephone companies in the mid-1990s, some long-distance firms, and seven regional phone monopolies resulting from AT&T having been split up in 1984. There were another eight or so major cable TV and satellite TV companies, each of the cable TV providers having a monopoly license where it operated, and each satellite TV firm had monopoly rights to part of the electromagnetic spectrum. The theory was that with digital communication, all these firms would leave their monopoly boundaries and begin to compete with each other and that phone and cable and satellite TV companies would go after one another's business. In addition, all sorts of new players were certain to enter the field now that the official monopoly licenses were ending and the digital gold mine was in sight. Images of the Wild West Internet were invoked to suggest an onslaught of new competitors in telecommunication and cable/satellite television. The principle was "competition everywhere," creating what Tim Wu called a "Hobbesian struggle of all against all."[57]

These telephone and cable giants came to tolerate and eventually support the long process of "deregulation" of their industries that came to a head in the 1990s, not because they eagerly anticipated ferocious new competition, but because they suspected that the new regime would allow them to grow ever larger and have more monopolistic power.[58] It was a cynical moment. The stated justification for deregulation was that these traditional phone and cable monopolies would be permitted to use their wires to compete with each other in local markets, creating bona fide competition. In exchange, restrictions on mergers would be relaxed, so the helpless giants could gird themselves for the coming competitive Armageddon.

It was all nonsense. The powerful incumbent players had sufficient monopoly power, commercial and political, to ensure that no new serious competitors emerged. In Texas, for example, SBC (the Baby Bell that later reconstructed AT&T) had nearly a hundred registered lobbyists working on a legislature of 181 members. Not surprisingly Texas passed laws making it very difficult for any newcomer to challenge SBC's telephone monopoly.[59] In most cases, the dominant players knew it was in their interest not to mess with another incumbent, and outsiders realized it was tantamount to torching their capital to try to break into these industries. The upshot has been a wave of massive mergers shrinking the number of telephone and cable powerhouses down to between six and ten, depending on one's criteria—less than half the total from the mid-1990s—with AT&T, Verizon, and Comcast emerging as dominant and much more profitable entities.

Deregulation has led to the worst of both worlds: fewer enormous firms with far less regulation. To top it off, the political power of these firms in Washington and state capitals has reached Olympian heights.[60] Accordingly, politicians pretty much ignored their platitudes about increasing competition. The George W. Bush administration, as Tim Wu puts it, "tended to agree that competition didn't necessarily require that there be any extant competitors."[61] These monopolists are the poster children for crony capitalism, which in theory promarket types despise but in practice invariably champion, at least when they're anywhere near political power.

Increasing monopoly power and crushing the threat of competition was all well and good, but it did not solve the problem posed by the Internet. The telephone companies provided the main wires for Internet access in the late 1990s, but the FCC required that they fulfill the "common carriage" statutes, which meant that the shrinking number of Baby Bells had to allow open access at nondiscriminatory prices for other firms to use their lines as Internet service providers (ISPs). This led to an explosion in the number of ISPs—it was a highly competitive market—in which AOL rose to the top by the end of the decade. The telephone companies despised this regulation, and through the courts and regulatory system they pushed to have it ended, so they could have exclusive rights to use their own networks for ISP purposes.[62] Otherwise, their future was pretty grim, renting out their dumb pipes for other people to use to get rich, especially as telephony would switch over to Internet protocols.

By the new decade, the fat cable pipes were brought online to provide broadband Internet access. The cable companies, too, initially had to follow the common-carrier provisions that telephone companies faced. Then, in 2002—very quietly, and with no debate or public hearing and scarcely a scintilla of news media coverage—the Bush administration's FCC reclassified cable modems as an information service, rather than a telecommunication service. It was a party-line decision, with Democrat Michael Copps providing the lone dissenting vote.[63] This change allowed cable to escape the common-carrier provisions. A cable company could be the *only* ISP to use its wires. The U.S. Supreme Court upheld the FCC's constitutional right to make this reclassification—though not necessarily agreeing with what the FCC did—in the 2005 *NCTA v. Brand X* case. Shortly thereafter, the FCC reclassified the phone companies' Internet access services as information services, so they, too, could avoid the open-access requirement. By this time, nearly 50 percent of independent ISPs had already gone out of business since 2000; and soon nearly all of the rest would follow. As a leading study put it, "Broadband competition in the United States has collapsed."[64] A crucial policy fight going forward is getting the FCC to reverse its 2002 decision and return both cable and telephone-based broadband to the telecommunication service classification.

This reclassification has had magnificent consequences for the bottom lines of a handful of telecommunication giants and disastrous implications for broadband development in the United States. Nearly 20 percent of U.S. households have access to no more than a single broadband provider—a monopoly. Using FCC data (that the commission acknowledges probably overstates the degree of actual competition), all but 4 percent of remaining households has, at most, two choices for wired broadband access, a duopoly comprised of the local monopoly telephone provider—which may or may not be aggressively pushing wireline broadband—and a cable company.[65] There is no incentive for these duopolists to expand the market if it means they must lower their monopoly prices and profits; hence the persistence of the "digital divide," which I turn to below. The Obama administration set aside $7.2 billion in stimulus money to bring high-speed Internet to underserved areas, and while it helped in some rural areas, "it had no impact on the broader competitive situation in the market for most American consumers."[66] Moreover, it gave the big players an indirect subsidy "because a lot of the projects that were supported then need to buy connectivity from the major telcos."[67]

The other great development is the rise of cell phones, smartphones, and wireless Internet access. With extraordinary corporate jujitsu and no public study or debate, the handful of old telephone companies have gobbled up spectrum and transitioned to becoming the dominant cell phone and wireless ISP providers. Four companies control around 90 percent of the U.S. wireless market, and two of them—AT&T and Verizon—control 60 percent of the market and have more than 90 percent of free cash flow.[68] It has become a classic duopoly, in which the smart play is to imitate the other firm. "AT&T and Verizon don't really compete with one another," a Consumers Union attorney commented. "They copy one another."[69] So it was that when AT&T put limits on the data customers were allowed to download in 2012, Verizon quickly followed suit.[70] A few months later, Verizon announced a new scheme to allow its customers to purchase a certain amount of wireless data capacity that could be spread across a family's digital machines.

The plan was devised to maximize Verizon's revenues. "Verizon is finally delivering something everybody wants," a telecommunication analyst at the research firm Ovum said, "in a way nobody wants." AT&T was expected to offer an almost identical plan in short order.[71]

What is the price of duopoly? *Americans pay an average of $635 per year for cell phone service; people in Sweden, the Netherlands, and Finland pay less than $130 for superior service.* Moreover, in 1997 cell phone firms invested a whopping 50 percent of every dollar of revenue in the cell phone network; today, with little competitive pressure, capital expenditures have fallen to 12.5 percent of revenues.[72] "AT&T doesn't want to invest more in this network than it absolutely has to," telecommunication expert Susan Crawford explains. "Building more towers and connecting all of them to fiber would bring down the value of its shares."[73] It's a textbook case of monopoly power, and it pays off. In 2011, AT&T and Verizon were the twelfth and sixteenth largest firms in the Fortune 500, with combined revenues of $230 billion and combined profits of $20 billion.[74]

The concern is not simply that each of the wired broadband and wireless realms are monopolistic; it is also that they are becoming what Harold Feld of Public Knowledge terms a cartel.[75] In 2011 and 2012, exclusive deals were engineered between the dominant cable companies and the telecommunication companies so they would work closely together on standards and integrate their services.[76] To some extent, they were made in recognition of the fact that cable had won the battle for wired broadband. By 2011, 75 percent of people adding broadband were choosing cable.[77] Cable firms agreed to give up their spectrum so the cell phone companies could have more of it, while the cell phone companies effectively withdrew from serious competition for wired broadband customers. The major development was when cable powerhouse Comcast and wireless giant Verizon reached a deal to market each other's services in December 2011, in the midst of a number of similar deals among the big players.[78] As Feld puts it, "these side agreements amount to a tacit agreement to divide up markets between them and avoid competition."[79]

In August 2012, the cartelization of the entire ISP market—wired and wireless—was effectively sanctioned when both the Justice Department and the FCC approved Verizon's deal to swap spectrum, divvy up the market, and collaborate with Comcast and the other major cable companies.[80] "These companies aren't competing anymore. Now they're partners," telecom industry analyst Jeff Kagan said. "All I see is bad."[81] "Instead of an arms race between telephone and cable incumbents," tech policy journalist Timothy Lee wrote, "we seem to be getting a truce."[82] Providers, Feld notes, can aggressively pursue "anticonsumer incentives with no consequence."[83] Considering the size and importance of the telecommunication and ISP markets to the economy, that is an extraordinary state of affairs.

The consequences of the monopoly system are evident. In 2000 the United States was a world leader in terms of broadband penetration and access, "12–24 months ahead of any European country," according to the Danish National IT and Telecom Agency.[84] Today the United States ranks between fifteenth and thirtieth in most global measures of broadband access, quality of service, and cost per megabit.[85] In a September 2011 global report from Pando Networks, the United States ranked twenty-sixth in the world in average consumer download speed.[86] A 2012 New America Foundation examination of twenty-two cities worldwide concluded that "U.S. consumers in major cities tend to pay higher prices for slower speeds compared to consumers abroad."[87] "Here's a big fact," the author of the FCC's National Broadband Plan, Blair Levin, stated in 2012: "For the first time since the beginning of the commercial Internet, the United States does not have a commercial wireline provider with plans to build a better network than the currently best available network."[88] Crawford notes that this means most Americans will never get access to "the speeds the rest of the world is used to."[89] The New America Foundation places the direct cost of monopoly in wireline to American consumers over the next decade at $250 billion.[90]

There is more than a little tragedy surrounding the emergence of the cartel. There exists a great deal of existing and potential unused spectrum that could be used to establish a superb wireless network alternative to the existing cartel and drive down prices.[91] As *The Economist* notes, the unused spectrum may offer a "third pipe" that can "rival cable and telephone broadband for access to the Internet."[92] What is the problem? The electromagnetic spectrum has been allocated in an "ad hoc, piecemeal system" by the government, generally in response to the pressures of the moment, be they commercial or military. Demand for spectrum for wireless applications is now doubling on an annual basis, hence the vaunted spectrum "shortage."[93] But, as Meinrath notes, "most spectrum lies fallow," as spectrum "utilization rates are in the single digits throughout most the country. It's not that folks are hogging spectrum, they're warehousing it—mothballing it away so no one else can use it."[94]

What exists is a "false scarcity" wherein AT&T and Verizon "continue to gobble up more and more of the spectrum capacity needed to provide wireless service."[95] Matt Wood of Free Press notes that "Verizon and AT&T have insurmountable advantages in the current system of spectrum allocation, which allows them to outbid everyone else—both in FCC spectrum auctions and on the 'secondary market' when other licensees look to sell—and then hoard the spectrum they have without really putting it to good use quickly enough."[96] In 2011, one industry trade publication reported that AT&T had license to $10 billion worth of spectrum that was lying fallow, while it lobbied to have more spectrum diverted to it.[97] This guarantees that no alternative can emerge.[98]

In a sane society, policy debates over spectrum would concern how best to utilize this public resource. As Peter Barnes argues, such a policy is not necessarily "socialist"—it would invigorate businesses by lowering their costs along with everyone else's and by dramatically improving service.[99] In the United States, the incumbents prevent such a debate, and politicians are quick to see selling off spectrum as a way to look like "deficit hawks," regardless of the shortsighted nature of such a policy. At any rate, AT&T and Verizon have propagated the notion that there is a spectrum shortage and they need to be able to grab even more. The cartel's claims have been dismissed by numerous experts with no material stake in the outcome. "Arguing that the nation could run out of spectrum is like saying it was going to run out of a color," David P. Reed, told the *New York Times*. As the *Times* reported, Reed, "one of the original architects of the Internet and a former professor of computer science and engineering at the Massachusetts Institute of Technology, says electromagnetic spectrum is not finite." Technologies exist to accommodate a dramatic increase in users, and the "shortage" can be solved by policy making.[100] As MacKinnon notes, "There is no sign that Congress is serious about tackling this core problem of monopoly and pseudo-monopoly held by many wireless and broadband companies in many parts of the country."[101]

Elements of the FCC and the government as well as the business community are concerned about this situation. After all, the digital economy depends upon ubiquitous high-speed Internet, but it is hamstrung by the cartel. One *Forbes* writer reflected the growing concern among businesses that America badly lags behind most advanced nations in broadband speed and prices. "This inferiority is almost purely a result of the lack of true competition and pro-consumer regulation in the telecom industry."[102] The President's Council of Economic Advisers issued a report in February 2012 calling for more spectrum to be auctioned to improve wireless broadband.[103] Later in 2012 a presidential advisory committee, including executives from Microsoft and Google, urged President Obama "to adopt technologies that would use radio spectrum more efficiently."[104] But while some in Washington might wish to see this new spectrum enable a credible challenger to the ISP cartel, the effects would not be felt for five to ten years, and there is no evidence that either political party wants to have a head-on collision with the cartel over what the cartel regards as a matter of life and death: maintaining its vise-like grip on Internet access. Those closest to the action in Washington are highly skeptical of any meaningful reform. The Obama-era FCC "has been willfully ignorant and avoided meaningfully addressing the dearth of competition in the US broadband industry," one high-level activist told me in 2012.[105] Meinrath concurred, calling the spectrum talk "window-dressing" and stating that "a more honest assessment would be that the FCC is actively supporting the telco cartels."[106] It was striking that when FCC chairman Julius Genachowski wanted to locate more spectrum in 2012, he was more comfortable lobbying the Pentagon to turn over some of its spectrum to private companies, rather than pursue the unused holdings of the cartel.[107] "The prospects for broadband competition are as bad as they've ever been," a leading public interest policy analyst observed in May 2012. "In fact, they're much worse than when we first started banging this drum 6 years ago."[108]

There is a striking comparison here to health care, for which Americans pay far more per capita than any other nation but get worse service, due to the parasitic existence of the health insurance industry. President Barack Obama said that if the United States were starting from scratch, it would obviously make more sense (from a public welfare and cost standpoint) to have publicly insured health care and no private health insurance.[109] The same logic applies to broadband Internet access. It is worth noting that this is how Senator Al Gore understood matters during his years in Congress, when he championed funding for the Internet. In 1990 he argued that the foundation for the "information superhighway" should be a public network analogous to the interstate highway system.[110] Commercial interests could use the network, much as commercial businesses use the highways. The telecommunication companies would have a role, get contracts, and gradually increase their role, but the government would be in the driver's seat, coordinate the system, and guarantee ubiquitous access and public interest standards.[111] That generally uncontroversial assessment was buried under an avalanche once Wall Street cast its eyes that way, leading Vice President Al Gore to start singing a different tune. It has long been forgotten.

The parallel with the health care situation can be expanded: Just as the health insurance companies have no interest in taking on unhealthy customers or people from "risky" demographic groups, who might hurt their bottom lines, the wired broadband providers have no desire to solicit customers in poor or rural areas, where the firms find either revenues are too low or costs are too high, or both. In a nation with as much inequality and poverty as the United States, that can be devastating. Wireline broadband costs nearly twice as much in the United States as in Sweden, for example, and prices increased nearly 20 percent from 2008 to 2010.[112] An extensive investigative report in 2012 revealed that as of December 2010, "40 percent of households did not have broadband connection in the home." Homes in wealthier neighborhoods subscribe to broadband in the 80 to 100 percent range, while impoverished households in the same city subscribe at half that rate. The poorest states in the nation all subscribe at under 50 percent. "Access to broadband has become critical for anyone to keep up in American society," the report observes. "Finding and applying for jobs often takes place entirely online. Students receive assignments via e-mail. Basic government services are routinely offered online." The digital divide thereby *accentuates* the gnawing inequality in the United States. The "solution" for the unwired is the cell phone with some Internet access, but as the report concludes, "a smart phone is no substitute for a home computer with a wire-line connection, at least not today."[113] And as we will see shortly, probably not tomorrow either.[114]

There are currently two great policy battles in the United States that may reduce the damage caused by the ISP cartel. First is the movement for local communities to establish their own broadband networks, "just as local governments a century ago wanted their communities to have affordable access to reliable electric power." Countless cities have been ignored or feel gouged by the cartel, and more than 150 of them throughout the nation have built their own networks. The private ISPs tend to be unwilling "to invest in next generation broadband networks except in the most lucrative markets."[115] To many of the communities left out in the cold, this is regarded as a matter of life and death. A 2012 study by the New America Foundation demonstrates that American universities are well positioned to be the "primary anchor institutions" that provide "robust physical infrastructure that can be leveraged to provide high-speed Internet access into communities."[116]

The cartel has responded to community broadband exactly as the health insurance industry did to the idea of a viable "public option" in the 2009–10 health care debates. It has deployed its vast resources and lobbying armada in what can only be described as withering attacks in nearly all states to make municipal broadband networks all but impossible, if not illegal. By 2012 nineteen states had passed such laws.[117] In North Carolina, for example, which passed a law restricting local governments from building broadband networks in 2011, the giant telecom companies and their trade associations gave nearly $1.8 million to North Carolina state candidates between 2006–11.[118] At the same time, that the total is *only* 19 states reflects the fact that popular campaigns to protect the right for communities to establish broadband networks have been able to thwart, or at least stall, the cartel. One *Economist* writer based in Atlanta raved about Chattanooga's municipally owned high-speed broadband network: "Meanwhile, here in Atlanta, a region of over 4m people, I'm stuck with mediocre Comcast service that conks out every time I look at it funny."[119] Once people experience community or municipal broadband, as in Santa Monica, California, it is much harder for the cartel's battalions of lobbyists and trunkloads of campaign donations to take it away.[120] In both 2005 and 2007, a bipartisan group of senators including John Kerry and John McCain introduced legislation that would have stopped states from blocking their cities and towns from building their own broadband networks. The cartel was able to derail the legislation then, but that approach remains the best immediate solution to the problem.

The second policy battle is over Net neutrality. This is a requirement that ISPs not discriminate among users, following the old common carrier requirements on the telephone monopoly. Technically, this meant ISPs "could not discriminate against packets moving across their networks."[121] In the 1990s many Americans assumed the Internet was a magical platform that let everyone have an equal right to speak, thanks to the technology. In fact, the democratic genius of the Internet was the *regulation* that prohibited ISPs from discriminating among legal Internet activities, so a punk rock or vegan website got the same treatment as Microsoft's website. The ISPs hated this regulation; if they could discriminate among users, they could effectively privatize the Internet and make it like cable television. For cartel members, it is less about their desire to censor dissident speech than their desire to extort extra fees from commercial players on their networks. AT&T CEO Ed Whitacre proclaimed as much in an interview with *BusinessWeek* in 2005. What Internet websites and applications "would like is to use my pipes for free, but I ain't going to let them do that."[122] Users did and do pay the ISPs to use their networks; what the cartel wanted was the right to discriminate, charge big users more, and collect additional undeserved "rents." In a world without Net neutrality, the potential for increased ISP profits was and is mind-boggling.

Business analysts and publications like *The Economist* argued that the obvious market solution to the problem was more competition. If consumers had choices, no one would ever sign up to an ISP that censored websites or discriminated among them. But the cartel made that about as realistic politically as passing a constitutional amendment outlawing heterosexuality, so the campaign for the maintenance of Net neutrality became the crucial battle to prevent the elimination of the Internet as an open public realm.

Led by Free Press, an enormous campaign mushroomed around 2005–6 to maintain Net neutrality. There was support on the political grounds that it was singularly dangerous to permit a small handful of private concerns to have a censor's power over what had become the primary marketplace of ideas. "In many countries," MacKinnon points out, "a lack of net neutrality makes censorship—whether by companies, government, or some mix of the two—much easier to implement and much less publicly visible, let alone accountable."[123] There was also support for Net neutrality from the business community, especially from powerful firms like Google, which did not want to be shaken down by ISPs in order to get on their networks. In 2008 a frustrated Vint Cerf, by then a Google executive, asked if it might not be better if the Internet data-pipe infrastructure were "owned and maintained by the government, just like the highways."[124] Candidate and later president Barack Obama loudly announced that he would "take a back seat to no one in my commitment to net neutrality," and that it would be the centerpiece of his communications policy regime.[125]

The formal Net neutrality policy that the FCC approved in December 2010 maintained effective neutrality for the wired ISPs but effectively abandoned it for the wireless ISPs, where much of the action was moving. "It's the internet vs. the schminternet," as Jeff Jarvis put it.[126] The actual policy closely approximated the agreement Google and Verizon had privately reached on Net neutrality in August 2010.[127] That meeting took on the air of the meeting of the five families in *The Godfather* to divvy up the illegal-drug trade in New York City. Jarvis termed it a "devil's pact," and it was a textbook example of how communication policy is made.[128] As of 2013, mobile phones have overtaken PCs as the most common way to access the Web, and that will be an increasingly proprietary world.[129] Nor will its influence end there. "The closed smartphone architecture is the canary in the coalmine for all of consumer computing," Harvard's Jonathan Zittrain says, concluding that "the PC is dead."[130]

Free Press, the New America Foundation, and most public interest advocates regarded the policy as a failure, an abandonment of the Obama administration's oft-stated position. The fingerprints of the wireless ISPs were all over it, and it was easy to see the fear the Obama administration had about antagonizing such a powerful and well-heeled lobby, especially with a billion-dollar election around the corner. Republicans opposed *any* Net neutrality regulations. The ISPs sensed weakness and pushed ahead in the courts to have even the FCC policy rejected, if not the very notion of Net neutrality. That is where the matter stands at this writing. If this stops being an issue among politicians, it will be because the cartel has won.

The *Titanic* Sails Again?

From the 1970s to the end of the 1990s, in a dramatic transformation, the U.S. media system came to be dominated by a handful of entertainment conglomerates—Time Warner, News Corporation, Viacom, Disney, General Electric, and one or two others. After a wave of ever larger mergers and acquisitions, these companies owned all the major television networks, many of the largest-market television stations, hundreds of radio stations, all the major film studios, many cable TV systems, most of the cable TV channels, and much of the music recording industry. These firms also had large stakes in magazine and book publishing, and a few newspapers. Some of them—like Sony, General Electric, and Disney—had extensive holdings outside traditional media. In just fifteen years, between 1984 and the end of the 1990s, the share of the five largest conglomerates in total media-sector revenues doubled to around 26 percent.[131] That may not sound like much by recent American standards, but the media sector includes as many as ten fairly distinct industries that traditionally often had their own unique firms. Several of these industries, like book publishing, had been rather competitive in the not too distant past.[132] This concentration would be somewhat akin to having five firms control 26 percent of the revenues of all branches of food production, grocery stores, and restaurants.

By 2000 there was also a second tier of a dozen or so lesser conglomerates that tended to be newspaper-based empires—like Gannett, the Tribune Company, Cox, the Washington Post and the New York Times—that had interests in television stations and publishing. These firms were pikers compared to the megaconglomerates, and they did not grow as quickly, but they were an important component of the media system, especially for journalism. Once one got past the first two dozen or so firms, the companies that remained were much smaller and less powerful. It was a quick trip from the redwood forest to the weeds. By the end of the 1990s, these two dozen largest firms were made up of what were once several hundred independent media companies as recently as the 1970s.[133]

By 2000 there were eighteen media and advertising firms that qualified for the Fortune 500, compared to eight in 1970; eight conglomerates qualified for the top 150, compared to two such firms in 1970.[134] Media concentration seems to many to violate the principle of open and diverse media required for a democratic culture. To the extent it was seen as affecting journalism, it became a growing concern.[135] These firms had gotten larger for the same reasons other capitalist firms get larger: bigness reduces risk and increases profitability, everything else being equal.[136] It's important to remember that conglomeration required a number of significant changes in federal laws and regulations—largely because most of these firms traded in radio and TV stations or cable TV systems, the licenses for which had strict ownership regulations to prevent monopoly—but media firms proved to be highly skilled at getting their way in Washington.

By the mid-1990s, for media moguls like Rupert Murdoch and Disney's Michael Eisner, it seemed the world was their oyster. But for all the depth and breadth of the empires they had constructed and despite all their political influence, the Internet seemingly posed a threat to their very existence. As Jaron Lanier put it, "the old-media empires were put on a path of predictable obsolescence."[137] The Internet appeared to pose this threat for three reasons. First, it opened the possibility of making it much easier for new players to enter media markets. As the Internet became the dominant platform, prospective entrants would no longer need major capital to get a broadcasting license or buy an existing film studio. With barriers to entry eliminated, the digital era might make it possible for another giant with an enormous bankroll, say a Microsoft or an AT&T, to successfully use the Internet as a platform to get in the media game, whereas it would have been unthinkable otherwise.

Like the telephone giants, the media conglomerates and their lobbyists argued that ownership regulations were no longer relevant to their industries and should be abolished. Why? Because as all media shifted to digital formats, the traditional distinctions among media sectors would disappear—a process called convergence—with a consequent tidal wave of digital competition. Media giants needed to be allowed to get much, much larger to withstand the impending competitive war. Otherwise they would likely die, and it would be unfair to force them to compete in the digital race for survival with their shoelaces tied together. Partially as a result of this argumentation, for example, the 1996 Telecommunications Act greatly relaxed radio station ownership rules, leading to massive consolidation in the next three years. This notion of new digital competition for the media giants was embraced by many digital activists in the 1990s, who thought the big media corporations were getting their just deserts. They would all soon be submerged by the Internet, with its unlimited number of websites.[138] All sorts of newcomers could enter what had been a restricted field, and if they could locate a following, they would be able to generate sufficient revenues to make a go of it. Jaron Lanier remembers the idealistic conviction that a digital utopia was around the corner in a cultural system soon to be liberated from the commercial monopolists.[139]

The second threat to the media conglomerates was the difficulty of getting customers to pay for media content online, because it was so ridiculously easy to copy and distribute perfect digital copies of music, films, TV shows, and the like at no charge. The Internet magnified the inherent problem with markets for cultural production and, in effect, made the commercial media system impossible. Copyright was finally overmatched. One could imagine the end of the recording industry, Hollywood, television, and book publishing. The prospective demise of the commercial media system could have generated public study and debate over how best to encourage cultural production and have cultural workers effectively compensated, that is, what policies could replace copyright in the digital era. But the media conglomerates had no interest in such a discussion, so it never occurred. Their business model is built on the dramatic expansion of copyright, and without it there would not be much of an industry.

Commercial media dealt with the public good of terrestrial radio and TV broadcasting by turning to advertising as the source of revenues. In theory this could have been part of a solution to their dilemma with the Internet. But all evidence suggested that people would never sit through thirty-second spots on their computer; they would go to another site. Advertising, which made television one of the great engines of profit for generations, was in the digital crosshairs. This was the third great threat posed by the Internet to the media conglomerates.

In combination, the three threats would take away audience with all sorts of new free offerings on the infinite World Wide Web. It would make "piracy" so rampant that there would be very little commercial incentive to produce content. Scarcity would no longer exist, so there could be no basis for markets.[140] And it would be impossible for advertising to bankroll Internet media, because customers would not tolerate it, and in the land of digital plenty, customers would have an infinite number of choices. This was enough to make any media CEO want to upload a résumé and look for a new field to conquer.

The Internet explosion of the 1990s scared the dickens out of the media giants, and they responded by doing what was second nature to them: buying the competition. They frantically spent billions of dollars gobbling up digital ventures so they would not be outflanked by any digital media upstarts. They would buy up everything they could on the Internet so no matter how it developed, they would own the damn thing. That experience is now chalked up as among the most insane flights of fancy in business history and an unmitigated disaster for the media giants, who acted as if they had only a matter of months until the Internet destroyed them. Some of the digital ventures they invested in were laughably implausible. The nadir came in January 2000 when the AOL–Time Warner merger was announced; AOL was the dominant partner in the deal even though it had just a smidgen of Time Warner's assets, sales, or profits. What AOL had was a mother lode of world-class hype. It soon became clear that once the Internet shifted from dial-up to broadband, AOL had no business model and was next to worthless.[141] How could Time Warner, the mightiest of the mighty media conglomerates, have missed something so elementary?

Despite the hit to corporate balance sheets due to the Internet bubble, in 2000 commercial media markets remained lucrative, and the immediate future looked just fine, especially for the Hollywood-based conglomerates. It would take widespread broadband to make the threats genuine. In the meantime, the media giants had oodles of cash and considerable lobbying power to try to redirect digital media before broadband hit full-force. They had also learned an important lesson by then: if the media giants couldn't find a successful business model for media online, no one else would either. To the extent that anyone could make a profit producing online media content, the media giants, with their vast collection of content and resources, had dramatic advantages over everyone else. This changed the nature of the struggle, lengthening their shelf life by decades, and, insofar as content had value, giving them considerable leverage.

The corporate media sector has spent much of the past fifteen years doing everything in its immense power to limit the openness and egalitarianism of the Internet. Its survival and prosperity hinge upon making the system as closed and proprietary as possible, encouraging corporate and state surreptitious monitoring of Internet users and opening the floodgates of commercialism.[142] By 2012, media firms were holding their own. Although asset-shuffling and deal making continued—Comcast, for example, bought a controlling interest in NBC Universal from General Electric in 2011—the degree of concentration has plateaued at around 2000 levels. The largest media firms maintained their grip, with about the same number ranking in *Fortune*'s top 150 and top 500 in 2011 as in 2000.[143]

The most important campaign has been to extend the scope and length of copyright and make enforcement as sweeping and penalties as onerous as possible. The copyright lobby has dominated congressional and regulatory deliberations. As MacKinnon put it, "The need to protect intellectual property has become a higher priority for many elected officials than due process—the presumption that a person is innocent until proven guilty."[144] Another major prong of this power grab was the development of digital rights management (DRM) technologies that imposed artificial limitations on the functionalities of digital devices and software.[145]

From 1998's Digital Millennium Copyright Act to the failed attempt in 2011–12 to pass the Stop Online Piracy Act (SOPA), copyright law has moved from the sleepy backwater of law school curricula—providing the rules of the road for a long-established commercial system—to the forefront as an offensive weapon for shaping our media and communication systems. SOPA would have given the government the power to shut down entire domains, with very little transparency and no meaningful repercussions for erroneous actions. It would have extended and legitimated the already extensive activities of ISPs to censor websites accused of "piracy," with minimal standards for due process and fairness. The measure, according to *Wired* magazine, also would have paved "the way for private rights holders to easily cut off advertising and banking transactions to what the bill's backers call 'rogue websites,' without court intervention." As Google's Sergey Brin told *The Guardian* in an interview, SOPA "would have led to the US using the same technology and approach it criticized China and Iran for using."[146] Representative Zoe Lofgren (D-CA) may have spoken with only a tad of hyperbole when she stated that its passage "would mean the end of the Internet as we know it."[147] The details were so frightening that *Wikipedia* closed its website for a full day in protest. Although defeated in 2012, the issue will return to Congress in coming years, perhaps in sheep's clothing.

Another measure of the power of the copyright lobby is how the federal government has made copyright enforcement the highest possible priority in trade deals and has pressured other governments to adopt U.S.-style laws and enforcement—to the point where a casual observer might think U.S. officials were on the media industry's payroll.[148] The United States has led the fight for the Anti-Counterfeiting Trade Agreement (ACTA), which as of 2012 had over thirty signatories and is in the process of being ratified. The United States kept top secret its core provisions until they were released by WikiLeaks in 2008. ACTA would empower governments to cut off Internet access for alleged copyright violators without due process and to remove content without proof of any violation. After worldwide protests, these stipulations were watered down grudgingly, but the concerns of copyright holders are clearly the point of the exercise and a higher priority than human rights. In July 2012 the European Parliament rejected ACTA, largely due to the public outcry over the onerous copyright extensions, which pretty much killed it. Attention then turned to the Trans-Pacific Partnership treaty being negotiated between the United States and Pacific Rim nations. Feld saw in those negotiations indications that the U.S. trade representative—after the publicity beating over ACTA—was beginning to recognize that a softer hand, and more acceptance of such matters as fair use and the public domain, might be necessary to gain passage of trade deals.[149] But some people close to the action do not expect meaningful changes in the U.S. position on copyright either internationally or domestically. "These efforts are absolutely independent of public input," James Losey told me.[150] Meinrath is dubious about the efforts of policy makers to appease concerned citizens about new copyright laws and treaties: "All multi-stakeholder efforts I've heard about have been more towards the PR BS side of the spectrum than anything meaningful."[151]

Note well, as MacKinnon chronicles, the lessons from China and Russia are that those governments routinely use copyright enforcement as a politically convenient cover for cracking down on dissent.[152] There is also a synergy of interests between the commercial forces that want to monitor people surreptitiously online to better sell them to advertisers and the copyright holders who want to monitor people online to see who might be using their material without permission.[153]

The irony is this: research demonstrates that while aggressively enforcing onerous copyright laws can quash dissent, because of the technology, that approach is ineffective at reducing the supply of "pirated" material online.[154] "In the long run," as David Friedman puts it, "simply enforcing existing law is not going to be an option."[155] Scholars like Pat Aufderheide and Peter Jaszi propose smart reforms, while others, like Yochai Benkler, Lawrence Lessig, and Friedman, demonstrate that there may be ways to make cultural production compatible with the Internet.[156] "I think we are at a point where we are asking whether you really need a film industry for a film to be made or a music industry to make music," Kickstarter co-founder Yancey Strickler put it in 2012.[157] The problem, of course, is that alternative approaches are not compatible with the media giants remaining enormous and enormously profitable.

Independent of the legislative front, in 2012 the media giants proceeded to work out private arrangements to enforce copyright to their satisfaction with the telecom cartel and Internet giants such as Google. The Center for Copyright Information was formed so that the ISPs would police their networks for "pirated" material. After six warnings, an infringing user would have the material significantly downgraded or removed. The exact manner in which the system would work has been obscure, as have been the rights of the accused. The potentially explosive plan was to go into effect in July 2012 but was delayed to work out the details. As one observer noted, the "ISPs are not the most popular companies, and playing policeman for Hollywood will not make that better at all."[158]

The media firms did get Google to agree to alter its search algorithms to favor copyrighted material in August 2012. Google preferred a private agreement to a bill like SOPA that could make more onerous and costly demands on it to police copyright. Websites that were repeatedly challenged on copyright grounds would be listed so deep into Google searches that they would effectively no longer exist. The concerns again are that the process is opaque and, as a public interest advocate told Talking Points Memo, "appears to incentive copyright holders to file many removal requests." Indeed, Google received copyright removal requests for over 4.3 million Web addresses within a thirty-day period during summer 2012, more than it received in all of 2009.[159] "Google has set up a system that may be abused by bad faith actors who want to suppress their rivals and competitors," one public interest lawyer stated.[160] As Free Press's Wood put it, "any number of deals that studios, ISPs, and search engine companies are ready, willing, and able to cut with each other" can threaten the open Internet just as much as "bad legislation."[161] Should private self-interested monopolies really be making secret policy that directs the future of cyberspace, without public awareness or participation?

The most significant development in the media giants' battle to stem "piracy" has been the emergence of Apple iTunes, Netflix, legal streaming systems, and e-books as ways to sell content online. Forty percent of Americans who said they had illegally downloaded videos said the legal proprietary streaming services made them less likely to do so.[162] By 2010 nearly a third of record companies' global revenues came from digital distribution, and the proportion was rising quickly. By 2011, Amazon's sales of e-books exceeded its sales of printed books.[163] One major publisher saw the percentage of its revenues from e-book sales increase from 11 percent in 2010 to 36 percent by the end of 2011, and this is the trend industrywide.[164] For the public, these legal alternatives are mixed blessings, because they are closed, proprietary systems devised to establish and maintain artificial scarcity, so as to give immense power to private monopolies. The problem for media giants is that they give firms like Apple and Amazon a great deal of power over pricing. The 2012 battle among Amazon, Apple, and book publishers over the pricing of e-books, for example, pointed to a future in which publishers may not be necessary, except in the sales of their existing copyrighted material. Hence the media giants are doubling down on their campaign for onerous copyright laws, extreme enforcement, and draconian penalties.[165]

Media conglomerate bottom lines notwithstanding, it remains uncertain if these proprietary systems can effectively generate a revenue base to sustain a large system of original cultural production. Lanier, for one, has abandoned his utopianism for what he terms empiricism. "To my shock, I have trouble finding a handful of musicians" (besides artists like Ani DiFranco) who have bypassed the corporate system and made a go of it online. "After ten years of seeing many, many people try," he concluded in his assessment of the Internet and culture, "I fear that it just won't work for the vast majority of journalists, musicians, artists, and filmmakers who are staring into career oblivion because of our failed digital idealism."[166]

The one truly hopeful sign for the media conglomerates is the extraordinary durability of television. In 2012 some $60 billion was spent on TV advertising, mostly flowing to the large conglomerates; online video received only $3 billion in advertising, although that was a 55 percent increase over 2011.[167] What is developing is a merger of sorts between digital television and the Internet. Online streaming currently reaches one third of all TV viewers on a weekly basis.[168] "Four to five hours per day is what Americans spend consuming video," Hulu CEO Jason Kilar noted, and the battle is on to see who controls that four to five hours, whether it is on a television, a laptop, or a smartphone.[169] According to Cisco Systems, video accounted for 40 percent of Internet traffic in 2012 and will account for around 60 percent in 2015.[170] As this is an advertising-supported area for the most part, the convergence is accelerating as digital television becomes "addressable" like the Internet. "Contemporary activities suggest," Joseph Turow writes, "that eventually there will be little difference between the 'internet' and 'television' in terms of advertisers' approach to people and their data."[171] The media conglomerates are working diligently to become the main content providers and to have control over the channels, whatever the precise medium.[172]

Firms like Apple, Amazon, and Google—not to mention the ISP cartel—are joining the battle to control video consumption, and are all scurrying to expedite and capitalize upon this marriage of digital TV and the Internet. As the *New York Times* puts it, these "battles are part of the larger war for three screens: smartphones, tablets, and televisions." A 2012 Pew survey determined that 52 percent of all adult cell phone users "incorporate their mobile devices into their television watching experiences."[173] Google's YouTube, for example, is launching one hundred TV-style advertising-supported Internet channels.[174] "We want to make all your screens work together in a unique and seamless way," a Microsoft executive explains. The growing consensus is that "whichever company ends up owning the living room, where most content is consumed, could own the entire sphere."[175]

It is unclear where this process will end up—and what the division of power will be among the corporate sectors—except that it is mostly being driven by advertising, in a form radically different from how it has been traditionally understood. The smart money says not to bet against the new digital giants as they square off with the media conglomerates for the largest slice of the pie.[176] Let's find out why.

5

The Internet and Capitalism II: Empire of the Senseless?

In this chapter I complete the analysis of the marriage of the Internet to really existing capitalism. I look at the new digital giants that have emerged and are increasingly the masters of the Internet—and masters of much of our social life. I then assess the extraordinary conversion of the Internet into an advertising-based medium, and how the new digital advertising industry is a radical departure from advertising as we have known it. Finally, I bring the government and the national security and military agencies into the picture, discussing their use of the Internet and how their operations mesh with those of the dominant commercial players. In all three sections, questions emerge about the compatibility of the capitalist-driven Internet with the requirements of effective self-government.

The New Digital Giants—Who and Why?

It is supremely ironic that the Internet, the much-ballyhooed champion of increased consumer power and cutthroat competition, has become one of the greatest generators of monopoly in economic history. Digital market concentration has proceeded far more furiously than in the traditional pattern found in other areas, described in chapter 2. As "killer applications" have emerged, new digital industries have gone from competitive to oligopolistic to monopolistic at breakneck speeds. To be clear, the Internet is still crystallizing as an area of capitalist development, and it appears to be dynamic, so not all of its characteristics are discernible. Nevertheless, the monopoly tendencies are powerful, and the existing giants appear poised for a long reign atop the U.S. and global political economy. At this point, one can only speculate as to whether any new digital monopoly giants will join them or the system is approaching consolidation.

In most Internet areas where profits can be generated, private interests have been able to convert beachheads into monopoly fortresses and generate endless profit. Google, for example, holds nearly 70 percent of the search-engine market. It may soon challenge the market share that John D. Rockefeller's Standard Oil had it its peak. Google already has 97 percent of the booming mobile search market.[1] Despite attacks by Apple and the growth of open-source Linux, Microsoft's Windows operating system continues to be used on more than 90 percent of all computers.[2] Apple, via iTunes, controls an estimated 87 percent market share in digital music downloads and 70 percent of the media-player market.[3] The iPad dominates the burgeoning tablet computer market.[4] "Ninety percent of the profits in the smartphone space are going to Apple and Samsung," a former Microsoft executive said in 2012. "There's no real sign that's changing anytime soon."[5] Amazon sells between 70 and 80 percent of both physical books and e-books online,[6] and eBay and Facebook, along with a handful of other giants, enjoy considerable monopolistic power as well. A recent analysis of economic inequality in the United States concluded that "the stupendous gains made possible by the technological advances of the information age have been almost entirely captured by a tiny elite."[7]

The monopolistic firms that have capitalized on the digital revolution have grown to world-historical proportions. In 2012, four of the ten largest U.S. corporations in terms of market valuation, including number one and number three, were Internet giants Apple, Microsoft, Google, and AT&T. Add IBM and that is five of the top ten. If one goes down through the top thirty, the list then includes Verizon, Amazon, Comcast, and Disney, as well as the Internet giants that depend less directly on the consumer market: Intel, Cisco, Qualcomm, and Oracle. That is thirteen of the top thirty firms. In comparison, the top thirty firms include only two of the "too big to fail" banks that have earned so much notoriety for their dominance of the political economy.[8] In short, the Internet monopolists sit at the commanding heights of U.S. and world capitalism. When *Fortune* magazine compiled its list of the top twelve entrepreneurs of the past generation, the founders of Internet giants Apple, Microsoft, Amazon, and Google occupied four of the top five slots.[9]

Why is monopoly so much more pronounced and so much more impervious to direct competitive challenge on the Internet than in the balance of the economy? The paradox is striking, because scarcity on the Internet has to be created and hence is artificial. As *Wired* editor Chris Anderson puts it, "Artificial scarcity is the natural goal of the profit-seeking."[10]

There are a few closely related explanations. First and most important, the Internet exhibits what economists term network effects, meaning that just about everyone gains by sharing use of a single service or resource. Information networks, in particular, generate demand-side economies of scale, related to the capture of customers, as opposed to supply-side economies of scale (prevalent in traditional oligopolistic industry) related to reduction in costs as scale goes up.[11] The largest firm in an industry increases its attractiveness to consumers by an order of magnitude as it gets a greater market share, and makes it almost impossible for competitors with declining shares to remain attractive or competitive. *Wired*'s Anderson puts the matter succinctly: "Monopolies are actually even more likely in highly networked markets like the online world. The dark side of network effects is that rich nodes get richer. Metcalfe's law, which states that the value of a network increases in proportion to the square of connections, creates winner-take-all markets, where the gap between the number one and number two players is typically large and growing."[12]

Bob Metcalfe, inventor of the Ethernet protocol that wires computers together, regarded the network effect as so prevalent that he formulated the law that goes by his name: the usefulness of a network increases at an accelerating rate as you add each new person to it.[13] Google search is an example; the quality of its algorithm improves with more users, leaving other search engines with a less effective and attractive product. Consider Facebook, which during 2012 exceeded one billion users worldwide. "Those who sign up (and it's free) have access to a wider circle. Those who don't can feel excluded," *The Economist* observed. "This powerful feedback loop has already made Facebook the biggest social-networking site in many countries. It accounts for one in seven minutes spent online worldwide."[14] Metcalfe's law was responsible for Rupert Murdoch being hoisted by his own petard. Murdoch's News Corporation spent $580 million for MySpace in 2005; at that moment MySpace had what looked to be a decent shot at grabbing a commanding lead in the nascent social-media market and getting a Google-type monopoly. It soon found itself in Facebook's rearview mirror and fading fast; Murdoch unloaded MySpace in 2011 for $35 million.[15]

There is also a flip side to Metcalfe's Law: those *excluded* from a network face an accelerating cost of exclusion. Depending on the importance of the network, the severity of the exclusion can be tantamount to nonpersonhood. This is a good way to understand the importance of battles for Net neutrality and universal affordable broadband.[16]

A second factor that encourages monopoly is the importance of technical standards, which become imperative if different firms and consumers are going to be able to use the Internet effectively. Once they are set, the firm that holds the patent or even a head start is off to the races. It is in the public interest that these standards not privilege a single firm, but that is not always possible. Smart firms do what they can to make their technical system the industry standard, hence giving them the pole position and a two-lap lead in a three-lap race. "I suppose I shouldn't say this," Bill Gates acknowledged back in 1996 when discussing the importance of setting industry standards favorable to Microsoft, "but in some ways it leads, in a product category, to a natural monopoly."[17] Microsoft has been able to exploit the dependence of a wide range of software applications on its underlying operating system in order to lock in its system seemingly permanently, allowing it to enjoy long-term monopoly-pricing power. Any competitor seeking to introduce a new, rival operating system, faces an enormous "applications barrier to entry."[18]

Some of this goes on beneath the surface. Consider the H.264 codec, owned by the MPEG LA group, with licenses held by Microsoft, Apple, and others. It is quickly becoming the standard for online video, currently getting 66 percent of the market. With a bottleneck on Internet traffic like this, the owners of H.264 can create many "billable moments." Economists often term shakedowns like this "economic rents," referring to the undeserved income economic actors receive by virtue of their ownership of a scarce resource, independent of the cost of production or reproduction.[19] Or consider wireless powerhouse Qualcomm. It controls 69 percent of the code division multiple access (CDMA) chipset market and 77 percent of the wireless chipsets in Android devices. Along with Broadcom, Qualcomm controls half of the key wi-fi chipset markets.[20]

A related factor that encourages monopoly is the widespread use of patents, to such an extent that Tim Berners-Lee would probably now regard the late 1990s, which he once deplored, as a golden age of openness. The U.S. Patent Office awarded 248,000 patents in 2011, 35 percent more than a decade earlier.[21] Patents are similar to copyright: by offering government protection for a temporary monopoly license, they have the necessary function of rewarding and therefore encouraging innovation; like copyright, patents have exploded in prominence in the digital era.[22] *Bloomberg Businessweek* terms the escalation in patents—Microsoft, for example, took out over 2,500 in 2010, compared to just a few hundred in 2002—as a "high-tech arms race." Two or three decades ago a machine might have five or ten patents, a patent expert noted. "Today, the phone in your pocket has about 5,000." Battles over patents among the digital giants are now routine. "We can sit by and watch competitors steal our patented inventions," Steve Jobs said in 2010, "or we can do something about it." He launched what was termed Apple's Jihad over patent rights in the courts.[23] When Google paid an "astonishing" $12.5 billion to purchase Motorola Mobility in 2011, it did so significantly for Motorola's 17,000 patents. These were a "trove of mobile patents" that would make Google's Android stand up to legal challenge and diminish the threat of any new market entrants.[24] "As tech companies snap up patents," *Politico* observed, "they are battling each other in courts around the world." One antitrust attorney called it mutually assured destruction. The certain loser: the smaller firms that "can't buy up 20,000 patents" or pay legal fees for endless court cases.[25]

In the same manner that copyright law has become a deterrent to creativity as much as a foundation for it, so it is with patents.[26] "The belief that stronger intellectual property protection inevitably leads to more innovations appears broadly wrong," the *Times* writes, because "innovation is often a cumulative process, with each step piggybacking on the ideas before it." Patents halt the process, but they are fantastic for protecting entrenched monopoly power, litigation costs notwithstanding. "Who has the patents?" Stanford economist Tim Bresnahan asks. "It's the guys who have been around awhile, not the guys who have done a lot of innovation lately." *Bloomberg Businessweek* notes that "startups no longer race headlong to develop prototypes as fast as possible. Instead, they must first protect them with bulletproof intellectual property portfolios that can take years to build." Patents, the *Times* concludes, allow "dominant businesses to stop future inventions that would disrupt their business model." The piece posits the radical idea that "perhaps software should not be patentable at all."[27] Berners-Lee, who will meet his maker as the genius scientist who gave us the World Wide Web but not as a billionaire, would likely agree.

All these factors explain how the profitability of the digital giants is centered on establishing proprietary systems for which they control access and the terms of the relationship, not the idea of an Internet as open as possible. Back in 2006, Jonathan Zittrain predicted that in the coming decade the personal computer would be replaced by a new generation of (proprietary) "information appliances." Tim Wu says he was "exactly right."[28] Apple was committed to this approach from the very beginning, and "Jobs's vision of a closed computer did not waver."[29] Wu notes that Apple's various devices were "Hollywood-friendly," and designed to work with a single ISP.[30] Technology writer Steven Johnson praised Apple for providing one of "the most carefully policed software platforms in history." The genius of the iPhone, for example, is that it is a "tethered" device, for which all the control is with Apple. As John Naughton put it, the Internet-connected mobile phone "is functional, enjoyable and perhaps even beautiful—but it is largely under someone else's control."[31] By 2008 Bill Gates conceded that Apple's closed system had proven to be the best approach.[32] The investment community agreed; by 2012 Apple was the most valuable company in the United States, worth over $550 billion. But Apple is hardly the only digital firm that can be so described. Facebook's genius is building a realm that is proprietary and a new essential layer for engaging with other websites.

Google, ironically, has voiced loud protests over the emergence of these "walled gardens" as the basis for the Internet. "The old internet is shrinking and being replaced by walled gardens over which Google's crawlers can't climb," John Battelle of the online advertising network Federated Media explained in 2012. "To many, the space outside Facebook will look more and more like an untamed space where scams, malware, and piracy thrive."[33] Google's Brin has been blistering in his criticism of Apple and Facebook for their "proprietary platforms" that are "stifling innovation and balkanising the web." He stated that he and co-founder Larry Page "would not have been able to create Google if the Internet was dominated by Facebook."[34] Nevertheless, Google has launched its own proprietary service, Google+, and Microsoft also has moved in a proprietary direction. Moreover both of them depended upon proprietary software, which may have been among the first apples eaten in the digital Garden of Eden. Google has been described as "the antithesis of the open-source movement."[35] And when matters turn to the preeminent issue of privacy, Google locks arms with Facebook, abandoning any claim to the moral high ground.

A key development that accompanies and enables proprietary systems is cloud computing, wherein each of the giants stores vast amounts of material on their battalions of servers. Users do not need to have massive computer memories to store their own material; they can—indeed, must—access everything they have from a small device just by gaining access to the cloud. There are still "little guys" who offer hosting services, and that is a constructive activity. At the other end of the spectrum, though, the digital monopolists, including Google, Facebook, Amazon, Apple, and Microsoft, have all invested to build enormous private clouds. Cloud computing is a brilliant way to make the Internet more efficient and less expensive to users and society, but whether having the preponderance of cloud capacity in the hands of a few giant firms is a wise policy is another matter altogether. The clouds can be a treasure chest full of valuable data for the giants to exploit.[36]

Cloud computing requires serious capital outlays—old-fashioned barriers to entry—which lock in oligopoly or monopoly. Consider Google, which spends many billions annually on computers so it can provide nearly instantaneous response to queries.[37] Any Google search query "fires up between 700 and 1,000 separate computers in several huge data centers around the United States."[38] Like the other giants, Google has enormous "server farms" all over the world to keep all this information in its cloud. The companies are secretive about their location and size, but evidence suggests a server farm is an enormous industrial undertaking that would have more than held its own in Akron, Ohio, or Gary, Indiana, in 1963 or in China today. Naughton describes one data center as being comprised of ten vast "rooms" with thirty thousand computers and a sizable industrial cooling system in each of them. In 2008 Google had nineteen such data centers in the United States and almost as many elsewhere.[39] Google was thought to be purchasing 15 percent of the servers being sold in the United States at the time.[40]

In combination, these factors demonstrate how absurd are the claims by giants like Microsoft and Google that "competition is a click away" and that they are in mortal fear for their very survival if someone were to develop a better algorithm in her garage.[41] Amazon, too, is more than an algorithm and a stack of patents. It has sixty-nine data and fulfillment centers in the United States, seventeen of which were built since 2011, with plans for more to come. It has a nonunion workforce; the working conditions in one of its main fulfillment warehouses in Allentown, Pennsylvania, were characterized by an investigative report as resembling "the onerous conditions so indelibly satirized by Charlie Chaplin in *Modern Times*."[42]

Today, the Internet as a social medium and information system is the domain of a handful of colossal firms. Each of these firms is centered on having a monopoly base camp that generates piles of cash. By some accounts, Apple had $110 billion in cash on hand in 2012, while Google had $50 billion, Microsoft had $51 billion, and Amazon had $10 billion.[43] Facebook pocketed $16 billion in cash from its IPO in May 2012, but even before that, it managed to make nearly two dozen acquisitions since 2010, topped by a $1 billion deal for Instagram.[44] The giants, the *New York Times* noted, comprise an "industry that seems to be more awash in money by the day."[45]

Protecting and preserving the monopoly base camp is job one, and everything follows from it. The best way to imagine the Internet is as a planet where Google, Facebook, Apple, Amazon, Microsoft, and the ISP cartel members each occupy a continent that represents their monopoly base camp. A mini-empire with a monopoly base camp like eBay is the equivalent of Japan. The traditional media giants have less leverage, so they are located on the equivalent of Hawaii, New Zealand, and Madagascar. (The pattern of merging with a larger digital giant, as NBC Universal did with Comcast, is a plausible outcome.) Those faltering digital contenders, like Netscape, AOL, and now Yahoo!, all failed to lock in monopoly power and found themselves in the middle of the ocean looking for an uninhabited island.[46] Twitter has been discussing some sort of formal alliance with Apple—up to a formal acquisition—"amid intensifying competition from the likes of Google and Facebook."[47] The goal of each empire is to conquer the world and prevent getting conquered by someone else. It is understood that no firm is an island, so to speak, and it cannot rest content with its monopoly base camp and let the world sail on by. The firms sometimes compete aggressively, while they simultaneously are each other's customers and find value in alliances with some empires against the others.[48] As one industry observer put it in 2012, these "companies can cooperate with each other and gouge each other's eye out and experience no dissonance."[49] This is where game theory probably best explains their behavior.[50]

With their mountains of cash and stock that is attractive in deals, and with the benefits of their existing monopoly base camp, the empires all try to move into adjacent areas and launch new monopoly services, in the hope that they will eventually pan out. Apple has been tremendous at this, creating new monopolistic industries out of whole cloth. Google has moved out from search to countless other areas over the past eight years; Gmail and YouTube are just the tip of the iceberg.[51] "When Facebook's photo service was introduced," Steven Johnson writes in *Wired*, "it almost instantly became the largest digital photo repository in the world, despite a feature set that was obviously inferior to those of competitors like Flickr and Photobucket."[52] Amazon hopes to use its e-commerce expertise from selling books to dominate nearly all e-commerce markets. Overall retail sales are pretty flat, so Amazon's growth, and that of other online retailers, will come at the expense of the "physical shops," as *The Economist* calls them.[53] As U.S. e-commerce is expected to climb from $176 billion in 2010 to $279 billion in 2015, Amazon's future looks bright. And the other empires are salivating to get a piece of the action.[54]

Amazon and its CEO, Jeff Bezos, understand the prerogatives of monopoly power as well as Jay Gould or John D. Rockefeller ever did; it uses its monopoly pricing power and market muscle to drive prospective competitors out of existence or into submission.[55] Then, like Rockefeller, it can set prices at the level that generates maximum profit.[56] "Amazon is a bully. Jeff Bezos is a bully," the CEO of one of the largest American book publishing houses said in a 2012 interview. "Anybody who gets that powerful can push people around, and Amazon pushes people around."[57] This is nothing new; Joseph Stiglitz describes how Microsoft used its "monopoly power" to crush Netscape in the 1990s.[58] Bill Keller writes about how Facebook disabled the game Critter Island in its system in 2010, and Critter Island went from 14 million users to zero in 48 hours.[59] What's the point of being a monopolist if you don't let everyone know who's boss?

The empires each spend many billions to purchase digital upstarts and midsize firms. Many familiar brand names on the Internet—from PayPal and YouTube to Skype and Hotmail—are owned by a giant. In 2011 alone, Google, for example, spent $14 billion to make eighty acquisitions.[60] Sometimes the firms are willing to overpay to lock in the potential of a new industry or to prevent another empire from getting the jump on them. As *The Economist* acknowledges, one of the benefits of being a cash-flush giant is that you are "rich enough to buy up potential rivals."[61] The fortunes being generated online go not only to the owners of the empires, but also to the owners of the upstarts that are sold to the empires. Mark Cuban, anyone? In fact, that is what many savvy entrepreneurs are aiming for, to get bought out by a giant.[62] For another independent giant empire—e.g., another Google or Facebook—to emerge would require the creation of a new digital industry that can avoid the thicket of patents and that can quickly be monopolized. Its owners must also avoid the great temptation to sell out at what would seem like an incredible price. The existing giants have it in their interests to minimize the possibility of another digital colossus emerging; though in a technologically fluid moment, the empires are not all-powerful.

Remember the classic Havana patio scene from *The Godfather* II, which I mentioned in chapter 3. The empires all agree it is their world and no one else's, and then they fight each other to control it. To the extent that there is competition in existing markets, it is because the giants decide to make a foray into enemy base-camp territory. No one else has a prayer. Fifteen percent of an existing market as number two can still be quite lucrative. So in one week in June 2012, Apple announced a series of new features to directly attack Google's monopoly markets, Google did the same to Microsoft, and Microsoft was reported to be about to launch a tablet computer to go after Apple.[63] When promising new areas emerge and it is unclear which empire will have the upper hand, the battle can be intense until the issue gets settled, which usually takes no more than a few years. So it is that most or all of the major empires are making (or preparing to make) plays in smartphones, search engines, tablet computers, Internet television, social media, e-books, games, e-commerce, and anything else that one of the other giants is currently prospering at doing and that has a growth horizon. Smartphones have opened up a new frontier of "over the top" services—including what are more commonly called apps—and the cartel and Internet giants are battling for dominance in new realms as these services emerge, as well as gobbling up new firms that show promise.[64]

Perhaps the most aggressive move by a giant in 2012 was Google launching its Google Fiber network in Kansas City. The Google system offered much higher speeds—as much as a hundred times faster than what is available in American "broadband" and similar to speeds increasingly found in other advanced nations. It was also an attack on the cable TV and satellite industry because it offered full-channel television access. It is unclear where this will go and how serious Google is about giving the cartel a run for its money. One activist in Washington said, "From what we've heard there are no plans for Google to build out in other cities or more broadly across the nation." Why? The "costs are tremendously high"—good old-fashioned barriers to entry—not to mention squaring off with the reigning heavyweight champion of lobbying forces.[65]

What is clear is that only an Internet giant like Google is in any position even to consider this sort of attack. At worst, it might provide all sorts of good publicity and increase Google's negotiating leverage with politicians and the cartel by acting as a shot across the bow at the cartel and even pushing it to get off its duff and join the twenty-first century, at least in wealthy communities. At best—and it is a long shot—Google might grab a nice profitable market share of the wireline ISP/pay television market. That would give Google more control over its own fate than any of the other giants.[66] In short, a smart, low-risk investment for a company with money to burn and the potential for a massive payoff.

Why the obsession with global domination or, as Peter Burrows put it, "to be everything to everyone"?[67] In the proprietary world, each empire wants to be as self-contained as possible and draw consumers into its world, where it will offer them an array of services and products and gather extensive data in its cloud to be mined for prospective advertisers. "The biggest tech companies are no longer content simply to enhance part of your day," the *New York Times* reported. "They want to erase the boundaries, do what the other big tech companies are doing and own every waking moment. The new strategy is to build a device, sell it to consumers and then sell them content to play on it. And maybe some ads too."[68]

The boundary between hardware and software has been obliterated by the likes of Apple, and Amazon and the others are racing to follow. "You need to control the hardware to control the overall experience," as one analyst puts it.[69] "It is about the ecosystem," another analyst stated. "The idea is to get consumers tied into that ecosystem as tightly as possible so they and their content are locked into one system."[70] The name of the game in these walled gardens is to exploit what economists now sometimes call an "enhanced surplus extraction effect"—that is, the increased ability to fleece those walled within.[71] Once an empire has you inside its confines, it is much easier for them to push the whole line of products on you. In effect, the giants are vying to be digital company stores in a national or global company town. Will it work? No one knows. "Who knows how the model is going to play out," one analyst observes. "Google doesn't know yet. But if you aren't building it today then you aren't winning in five years."[72] The present logic points toward possibly even fewer megagiants once everything shakes out.

In Praise of Monopoly?

According to conventional economic theory, concentration in markets is bad for the efficient allocation of resources in an economy. Monopoly is the enemy of competition, and competition is what keeps the system honest. It is monopoly power, for example, that makes it possible for Facebook to disregard its users' concerns about privacy; in a competitive market consumers would be able to switch to a more privacy-friendly social medium.[73] Without effective competition, capitalism loses much or all of its justification to exist, its claims to be a rational and fair system compatible with political democracy. Some economists acknowledge that such monopolies have emerged but claim they will be only temporary due to the technological dynamism of the digital world. The assumption is that new technology will beat down the walls erected around any monopolistic market in a Schumpeterian wave of creative destruction.[74] But there is little evidence to support this claim. Given these giant firms' enormous size and financial and political power, there may be some reshuffling of the deck, but, barring political intervention, some version of these giant monopolies is likely here for the duration.

For *Wired*'s Chris Anderson, the new world order of monopoly *über alles* is simply the way of the world: "A technology is invented, it spreads, a thousand flowers bloom, and then some one finds a way to own it, locking others out. It happens every time. . . . Indeed, there has hardly ever been a fortune created without a monopoly of some sort, or at least an oligopoly. This is the natural path of [capitalist] industrialization: invention, propagation, adoption, control. . . . Openness is a wonderful thing in the nonmonetary economy. . . . But eventually our tolerance for the delirious chaos of infinite competition finds its limits."[75] As PayPal founder and billionaire Peter Thiel now tells students attending his lectures at Stanford, the moral of the story is that it is time to grow up and accept the new monopoly system. Competition is overrated, even destructive, and capitalism works better with a handful of monopolists "doing something so creative that you establish a distinct market, niche and identity. You've established a creative monopoly and everybody has to come to you if they want that service." In this view, it is these entrepreneurs behind the handful of monopolies who are the progressive force in society.[76]

In fact, as this chapter has demonstrated, none of this was natural, nor does it reflect "our" preferences; "we" have had little say in the matter. The ISP cartel and the digital empires can appear far less benevolent if one is not looking through the rose-tinted glasses of Thiel's asset portfolio. None of these monopolies would have been possible without supportive and enabling government policies on a range of issues, as well as considerable previous investments by the government, a point lost in Thiel's self-congratulatory paean. If actions speak louder than words, the giants know full well that their existence depends upon favorable regulation and taxation policies. Their existence is predicated upon a government that not only accepts but expedites and facilitates their economic power. Facebook, as Lori Andrews observes, could not exist unless there were laws preventing it from being "sued for invasion of privacy, defamation, or criminal acts based on people's postings." As she observes, "all the rights run in one direction. Facebook holds the cards, and its citizens have little recourse—other than to leave the service entirely."[77] But don't hold your breath waiting for Thiel or the giants to acknowledge the great debt they owe the government and to society. As two scholars observed wryly, "People care more about what unjustly harms them than about what unjustly benefits them."[78]

Nearly everything about the way the digital giants conduct their operations smacks of antitrust violations, or at least violations of the spirit in which the relevant statutes were passed a century ago. To put it politely, antitrust law enforcement has been malleable. Enforcement has declined over the past three decades, and—notwithstanding the integrity and commitment of many public servants—is seemingly more often deployed when business competitors complain about the dominant firm in a market than as the result of popular concerns or empirical reality. Such was the case with Microsoft in the 1990s.[79] By 2012 the monopolistic propensities of the giants again were drawing attention from the Federal Trade Commission (FTC), the Justice Department, and Congress. Several of the giants, like Apple, Amazon, and Facebook, were embroiled in a variety of cases and negotiations. Google, in particular, was being pressed by the FTC over whether "Google has abused its dominance by manipulating its search results, making it less likely that competing companies or products will appear at the top of a results page."[80]

In much economic theory, such monopolies should either be publicly owned or, at the very least, heavily regulated to prevent abuses, especially as they often tend to monopolize crucial public functions.[81] If they can be effectively reformed into competitive industries, that route should be considered too, though—for the reasons mentioned above, and as *Wired*'s Chris Anderson and monopoly enthusiast Peter Thiel would agree—the monopolistic pressures in this sector makes that mostly unrealistic. The free-market option does not compute. André Schiffrin, founder of The New Press, suggests that the option of public ownership is a debate we should be having about Google.[82] The World Wide Web has thrived in the public domain; why not Internet search?

Yet corporate political power has basically eliminated the threat of public ownership, as well as credible regulation in the public interest. "All too often policymakers thinking to regulate Google have preferred to treat it as an equal of Human Rights Watch rather than of Halliburton," Evgeny Morozov writes, adding that "if we are serious about making the Internet deliver on its democratic potential, we will need to reconsider this attitude."[83] The regulation that remains, antitrust or otherwise, is done as much to guarantee the existence of profitable firms and industries as it is to protect public interest values threatened by commercial monopolies. The range of legitimate political debate cannot question the propriety of these giant firms; it can only nibble around the edges.

None of the government's current activities toward the new giants is remotely close to life-threatening. Even at their most rigorous, contemporary U.S. or European antitrust regulators have no apparent problem with markets as long as there are two or three players with double-digit market shares. The regulators seem to be waving a white flag before the market reality of contemporary capitalism, except for the most egregious monopolies.[84] The single greatest antitrust threat to Google and the other giants comes from the European Union, which does not necessarily regard the American-based giants as the home team. By 2012 the EU was in intense negotiations with Google over its monopolistic practices; Google has 85 percent of the European search market, some 15 percent more than its U.S. position.[85] The FTC was in regular communication and collaboration with the EU officials. A concern from Google's perspective was that a formal European antitrust case against Google might embolden American regulators and give them powerful ammunition.[86]

All of this points in one direction: the Internet giants need to follow the path of the cartel and the copyright lobby and add nuclear weaponry to their lobbying army. With "big policy issues looming," one tech insider said, the giants "need to engage today to protect their long-term interests in Washington."[87] They are doing just that.[88] Google spent $5 million on Washington lobbying during the first three months of 2012, an amount nearly equal to its entire 2011 spending on lobbying, which itself had doubled Google's 2010 spending.[89] Facebook, too, fattened its D.C. lobbying team, part of its work being to help members of Congress integrate Facebook into their election campaigns as well as constituent relations.[90] The spending of individual firms is just a small part of the lobbying effort; there are several trade associations representing the Internet giants, each with budgets in the tens of millions of dollars.[91] The digital empires have a long way to go to catch up with the ISPs or the media giants on the lobbying front, but they are starting to close the gap. Given their extraordinary size and wealth and the corruption of the political system, they should have commensurate political power in Washington in short order.

Some sense of the rapidly growing power of the digital giants comes when one looks at international politics, where the giants play a foundational role. Facebook's Mark Zuckerberg was invited to the 2011 G8 meetings, where he sat at the table and discussed world politics.[92] MacKinnon characterizes "Facebookistan" and "Googledom" as virtual nation-states obsessed with limiting the ability of governments anywhere to interfere with their profitability and growth, which is their driving concern. The U.S. government—the same one that is theoretically working to regulate the giants domestically—generally acts as their powerful advocate globally. "Right now our social contract with the digital sovereigns is at a primitive, Hobbesian, royalist level," Mackinnon writes. "If we are lucky we get a good sovereign, and we pray that his son or chosen successor is not evil. There is a reason most people no longer accept that sort of sovereignty."[93]

One test for how effective the U.S. government can be in regulating the digital giants will be the matter of taxation.[94] Because of the fluid nature of the digital economy, Internet firms have been able to take advantage of the federal income tax code, devised for brick-and-mortar businesses, to move a disproportionate amount of their profits earned in the United States to accounts in foreign low-tax nations and dramatically reduce what they pay in taxes overall, in particular to the U.S. government. Nicholas Shaxson describes aspects of the process in his 2011 book, *Treasure Islands*:

> In October 2010 a Bloomberg reporter explained how Google Inc. cut its taxes by $3.1 billion in the previous three years through transfer pricing games known by names such as the "Double Irish" and the "Dutch Sandwich," ending up with an overseas tax rate of 2.4 percent. The problem is getting worse. Microsoft's tax bill has been falling sharply, for similar reasons. Cisco is at it. They are all at it. Transfer pricing alone costs the United States an estimated $60 billion a year—and that is just one form of the offshore tax game.[95]

Apple, for example, has pioneered sophisticated accounting techniques that—although probably technically legal—are extraordinarily damaging to U.S. tax revenues. It paid less than 10 percent in taxes on its $34.2 billion in 2011 profits; Walmart, for the sake of comparison, paid taxes at a 24 percent rate on $24.4 billion in 2011 profits, the average rate for nontech companies. High-tech firms effectively pay a third less in taxes on the same amount of profits as the balance of the U.S. corporate community.[96]

It will be a test of the political system to see if it can get the high-tech sector to pay what other firms do, and help address the nation's deficit problems that are the purportedly the overriding concern of so many politicians. A problem for Apple and its fellow Internet giants is that the profits they allocate to foreign locales cannot be repatriated to the United States without paying U.S. taxes. To get around this, the digital giants are launching a lobbying campaign to establish a "repatriation holiday." The last such corporate tax repatriation was in 2004. This would allow for a brief amnesty period during which American businesses could return these foreign profits to the United States without owing any taxes on them.[97] Then the whole process would begin again.

As the authors of a 2011 report by the New America Foundation put it, on its present course, "the Internet will devolve into a feudalized space—one that limits democratic freedoms while enriching an oligopoly of powerful gatekeepers."[98] It is a world that would have been considered impossible not too long ago, but it is the destination where one inevitably arrives when really existing capitalism is behind the wheel.

Our Master's Voice—Loud and Clear?

In 1934 journalist and ex-adman James Rorty's seminal work, *Our Master's Voice: Advertising*, was published. This was a historical moment when advertising was relatively unpopular and more than a little controversial. Reformers were marshaling widespread antipathy to broadcast advertising in their campaign to establish a large nonprofit and noncommercial sector in American radio. Radio inventor Lee DeForest so detested broadcast advertising and its "moronic fare" that in the early 1930s he attempted to invent a device that would automatically mute radio advertisements and then return the volume to audible levels when the programming resumed.[99] The consumer movement, as Inger L. Stole has chronicled, organized campaigns for federal laws that would provide rigorous regulation of advertising so that it would provide accurate and useful information to consumers, not propaganda to confuse them.[100] Rorty's jeremiad against his former profession ultimately came down to one crucial point: advertising was the voice of corporations and the wealthy who owned them; its ultimate effect was to spawn a culture that cemented their power. In particular, its role as paying the piper gave the masters control over the very media system a free people required to address corporate power.[101]

This radical critique of advertising and the attendant political movements receded from public view in the postwar decades, but advertising remained largely suspect, fodder for comedy due to its insincerity, absurdity, and asininity, as piles of *Mad* magazines or parodies on *Saturday Night Live* attest. Meanwhile, considerable scholarship examined the dubious contribution of advertising to the content of American entertainment and journalism. When the Internet emerged, the notion that it would be a distinctly noncommercial space was uncontroversial and widely embraced. I was there and I can tell you that in the early 1990s no one was bellyaching about a lack of advertising on the Internet, or a shortage of advertising anywhere else for that matter.

But the notion of a commercial-free Internet was quickly challenged in the 1990s on two fronts. First, major advertising corporations, Rorty's "masters," were alarmed by the idea that they could not effectively market their products to prospective consumers online. Procter & Gamble CEO Edwin Artzt had the "chilling thought," as Joseph Turow chronicles in his superb book *The Daily You*, "that emerging technologies were giving people the opportunity to escape from advertising's grasp altogether." By the mid-1990s, Artzt had made this a central concern, and he implored major advertisers to respond to the threat of the Internet in the same way advertising had conquered previous media: "Let's grab all this new technology in our teeth once again and turn it into a bonanza for advertising."[102]

One way to make the Internet more ad-friendly would be to support the creation of technical standards for *cookies*, small files secretly downloaded to users' computers that would make it possible to track Internet users surreptitiously and create profiles of their activities so as to segment them for marketing. Websites could then "quietly determine the number of separate individuals entering various parts of their domains and clicking on their ads.[103] The counterculture types at the Internet Society's Internet Engineering Task Force had an adverse reaction, offering a proposal that cookies "should be shut off unless someone decides they're willing to accept them." This standards battle became the first policy fight over advertising. As one ad industry executive said, "What concerns us is the tone of the proposal, which is that advertising is not good for us, so we want to avoid it." Netscape and Microsoft bowed to the commercial pressures in designing their Web browsers.[104] Though scholars, activists, and Internet purists expressed alarm about invasions of privacy, in one fell swoop, the nature and logic of the Internet had been turned on its head—though it would not be fully apparent for at least a decade.[105]

But this still did not solve the problem. Most of the corporate advertising done online in the late 1990s was ineffectual. One expert termed the click-through rates on Internet ads as "miserable," less than one half of one percent.[106] Maybe the idealists were right and the Internet simply was not going to be a sales medium because users could not be held hostage.

The second factor behind the drive to make advertising effective online was the need to have a source of revenue for online content and services. The idea of converting the computers into vending machines and having a pay-per-view system was unrealistic for the foreseeable future. On the one hand, the Internet founders would never approve such a radical change in the system, nor would the public, as it had already tasted the openness of the Web. On the other hand, if websites tried to sell access to their content, usage tracking quickly established that most Internet users would ignore those sites and move on to the infinite world of free content. A handful of prominent brands like the *Wall Street Journal* or ESPN might make a go of it, but for everyone else, *fuhgetaboutit*. As all the other alternatives stepped backward, advertising was left as the only answer to the question of how the commercial Internet could be funded. The emergence of widespread broadband early in the 2000s helped the cause a lot; now advertising could use compelling audiovisual messages as on television. Tools for surreptitious monitoring, like cookies, were augmented and dramatically improved. But the problem remained: how to get people to pay attention to and respond to the commercials; all hands were summoned to the task. "The best minds of my generation," an early Facebook employee told *The Atlantic*'s Alexis Madrigal, "are thinking about how to make people click ads."[107]

The great development in recent years has been the emergence of advertising that targets people based upon detailed information gleaned surreptitiously from their Internet activities. "What was once an anonymous medium where anyone could be anyone," Eli Pariser wrote in 2011, "is now a tool for soliciting and analyzing our personal data."[108] U.S. Internet advertising totaled $40 billion in 2012—topping the total amount going to all print media for the first time—and was expected to increase to as much as $60 billion in 2014 and then $80 billion annually by 2016.[109] Borrell Associates estimates that ads placed on mobile apps will increase from $1.25 billion in 2011 to $21.2 billion in 2016.[110] (The United States accounts for just under one half of global Internet advertising.[111]) Internet advertising is on an explosive trajectory to gobble up an ever increasing portion of all advertising expenditures for the foreseeable future, and television advertising, to the extent it remains distinct, is becoming much more like Internet advertising.

Nothing exemplifies this emergence of advertising on the Internet more than the meteoric rise of Google. Google search advertising accounts for one half of all U.S. Internet advertising revenues—the other type of online advertising is called display advertising—and Google generated $36 billion in global ad revenue in 2011.[112] It has taken the logic of commercial broadcasting—"If you're not paying for something, you're not the customer; you're the product being sold"—and elevated it to unimagined heights.[113] Or, as Bruce Schneier puts it, "Google has great customer service. Problem is, you're not the customer."[114] With scores of distinct Internet services collecting data on people online, Google can target advertising as no other firm has ever been able to do.

Except for Facebook. Beyond the hubbub surrounding its dramatic 2012

IPO, with its equally dramatic ascension and decline, something extraordinary is occurring with social media. Facebook is "more than the world's largest social network, it is a fast-churning data machine that captures and processes every click and interaction on its platform."[115] By 2011 Facebook became the first website with a *trillion* page views in a month. More than half of its more than one billion users check it every day; in America half of eighteen- to thirty-four-year-olds check it within minutes of waking up, and 28 percent do so before getting out of bed. Americans spend, on average, 20 percent of their online time exclusively on Facebook. In a single day, 300 million photographs are uploaded; on the weekend, the figure jumps to 750 million.[116] "Facebook will have more traffic than anyone else, and they'll have more data than anyone else," one investment analyst observed in 2012. "So, unless they are impervious to learning how to monetize that data, they should be the most valuable property on the Internet, eventually."[117] Corporate America is excited to burrow its way into this mother lode of data. "We're going to get a ton of new ideas," Frito-Lay's North American chief marketing officer stated.[118] "Facebook is unilaterally redefining the social contract," Lori Andrews writes, "making the private now public and the public now private."[119]

The digital advertising industry goes far beyond Google and Facebook. Turow documents how Madison Avenue ad agencies have been reconfigured so that media buying, once the somewhat perfunctory function of locating media to place ads, has become arguably the most important part of the operation. Moreover, Google, Microsoft, Yahoo!, and AOL have each established advertising networks to place advertising on websites. This Big Four accounted for 28 percent of online display ad revenue in 2008.[120]

Gathering as much information as possible on Internet users and knowing where to reach them online is the key to securing ad dollars. Turow calls it "one of history's most massive efforts in stealth marketing."[121] Our era has come to be "epitomized by Big Data," a report in *The Guardian* states.[122] "Personal data is the oil of the information age," writes a *New York Times* reporter.[123] "Every day most if not all Americans who use the Internet," Turow notes, "are being quietly peeked at, poked, analyzed, and tagged as they move through the online world."[124] The online advertising industry, says Jeff Chester, has turned the Internet into "a digital data vacuum cleaner on steroids."

And it's not just Google or Facebook or the ISP cartel tracking people.[125]

"Your smooth new iPhone knows exactly where you go, whom you call, what you read," Pariser writes. "With its built-in microphone, gyroscope, and GPS, it can tell whether you're walking or in a car or at a party."[126] Two investigative reporters for ProPublica concluded their examination of smartphones by writing, "Let's stop calling them phones. They are trackers."[127] A 2010 *Wall Street Journal* investigation of 101 smartphone apps for Apple iPhone and Android found that 56 of these apps "transmitted the phone's unique device ID to other companies without users' awareness; 47 transmitted the phone's location in some way," and 5 sent "age, gender and other personal details to outsiders."[128] On the Internet, the *Wall Street Journal* concluded, businesses know immense amounts about individuals, who remain "anonymous in name only."[129]

In fact, it is more accurate to say that the Internet is swarming with mostly anonymous and unaccountable companies tracking anything that moves. The *Wall Street Journal* examination determined that the top fifty websites in the United States installed, on average, sixty-four pieces of tracking technology on the computers of visitors.[130] In 2012 *The Atlantic*'s Madrigal investigated who exactly was monitoring his online activities over a thirty-six-hour period. He discovered there were 105 companies that were tracking him and collecting data. Many of the companies were collecting the data to sell to other companies. "Right now," he concluded, "a huge chunk of what you've ever looked at on the Internet is sitting in databases all across the world." What individual anonymity that remains is little consolation to Madrigal. "The results of this process are ineluctable. Left to their own devices, ad tracking firms will eventually be able to connect your various data selves. And then they will break down the name wall, if they are allowed to."[131] A month after Microsoft purchased Skype in 2011, Microsoft patented a "legal intercept" technology that could "silently copy" every communication done on VOiP services like Skype. Microsoft refuses to say whether the technology is integrated into Skype's architecture.[132]

Viktor Mayer-Schönberger regards this as nothing less than a "redistribution of information power from the powerless to the powerful."[133] The greatest fear of Schneier's—arguably the leading global expert on computer security—is not cyberterrorism, cybercrime, identity theft, WikiLeaks, or illegal downloads of music and Hollywood films. According to the *New York Times*, it is "ubiquitous surveillance" conducted by "private companies and government agencies advancing their own interests, whether for surveillance or commerce."[134] "You need to know one simple truth," investigative journalist David Rosen wrote after a detailed examination of the subject: "You have no privacy with regard to your electronic communications. Nothing you do online, via a wireline telephone or over a wireless device is outside the reach of government security agencies and private corporations."[135] "Given enough data, intelligence and power," one technology journalist said, "corporations and governments can connect dots in ways that only previously existed in science fiction."[136] Need it be added that this was invariably *dystopian* science fiction?

This may be the great Achilles' heel of the Internet under capitalism: the money comes from surreptitiously violating any known understanding of privacy. The business model for Google and Facebook, and to a certain extent for all Internet firms, as Jaron Lanier put it, requires "a magic formula to appear in which some method of violating privacy and dignity becomes acceptable."[137] As the *New York Times*'s Keller puts it, the challenge these firms face is "how to sell us on without creeping us out."[138] This is not an issue the Internet giants are keen to open up for public discussion or debate, and for good reason. When Senator Claire McCaskill (D-MO) held a privacy hearing in 2010, she was astounded to learn how the Internet actually functioned. "I understand that advertising supports the Internet, but I am a little spooked out," she said. "This is creepy." An industry consultant acknowledged that as marketers pushed ever further into the data, there was an "ick factor."[139]

Polling data confirms widespread antipathy to online attacks on privacy. A 2008 survey by *Consumer Reports* found that "93 percent thought Internet companies should always ask for permission before using personal information, and 72 percent wanted the right to opt out of online tracking." A 2009 study by Princeton Survey Research Associates found that 69 percent thought the United States should adopt a law "giving people the right to learn everything a website knows about them."[140] A 2012 survey of U.S. smartphone users found 94 percent consider online privacy an important issue and 55 percent say it is something they think of often. Sixty-two percent of respondents were aware they were being tracked by advertisers—though not necessarily aware of the extent of the tracking—but only 1 percent "liked" being surreptitiously pursued.[141] Turow has conducted a series of surveys over the past seven years and generated similar results. He found that "unlike what many have suggested, attitudes toward privacy expressed by American young adults (age eighteen to twenty-four) are not nearly so different from older adults." In short, young people immersed in smartphones and social media want their privacy too. If the will of people were honored, Internet advertising as it has evolved might be effectively ended.[142] The Internet giants "sell this extremely creepy intrusion as a great boon to your life because they can tailor services to your needs," a legal expert in privacy and computer crime told the *New York Times* in 2012. "But do most people want to give that much away? No."[143]

The system appears safe from political challenge, however, and the polling data offers a good part of the answer there too.[144] Surveys reveal spectacular ignorance by most Americans about what is actually occurring to them and their data online. Turow calls the ignorance level "distressing" and notes that it is worse among younger people and that it has not improved with increased exposure to the Internet.[145] Only a small number of people are aware, for example, that over half of the roughly 84 data categories Facebook collects about its users are not available for them to see.[146] One source estimates that only 29 percent of the information Facebook possesses on any given user is available through the site's tools. Nor is there any right under U.S. law to ask a company to hand over the information it holds on you.[147] When a person follows the online protocol to opt out and thinks she has stopped data tracking, she has stopped getting targeted ads from only the one specific company. Data tracking continues unabated and there is no way to stop being tracked online.[148] In part, these misconceptions are due to the lack of media coverage or political interest in the matter. In part they are due to the official "privacy statements" of firms like Google and Facebook, which are worthless. A 2008 study by Carnegie-Mellon researchers concluded that these privacy statements are "hard to read, read infrequently, and do not support rational decision making."[149] "Legal and technology researchers," the *New York Times* reported in 2012, "estimate that it would take about a month for Internet users to read the privacy policies of all the Web sites they visit in a year."[150]

By 2010–12, online privacy had become a political issue throughout Europe, and the FTC had gotten into the game.[151] It has probably done the best it can in unsupportive political terrain, issuing critical reports on online privacy in December 2010 and March 2012,[152] and reaching a settlement with Facebook in November 2011, after accusing the company of making claims about how it used its data that were "unfair and deceptive, and violated federal law."[153] In August 2012 the FTC fined Google $22 million in a privacy case, but there was no indication this would lead to any substantive change in Google's operations.[154] As a writer for *Slate* put it, the fine amounted to "approximately 0 percent of revenues." As part of the settlement, Google did not have to admit to any wrongdoing.[155] There is little evidence at this writing that the FTC or Congress will get much more aggressive, in large part because of the political power of the Internet giants, which desperately need to expand their data collection to make profits. Even under the glare of attention in Europe in 2012, and knowing it would generate criticism, Google instituted a new privacy policy by which it consolidates all the data from sixty different Google activities into a single database.[156] Twitter acknowledged in 2012 that its future was dependent upon addressing the concerns of advertisers and that this was not an optional course.[157]

The Internet giants apparently reckon that their political muscle, combined with the importance of the Internet to the economy, makes their data-tracking systems untouchable. One investors' report states that "government regulations and consumer pushback" over privacy are a, perhaps *the*, core threat to Internet advertising.[158] As *The Economist* put it, at this point anything that handcuffed Internet advertising "would severely disrupt the internet economy."[159] In February 2012, the Obama administration said that privacy standards were important, but they had to allow "electronic commerce to grow."[160]

In Washington, industry self-regulation is the preferred foundation for any solution to the privacy issue, and the FTC acknowledges the centrality of "strong and enforceable self-regulatory initiatives."[161] Smarter figures in the Internet community know this is a problem that needs to be addressed to assuage growing public concerns. "Privacy is a source of tremendous tension and anxiety in big data," a Microsoft executive acknowledged. "Technologists need to re-engage with regulators."[162] Microsoft went so far as to make the FTC's favored "Do Not Track" the default option in its Internet Explorer 10 in 2012.[163] This works like the Do Not Call registry. This will not stop tracking, but it might limit some targeted advertising, although the system seems to be largely voluntary and difficult to enforce. It is a public relations victory, though, almost certainly sufficient for politicians to go back to sleep on the matter. *The Atlantic*'s Madrigal, after going through a maze of these corporate self-regulatory privacy schemes, came to regard them as self-serving time wasters.[164] If Congress does eventually adopt formal online privacy protections, it will do so only in a manner that will get a sign-off from Google, Microsoft, Apple, and the other giants, according to the *New York Times*.[165]

We should also expect world-class public relations campaigns extolling all the rights consumers have online, how strong the privacy standards are, and how wonderful the Internet is, thanks to advertising. It is not going to be an easy campaign. As *The Economist* puts it: "Everyone hates digital ads."[166] A report on digital commerce by Forrester Research led to this conclusion: "Consumers aren't saying, 'Oh, I really want to be able to connect with companies and brands.'"[167] Some liberals and progressives will trumpet corporate self-regulation as well, for a variety of reasons.[168] Jeff Jarvis, for example, argues that we should not "become too obsessed with privacy." A key reason is that Jarvis admits he is an "apologist of advertising"—even though "most advertising sucks"—because "advertising is the most visible means of support for journalism and media" online.[169] But this attitude raises a question: is advertising generating sufficiently useful online content to justify the price people are paying?

The commercial media system online is nascent in some respects and will not crystallize for many years, so there are unforeseeable twists and turns ahead. But the preliminary indications are that the relationship of advertising to content production is going to be rather different online than it was for twentieth-century media, and that Jarvis's defense is unlikely to apply. Recall from chapter 3 that during most of the twentieth century, the relationship of advertising to media was ambiguous. On the one hand, it did provide the funds that subsidized much of the media on recognized terms. "The social contract between advertisers and publishers used to be that publications gathered particular types of people into something called an audience," Madrigal writes, "then advertisers purchased ads in that publication to reach that audience."[170] The same was true for broadcasters. Advertisers were, in effect, forced to bankroll media content if they wanted to reach their target audience. Because the media firms had leverage in the oligopolistic marketplace, they "often saw value in maintaining credibility with audiences, advocacy groups, and government regulators by adopting policies and principles that sometimes conflicted with the advertisers' direct interest in getting the most for their money."[171]

However, one should not exaggerate how much integrity and commitment to public service these media firms had in their relationships with advertisers. It is probably more accurate to say that they had enough leverage to pursue sufficiently credible editorial policies that protected their long-term profitability by not succumbing to short-term commercial pressures or opportunities. Moreover, as has been amply demonstrated in the literature, advertising had a powerful direct and indirect effect on the nature of media content in the predigital era, often for the worse. It was hardly a form of support that came without strings attached.[172]

The balance of power began shifting with the emergence of cable and then satellite television systems, with their plethora of channels. Although most of the channels were owned by the same handful of conglomerates, each of the channels still was competing for advertising dollars, so there was a lot more "supply," and advertisers now had more options. When digital video recorders came along, advertisers became concerned that their ads were going to be skipped over by empowered viewers. Marketers began to demand and get "product placement" in programs. The media conglomerates were eager to make money, so there was no apparent period of moral angst as they weighed their options. "Branded" entertainment became more common. This meant "embedding products in the plots of television shows and movies, making it difficult to ignore them."[173]

The Internet supercharges this tendency, as there are countless websites chasing after a finite pool of ad dollars. "If publishers of all sorts—print, electronic, digital—want to survive on advertising," ad agency executive Rishad Tobaccowala explained to Turow, "they will have to adapt to their advertising masters' new demands."[174] Media firms are aggressively pursuing advertisers to get programming along these lines, and it is now so common online that it is barely noticed any longer. "Rather than doing advertising and P.R. only," a corporate brand manager working on Web entertainment stated in 2012, "we are part of the cultural conversation. When you encounter the brand through entertainment content, the conversation at the water cooler is very different." The chief creative officer at BBDO North America said, "Hollywood and advertising agencies have tried to work together before, but this time has been a positive transmogrification to something really different, and the walls came down, and now there's this."[175]

In short, the balance of power has shifted, giving advertisers much greater explicit influence over media content.[176] "The new system is forcing many media firms to sell their soul for ad money," Turow states.[177] This on its own is an astonishing development that, according to most scholarship, portends grave consequences for the quality and nature of journalism and entertainment media.

But that is hardly the worst of it. The Internet has not simply made media outlets more desperate to please advertisers; it has made them increasingly irrelevant. "Marketers haven't ever wanted to underwrite the content industry," Tobaccowala told Turow. "They've been forced."[178] Those days are over. "Advertisers are increasingly indifferent to the context in which messages appear" online, "at least compared with other media," the Pivotal Research Group reported in 2012.[179] Online media—or "publishers" in the emerging vernacular—no longer sell many of the ads appearing on their websites.[180] "Up to 80% of interactive ads are sold and resold through third parties," one industry source reports, "and advertisers don't always know where their ads have run."[181] Turow notes that the evidence suggests that in an environment where advertisers purchase ads in real time (meaning they appear almost immediately), reaching untold numbers of target demographic members, they are mostly indifferent to the quality of the surrounding content on any of the thousands of places their ads might instantly appear. The system allows advertisers to "buy" desired individuals "automatically, and in real time, on whatever page they've landed."[182] As Madrigal puts it, "Now you can buy the audience without the publication."[183] Media in the traditional sense are almost unnecessary.

In 2003 digital publishers "received most of every dollar advertisers spent on their sites," Pariser reports. In "2010, they only received $.20."[184] The missing 80 percent was going to ad networks and people who handle data. For publishers who want to attract ads, it is becoming more important to have quality detailed data on their Web clientele that can be packaged and sold by third-party wholesalers than it is to have quality content, or any content at all. *Smart* or *targeted* advertising is the term for what is emerging, and it is quickly becoming the basis for much of Internet advertising. For that reason, retail websites like Target.com are now becoming major advertising sites because they have so much traffic and collect such extensive data.[185] "Content is no longer king," *The Economist* proclaims. "Information about users is what really matters."[186] Turow concludes, "The emerging trajectory suggests that apart from a relatively few elite-oriented publishers (*New York Times*, *Atlantic*, and the like), the pressure to bring personalization synced to marketing goals will be difficult for companies to avoid if they want to survive."[187] This should not really be a surprise; advertisers always supported media for opportunistic reasons, because they had no better options. Now they have better options, and consequently much of the media can get thrown overboard.

The profit motive pushes this process into new and dangerous frontiers quickly. Increasingly, research—"persuasion profiling"—determines what types of sales pitches are most effective with each individual, and ads are tailored accordingly. Moreover, researchers are now working on "sentiment analysis," to see what mood a person is in at a particular moment and what products and sales pitches would be most effective.[188] Advertisers are at work developing emotional analysis software so webcams can monitor how one's face responds to what is on the screen. "One way to persuade internet users to grant access to their images," *The Economist* notes, "would be to offer them discounts or subscriptions to websites."[189] Pariser chronicles a range of developments on the horizon, including making machines more "human." Such machines-*cum*-humans can then establish "relationships" with actual people and get even more information from them.[190]

Nielsen research reveals that people put far more stock in peer recommendations and crowd-powered ratings than they do in traditional advertising, so considerable effort is going into making covert sales pitches.[191] Commercializing friendship is a killer app.[192] Facebook is ideal for this. "On Facebook, you take friends into account," an ad executive explained to Turow. "So-and-so liked this; you will too. People find that creepy in the beginning, but . . . they slowly get used to it."[193] A 2011 Duke University survey of corporate marketing officers found that they expected to allocate no less than 18 percent of their advertising budgets to social media within five years.[194]

The problems faced by traditional media do not mean that advertisers and the emerging system are entirely agnostic about content. Preliminary research suggests that the content of a website *does* influence the success of an ad. The issue is whether the effect is enough to justify any subsidy of the media content by the advertiser.[195] Sometimes advertisers simply "cut out the middleman" and produce the content themselves in a manner that has the sole objective of selling the product. The logic of the system is that it personalizes content for individuals, and the content is selected based on what is considered most likely to assist the sale. Pariser's *Filter Bubble* documented how the Internet is quickly becoming a personalized experience wherein people get different results on Google searches for identical queries, based on their history. They are soon to get different websites on the screen than other people who enter the same URL. These developments are driven in toto by advertising and commercialism.[196] Indeed, with the appearance of "content farms," an industry has emerged that produces content on demand to provide access to desired consumers for advertisers. Google's former CEO Eric Schmidt notes that individual targeting "will be so good it will be very hard for people to watch or consume something that has not in some sense been tailored for them."[197]

All of this has a long way to go, but some things are already crystal clear: the notion in the 1990s that the Internet would empower individuals and make them masters of their digital fate has been turned on its head. The idea that people would join together in a shared global commonwealth is a distant memory. "The way the Internet has gone sour," Lanier laments, "is truly perverse."[198] While "in many cases this provides for happier, healthier lives," Pariser concludes, "it also provides for the commercialization of everything—even of our sensory apparatus itself."[199] And much as Rorty framed the matter in 1934, Turow concludes that the evidence points in one direction: "The centrality of corporate power is a direct reality at the very heart of the digital age."[200] In 1935, *New Republic* editor Bruce Bliven characterized himself as among those "who find advertising so obnoxious that they wish the radio had never been invented."[201] One wonders if the Internet will produce its modern Blivenites—or if, as with broadcasting, people will come to accept its degradation as the natural way of the world and barely recognize, let alone question, what is taking place.

A Military-Digital Complex?

In his farewell address in 1961, President Dwight D. Eisenhower ominously warned about the military-industrial complex that had emerged as a cornerstone of the American political economy in the postwar years, with powers previously unknown in American history. The former Supreme Allied Commander in Europe during World War II decried the shared interests of warmakers, large corporations, and politicians that would render the public largely powerless to provide any opposition. In grave terms he charted how this could lead to the end of any humane or democratic society in the war-fearing spirit of James Madison and Thomas Jefferson. It was one of the most extraordinary speeches by a president or any political leader in American history.[202] His warnings had no effect precisely for the reason he expressed concern: there were many powerful elements of society that benefited from a permanent wartime economy, and no powerful elements that were significantly harmed by a permanent wartime economy.

Eisenhower's words were accurate at the time, and his analysis has proven depressingly prescient. Except for a brief hiccup in the 1970s in the aftermath of the Vietnam War, the system has been unchallenged. Military and national security spending has continued to grow and has remained a large and constant part of the economy. By 2012 the United States spent roughly $1 trillion on the military annually, when all the wars, nuclear weapons, secret budgets, and interest payments on debt are taken into consideration.[203] America has around 5 percent of the world's population but 50 percent of global military spending. "We don't have any enemies in Congress," a senior defense official told Rachel Maddow in 2011. "We have to fight Congress to cut programs, not keep them."[204] When Americans are directly informed of how much the government actually spends on the military compared to other programs, a significant percentage, arguably a strong majority, believe the military is a logical place for sharp cuts in government spending.[205]

Military spending plays a central role in the economy. It provides demand for goods and services without putting any products on the market that compete with those produced in the private sector, so it is a definite stimulus to production and an antidote to stagnation. Military spending is also a windfall for the firms that are the recipients of military contracts, especially as an increasing portion of the budget is outsourced. Military spending has been the basis for much of the research and development spending in high technology in the United States. As I discussed in chapter 4, its role has been and remains crucial to the development of the commercial Internet. Many economists rightly point out that there are far more effective ways for the government to spend money to stimulate economic growth or spur research, but those options either have no political support from powerful lobbies or face ferocious opposition from them. The late Chalmers Johnson wistfully hoped the United States could eliminate its empire and return to being a republic, in a soft landing. The evidence suggests that the national security state is as much a part of really existing American capitalism as the large corporation, Wall Street, or advertising. A campaign to end it is, in effect, a campaign to radically reform or replace capitalism as we know it.

The transition from the Cold War, in which America's antagonists were known and the conflicts could (and did) eventually end, to the so-called War on Terror, in which the enemies are largely unseen and their activities unknown, has been a boon for the national security state. The War on Terror will last as long as our leaders tell us it must last; in other words, it is permanent. Americans now live in an Orwellian world where leaders periodically warn them about some evil "Eurasia" to get the blood boiling, but there is no need to provide evidence or context. The leaders are to be trusted, their budgets approved; to challenge them is to be unpatriotic, if not treasonous.[206] Dissidents are parked on some university campus or at a community radio station. Nothing much changes, regardless of which party is in power, and what little political debate exists is fatuous. "Our national security isn't much related to its stated justifications anymore," Maddow notes.

> To whatever extent we do argue and debate what defense and intelligence policy ought to be, that debate—our political process—doesn't actually determine what we ought to do. We're not directing that policy anymore; it just follows its own course. Which means we've effectively lost control of a big part of who we are as a country. And we've broken faith with some of the best advice the founders ever gave us.[207]

In the last decade, federal spending on intelligence has ballooned some 250 percent to around $100 billion annually, though most of the intelligence budgets are secret, so the best one can do is guess. The national security state has gone places Stanley Kubrick and Terry Southern could have barely imagined when they wrote the screenplay for *Dr. Strangelove*. In 1995 the government classified 5.6 million documents; in 2011 it classified 92 million documents. Or consider this: in 1996 the government *declassified* (i.e., made public) 196 million pages of documents; in 2011 it declassified just under 27 million pages. The U.S. government spends, by conservative estimate, $13 billion annually to make and keep secret government information.[208] As Fareed Zakaria puts it:

> Since September 11, 2001, the U.S. government has created or reconfigured at least 263 organizations to tackle some aspect of the war on terror. Thirty-three new building complexes have been built for the intelligence bureaucracies alone, occupying 17 million square feet—the equivalent of 22 U.S. Capitols or three Pentagons. The largest

> bureaucracy after the Pentagon and the Department of Veterans Affairs is now the Department of Homeland Security, which has a workforce of 230,000 people.[209]

The resulting national security complex is almost unimaginable, like trying to compute the distance from earth to a far-off galaxy in millimeters. Over 850,000 people have top-secret clearances. Some 1,300 government agencies and 2,000 private companies are collecting intelligence and have top-secret clearance. It is a massive self-interested bureaucracy with no public accountability and barely a trace of congressional oversight.[210] "The complexity of this system defies description," a retired U.S. Army intelligence specialist told the *Washington Post*. "We can't effectively assess whether it's making us more safe."[211]

The Internet has been embraced by the military and national security agencies, which are determined to make it their own. It "is a surveillance tool made in heaven," John Naughton writes, "because much of the surveillance can be done, not by expensive and fallible human beings, but by computers."[212] In 2012 the U.S. military formally stated that it "intended to treat cyberspace as a military battleground," and the most important battleground at that.[213] The National Security Agency is completing a $2 billion complex in Utah that will be the cumulonimbus of Internet clouds. Its "near-bottomless databases" will include "the complete contents of private e-mails, cell phone calls, and Google searches, as well as all sorts of personal data trails." The NSA then has enormous capacity to slice and dice the contents. As James Bamford observes, for the first time since Watergate, "the NSA has turned its surveillance apparatus on the US and its citizens."[214]

This is just part of the intrusion, as incredible as that may seem.[215] "The U.S. government," former Sun Microsystems senior engineer and cybersecurity expert Susan Landau writes, "has embarked on an unprecedented effort to build surveillance capabilities into communication infrastructure."[216] And Naughton writes, "Most Internet users would be shocked if they realized the extent to which their online activities are already under surveillance" by the government. "I suspect many are unaware of the laws that permit such surveillance."[217] Zakaria reports:

> The rise of this national security state has entailed a vast expansion in the government's powers that now touch every aspect of American life,

even when seemingly unrelated to terrorism. Some 30,000 people, for example, are now employed exclusively to listen in on phone conversations and other communications within the United States.[218]

What is the relationship of the government, especially the national security state, to the ISP cartel and the digital giants? The evidence suggests it is complementary and collegial, even intimate. For national security agencies, the advantages are clear. As UCLA law professor Jon Michaels noted in a 2008 study, "Participating corporations have been instrumental in enabling U.S. intelligence officials to conduct domestic surveillance and intelligence activities outside of the congressionally imposed framework of court orders and subpoenas, and also outside of the ambit of inter-branch oversight."[219] In addition, the Internet giants can provide extraordinary access to information that would be much more difficult for the government to get on its own.

For the Internet giants, the reasons for collaboration are many.

- There is a great deal of money to be made providing data services for the government. As Heather Brooke puts it, "Dozens of commercial data brokers compete to sell data to the government."[220]
- The military generates many of the new technologies that Internet giants can exploit commercially.
- The giants have a great deal at stake in government subsidies, regulations, taxation, and antitrust oversight. They have no interest in antagonizing the government by not playing ball with the military and intelligence agencies.
- Outside the United States, the U.S. government is an aggressive advocate for the Internet giants, and they therefore want to reciprocate and have the government in their debt.
- Much of the military's cyberwarfare planning addresses protecting U.S. intellectual property, patents, and copyright. The government is like a private police force for the Internet giants, corporate media, and all businesses that rely on patents and copyright.[221]

In short, the rational course for these firms—even the ones not presently working closely with the military and security agencies—is to cooperate with the national security state. Any other course of action would threaten their profitability. It's a no-brainer.

Of course, there is almost certainly patriotic sentiment among some executives at the giants, which reinforces or guides the choices they make. But the Internet firms are not people; they are bloodless institutions legally chartered to maximize profits by any (legal) means necessary. Many of the same patriotic firms have had few qualms about "selling surveillance and censorship technology to the most heinous regimes in the world," as Morozov puts it.[222] The Tunisian government that was overthrown in 2011, for example, used "deep-packet inspection" technology it purchased from the American firm Narus, a subsidiary of Boeing, to monitor the online activities of dissidents and eliminate them. Pakistan and Saudi Arabia are two more of Narus's authoritarian clients. China expert Rebecca MacKinnon argues that U.S. investors and firms play a central role in the Chinese government's ability to convert the Internet into a relatively harmless medium. It is "more than likely," she observes, that "the Internet's pervasive use in China will actually help *prolong* the Communist Party's rule of China rather than hasten its demise."[223] For a firm like Google, there is an immense amount of money to be made providing security tools to governments and corporations and not as much of a market for supporting dissidents, especially those who have the misfortune of living in countries with governments that have close relations with the U.S. government.[224] The evidence is clear: the Internet corporations place a lower priority on human rights and the rule of law than they do on profits.

We must assume that the vast majority of collaborations between the national security state and the Internet giants are not known—both sides have every incentive to keep them secret—but enough has slipped through the cracks to give us pause. In 2001 the NSA started an illegal warrantless wiretapping program on U.S. citizens, monitoring telephone calls with deep-packet inspection technology. It received the unconditional cooperation of AT&T, Verizon, and all the other telecom companies except Qwest. The Bush administration threatened Qwest that it would lose future lucrative government contracts if it did not cooperate. The other firms received hundreds of millions of dollars for their participation. In a subsequent shareholder lawsuit over the sale of Qwest, documents were released that "revealed an extraordinary degree of cooperation between the various military and intelligence branches of the government—particularly the Pentagon and the NSA—and the private telecommunication corporations." The documents demonstrated, as Glenn Greenwald put it, "that the telecom corporations and the military and intelligence agencies of the federal government were so close as to be virtually indistinguishable."[225]

The telecom giants understood that their actions were in clear violation of the Foreign Intelligence Surveillance Act (FISA), a law for which their own lawyers in the 1970s had written the precise clauses so there could be no confusion or ambiguity.[226] The operation was seen as so "shockingly lawless that even Bush's own top DOJ [Department of Justice] officials had revolted when they learned of it."[227] These corporations had committed the sorts of felonies that lead to severe jail time for those unconnected to power. When the operation became public—thanks to a whistleblower—no prosecutions were made, no heads rolled. Instead, Congress passed a full *retroactive* immunity for the telecom firms in 2008, with bipartisan support. This effectively made the program legal. The Obama administration tightened regulations to make it *more* difficult for whistleblowers to avoid prosecution. And the domestic spying program proceeded full steam ahead. By 2010, the *Washington Post* reported, "Every day, collection systems at the National Security Agency intercept and store 1.7 billion e-mails, phone calls and other types of communications."[228]

The domination of the Internet by a handful of monopolists, as well as the emerging cloud structure of the Internet, is perfect for the government. It need deal with only a handful of giants to effectively control the Internet. The consequences of this became striking in the wake of the brouhaha surrounding WikiLeaks after it released government documents in 2010. The "U.S. government response to WikiLeaks," MacKinnon writes, "highlights a troubling murkiness, opacity, and lack of public accountability in the power relationships between government and Internet-related companies." Amazon booted WikiLeaks off its servers, and the site immediately collapsed, as there was nowhere else to go.[229] Apple pulled a WikiLeaks app from its store.[230] Monopolist PayPal—as well as MasterCard, Visa, and Bank of America—also severed ties to WikiLeaks. There is no evidence that the executive branch made any explicit demand of the firms to do what they did; it appears they acted proactively, possibly egged on by all the saber rattling and macho talk coming from Capitol Hill.[231] The firms responded to vague claims of illegality on the part of WikiLeaks, but no charges had been filed, nor had anyone been convicted. "We have a problem," MacKinnon concludes.

> The political discourse in the United States and in many other democracies now depends increasingly on privately owned and operated digital intermediaries. Whether unpopular, controversial, and contested speech can exist on these platforms is a decision left to unelected corporate executives who are under no legal obligation to justify their actions. The response to WikiLeaks's release of classified cables is a troubling example of private companies' unaccountable power over citizens' political speech, and of how government can manipulate that power in informal and thus unaccountable ways.[232]

The list of such malfeasances continues. In April 2012 the American Civil Liberties Union (ACLU) released 5,500 pages of documents demonstrating that most police departments in the country tracked suspects and others by using their cell phones without warrants, hence illegally. The ISP cartel not only cooperated, but was sometimes paid, the price ranging from a few hundred dollars for providing a suspect's physical location up to $2,200 "for a full-scale wiretap."[233] In 2012 it came out that the Department of Homeland Security was routinely scouring social media like Facebook and Twitter with a list of several hundred keywords. Its purpose was, among other things, to assess "public reaction to major governmental proposals with homeland security implications."[234] If it needs help, LexisNexis has developed a product "to give government agents information about what people do on social networks."[235]

The capper came in July 2012 when it was revealed, in response to a congressional inquiry, that cell phone companies had responded surreptitiously to fully 1.3 million demands for subscriber information from law enforcement agencies. "I never expected it to be this massive," said Representative Edward Markey, the Massachusetts Democrat, who launched the inquiry. AT&T handles seven hundred requests per day, and, like the other cell companies, is compensated for its assistance.[236] AT&T now has one hundred full-time employees whose job is to review and respond to law enforcement requests; Verizon has seventy.[237] With this explosion in easy access to mobile phones, traditional wiretapping—with its more "stringent legal standards," which might actually protect a citizen's constitutional rights—has sharply declined. There were only 2,732 nationwide in 2011, a 14 percent drop from 2010. The *New York Times*, to its credit, editorialized against the cell phone spying, wondering if privacy even continues to exist.[238]

Since September 11, 2001, when it comes to spying on Americans, the Federal Bureau of Investigation has increasingly turned to the National Security Letter (NSL), an administrative demand letter or subpoena requiring neither probable cause nor judicial oversight. As David Rosen puts it:

> In effect, an NSL overrides 4th Amendment guarantees safeguarding an American's right [to be free] from unreasonable search and seizure. Between 2000 and 2010 (excluding 2001 and 2002, for which no records are available), the FBI was issued 273,122 NSLs; in 2010, 24,287 letters were issued pertaining to 14,000 U.S. residents. Even more alarming, if a company, journalist, person or attorney receives an NSL, they are barred from informing anyone, including the press, about the order. And the NSL is but one of an expanding number of means employed by the surveillance state to spy on an evergrowing, in effect unknowable, number of Americans.[239]

Google co-founder Sergey Brin told *The Guardian* in 2012 that "the company was periodically forced to hand over data and sometimes prevented by legal restrictions from even notifying users that it had done so."[240] According to *The Economist*, Google received at least ten thousand requests for information from law enforcement and national security agencies in 2011—not necessarily all NSLs—and Google acknowledged that it complied with 93 percent of government requests.[241] The only telecom company that has stood up to the government and gone to court to challenge the constitutionality of NSLs is Working Assets. It operates Credo Mobile, a relatively minuscule firm with explicitly liberal politics that directs a portion of its revenues to progressive causes. (That is generally why its preponderantly left-leaning customers sign up for its service.) The case is winding its way through the court system at this writing.[242]

Policing the Internet with minimal public interference is a front-burner issue in Washington. In April 2012 the U.S. House of Representatives passed the Cyber Intelligence Sharing and Protection Act (CISPA), which would allow for the sharing of Internet traffic information between the U.S. government and certain technology and manufacturing companies. The stated aim of the bill is to help the government investigate cyber threats and ensure the security of networks against cyber attack. It has been unanimously criticized by organized advocates of Internet privacy and civil liberties, such as the

Electronic Freedom Foundation, the ACLU, Reporters Without Borders, and Mozilla, which regard it as the most sweeping anti–civil liberties legislation yet proposed. As Free Press put it, CISPA would allow companies and the government to legally bypass privacy protections and spy on e-mail traffic, comb through text messages, filter online content, and block access to websites. It would permit companies to give the government its users' Facebook data, Twitter history, and cell phone contacts. It would also allow the government to search e-mail using the vaguest of justifications without any real legal oversight. CISPA also contains sweeping language that could be used as a blunt weapon to silence whistleblower websites like WikiLeaks and the news organizations that publish their revelations.[243] "I'm not convinced that Congress even comprehends the insanity of the laws they're passing right now," one of the leading experts on Internet policy told me in May 2012.[244]

The Internet giants all supported the legislation, either aggressively or tacitly, for four reasons. First, it gave them legal cover for what they were already doing surreptitiously with the government, much of it in the gray area of questionable legality. Second, it also opened new vistas for work with the government, which would offer remuneration as well as immunity from prosecution. Indeed, some of this work could develop useful commercial applications, particularly for the online advertising industry. Third, it would keep the giants on good terms with the government, which is very much in their interests. Fourth, CISPA was voluntary, and corporations could decline to participate, which they may want to do if the costs of the government request are damaging. (The fact that none ever challenged NSLs suggests refusal on grounds of principle wasn't on the grid of responses.)

Senate Democrats refused to support CISPA, to some extent due to opposition on civil liberties grounds, so the Senate produced its own "cybersecurity bill" with the strong support of President Obama, Democrats, and the military.[245] The Senate version of the bill was filibustered by the Republicans and failed to earn the necessary filibuster-defeating majority in August 2012, "losing" 52–46. A major change, and a stated reason most Republican Senators voted against the bill, was that it required corporations to do some of what had been voluntary in the House's CISPA. The Senate bill was seen as possibly forcing "privately owned companies to spend what's needed to protect our critical infrastructure, even if that spending drives down profits for a time," Jeffrey Carr, founder of boutique cybersecurity firm Taia Global, told

Talking Points Memo's Carl Franzen. Many security experts disputed the bill's ability to actually better protect the United States from cyberattacks.[246] In terms of civil liberties and privacy, and general public interest policy making, Meinrath says both the House and Senate bills were "atrocious."[247]

With SOPA in 2011 and CISPA and "cybersecurity" in 2012, all signs point to the legislative thrust being in one direction: shrinking the rights of citizens and expanding the unaccountable prerogatives of the national security state and the Internet giants. Depending upon the makeup of Congress, the logic suggests the Internet giants will have to be given better terms and a few crumbs will have to be thrown to civil libertarians to get the bills passed, and those are not insurmountable obstacles in contemporary American politics. "In a war of attrition where one side has infinite money and resources and the other only has volunteers," one activist said, "that's a bleak future."[248] The difficulty of stopping this trend is elevated by a thoroughgoing lack of news media coverage, so the vast majority of Americans are understandably clueless. As one reporter noted,

> Even after passing the House, the White House press pool has never asked a single question about CISPA at the daily press briefing, let alone in discussion with the president or senior officials. Out of all public transcripts and statements, there is only a single CISPA reference on the White House website, from the administration's proactive policy announcement. (There are over seventy references to "long form birth certificate," to compare another topic.)[249]

A Free Press organizer summed up the situation: "Unless we get mass organized behind a universal set of Internet freedom principles, we'll be playing defense on bad legislation until we lose."[250] The good news is the energy created by the campaigns against SOPA and CISPA and mounting concerns about privacy, monopoly, and digital censorship helped Free Press generate a broad coalition of some two thousand groups to organize popular support for protecting and expanding what it terms "Internet Freedom." Its "Declaration of Internet Freedom" exploded into global prominence in the summer of 2012 and was translated into seventy languages in its first month.[251] This is one of the central political fights of the times.

There are legitimate security concerns for any government, and in times of war the stick can be bent temporarily toward greater security at the expense of freedom. There are also certainly legitimate security concerns surrounding the Internet and the threat of cyberwarfare. But we are entering dangerous new terrain. "When privacy is balanced against security, the scale is rigged so security will win out nearly every time," privacy expert Daniel Solove wrote.[252] "In the past, the U.S. government has built up for wars, assumed emergency authority and sometimes abused that power, yet always demobilized after the war," Zakaria observed in 2012. "But this is, of course, a war without end."[253] The system that has emerged is an open invitation to abuse, which should remind us all of James Madison's warning cited in chapter 2: "No nation can preserve its freedom in the midst of continual warfare."[254]

"Every incentive in a state bureaucracy," Siva Vaidhyanathan writes, "encourages massive surveillance." Nothing pushes hard in the opposite direction.[255] Cybersecurity expert Landau notes that "when surveillance mechanisms are easy to turn on, the chance of misuse is high."[256] Moreover, there is now an industry poised to make terrific profit through participating in and extending the national security apparatus. No one, except a handful of civil liberties lawyers, is making a dime slowing down surveillance. Without accountability, this is a recipe for disaster. For any national security agency, there is no credible penalty for overreach, but careers can end for underreach. The Electronic Freedom Foundation published a report in 2011 based on a comprehensive review of FBI documents and concluded that "intelligence investigations have compromised the civil liberties of American citizens far more frequently, and to a greater extent, than was previously assumed."[257]

What little examination has been made, for example, of the government's process for classifying material as top secret indicates that it is often more about keeping the truth about government malfeasance and incompetence from the public than it is about safeguarding necessary secrets. Award-winning journalist Sanford J. Ungar noted in the *Columbia Journalism Review* that WikiLeaks should have drawn attention to "an obvious underlying problem: that the obsessive over-classification of US official information has reached a point where it is impossible to know with confidence what truly deserves to be kept secret and how that can be done effectively." Ungar quotes Erwin Griswold, the U.S. solicitor general in charge of prosecuting the Pentagon Papers case for the Nixon administration, who later renounced his position; Griswold noted in 1989 that "the principal concern of the classifiers is not with national security, but rather with government embarrassment of one sort or another." Griswold added that "apart from details of weapons systems, there is very rarely any real risk to national security from the publication of facts related to transcriptions in the past, even the fairly recent past."[258]

Griswold's era looks benign compared to the contemporary United States. In 2011, Michael Hastings, one of the few reporters who is on this beat, wrote, "Over the past ten years the government has acquired a security fetish, classifying over 2.6 million new secrets." He notes, like Griswold, that analysts have "pointed out that one of the main reasons the government tried to hold on so tightly to its documents wasn't that their release would hurt national security, the catchall justification to classify, but that the government wanted to prevent embarrassment."[259] "The world of secret knowledge is far larger than the world of public knowledge," Stanford's Robert Proctor told Chris Hayes. "In the U.S. there are four thousand censors who just work on censoring nuclear secrets. We live in this world where the public knowledge is just a tiny fraction of secret military knowledge."[260]

It is not just incompetence or banality that should concern us. Governments, even democratic ones, are capable of acting unconscionably and undermining the very freedoms that are necessary for self-government to be effective. When they grow secretive, the likelihood that they are representing powerful interests grows. Everyone understands that governments often identify their enemies as terrorists to justify persecuting them; it is par for the course in authoritarian nations. But Americans need to look in the mirror. When the U.S. government turns to domestic spying and illegal harassment of citizens, it rarely if ever has been known to go after billionaires, corporate CEOs, or their advocates; it has a track record of using its spying powers domestically on, among others, law-abiding and nonviolent dissident groups that challenge entrenched wealth and privilege. When one sees how peaceful Occupy protesters have been made the target of Homeland Security covert scrutiny here in the United States—while the bankers whose dubious shenanigans helped drive the economy off a cliff waltz free—the dimensions of the problem grow stark.[261] It invokes the darkest and most dangerous moments in American history, from the Alien & Sedition Acts, the Fugitive Slave Act, and Jim Crow to the Palmer Raids, McCarthyism, and COINTELPRO. But now the state has technological powers previously unimaginable.

The great defense of capitalism as the economic system best suited for democratic governance and political freedom—made by Milton Friedman and others—is that the private sector is competitive and independent of the government, thereby providing an autonomous and occasionally adversarial source of power. As this chapter demonstrates, that notion of capitalism and democracy has blown up like a trick cigar on April Fool's Day. Without meaning to be pejorative or alarmist, it is difficult to avoid noting that what is emerging veers toward a classic definition of fascism: the state and large corporations working hand in hand to promote corporate interests, and a state preoccupied with militarism, secrecy, propaganda, and surveillance.[262] People who are uppity and nonviolently resist the system are the enemy. In such an environment, political liberty is at risk.

The founders of the American republic, to their immense credit, understood this dilemma. For that reason, they regarded the press system as the key institution that would keep people informed of what was taking place and give citizens the capacity to resist tyranny and protect their freedoms. It is the news media that must expose the duplicity and crimes of those in power. So how are these crucial institutions faring in the age of the Internet? A great deal rides on the answer. That is the question for the next chapter.

6

Journalism Is Dead! Long Live Journalism?

"Journalism is dead! Long live journalism!" So goes the mantra of the new conventional wisdom. The bad news is that the Internet has taken the economic basis away from commercial journalism, especially newspapers, and left the rotting carcass for all to see. The Internet is providing intense competition for advertising, which has traditionally bankrolled most of the news media. In 2000, daily newspapers received nearly $20 billion from classifieds; in 2011 the figure was $5 billion. A free ad on Craigslist generally gets more responses. Display advertising fell from around $30 billion to $15 billion in the same period. Combined newspaper advertising revenues were cut in half from 2003 to 2011.[1] In 2011 newspapers still received 25 percent of all advertising expenditures despite getting only 7 percent of consumers' media time. By all accounts, the industry remains in free fall.[2]

The Internet has also taken away readers, who can find online for free much of the journalism they might want. A large and growing number of Americans, especially younger ones, get their news from comedy programs.[3] A 2011 Pew Research Center survey found that computer tablets were booming among traditional newspaper readers, and 59 percent of the respondents said the tablet had replaced "what they used to get" from a newspaper.[4] And as the content of newspapers gets skimpier, the product becomes that much more unappealing, making it that much more difficult to get people to subscribe to cover the lost advertising revenues. A 2011 survey determined that only 28 percent of American adults thought it would have a major impact on them if their local newspaper disappeared; 39 percent said it would have no impact whatsoever.[5] By any reckoning, this onetime ubiquitous medium is in its death spiral.

It is not just newspapers, though they are being hit hardest; all commercial news media are in varying stages of decay. But newspapers are by far the most important, because they are where the vast majority of original reporting is done, and no other media have emerged to replace them. Harvard's Alex S. Jones estimates that 85 percent of all professionally reported news originates with daily newspapers, and he notes that he has seen credible sources place that figure closer to 95 percent.[6] Commercial radio news barely exists at all, and much of what remains on commercial television can be called news only by a loose definition of the term.

But fear not, we are told. Here's the good news: The same Internet that has slain the news media will provide ample journalism eventually, in an almost certainly superior form. In no other area have the celebrants been so emphatic.[7] Jeff Jarvis asserts, "Thanks to the web . . . journalism will not only survive but prosper and grow far beyond its present limitations."[8] All we need to do is get out of the way and let free markets work their magic on revolutionary technologies.

Clay Shirky wrote in his influential 2009 essay, "Newspapers and Thinking the Unthinkable," that "this is what real revolutions are like," adding, "the old stuff gets broken faster than the new stuff is put in its place." Shirky counsels patience. "Nothing will work, but everything might. Now is the time for experiments, lots and lots of experiments, each of which will seem as minor at launch as Craigslist did, as Wikipedia did, as *octavo* volumes did." He adds, "In the next few decades, journalism will be made up of overlapping special cases. . . . Many of these models will fail. No one experiment is going to replace what we are now losing with the demise of news on paper, but over time, the collection of new experiments that do work might give us the journalism we need."[9]

Yochai Benkler suggests that the new journalism will be so radically different from the old that traditional concerns about resource support are no longer of pressing importance. We can have a leaner journalism, and it will still be much better, thanks to the Internet. He writes: "Like other information goods, the production model of news is shifting from an industrial model—be it the monopoly city paper, IBM in its monopoly heyday, or Microsoft, or Britannica—to a networked model that integrates a wider range of practices into the production system: market and nonmarket, large scale and small, for profit and nonprofit, organized and individual. We already see the early elements of how news reporting and opinion will be provided in the networked public sphere."[10] Likewise, Shirky, in a major address on the state of the news media at Harvard in 2011, basically ignored the issue of resources and economic support.[11]

The enthusiasm of the celebrants for the Internet as the basis for journalism's revitalization is understandable, for four putative reasons. First, there are an exponentially greater number of people who are able to participate as journalists online because barriers to entry are all but eliminated. "We are all journalists, now," as the saying goes.[12] Second, newly christened journalists, like everyone else, can have access to the world's information at a second's notice, far beyond what anyone could have accessed in the past. All they need to do is develop their skills at surfing the Web. Third, journalists will be able to collaborate and draw from the intelligence and labor of countless others in a networked environment, so that the whole will be far greater than the sum of its parts. Fourth, the Internet dramatically lowers the cost of production and effectively eliminates the cost of distribution, so a journalist can have a digital readership in the tens of millions with barely any budget at all.

So while the Internet might undermine the viability of the existing commercial news media, unless they change, it will also provide a far more glorious and democratic replacement. All that needs to be done is to keep the government censors at bay, and even the censors will have a very difficult time wrestling this magical technology to the ground.

This is an intoxicating prospect. There are numerous great journalists, like Glenn Greenwald, whose work exists only because of the factors above. Concerned citizens can locate a treasure trove of information online. The Arab Spring demonstrates that the powers-that-be face an unprecedented threat to their existence from aroused and empowered populations. For the most exuberant among us, the newest wave of technologies may have already ushered in the next glorious period. "There's no longer any need to imagine a media world where you create, aggregate and share freely and find credible, relevant news and information by using recommendations from peers you trust," Rory O'Connor writes, "because that world is already here."[13] Peter Diamandis and Steven Kotler write that "the free flow of information enabled by cell phones replaces the need for a free press."[14]

Perhaps no issue is of greater importance to the future than how accurate these hopeful perspectives prove to be. Two matters are beyond debate: First, journalism in the manner I described it in chapter 3 is mandatory, not only so people can participate in the central political and communication policy issues outlined in this book, but also so there can be a democratic society wherein individual liberties are meaningful. Second, current journalism is in decline and disarray. If there are any doubts about the second point, the evidence presented below should eliminate them. We are in a political crisis of existential dimensions.

Two outstanding questions arise. First, will the Internet, the profit motive, citizens, and assorted nonprofit groups combine in some manner to generate a higher grade of journalism sufficient to empower self-government? I argue herein, drawing from the foundation I provided in chapter 3, that the celebrants have either greatly undervalued the importance of having independent competing institutions and resources to do journalism—especially living wages for reporters—or they have overestimated the capacity of the market to produce such a system, or both. Moreover, the celebrants tend to be naive about the endemic problem of commercialism for democratic journalism, in the form of both private ownership and advertising support. As I assess the state of journalism in the United States today, it becomes evident that the Internet is not the cause of journalism's problems. Digital technology has only greatly accelerated and made permanent trends produced by commercialism that were apparent before the World Wide Web, Craigslist, Google, or Facebook existed.

I then look at the various efforts at generating digital journalism by the traditional news media, entrepreneurs, citizen journalists (a colloquial term for unpaid journalists), and nonprofit organizations. Although I find scant evidence that what is occurring online today could plausibly generate a popular journalism sufficient for a free and self-governing society, the notion that the Internet *could* provide the *basis* for a radically improved democratic journalism is another matter altogether. There I believe the celebrants are clearly on to something very big.

This leads to the second outstanding question: if the market, philanthropy, and new technologies are inadequate, how can we have a journalism system sufficient for a free and self-governing society? I return to the point first made in chapters 2 and 3: the solution to the problem of generating sufficient journalism begins with the recognition that it is a public good. Journalism is something society requires but that the market cannot generate in sufficient quantity or quality. The market is incapable of solving the problem, no matter how fantastic the technologies. Advertising disguised the public-good nature of journalism for the past 125 years, but now that it has found superior options, the truth is plain to see. That means that any realistic notion of a credible Fourth Estate will require explicit public policies and extensive public investments, or what are also termed subsidies. I look at the enormous and striking role of journalism subsidies in American history—especially in the "pre-advertising" era—as well as the continued importance of public investments in journalism in the most democratic nations in the world today. I conclude by assessing what a powerful digital free press might look like.

Farewell to Journalism?

The notion that journalism was in severe crisis became common by 2006 or 2007, then escalated into a major theme following the economic collapse of 2008–9, when hundreds of newspapers and magazines shut their doors. Optimists hoped the economic recovery would put commercial journalism back on solid footing and allow breathing space for a successful transition to the Internet; instead newspaper layoffs increased by 30 percent in 2011 compared to 2010.[15] The next recession could devastate the remaining commercial news media.

In 2012 the President's Council of Economic Advisers described the newspaper industry as "the nation's fastest-shrinking industry."[16] A survey of two hundred possible careers by CareerCast.com listed "newspaper reporter" as the fifth worst job one could have in terms of making a living. The worst job? A lumberjack. Broadcast journalists hardly fared better, ranking as the ninth worst job.[17] Some sense of the collapse: in 2012 the legendary *Philadelphia Inquirer* and its sister properties sold for just 10 percent of what they sold for in 2006.[18]

Speaking of Philadelphia, consider the findings of the Project for Excellence in Journalism in 2006 on the changes in Philadelphia's journalism over the preceding three decades:

> There are roughly half as many reporters covering metropolitan Philadelphia, for instance, as in 1980. The number of newspaper reporters there has fallen from 500 to 220. The pattern at the suburban papers around the city has been similar, though not as extreme. The local TV stations, with the exception of Fox, have cut back on traditional news coverage. The five AM radio stations that used to cover news have been

reduced to two. As recently as 1990, the Philadelphia Inquirer had 46 reporters covering the city. Today it has 24.[19]

As bad as it seemed at the time, 2006 looks like a golden age for journalists compared to today. In 2010–12, I visited two dozen American cities to discuss the state of journalism. In virtually every city I would ask veteran news professionals what was the percentage of paid journalists in their community working for all media compared to the 1980s. The general response, after serious contemplation, was in the 40 to 50 percent range, with several cities considerably less than that. In June 2012, in one fell swoop, Advance Publications eliminated over one half of the remaining editorial positions—some four hundred jobs—at three newspapers that served three of the four largest cities in Alabama.[20] Such drastic layoffs have become so common that they are barely news stories any longer—or maybe there just aren't people left to cover them.

A familiar story came when I visited Peoria, Illinois, in 2011 and learned that the once highly regarded *Peoria Journal-Star* had its editorial staff slashed in half since 2007 when GateHouse Media had purchased it. This led to political controversy as the mayor and city council realized that the citizens of Peoria had far less chance to understand what was going on in their community. At the same time that GateHouse was claiming dire circumstances forced it to slash budgets to the bone, it paid out $1.4 million in executive bonuses and $800,000 to its CEO.[21] Jim Romenesko noted that corporate CEOs at nine of the largest newspaper-owning firms had compensation packages in 2011 ranging from $3 million to $25 million each—with the average around $9.5 million—and in nearly every case corporate revenues and earnings had fallen.[22] Perhaps the only good news is that the journalism crisis has yet to reach the boardroom. That is hardly consolation for anyone else. "I don't know anybody from my profession," a former *Seattle Times* reporter said in 2011, "who isn't heartbroken, devastated, terrified, scared, enraged, despondent, bereft."[23] As bad as it is, all signs point to it getting even worse, if that is possible. "Most newspapers are in a place right now that they are going to have to make big cuts somewhere and big seams are bound to show up at some point," a media business analyst at the Poynter Institute said in July 2012.[24]

It is hard to avoid what seems like the obvious conclusion: corporations and investors no longer find journalism a profitable investment.[25] If anything, they are stripping what remains for parts and milking monopoly franchises until they run dry. That leads to an immediate problem for a society that has entrusted its news media to the private sector: a 2011 FCC study on the crisis in journalism concluded that "the independent watchdog function that the Founding Fathers envisioned for journalism—going so far as to call it crucial to a healthy democracy—is at risk."[26]

In addition, "the falling value and failing business models of many American newspapers," as David Carr of the *New York Times* puts it, is leading to a situation in which "moneyed interests buy papers and use them to prosecute a political and commercial agenda." Carr cites San Diego as exhibit A; the *U-T San Diego* (formerly the *San Diego Union-Tribune*) was purchased in November 2011 by right-wing billionaire Douglas F. Manchester, whose anti–gay rights politics gained him notoriety. "We make no apologies," Manchester's chief executive states. "We are very consistent—pro-conservative, pro-business, pro-military." The newspaper also has a tendency to equate what is good for San Diego's future with what is good for Manchester's net worth. "There is a very real fear here," a San Diego journalist said in 2012, that the *U-T San Diego* "will not be advocating for the public's good, but the owner's good instead."[27] David Sirota has chronicled the return of monopoly press lords and their effect on communities ranging from San Diego and Denver to Chicago and Philadelphia: "Private newspaper owners have vaulted themselves into a historically unique position, which enables them to sculpt the news to serve their personal interests while circumventing the costs that come with true adversarial journalism."[28] It was this type of journalism that produced the crisis that led to the rise of professional journalism a century ago. The system is unraveling.

Let's look more closely at what the crisis means in terms of actual reporting. The point is not to romanticize what is being lost; as discussed in chapter 3, U.S. professional journalism even at its peak in the late 1960s and 1970s had significant flaws. Many of the problems with journalism today can still be attributed to some of the weaknesses of the professional code, such as reliance upon official sources to set the boundaries of legitimate debate. That being said, it also had its virtues, not the least of which was a relatively serious commitment to covering much of public life, from small communities to major cities and the world. There was "a firewall between the news divisions and the corporate structure," veteran broadcast journalist Dan Rather recalls from the 1960s and 1970s. "That's all gone now. Out the window."

The flip side of corporatization of the news, to Rather, is the "trivialization" of the content. An increasing portion of news has gone over to inexpensive-to-cover entertainment, celebrity, gossip, crime, and lifestyle journalism—"soft news." Commercial values have increasingly permeated—or, to old-timers like Rather, subverted—the professional code.[29]

A study on the crisis was released by the Pew Center for the People and the Press in 2010; it examined in exhaustive detail the "media ecology" of the city of Baltimore for one week in 2009.[30] The object was to determine how, in this changing media moment, "original" news stories were being generated, and by whom. They tracked old media and new, newspapers, radio, television, websites, blogs, social media, even Twitter tweets from the police department.

Despite the proliferation of media, the researchers observed that "much of the 'news' people receive contained no original reporting. Fully eight out of ten stories studied simply repeated or repackaged previously published information." And where did the "original" reporting come from? More than 95 percent of original news stories were still generated by old media, particularly the *Baltimore Sun* newspaper. It gets worse: The *Sun*'s production of original news stories was down more than 30 percent from ten years ago and a whopping 73 percent from twenty years ago.

Back in the 1980s and 1990s, Ben Bagdikian chronicled the declining numbers of independent news media due to the wave upon wave of mergers and acquisitions and the entrance of large conglomerates as central players. He warned of the dire consequences for journalism and democracy caused by media monopoly. Internet celebrants consigned Bagdikian and other old-media fuddy-duddies to history's dustbin; they believed that the last thing anyone had to worry about now was a lack of distinct voices or competition. How ironic then that the Internet appears to have all but finished off the job that the market began. By 2012, the newspaper industry was "half as big as it was seven years ago," according to Carr of the *New York Times*. "Quite a few of the mid-size regional and metropolitan dailies that form the core of the industry have gone off a cliff."[31]

In the Internet era, the *New York Times* probably plays a much larger role in national and international journalism than it ever did in previous generations, despite its own significant cutbacks.[32] It does so because most of the other major news media have abandoned their networks of national and international bureaus altogether.[33] As a recent history of the *Times* from

1999–2009 concludes, it has become "the worst newspaper in the world—except for all others."[34]

Dan Rather counted in his research between forty and fifty independent news media organizations that had the resources and a commitment to cover politics at the national level in the 1950s and 1960s. Most of these businesses did journalism as their exclusive or primary undertaking. That world is long gone, as a handful of conglomerates dominate the few remaining national newsrooms, and news is generally a small part of a broader corporate empire. As Rather put it in 2012:

> Whether you're a conservative or a liberal or a progressive, a Democrat or a Republican, everybody can be and should be concerned about this: the constant consolidation of media, particularly national distribution of media . . . few companies—no more than six, my count is four—now control more than 80 percent of the true national distribution of news. These large corporations, they have things they need from the power structure in Washington, whether it's Republican or Democrat, and of course the people in Washington have things they want [in] the news to be reported. To put it bluntly, very big business is in bed with very big government in Washington, and has more to do with what the average person sees, hears, and reads than most people know.[35]

Rather's words are particularly striking in light of the conclusion of chapter 5: if the news media are to be the institution that protects the public from the collusion of very big business and the government, especially the very big national security state, its current industrial structure seems to be precisely the opposite of what is needed.

The shrinkage has had devastating implications for political journalism. The numbers of foreign bureaus and correspondents, Washington bureaus and correspondents, statehouse bureaus and correspondents, down to the local city hall, have all been severely slashed, and in some cases the coverage barely exists any longer.[36] In an era of ever greater corruption, the watchdog is no longer on the beat. Some of the biggest political scandals in Washington in the past decade—the ones that brought down Jack Abramoff, Tom DeLay, and Randy "Duke" Cunningham—were all started by a daily newspaper reporter's investigation. Those paid reporting positions are now gone, and those reporters no longer draw a paycheck to do such work. This means the next generation of corrupt politicians will have much less difficulty as they fatten their bank accounts while providing their services to the highest bidder. Throughout the nation, most government activity is taking place in the dark compared to just one or two decades ago.

Everywhere it is the same: far fewer journalists attempting to cover more and more.[37] It's like an NFL team trying to stop the Green Bay Packers with only two players lined up on the defensive side of the line of scrimmage. Broadcast journalism hardly has any players either. By 2012 it was common practice for competing broadcast stations to pool their news resources and provide the same news on different channels in the same market. This practice is of dubious legality but takes place in at least 83 of 210 television markets; it allows stations to slash their labor costs. As the FCC observes, the remaining reporters and editors "are spending more time on reactive stories and less on labor-intensive 'enterprise' pieces." Television reporters "who once just reported the news now have many other tasks, and more newscasts to feed, so they have less time to research their stories."[38]

For a chilling account of what the loss of journalism means, consider the explosion that killed twenty-nine West Virginia coal miners in 2010. Following the disaster, the *Washington Post* and *New York Times* did exposés and discovered that the mine had had 1,342 safety violations in the preceding five years, 50 in the previous month alone. This was big news. "The problem," the FCC notes, "is that these stories were published after the disaster, not before—even though many of the records had been there for inspection."[39] Josh Stearns perceptively writes that "we are entering an era of 'hindsight journalism,' where some of the most important stories of our time emerge after the fact. This kind of journalism shines a spotlight on critical issues, but serves as more of an autopsy than an antiseptic. It dissects issues like specimens, instead of shining a light on problems before or as they emerge."[40]

It is especially disastrous at the local level, where smaller news media and newsrooms have been wiped out in a manner reminiscent of a plague. Research affirms that there is "an explicit relationship between local and community news, local democracy, community cohesion, and civic engagement." When people living in a community no longer have credible news that covers their community and draws it together, the American system is suddenly on quicksand.[41] In 2012 the *New Orleans Times-Picayune* became the first major daily newspaper to restrict publication to three days a week.

What does that mean for the roughly one third of New Orleans residents who have no Internet access?[42] The *Los Angeles Times* is now the primary news medium for eighty-eight municipalities and 10 million people, but its metro staff has been cut in half since 2000. The staff "is spread thinner and there are fewer people on any given area," Metro editor David Lauter laments. "We're not there every day, or even every week or every month. Unfortunately, nobody else is either."[43]

Consider the farcical nature of American elections. Local elections, indeed nearly all non-presidential elections, barely get any news coverage, and what coverage they do get is generally inane, often driven by the TV ads and comprised of assessments of PR strategies, gaffes, and polling results. As for the presidential election, its coverage is generally endless and meaningless. Those with the most money to purchase the most ads can dominate political discourse. How can people effectively participate in electoral politics if they have little idea about the candidates, not to mention the issues? The logical course is to opt out, rather than be drowned in a pool of slime, spin, clichés, and idiocy. Where does that leave governance?

In a nation like the United States, the poor and marginalized are hardest hit. They are the least attractive group commercially, so labor news and news aimed at the bottom third or half of the population began to decline decades ago. Communities of color, which have traditionally gotten short shrift in the mainstream commercial news media, have seen many of the hard-won gains in diversifying newsrooms wiped out in the past five years. A 2012 American Society of News Editors report stated, "Across all market sizes, minority newsroom employment is still substantially lower than the percentage of minorities in the markets those newsrooms serve."[44]

The Pew Center conducted a comprehensive analysis of the sources for original news stories in its 2009 study of Baltimore. It determined that fully 86 percent originated with official sources and press releases. A generation earlier, PR accounted for more like 40 to 50 percent of news content. These stories were presented as news based on the labor and judgment of professional journalists, but they generally presented the PR position without any alteration. As the Pew study concludes, "the official version of events is becoming more important. We found official press releases often appear word for word in first accounts of events, though often not noted as such."[45]

So there may not be much journalism, but there still is plenty of "news." On the surface, it can seem as though we are inundated with endless news.

Increasingly, though, it is unfiltered public relations generated surreptitiously by corporations and governments in a manner that would make Walter Lippmann—whose vision guided the creation of professional journalism in the 1920s—roll in his grave. In 1960 there was less than one PR agent for every working journalist, a ratio of 0.75 to 1. By 1990 the ratio was just over 2 to 1. In 2012, the ratio stood at 4 PR people for every working journalist. At the current rates of change, the ratio may well be 6 to 1 within a few years.[46] Because there are far fewer reporters to investigate the spin and press releases, the likelihood that they get presented as legitimate news has become much greater.[47] "As a direct result of changing media platforms," one 2011 media industry assessment of the future of journalism put it, "PR pros are now a part of the media in a way they have never been before."[48]

Is it a surprise that Gallup found that Americans' confidence in television news dropped to an all-time low in 2012 and is not even half of what it was less than two decades earlier?[49] Or that there has understandably been an increase in the number of people, to nearly one in five, who state they have gone "newsless"—not even glancing at Internet headlines—for the day before the poll? Who could blame them? By 2009 nearly a third of Americans aged eighteen to twenty-four years were thus self-described.[50] Forty years ago, young Americans followed the news at the same rate as their parents and grandparents.

Note that the decline of journalism was well established long before the Internet had any effect.[51] The big change came in the late 1970s and 1980s, when large corporate chains accelerated their long-term trend of gobbling up daily newspapers and becoming conglomerates, sometimes with broadcast stations and networks under the same umbrella as newspaper empires. Family owners sold for a variety of reasons, and corporations came in to milk the cash cow. The corporations paid top dollar to get these profit machines, and they were dedicated to maximizing their return. They quickly determined that one way to increase profits even more was to slice into the editorial budget; in a monopoly there is little pressure to do otherwise, and with the money flowing, who worries about the long-term implications?[52]

It was then, when they were still swimming in profits, that managers began to satisfy the demand from investors for ever-increasing returns by cutting journalists and shutting news bureaus. By the late 1980s and early 1990s, prominent mainstream journalists and editors like Jim Squires, Penn Kimball, John McManus, and Doug Underwood were criticizing the news industry or leaving it in disgust because of the contempt corporate management displayed toward journalism.[53] By the end of the century, the trickle out was more like an exodus.

The 1990s were a period of tremendous profitability for newspapers and broadcast networks, as well as rapid growth for the economy. It was also a decade of considerable population growth. The Internet had become a big deal on Wall Street but had yet to do much more than hypothetical damage to journalism business models. Yet from 1992 to 2002, the editorial side was reduced by six thousand broadcast and newspaper jobs.[54] By the end of the 1990s, the number of foreign correspondents working for American newspapers and television networks had already been greatly reduced, as had the number of investigative reporters.[55] At the dawn of the new century, editors and observers were vocal, at times almost apoplectic, in their alarm at the policies that were devastating newsrooms.[56] In 2001 a team of leading journalists and scholars concluded, "Newspapers are increasingly a reflection of what the advertisers tell the newspapers some of us want, which is what the financial markets tell the newspapers they want."[57] It was already clear that this was a recipe for disaster.[58]

This is the actual history of journalism under really existing capitalism. Celebrants who think the market will rejuvenate journalism online and produce better results have yet to come to terms with this record and explain why digital commercial news media would be any different or better. Right now it looks a whole lot *worse*.

Digital Journalism: Gold Mine or the Shaft?

The decline of journalism over the past generation, which has accelerated in the last decade, would be a less pressing concern if the existing news media were making a successful digital transition, or if the Internet was spawning a credible replacement in the manner Benkler envisions. The evidence provided above suggests on balance that emerging digital news media are having a negligible effect upon the crisis in journalism. It certainly is not due to a lack of effort, as commercial news media have been obsessed with the Internet since the 1990s; they understood that it was going to be the future.

For traditional news media, it has been a very rocky digital road. A 2012 report based on proprietary data and in-depth interviews with executives at a dozen major news media companies found "the shift to replace losses in print ad revenue with new digital revenue is taking longer and proving more difficult than executives want and at the current rate most newspapers continue to contract at alarming speed." For every seven dollars of print advertising lost there is only one new dollar of Internet ad revenues; the executives said it "remains an uphill and existential struggle."[59] The newspaper industry's percentage of overall Internet advertising fell to 10 percent in 2011, an all-time low; it had been 17 percent in 2003.[60] "There's no doubt we're going out of business right now," one executive said.[61] By all accounts, the "clock continues to tick" for old media to find a way to survive online in the inexorable transition to the Internet.[62]

It is both tragic and pathetic to see dedicated journalists obsessing over how to keep their newsrooms alive. "We have to find a business model that works—we have to," *Christian Science Monitor* editor Marshall Ingwerson told NYU media scholar Rodney Benson. "This is the word I hated but in the last five years has become universal—we have to monetize. How do we monetize what we do? Same as everybody else."[63] Journalists have been inundated with lectures that they "require an embrace of new technologies and a ruthless but necessary shedding of the old ways of doing business. It should have happened already. It must happen now."[64]

The assumption is that there *has* to be a way to make profits doing digital journalism if journalists and owners simply wise up and get with the program. Over the past few years, many American newspapers have been purchased on the cheap by hedge funds—nearly a third of the twenty-five largest dailies are now so owned—the subtext being that these business geniuses can generate profits where dummkopf journalism industry types have failed.[65] As John Paton, the journalist-*cum*-CEO for a newspaper company purchased by the Alden Global Capital hedge fund in 2011, put it: "We have had 15 years to figure out the web and, as an industry, we newspaper people are no good at it."[66] Apparently, neither are the hedge fund managers. David Carr wrote in July 2012 that "hedge funds, which thought they had bought in at the bottom, are scrambling for exits that don't exist."[67]

Few wish to consider the obvious question: what if it is simply impossible to generate commercially viable popular journalism online, let alone journalism adequate for a self-governing people? What then?

In the meantime, news media corporations work furiously to find their digital Shangri-La. The primary course for traditional news media has been to pursue digital advertising dollars, with disappointing results. Most websites for publishers and broadcasters primarily run generic banner ads, "among the least trusted sources of commercial information," according to consumer surveys.[68] These are rapidly falling out of favor with advertisers. Digital news sites have been laggards in "using technology that would customize ads based on their users' online behavior."[69] Moreover, as much as 80 percent of digital newspaper advertising is placed through networks that take a 50 percent cut of the action. This means a paper's revenues for a thousand viewers (CPM in industry parlance) can be as little as 2 or 3 percent of its CPM for print readers.[70] Worse yet, as discussed in chapter 5, much of local marketing—once the bread and butter of news media—as it goes digital does not support media content sites or independent content sites of any kind.[71] "A consensus has emerged that website advertising," a respected 2011 industry report said, "its rates driven down by massive available inventory, will probably never sustain a comprehensive daily news report."[72]

However, digital advertising provided newspapers over $3 billion in revenues in 2011, far exceeding all other forms of Internet revenues. It is not going to be abandoned even if no one expects it to grow very much.

With the possibility fading for digital advertising to serve as a panacea, attention has returned to making people pay for their news online.[73] This has worked for a handful of prominent newspapers like the *Wall Street Journal* and *Financial Times*, with well-heeled readers and specialized business content. The *New York Times* has also done well, enrolling nearly four hundred thousand subscribers since it introduced its pay system in 2011. The *Washington Post*, on the other hand, dismisses paywalls as "backwards-looking." CEO Don Graham claims they can work only for papers like the *Times* and the *Journal* that have paid circulation spread across the nation.[74] Paywalls have been a flop otherwise, and a study of three dozen papers that attempted to do so found only 1 percent of users opted to pay.[75] Nevertheless, by 2012 some 20 percent of America's 1,400 daily newspapers were planning to charge for digital access, and some firms, such as Gannett, claimed they were generating significant revenue.[76] They are inspired by the success of dailies doing so in places like Finland and Slovakia.[77] The key, apparently, is to be able to offer a lot of content at a low price—ideally by numerous newspapers combined—which might be easier in a small nation with a distinct language than in the United States, where English-language material grows like kudzu online. Whether there is an endgame is unclear—subscribers have never provided sufficient revenues for news media—and it appears as much an act of desperation as vision. Of course, there is no time to be concerned with the externality that paywalls invariably cut many people off from access to the news, with all that suggests about their undemocratic character.

The latest hope is that the rapid emergence of mobile communication will open up new ways to monetize content. By 2012 a clear majority of Americans are getting some local news on their cell phones, and that number is growing. Best of all, the mobile world is increasingly proprietary, so there might be sufficient artificial scarcity to encourage people eventually to pay for news apps. Rupert Murdoch announced his iPad-only newspaper, *The Daily*, in 2011, and by 2012 the price had been lowered, some content was being offered for free, and it had been extended to smartphones. With a hundred thousand subscribers paying a couple dollars per month, "it's going to need more than that to move from interesting experiment to profitable."[78] The news app idea still has a long way to go before it can be realistic. In 2011, 11 percent of the American adult population had a news app, but nearly 90 percent of them got the app for free. Only 1 percent of the adult population paid for one. There is little reason yet for thinking news apps could get anywhere close to supporting the network of newsrooms that once dotted the landscape. It did not help the case that News Corporation laid off 29 percent of *The Daily*'s full-time staff in 2012. But it may be the last best hope.[79]

The point of professional journalism in its idealized form was to insulate the news from commercialism, marketing, and political pressures and to produce the necessary information for citizens to understand and participate effectively in their societies. In theory, some people were not privileged over others as legitimate consumers of journalism. That is why it was democratic. There was one set of news for everyone. It was a public service with an ambiguous relationship with commercialism; hence the professional firewall. Journalists made their judgment calls based on professional education and training, not commercial considerations. That is why people could trust it. The core problem with all these efforts to make journalism pay online is that they accelerate the commercialization of journalism, degrading its integrity and its function as a public service. The cure may be worse than the disease.

So it is that top editors at the venerable *Washington Post* "have embraced the view that studying [Internet user] traffic patterns can be a useful way to determine where to focus the paper's resources."[80] They are desperate to find the content that will appeal to desired consumers *and* to the advertisers who wish to reach affluent consumers. In this relationship, advertisers hold all the trump cards, and the news media have little leverage. In the emerging era of "smart" advertising, this means shaping the content to meet the Internet profiles of desired users, even personalizing news stories alongside personalized ads. The best stories for selling tend to be soft news. "The challenge," Joseph Turow writes, has been "trying to figure out how to carry out editorial personalization in a way that wouldn't cause audiences to freak out." He points out that all the logic of the system points to advertisers demanding that *they* get sympathetic editorial mention as well. Research shows that that makes for a far more successful sales pitch. As one frustrated editor put it, "This crap may be groovy, but it still stinks."[81]

Nothing much changes when one looks at the new companies that have emerged to use the Internet as a battering ram to enter the news media industry. "All these people who forecast the end of newspapers because of the decline in advertising and users being unwilling to pay for content can't explain how the new Internet journalism websites are going to survive or even thrive—since most of them, too, need paid ads and/or subscribers," said Greg Mitchell, the longtime editor of *Editor & Publisher*. "I just don't get it."[82]

The new commercial ventures range from "content farms" to apps to major efforts to establish newsrooms and re-create a sense of news media online. The content farms, like Demand Media and Associated Content, have "embraced the attrition of the church-state boundary and turned it into a business model."[83] These firms hire freelancers to produce articles quickly and cheaply to respond to popular search terms, and then sell advertising to appear next to the article. The needs of advertisers drive the entire process.[84] The key to commercial success is producing an immense amount of material inexpensively; the leading content farms can generate thousands of pieces of text and video on a daily basis.[85]

Pulse has emerged as one of the leading commercial news apps, with 13 million smartphone users who get it for free. Pulse aggregates other firms' news and makes its money working with advertisers and merchants. It is moving into "branded-content advertising," by which ads get slotted next to appropriate stories for individualized users. The outstanding question is whether Pulse will generate a workable business model and then can establish a monopoly position due to its scale and network effects, like Twitter. By

2012 it moved aggressively to provide local news—with the ability to place advertising in real time that addresses one's exact location—and become a global operation; the service is already available in eight languages. Pulse does not generate original news, and its founders concede that they don't know much about journalism.[86] Nor do any of the other mobile aggregators generate any original journalism,[87] but some of their revenues will probably end up in the hands of other news media and may eventually contribute to paying actual journalists.

The journalism company that has made the greatest impact online has been AOL, which was tenuously married to Time Warner for a decade until it went independent again in 2009. AOL purchased Patch around then, to be a "hyperlocal" digital news service, with branches in some 860 communities, supported by advertising. In other words, it would be like a digital newspaper but without the massive production expenses. A detailed and largely sympathetic *Columbia Journalism Review* account of a Patch editor in upstate New York described how the service logically focused on more affluent communities. After months of keeping the editorial and commercial sides distinct, that strategy was thrown overboard as the enterprise foundered; editors worked with the ad staff, among other things "drumming up ad sales leads." The editors were then directed to favor content that would get people to the site and also to cultivate "user-generated free content." Patch lost $100 million in 2011, and is estimated to have lost another $150 million in 2012. As David Carr puts it, Patch "is no closer to cracking the code."[88] While it may eventually get into the black, it will do so at the expense of sacrificing much of the journalistic vision it had at its launch.[89]

Patch is evolving toward the *Huffington Post* business model: rely on volunteer labor, aggregate content from other media, emphasize sex and celebrities to juice the traffic, and generate some of your own content if you can afford to do so.[90] As fate had it, AOL purchased the *Huffington Post* in 2011. An internal memo on journalism from AOL CEO Tim Armstrong at the time captured the commercial logic: he ordered the company's editors to evaluate all future stories on the basis of "traffic potential, revenue potential, edit quality and turnaround time." All stories, he stressed, are to be evaluated according to their "profitability consideration."[91] As one 2011 media industry assessment of the future of journalism put it, this is "good news for public relations professionals who are trying to pitch stories," because "these sites will be looking for more content to fill their pages."[92]

Armstrong's memo raises the question: What happens when a story—like that of a distant war or the privatization of a local water utility—fails to achieve proper "traffic potential, revenue potential"? What if no PR spinmeister wants to push it and provide free content? Does it disappear off the radar—and with it the ability of citizens to know what is being done in their name but without their informed consent? That might be a smooth ride for the CEOs, but it's a clunker for a democratic society.

Two aspects of capitalism and the Internet loom large in digital journalism. First, if anyone can make money doing online journalism, it will almost certainly be as a very large, centralized operation, probably a monopoly or close to it. The Internet has proven to be more effective at centralizing corporate control than it has been at enhancing decentralization, at least in news media. "We are probably far more centralized than we were in the past," one executive said.[93]

To some extent it is because human beings are capable of meaningfully visiting only a small number of websites on a regular basis. The Google search mechanism encourages concentration because sites that do not end up on the first or second page of a search effectively do not exist. As Michael Wolff puts it in *Wired*, "The top 10 Web sites accounted for 31 percent of US pageviews in 2001, 40 percent in 2006, and about 75 percent in 2010."[94] By 2012, according to the Web traffic measurer Experian Hitwise, 35 percent of all Web visits now go to Google, Microsoft, Yahoo!, and Facebook. (The same firms get two thirds of online ad revenue.) And, ironically, as Matthew Hindman points out, personalization of websites "systematically advantages the very largest websites over smaller ones."[95] A paradox of the Internet, John Naughton writes, "is that a relatively small number of websites get most of the links and attract the overwhelming volume of traffic." If your site isn't in that elite group, it will likely be very small, and stay very small.[96]

As Matthew Hindman's research on journalism, news media, and political websites demonstrates, what has emerged is a "power law" distribution whereby a small number of political or news media websites get the vast majority of traffic.[97] They are dominated by the traditional giants with name recognition and resources. There is a "long tail" of millions of websites that exist but get little or no traffic, and only a small number of people have any idea that they exist. Most of them wither, as their producers have little incentive and resources to maintain them. There is also no effective "middle class" of robust, moderate-size websites; that segment of the news media system has been wiped out online, leading Hindman to conclude that the online news media are *more* concentrated than in the old news media world.

This seems to be the way of the digital world. Because the returns are so low and the marginal costs of adding new users are zero, profits are possible only by having massive scale. The "best bet for making money," *The Economist* states, "is to pull in more readers for the same content." And when a player gets that large, there usually isn't much room for anyone else. "There will be fewer national news outlets" in the digital world.[98] The grand irony of the Internet is that what was once regarded as an agent of diversity, choice, and competition has become an engine of monopoly. As to journalism, it is unclear if *anyone* can make a go of it commercially, beyond material aimed at the wealthy and the business community.

The second aspect of the capitalism-Internet nexus at the heart of the online journalism business model is an understanding that the wages paid to journalists can be slashed dramatically, while workloads can be increased to levels never before seen. Armstrong's memo states that all of AOL's journalistic employees will be required to produce "five to 10 stories per day." Tim Rutten of the *Los Angeles Times* captured the essence of this requirement in his assessment of AOL's 2011 purchase of the *Huffington Post*: "To grasp the Huffington Post's business model, picture a galley rowed by slaves and commanded by pirates." In the "new-media landscape," he wrote, "it's already clear that the merger will push more journalists more deeply into the tragically expanding low-wage sector of our increasingly brutal economy."[99]

With massive unemployment and dismal prospects, the extreme downward pressure on wages and working conditions for journalists is the two-ton elephant that just climbed into democracy's bed. "In the new media," Rutten concludes, we find "many of the worst abuses of the old economy's industrial capitalism—the sweatshop, the speedup, and piecework; huge profits for the owners; desperation, drudgery, and exploitation for the workers. No child labor, yet, but if there were more page views in it . . ."[100] David Watts Barton left the *Sacramento Bee* in 2007 to work at the *Sacramento Press*, a hyperlocal digital news operation. In the *Columbia Journalism Review*, he described the extreme difficulty of producing credible journalism based on volunteer labor. "Editing costs money. Citizen journalists are cheap and they can even be good. But even great journalists need some editing; citizen journalists need a lot of it. . . . Without journalism jobs, we don't have journalism."[101]

Commercial media's attitude toward journalism labor became apparent in the Journatic brouhaha following a whistleblower's exposé aired on public radio's *This American Life* in the summer of 2012. Journatic is a shadowy "hyperlocal content provider" that reportedly eschews publicity to the point where its site contains code that lessens its appearance in Google search results. It contracts with dozens of U.S. commercial news media to provide local coverage, including *Newsday*, the *Houston Chronicle*, the *San Francisco Chronicle*, and the GateHouse newspaper chain. The Journatic business model is premised on the idea that doing routine local news with actual paid reporters is no longer a viable option for many American news media, so it provides a discount alternative.

Journatic's local coverage is provided by low-paid writers and freelancers in the United States and, ironically enough, the Philippines, where Journatic hires writers "able to commit to 250 pieces/week minimum" at 35 to 40 cents a piece. Journatic CEO Brian Timpone says that the compensation was "more than most places in the Philippines." They produce stories under bogus "American-sounding bylines" that make it seem as if they are based in the local community running the stories. Part of the reason aliases are used is that it would be suspicious to readers and other journalists if they saw the number of articles a single writer produced, not to mention the importance of maintaining the illusion that these are local reporters.

Not surprisingly, these stories are "little more than rewritten news releases," as the whistleblower put it. They also contain a considerable number of errors, fabrications, and instances of plagiarism.[102] But to the casual reader of a Journatic client, it would seem the newspaper or website was chock-full of original local material.

The Tribune Company, which owns the *Chicago Tribune*, invested in Journatic in April 2012 and outsourced coverage for the Chicago area's ninety TribLocal websites and twenty-two weekly editions to it. TribLocal laid off half of its forty staffers when it contracted with Journatic, and its output tripled. When word got out, ninety members of the *Chicago Tribune* newsroom presented a petition protesting Journatic's role. On July 13 the company indefinitely suspended use of Journatic in its papers, but the hyperlocal content provider is still very much in action in other markets, waiting for the bad publicity to blow over.

This is hardly the end of the story. A Pasadena publisher, James Macpherson, stated he wanted to "defend the concept" of outsourcing, claiming that "Journatic has done it quite shabbily." His firm had begun outsourcing journalism to India in 2007, but the program was postponed soon thereafter as he was apparently ahead of his time. Macpherson uses Internet software developed by Amazon in 2012 to contract with freelance reporters all over the world and says, "I outsource virtually everything. I am primarily looking for individuals who I can pay a lower rate to do a lot of work." He concedes there are limitations: "There is no way someone in Manila can possibly understand what is happening in Pasadena." But the economics are such that Macpherson argues outsourcing is inevitable: "The real lesson of Journatic is that outsourcing is not going to go away."[103]

As journalism becomes increasingly rote, the logical question becomes who needs human labor at all? StatSheet, a subsidiary of Automated Insights, uses algorithms to turn numerical data into narrative articles for its 418 sports websites. Automated Insights now also computer-generates ten thousand to twenty thousand articles per week for a real estate website, and the emerging computer-generated content industry is convinced that algorithms will become a key part of writing news stories in the near future. "I am sure a journalist could do a better job writing an article than a machine," says a real estate agency CEO who contracted with Automated Insights, "but what I'm looking for is quantity at a certain quality."[104] Who knows—maybe we will someday look back at Journatic as a golden age of journalism.

In short, the Internet does not alleviate the tensions between commercialism and journalism; it magnifies them. With labor severely underpaid or unpaid, research concludes that the original journalism provided by the Internet gravitates to what is easy and fun, tending to "focus on lifestyle topics, such as entertainment, retail, and sports, not on hard news."[105] As traditional journalism disintegrates, no models for making Web journalism—even bad journalism—profitable at anywhere near the level necessary for a credible popular news media have been developed, and there is no reason to expect any in the future.[106]

There is probably no better evidence that journalism is a public good than the fact that none of America's financial geniuses can figure out how to make money off it. The comparison to education is striking. When managers apply market logic to schools, it fails, because education is a cooperative public service, not a business. Corporatized schools throw underachieving, hard-to-teach kids overboard, discontinue expensive programs, bombard students with endless tests, and then attack teacher salaries and unions as the main impediment to "success."[107] No one has ever made profits doing quality education—for-profit education companies seize public funds and make their money by *not* teaching.[108] That's why the elite managers send *their* own children to nonprofit schools, generally private but sometimes public in the affluent suburbs, while other children are hung out to dry in the marketplace. Education is, in short, a public good. In digital news, the same dynamic is producing the same results, and leads to the same conclusion.

Fighting for the Public Good

The severity of the crisis in journalism is difficult to ignore, especially for those in politics who have seen the number of reporters following them diminish rapidly. By 2008 many politicians were commenting on how difficult it had become to get press coverage in their districts or on the issues they cared about. On the campaign trail, U.S. senators who once had entourages of reporters following them like they were heavyweight champions suddenly found themselves traveling with one or two staffers and few others. By 2010 the FCC and the Federal Trade Commission had each created task forces to study the crisis in journalism and propose solutions. The Democratic Caucus in Congress established an informal inquiry too. Hearings were held in both the House and Senate. Nothing has resulted, but these inquiries were unprecedented in American history.[109]

The lack of action was due in part to a lack of public outcry and pressure. The extent of the crisis in journalism is underappreciated by most Americans, including many serious news and political junkies. The primary reason may well be the Internet itself. Because many people envelop themselves in their favored news sites and access so much material online, even surfing out onto the "long tail," the extent to which we are living in what veteran editor Tom Stites terms a "news desert" has been obscured.[110] Moreover, using dissident websites, social media, and smartphones, activists have sometimes "bypassed the gatekeepers" in what John Nichols calls a "next media system."[111] Its value is striking during periods of public protest and upheaval.

But the illusion that this constitutes satisfactory journalism is growing thinner. Nothing demonstrates the situation better than the release by WikiLeaks of an immense number of secret U.S. government documents between 2009 and 2011. To some this was investigative journalism at its best, and WikiLeaks had established how superior the Internet was as an information source. It clearly threatened those in power, so this was exactly the sort of Fourth Estate a free people needed. Thanks to the Internet, some claimed, we were now truly free and had the power to hold leaders accountable.[112]

In fact, the WikiLeaks episode demonstrates precisely the opposite. WikiLeaks was not a journalistic organization. It released secret documents to the public, but the "documents languished online and only came to the public's attention when they were written up by professional journalists," as Heather Brooke put it. "Raw material alone wasn't enough."[113] Journalism had to give the material credibility, and journalists had to do the hard work of vetting the material and analyzing it to find out what it meant. That required paid, full-time journalists with institutional support. The United States has too few of these, and those it has are too closely attached to the power structure, so most of the material still has not been studied and summarized for a popular audience—and it may never be in our lifetimes.

Moreover, there was no independent journalism to respond when the U.S. government launched a successful PR and media blitz to discredit WikiLeaks. Attention largely shifted from the content of these documents to overblown and unsubstantiated claims that WikiLeaks was costing innocent lives, and to a personal focus on WikiLeaks leader Julian Assange. Glenn Greenwald was only slightly exaggerating when he stated that "there was almost a full and complete consensus that WikiLeaks was satanic." The onslaught discredited and isolated WikiLeaks, despite the dramatic content that could be found in the documents WikiLeaks had published. The point was to get U.S. editors and reporters to think twice before opening the WikiLeaks door. It worked.

Many journalists elsewhere rallied to defend basic principles about transparency and speaking truth to power. The material they assessed and made public energized a wave of global democratic movements, even contributing to peaceful political revolutions. In the United States, nothing of the kind occurred, and WikiLeaks has had no effect on democratizing *our* politics or calling *our* leaders to account. The responses of U.S. journalists and commentators to the WikiLeaks revelations were often indistinguishable from those of the government spin doctors. Greenwald ended up defending WikiLeaks on numerous broadcast news programs and discovered that his on-air opponents were often working reporters: "There wasn't even really a pretense of separation between how journalists think and how political functionaries think."[114]

When the U.S. government and the Internet giants took steps to render WikiLeaks ineffective, even though no one connected with it had been charged with, or convicted of, any crime for its publishing activities, what passes for U.S. journalism stood by meekly. How revealing that a news media that almost never does investigative work on the national security state or its relations with large corporations does not come to the defense of those who have the courage to make such information public! As the Obama administration, like those before it, has pursued extraordinary measures to limit public access to information and to punish whistleblowers, a credible independent news media in a free society would have led the charge to publicize its secrecy and actively oppose it.[115] All the signs suggest that WikiLeaks, rather than being the harbinger of a new era, may have been the last gasp of an old one.

This also touches on the limitations of blogs, which not long ago were heralded as "little First Amendment machines. They extend freedom of the press to more actors."[116] Blogs provide commentary, sometimes expert commentary, but they tend to rely upon others' reporting upon which to comment. Without a credible journalism, blogs have value only to the extent they produce original research, which is difficult unless one can do it full-time with institutional support. Moreover, Hindman's research on online media concentration applies just as much, if not more, to the blogosphere. He found its traffic is highly concentrated in a handful of sites, operated by people with astonishingly elite pedigrees.[117]

There is one exciting new hope for digital journalism that has emerged in the past few years: online nonprofit news media. A number of outlets have been created that are dedicated to doing journalism in the public interest. What we have done "was out of seeing where the business model is headed, off a cliff," the editor of the *Voice of San Diego* told NYU's Benson, "and if we want to keep this public service alive we needed to fund it in a different way." "I say good riddance" to having to rely on advertising and generating profits, the editor of the *SF Public Press* told Benson. "It was a bad marriage to begin with and it skewed coverage. And it foreclosed discussion of people and communities who were not targets of advertising."[118] Founders of these organizations see the gaping void in American journalism and wish to fill it.

The great question, then, is whether this new wave of nonprofit news media can rejuvenate American journalism and steer it away from the commercialism that was eating at its foundations. If it can, public ennui and governmental inaction are justified. Yankee ingenuity will have licked the problem. Best of all, there will be little government or commercial involvement with journalism; it will be a genuine public sphere.[119]

Some of these nonprofit ventures are local, like *MinnPost* and the aforementioned *Voice of San Diego*, and some are national, like *ProPublica*, which, in 2010, was the first digital news medium to win the Pulitzer Prize for reporting. Many are staffed by superb journalists who once worked in commercial news media. Young and enthusiastic new journalists are entering the field in this sector. A 2011 study by the Investigative Reporting Workshop determined that the top seventy-five nonprofit news operations had 1,300 employees and combined annual budgets totaling $135 million. (This includes *Consumer Reports*, which accounts for nearly half the total staff and one third of the budgets.)[120] Since 2008, there has been a spike in Internal Revenue Service (IRS) applications for nonprofit status from journalism organizations, almost entirely for digital operations.[121] "This sector has absolutely ballooned," I was told by Josh Stearns, the Free Press activist who works in the area.[122] How many of these new nonprofit digital news ventures are there? "It's scores, not dozens, maybe hundreds, probably a lot more than anyone knows," says the Knight Foundation's Eric Newton, who monitors and encourages such activity for a living.[123]

Nevertheless, the impact of the nonprofit sector may be less than the sum of its parts. "Investigative nonprofits," as Newton put it, "are 'punching above their weight,'" meaning that "the total community reached is still not close to the for-profits."[124] They are usually most successful when a mainstream news organization picks up their work. That is often the approach of *ProPublica*, which won the first of its two Pulitzers for a piece that ran in the *New York Times Magazine*. In this scenario, the nonprofit sector is providing a subsidy to commercial news media.

There is also a push for nonprofit activist groups—nongovernmental organizations, or NGOs—to become direct producers of online journalism in the areas where they have expertise.[125] With the collapse of traditional newsrooms, public interest NGOs are doing their own reporting so they can pursue stories relating to their work. "What's a nonprofit digital news operation? Consumer Reports online?" asks Newton. "The highly ethical digital info gathering part of Human Rights Watch?"[126] In 2011, for example, the Center for Media and Democracy (CMD) produced award-winning exposés of the secretive and corporate-dominated American Legislative Exchange Council (ALEC). A few years earlier, the work might have been done by traditional journalists, but there were simply too few left to take on that assignment.

As exciting as it is to have NGOs get into the journalism business, we should not romanticize the development and make a virtue out of a necessity. In my experience, most of these groups would prefer that there be independent journalism organizations doing the hard investigative work they are being forced to do. It would allow them to use their very scarce resources for their core research, advocacy, and service. Most important, it would give the findings far more legitimacy and have greater public impact than when they come from an interested party. In a world where most journalism emanates from interested parties, it will be hard for NGOs to rise above the clatter that the corporate-funded groups produce, because the latter have exponentially greater resources. The work of the CMD on ALEC, for example, went mainstream when it was picked up and pushed along by the *New York Times* a full year after the CMD broke the story.[127]

The good news for both NGO journalists and the new sector of digital nonprofit news media is that by dispensing with print, they lop off at least 30 percent of the costs of production and distribution for a traditional newspaper or magazine.[128] This is one of the factors that allows celebrants to wax rhapsodic about the postmaterial nature of networked journalism. The bad news is that losing 30 percent of costs still leaves this sector well under water. These digital nonprofit news media are underfunded, and there is no reason to think they will ever generate much more resources than they currently have. To put this sector in context, it has, at most, a few thousand employees, compared to the 120,000 full-time paid journalists our country had two decades ago.[129] Moreover, none of these ventures is pointed toward large-scale growth. Even in the assessments of their most enthusiastic supporters, they are far more likely to go under. In fact, this is probably about as good as it gets, barring the sort of radical policy proposals I make in the next section. Once one gets past the seventy-five largest nonprofit news organizations, one is deep in the weeds of very small, marginal shops. "None has developed a clear business model," a Knight Foundation study concluded.[130]

Individual donations and foundation grants have been the basis of revenues, but these have distinct limits and invite problems. Experience with public broadcasting shows that people will pay, but there is an upper limit that is far below the money needed. Individuals gave $730 million to all public and community broadcasting stations in 2009. The total has not grown as a percentage of public media revenues over the past decade, and only a fraction of that went toward journalism.[131] The *SF Public Press* made a concerted effort to establish a "PBS model" for donations to support itself, but the donations amount to only between 7 and 12 percent of its meager $80,000 annual budget.[132] Even if the donation approach were to become viable, there is an additional concern: it tends to extend the privileges of the upper-middle and upper classes into the digital future.

This brings us to foundations. As the newspaper meltdown unfolded early in 2009, a movement was afoot to establish nonprofit newspapers and/or endowed newspapers, to be supported by philanthropy. As the longtime head of the Center for Public Integrity, Charles Lewis, put it, "It's time for civil society, especially the nation's foundations and individuals of means, to collaborate with journalists and experts who understand the changing economics of journalism in an imaginative, visionary plan that would support our precious existing nonprofit institutions and help to develop new ones."[133] Since 2005, Jan Schaffer of American University estimates that foundations have donated at least $250 million to U.S. nonprofit journalism ventures.[134]

The problems with foundations as a form of support are threefold. First, they do not have anywhere near enough money to bankroll even a large chunk of journalism. They have a lot of other issues on their plates. *The Economist* notes that foundations "can only be a partial solution to the woes of newspapers."[135]

Second, foundations are hardly value-free or neutral institutions. They have their own pet causes and axes to grind, and they are often associated with powerful people and institutions. Sometimes they will fund coverage only of certain types of stories that they have an interest in. Foundations are generally accustomed to having their grantees give them what they want. Exceptions notwithstanding, they are not going to cut big checks and then head off to the beach. In an environment where many nonprofit journalists are wondering where their next meal is coming from, that gives foundations extraordinary implicit or explicit power over the content—largely unaccountable power.

Third, most foundations provide only limited-term support, often for periods of three years or less, to new enterprises. Foundation boards and directors like to spawn groups, not bankroll them in perpetuity. "It is worth noting that many of these are start-ups within their first three years," Stearns said when chronicling the state of nonprofit news ventures. "Once the start-up funding disappears it is unclear how many will survive."[136] John Bracken of the Knight Foundation, the leading funder of nonprofit journalism, warns start-ups that "we will not be providing perpetual support."[137]

It is striking that the leading foundations involved in funding and studying nonprofit news ventures apparently have no idea, after years of experience, how these operations can ever become sustainable. Foundation officials are reduced to recycling platitudes and buzzwords like those that hedge fund managers are directing at old-fashioned newspaper people on the commercial side. The Knight Foundation president said, "We're interested in new and different ways of doing things. . . . Folks who can be nimble and change are going to do better in the future than those who are slow to change."[138] Jeff Jarvis told grantmakers in 2011 that digital nonprofit news media need to focus on figuring out "which financial models work." A 2011 Pew Research Center report says the most "promising experiments in community news" are "coming from people who embrace business entrepreneurship and digital innovation."[139] Newton argues that "digital nonprofits need a diverse revenue stream to survive."[140] He says the days of getting a grant and concentrating on doing great journalism are over. Digital nonprofits must spend "substantial amounts of money on such items as technology, sales and marketing."[141] He believes digital nonprofit media should embrace the use of unpaid labor: "The new digital models are different types, citizen/volunteer/freelance/traditional/mixed."[142]

In effect, this approach admits defeat and then tries to declare victory.[143] It clings desperately to the faith-based conviction that everything will somehow eventually work out in the absence of any public policy intervention, while conceding that there will be an indefinite period during which the resources going to journalism are certain to decline precipitously. During that interregnum, anywhere from one to five decades, we apparently will have to get by on chewing gum and baling wire. Newton, to his credit, has pondered the implications of this approach:

> News, like life, finds a way. My long-term optimism is tinged with worry about the current state of things. Eventually is not the same as

> immediately. While we are waiting for the huge new age—two-way, not one-way; digital, not industrial; networked, not broadcast—to take hold, a lot of bad things are happening. Whenever traditional journalism decreases, for example, public corruption increases. Sometimes I wonder: How much corruption and confusion can one country take?[144]

Newton is right: this is a dubious strategy. In view of the immense problems before us, it strikes me as tantamount to social suicide.

Perhaps the most sobering development of recent times concerns *The Guardian*, arguably the best English-language newspaper in the world, with an enormous online readership. As a report by *The Economist's More Intelligent Life* notes, "The *Guardian* has been having an astonishing run." Few newspapers have embraced the Internet with such fury and apparent success. In terms of reach and impact, "the *Guardian* is doing better than ever." The success is due in part to *The Guardian* being a nonprofit, with a singular devotion to journalism above all else. There are no investors weighing their stake in *The Guardian* against other more profitable options. The Scott Trust—established in the 1930s by the family owners—has been well managed and has a "war chest" of roughly $250–300 million to cover operating losses, though CEO Andrew Miller says that amount will cover at most another three to five years. But even *The Guardian* cannot find a way to break even without cutting resources or commercializing its operations beyond the traditional role of advertising. Both options undermine quality and put the paper and its website on a downward spiral. *Guardian* employees are aware of the dilemma; reporter Nick Davies says it is impossible to see how investigative journalism can survive on the current trajectory. If an operation like *The Guardian*, with its support structure, vast resources, enormous scale, and popularity, cannot transition to the digital age and maintain quality—and might not even survive—what hope is there for anyone else?[145]

In my view, we are better off admitting what is plainly obvious: there is no business model that can give us the journalism a self-governing society requires. What we need is a significant body of full-time paid journalists, covering their communities, the nation, the world, in competition and collaboration with other paid journalists. There need to be independent newsrooms where journalists who are secure enough in their livelihoods to focus on their work can collaborate and receive professional editing, fact-checking, and assistance. There needs to be expertise, developed over years of trial and error, in vital areas of specialty, and paid journalists accountable for those beats. We need journalists trained in languages, history, and culture to work international beats with the credentials to protect them from government harassment. Great media institutions need to compete with other great media institutions, giving citizens solid choices and distinct perspectives.

And all of this media must be digital, perhaps with an old-media overlay during the interregnum. Digital technologies can make the system much more accessible and economically cost-efficient, and it can allow a much larger role for citizens to participate. That is what is so exciting about the world Benkler and the other celebrants envision. I can see a new and dramatically superior caliber of journalism emerging as a result of the Internet. It will be a journalism that will overcome the great limitations of professional journalism as it has been practiced in the United States: among other things, reliance upon the narrow range of opinion of people in power as the legitimate parameters of political debate, with a bias toward seeing the world through upper-class eyes. It will be a journalism that can truly open up our politics in the manner democratic theory envisions.

However, for this to happen there must be major public investments, and these funds must go to the development of a diverse and independent nonprofit sector. The future of journalism otherwise will likely approach what education would be like if all public investments were removed. With no such investments, our education system would remain excellent for the wealthy, who can afford private schools, mediocre for the upper-middle class, and nonexistent or positively frightening for the increasingly impoverished middle and working classes, the majority of the nation. To the extent it even existed, it would depend upon volunteer labor. It would be a nightmare unsuitable for any credible democratic or humane society. We wouldn't accept this model for public education. Nor should we for journalism.

But wait, don't government subsidies for journalism violate everything America stands for? Aren't they an affront to the most elementary notions of freedom and democracy? Isn't it better to risk going down in flames as a failed state than to open *that* Pandora's box?

Baseball, Hot Dogs, Apple Pie . . . and Public Investments in Journalism?

In 1787, as the Constitution was being drafted in Philadelphia, Thomas Jefferson was ensconced in Paris as this young, undefined nation's minister to France. From afar he corresponded on the matter of what was required for successful democratic governance. The formation of a free press was a central concern. Jefferson wrote:

> The way to prevent these irregular interpositions of the people is to give them full information of their affairs thro' the channel of the public papers, and to contrive that those papers should penetrate the whole mass of the people. The basis of our governments being the opinion of the people, the very first object should be to keep that right; and were it left to me to decide whether we should have a government without newspapers, or newspapers without a government, I should not hesitate a moment to prefer the latter. But I should mean that every man should receive those papers and be capable of reading them.

For Jefferson, having the right to speak without government censorship is a necessary but insufficient condition for a free press and therefore democracy, which also demands that there be a literate public, a viable press system, and easy access to this press by the people.

But why, exactly, was this such an obsession to Jefferson? In the same letter, he praised Native American societies for being largely classless and happy, and he criticizes European societies—like the France he was witnessing firsthand on the eve of its revolution—in no uncertain terms for being their opposite. Jefferson also highlighted the central role of the press in stark class terms when he described its role in preventing exploitation and domination of the poor by the rich:

> Among [European societies], under pretence of governing they have divided their nations into two classes, wolves and sheep. I do not exaggerate. This is a true picture of Europe. Cherish therefore the spirit of our people, and keep alive their attention. Do not be too severe upon their errors, but reclaim them by enlightening them. If once they

> become inattentive to the public affairs, you and I, and Congress, and Assemblies, judges and governors shall all become wolves. It seems to be the law of our general nature, in spite of individual exceptions; and experience declares that man is the only animal which devours his own kind, for I can apply no milder term to the governments of Europe, and to the general prey of the rich on the poor.[146]

In short, the press has the obligation to undermine the natural tendency of propertied classes to dominate politics, open the doors to corruption, reduce the masses to powerlessness, and eventually terminate self-government.

James Madison was every bit Jefferson's equal in his passion for a free press. Together they argued for it as a check on militarism, secrecy, corruption, and empire. Near the end of his life, Madison famously observed, "A popular government without popular information or the means of acquiring it, is but a Prologue to a Farce or a Tragedy or perhaps both. Knowledge will forever govern ignorance, and a people who mean to be their own Governors, must arm themselves with the power knowledge gives."[147]

They were not alone. In the early republic, with no controversy, the government instituted massive postal and printing subsidies to found a viable press system. There was no illusion that the private sector was up to the task without these investments. The very thought would be unthinkable for generations. For the first century of American history, most newspapers were distributed by mail, and the Post Office's delivery charge for newspapers was very small. Newspapers constituted 90 to 95 percent of its weighted traffic, yet provided only 10 to 12 percent of its revenues. The Post Office then was by far the largest and most important branch of the federal government, with 80 percent of federal employees in 1860.[148]

In the haze of the past century of commercially driven news media, we have lost sight of the fact that the American free-press tradition has two components. First is the aspect everyone is familiar with, the idea that the government should not exercise prior restraint or censor the press. The second, every bit as important, is that it is the highest duty of the government to see that a free press actually exists so there is something of value that cannot be censored. Although this second component of the American free-press tradition has been largely forgotten since the advent of the corporate-commercial era of journalism, the U.S. Supreme Court, in all relevant cases, has asserted its existence and preeminence. Justice Potter Stewart noted, "The Free Press guarantee is, in effect, a *structural* part of the Constitution" (Stewart's emphasis). "The primary purpose of the constitutional guarantee of a free press was," he added, "to create a fourth institution outside the Government as an additional check on the three official branches." Stewart concluded, "Perhaps our liberties might survive without an independent established press. But the Founders doubted it, and, in the year 1974, I think we can all be thankful for their doubts."[149] In his opinion in the 1994 case *Turner Broadcasting System v. FCC*, Reagan appointee Justice Anthony Kennedy concluded, "Assuring the public has access to a multiplicity of information sources is a governmental purpose of the highest order."[150]

How big were these public investments in journalism (or press subsidies) in contemporary terms? In *The Death and Life of American Journalism*, Nichols and I calculated that if the U.S. federal government subsidized journalism today at the same level of GDP that it did in the 1840s, the government would have to invest in the neighborhood of $30 billion to $35 billion annually. In his *Democracy in America*, Alexis de Tocqueville wrote with astonishment of the "incredibly large" number of periodicals in the United States and concluded that the number of newspapers was in direct proportion to how egalitarian and democratic the society was.[151] The robust press had little to do with free markets and everything to do with subsidies that dramatically lowered the costs of publishing and provided additional revenues from printing contracts. As late as the 1910s, when Postmaster General Albert Burleson questioned the need for newspaper and magazine postal subsidies, he was roundly dismissed as someone who knew little about news industry economics.[152] To Americans of all political persuasions—and especially to progressive political movements like the abolitionists, populists, and suffragists—even during the most laissez-faire periods in American history, the necessity of a large public investment in journalism was a given.

Federal press subsidies—e.g., postal subsidies and paid government notices—have diminished in real terms to only a small fraction of their nineteenth-century levels, though they remain to the present day. Public broadcasting is the most visible investment by government in media, and it receives approximately $1 billion in public support, but only a small portion of that supports journalism. State and local governments, as well as public universities, provide much of this public subsidy, with only about $400 million coming from the federal government.

There are legitimate concerns about government control over the content of journalism, and I reject any investments that would open the door to that outcome. I also understand that a government with a massive military and national security complex, like the United States, could be especially dangerous with the keys to the newsroom, but we could fund real journalism with some of the roughly $5 billion currently used annually by the Pentagon for public relations.[153] Moreover, the United States, for all of its flaws, remains a democratic society in the conventional modern use of the term. Our state is capable of being pushed to make progressive moves as well as regressive ones.

This is a crucial distinction. Most opponents of press subsidies assume that the places to look for comparison purposes are Nazi Germany, Stalin's Russia, Pol Pot's Cambodia, and Idi Amin's Uganda. If a dictatorship or authoritarian regime subsidizes journalism, the "news" will be propaganda designed to maintain an antidemocratic order. But that does not mean the same outcome necessarily occurs when democratic nations institute press subsidies. What happens when we look at nations with multiparty democracies, advanced economies, the rule of law, electoral systems, and civil liberties?—places like Germany, Canada, Japan, Britain, Norway, Austria, the Netherlands, Denmark, Finland, Belgium, Sweden, France, and Switzerland.

For starters, all these nations are huge government investors in journalism compared to the United States. If America subsidized public media at the same per capita rate as nations with similar political economies, like Canada, Australia, and New Zealand, U.S. public broadcasters would have a government investment in the $7 billion to $10 billion range. If America subsidized public media at the same rate as nations along the lines of Japan, France, or Great Britain, the total would be $16 billion to $25 billion; if at the same rate as Germany, Norway, or Denmark, $30 billion to $35 billion.[154]

These estimates do not even factor in the extensive newspaper subsidies that several democracies employ. If the U.S. federal government subsidized newspapers at the same per capita rate as Norway, it would make a direct outlay of approximately $3 billion annually. Sweden spends slightly less per capita, but has extended the subsidies to digital newspapers. France is the champion at newspaper subsidies. If a federal government subsidy provided the portion of the overall revenues of the U.S. newspaper industry that France does for its publishers, it would have spent at least $6 billion in 2008.[155]

I have had the privilege of traveling to many of these nations in recent years, and my impression is that these nations are far from police states, nor do their extensive public media systems and journalism subsidies evoke comparisons to a sham democracy, let alone a one-party state. But appearances can be deceiving, and one prefers harder evidence, from unimpeachable sources that would not necessarily be inclined to endorse public press investments.

I start with Britain's *The Economist*, a business magazine keenly in favor of capitalism, deregulation, and privatization, unsympathetic toward large public sectors, labor unions, or anything that smacks of socialism. Every year *The Economist* produces a highly acclaimed Democracy Index, which ranks all the nations of the world on the basis of how democratic they are. In 2011 only twenty-five nations qualified as democratic. The criteria are: electoral process and pluralism, functioning of government, political participation, political culture, and civil liberties. The United States ranks nineteenth by these criteria. Most of the eighteen nations ranking higher had government media subsidies on a per capita basis at least ten or twenty times that of the United States. The top four nations on the list—Norway, Iceland, Denmark, and Sweden—include two of the top three per capita media subsidizers in the world, and the other two are dramatically ahead of the United States. These are the freest, most democratic nations on earth according to *The Economist*, and they all have perfect or near-perfect scores on civil liberties. The United States is tied for the lowest civil liberties score among the twenty-five democracies, and on this issue trails twenty nations described as "flawed democracies" in *The Economist*'s rankings.[156]

Although all of the Democracy Index criteria implicitly depend to a large extent upon having a strong press system—and the report specifically discusses press freedom as a crucial indicator of democracy—freedom of the press itself is not one of the six measured variables. Is there a more direct source on press freedom?

Fortunately, there is. The Democracy Index can be supplemented with the research of Freedom House, an American organization created in the 1940s to oppose totalitarianism of the left and right, which with the coming of the Cold War emphasized the threat of left-wing governments to freedom. Freedom House is very much an establishment organization, with close ties to prominent American political and economic figures. Every year it ranks all the nations of the world on the basis of how free and effective their press systems are. Its research is detailed and sophisticated, particularly concerned with any government meddling whatsoever with private news media. For that reason, all communist nations tend to rank in a virtual tie for dead last as having the least free press systems in the world. Freedom House is second to none when it comes to having sensitive antennae to detect government meddling with the existence or prerogatives of private news media.

Freedom House hardly favors the home team. In 2011 it ranked the United States as being tied with the Czech Republic as having the twenty-second freest press system in the world. America is ranked so low because of failures to protect sources and because of the massive economic cutbacks in newsrooms that have been chronicled in this chapter.

Freedom House's list is dominated by the democratic nations with the very largest per capita journalism subsidies in the world. The top nations listed by Freedom House are the same nations that top *The Economist*'s Democracy Index, and all rank among the top per capita press subsidizers in the world.[157] In fact, the lists match to a remarkable extent. That should be no surprise, as one would expect the nations with the freest and best press systems to rank as the most democratic nations. What has been missing from the narrative is that *the nations with the freest press systems are also the nations that make the greatest public investment in journalism* and therefore provide the basis for being strong democracies.[158]

Freedom House research underscores the fact that none of these successful democracies permit the type of political meddling that is common in U.S. public broadcasting, particularly by those politicians who want to eliminate public broadcasting, with no sense of irony, because it has been "politicized."[159] Matt Powers and Rodney Benson conducted a thorough analysis of media laws and policies in fourteen leading democracies and "found that all of these countries have self-consciously sought to create an arm's-length relationship between public media outlets and any attempt at partisan political meddling."[160] They conclude:

> What matters for both public and private media are the procedures and policies in place to assure both adequate funding and independence from any single owner, funder or regulator. Inside corporate-owned newsrooms, as profit pressures have increased, informal walls protecting the editorial side from business interference have crumbled. In contrast, the walls protecting public media are often made of firmer stuff such as independent oversight boards and multiyear advance

funding to assure that no publicly funded media outlet will suffer from political pressure or funding loss because of critical news coverage.[161]

"I'd like to think that this finding rather than our calculation of funding is the major contribution of our study," Benson told me.[162]

Although no nation is perfect and even the best have limitations, these examples consistently demonstrate that there are means to effectively prevent governments from having undue influence over public media operations, much as in the United States we have created mechanisms to prevent governors and state legislatures from dictating faculty research and course syllabi at public universities. In other democratic nations, public broadcasting systems tend to be popular and are defended by political parties throughout the political spectrum. Even in the United States, despite its paltry budgets and spotty performance, public broadcasting routinely polls as one of the most popular government programs.[163]

One other annual survey presents supporting evidence. Since 2002 Reporters Without Borders has produced a highly respected annual world press freedom index that ranks all nations in terms of how freely journalists can go about their work without direct or indirect attacks. The survey does not address the quality of the journalism, but only how unconstrained journalists are to cover their communities and beats without violence or harassment. The United States plummeted to forty-seventh in the world in 2012, largely because of the mushrooming practice of police arresting and sometimes beating up journalists who dare to cover and report on public demonstrations. As journalism weakens, the state has less fear of harassing members of the Fourth Estate, who are seen as unduly interested in issues the state prefers not to be covered. The dozen or so nations that scored well above the rest of the world in terms of press freedom were pretty much the exact same nations that dominated the other two lists, those that have the largest public investments in journalism.[164] Table 1 puts all these studies together.

Research also demonstrates that in those democratic nations with well-funded noncommercial broadcasting systems, political knowledge is higher than in nations without them and the information gap between the rich and the working class and poor is much smaller.[165] Stephen Cushion's recent research confirms this pattern. He notes that public service broadcasters tend to do far more election campaign reporting than their commercial counterparts. One conclusion of Cushion's is especially striking: those

Table 1. Journalism funding and democracy

Press Freedom (Reporters Without Borders)		Freedom of Press (Freedom House)		Democracy Index (*The Economist*)		Funding for Public Media		
Country	**Rank**	**Country**	**Rank**	**Country**	**Rank**	**Country**	**Rank**	**Per capita**
Finland	1	Finland	1	Norway	1	Norway	1	$130.39
Norway	2	Norway	2	Iceland	2	Denmark	2	$109.96
Estonia	3	Sweden	3	Denmark	3	Finland	3	$104.10
Netherlands	4	Belgium	4	Sweden	4	United Kingdom	4	$88.61
Austria	5	Denmark	5	New Zealand	5	Belgium	5	$74.00
Iceland	6	Luxembourg	6	Australia	6	Ireland	6	$61.28
Luxembourg	7	Netherlands	7	Switzerland	7	Japan	7	$57.31
Switzerland	8	Switzerland	8	Canada	8	Slovenia	8	$52.34
Cape Verde	9	Andorra	9	Finland	9	Netherlands	9	$49.50
Canada	10	Iceland	10	Netherlands	10	France	10	$45.62
Denmark	11	Liechtenstein	11	Luxembourg	11	Australia	11	$35.86
Sweden	12	St. Lucia	12	Ireland	12	New Zealand	12	$28.96
New Zealand	13	Ireland	13	Austria	13	Canada	13	$27.46
Czech Republic	14	Monaco	14	Germany	14	Germany	14	$27.21
Ireland	15	Palau	15	Malta	15	South Korea	15	$9.95
U.S. rank	47	*U.S. rank*	22	*U.S. rank*	19	*U.S. spending*		$1.43

Sources: This table is reproduced from Josh Stearns, *Adding It Up: Press Freedom, Democratic Health, and Public Media Funding* (Washington, DC: Free Press, Jan. 26, 2012), savethenews.org/blog/12/01/26/adding-it-press-freedom-democratic-health-and-public-media-funding. The data are from: "Press Freedom Index 2011–2012," (Paris: Reporters Without Borders, 2011), en.rsf.org/press-freedom-index-2011–2012, 1043.html; Karin Deutsch Karlekar and Jennifer Dunham, *Press Freedom in 2011* (Washington, DC: Freedom House, 2011), freedomhouse.org/sites/default/files/FOTP%20 2012%20Booklet.pdf (ties not represented here); "Democracy Index 2011," *The Economist*, eiu.com/democracyindex2011; and "Funding for Public Media," Free Press, based on 2008 budget numbers, freepress.net/public-media. I thank Josh Stearns for the data and Jamil Jonna for the formatting.

nations with strong public broadcasting have more *substantive* campaign coverage, i.e., news about policy that can help inform citizens about the relative merits of a political party or a particular politician. Moreover, good public broadcasting holds commercial broadcasters to higher standards than they have in nations where public broadcasting lacks resources for campaign coverage.[166]

Likewise, in a manner that recalls the U.S. postal subsidies of the nineteenth century and that might baffle contemporary Americans cynical about the possibility of democratic governance, newspaper subsidies tend to be directed to helping the smaller and more dissident newspapers, without ideological bias, over the large successful commercial newspapers.[167] Recent research on the European press concludes that as journalism subsidies increase, the overall reporting in those nations does not kowtow but in fact grows *more* adversarial to the government in power.[168]

The point is not to romanticize other democratic nations or put them on a pedestal. Journalism is in varying degrees of crisis in nations worldwide. Resources for journalism are declining in other countries, too, even though public investments provide a cushion.[169] Moreover, the quality of journalism is hardly guaranteed even with greater resources.[170] Resources are simply a necessary precondition for sufficient democratic journalism.

Public investments in journalism are compatible with a democratic society, a flourishing uncensored private news media, and an adversarial journalism. The evidence is clear: the problem of creating a viable free press system in a democratic society is solvable. There may not be a perfect solution, but there are good, workable ones. And in times like these, when the market is collapsing, they are mandatory. The late James Carey—perhaps the dean of American journalism scholars, and no fan of government involvement with the press—said in 2002, "Alas, the press may have to rely upon a democratic state to create the conditions necessary for a democratic press to flourish and for journalists to be restored to their proper role as orchestrators of the conversation of a democratic society."[171]

In my other works, I have outlined a number of concrete suggestions to spawn a democratic journalism—including an immediate expansion of public, community, and student media. It is imperative that we develop a heterogeneous system, with different structures and subsidy systems, and significant nonprofit competition. There is little doubt that if Americans spent one tenth as much time devising creative policy proposals and public funding mechanisms as they do to trying to figure how to sell people stuff online, we could have a boatload of brilliant propositions to consider. Here I will mention only one, because it pertains directly to how best to capture the genius of the digital revolution and harness that potential for a credible journalism system.

This idea was first developed by the economist Dean Baker and his brother Randy Baker; Nichols and I have embellished their core concept and called it the citizenship news voucher. The idea is simple: every American adult gets a $200 voucher she can use to donate money to any nonprofit news medium of her choice. She will indicate her choice on her tax return. If she does not file a tax return, a simple form will be available to use. She can split her $200 among several different qualifying nonprofit media. This program would be purely voluntary, like the tax-form check-offs for funding elections or protecting wildlife. A government agency, probably operating out of the IRS, can be set up to allocate the funds and to determine eligibility according to universal standards [like those granting 501(c)(3) nonprofit status] that err on the side of expanding rather than constraining the number of serious sources covering and commenting on the issues of the day.

This funding mechanism would apply to any nonprofit medium that does exclusively media content. The medium could not be part of a larger organization that has any nonmedia operations. Everything the medium produces would have to be made available immediately by publication on the Internet, free to all. It would not be covered by copyright and would enter the public domain. The government would not evaluate the content to see that the money is going toward journalism. My assumption is that these criteria would effectively produce the desired result—and if there is some slippage, so be it. Qualifying media ought not be permitted to accept advertising; this is a sector that is to have a direct and primary relationship with its audience. Qualifying media could accept tax-deductible donations from individuals or foundations to supplement their income.

With advertising banned from this new Internet sector, the pool of advertising that exists could be divvied up among newspapers and commercial media, especially commercial broadcasters. This would give commercial media a better crack at finding a workable business model. I would also suggest that for a medium to receive funds, it should have to get commitments for at least $20,000 worth of vouchers. This requirement would lessen fraud and also force anyone wishing to establish a medium to be serious enough to get at least a hundred people to sign on. (In other words, you can't just declare yourself a newspaper and deposit the voucher in your bank account.) There will be some overhead and administration for the program, but it would be minimal.

The voucher system would provide a way for the burgeoning yet starving nonprofit digital news sector to become self-sufficient and have the funds to hire a significant number of full-time paid workers. It could be as much as an annual $30 billion to $40 billion shot in the arm. All those nonprofit digital news operations would finally have a prayer of survival and growth, because this is a policy that recognizes journalism for what it is—a public good.

Imagine a website in the blogosphere right now covering national politics, producing some great content, getting hundreds of thousands of regular visitors, but depending on low-paid or volunteer labor and praying for advertising crumbs or donations for revenue. Now the site goes formally nonprofit, stops obsessing over advertising, and appeals directly to its readers. Imagine this outfit getting twenty thousand people to steer their vouchers into its accounts. That is $4 million, enough to have a well-paid staff of fifty full-time journalists, as well as ancillary staffers. Consider what a Web news service could do with *that*. And then start thinking about how motivated the reporters and editors would be to break big stories, maintain high quality, and keep attracting the vouchers.

Or imagine that you live in a city with deplorable news coverage of your community or neighborhood, as more and more Americans do. If someone starts a local news outlet and gets a thousand people to give her group their vouchers, that would provide a nice start-up budget of $200,000. For that money, a group can have several reporters covering the turf and build a real following.

Vouchers also would allow newcomers to enter the fray and hence encourage innovation. A group could raise start-up funds from donations or philanthropy, get under way, and then appeal directly for voucher support. In this model, philanthropists would have much greater incentive to put money into journalism because there would be a way for their grants to lead to self-sustaining institutions. The voucher system would produce intense competition because a medium cannot take its support for granted. It would reward initiative and punish sloth. It would be democratic because rich and poor would get the same voucher. And the government would have no control over who'd get the money, whether left, right, or center. It would be an enormous public investment, yet be a libertarian's dream: people could support whatever political viewpoints or organizations they preferred or do nothing at all.

As Dean Baker puts it, this is an economic model that recognizes that old-fashioned media economics no longer work in the Internet era. You can't produce a digital product, take it to market, and sell it. And you can't get advertisers to bankroll your operation. The rational policy solution is to give media producers—journalists, in this case—money up front and then make what they produce available to all for free online. Embrace the digital revolution; don't try to fight it with electronic barbed wire, paywalls, hypercommercialism, and spying on users. Citizenship news vouchers would fill the Web with large amounts of professional-quality journalism and provide a genuine independent journalism sector. Moreover, all the material developed through the program can be used by commercial news media however they see fit. They simply cannot monopolize it or restrict access to it. But if they can add value, more power to them.

When Dean Baker first broached this idea, well over a decade ago, it was dismissed as utopian and absurd. After Nichols and I wrote about it in *The Death and Life of American Journalism*, we visited officials connected to both the FCC's and the FTC's formal panels that were studying the crisis in journalism in 2010. Each of them had read the book closely. Each stated, almost immediately upon meeting us, that the citizenship news voucher represented exactly the sort of thinking that was necessary if there was going to be much journalism going forward.[172] In critical junctures, once unthinkable ideas can become thinkable in a hurry.

Regrettably, this suggested reform, like many others, is not being considered. After acknowledging its value, the FTC and FCC journalism officials conceded that they could not endorse such a "radical" proposal for fear that political attacks would destroy their work altogether. There are two main reasons for this fear. First, there is the still-prevalent idea that "subsidies are un-American but profits are all-American." One can only hope that this response is weakening due to the severity of the crisis and the mounting evidence that public investments in journalism are not only compatible with democracy, but mandatory for its survival. There has been some movement, but nowhere near enough. In 2011 a comprehensive analysis on the journalism crisis by Columbia faculty members still concluded that "it is ultimately up to the commercial market to provide the economic basis for journalism."[173] What Todd Gitlin said over three years ago is even more urgent today: "We are rapidly running out of alternatives to public finance. It's time to move to the next level and entertain a grown-up debate among concrete ideas."[174]

The second factor is the more intransigent one and goes back to Jefferson's assessment of the situation in 1787. There is one group that definitely benefits from a lack of journalism and from information inequality: those who dominate society. They do not wish to have their privileges or affairs examined closely, either in politics or commerce—if the two are still separable. The Wall Street banks, energy corporations, health insurance firms, defense contractors, agribusinesses—powerful interests of all sorts—do not want their operations or their cozy relations with the government exposed for all to see, nor do the politicians who benefit from these relationships. These are Jefferson's wolves. None of them desires a journalism that will engage the electorate and draw the poor and working class into the political system. These powerful forces oppose anything that would open and enhance our news media, and they will aggressively oppose any campaign for press subsidies like public media or citizenship news vouchers. They might not say so in public, but their actions speak louder than words. Journalism? No, thank you.

Not all wealthy people are content with a world that lacks democratic journalism. True free-market capitalism would even benefit from a strong press system. But none of the rich have a material stake in pushing the cause, so it founders. Our political system has become so corrupt that it is losing the capacity to address problems that threaten its own existence. Instead, the main issues placed before policy makers are making what seem like endless cuts in social programs, lowering taxes on business and the wealthy, ignoring necessary environmental protections, increasing "national security" spending, and corporate deregulation.

As of 2013, it seems obvious that if the Internet is really reviving American democracy, it's taking a roundabout route. The hand of capital seems heavier and heavier on the steering wheel, taking us to places way off the democratic grid, and nowhere is the Internet's failure clearer or the stakes higher than in journalism.

7

Revolution in the Digital Revolution?

The Internet and the broader digital revolution are not inexorably determined by technology; they are shaped by how society elects to develop them. Reciprocally, our chosen way of development will shape us and our society, probably dramatically. I have highlighted a number of policy issues and suggested the type of reforms we ought to be debating, which could put the Internet and our society on a very different trajectory. These issues include:

- Establishing comprehensive media literacy education in schools to give people a critical understanding of digital communication;
- Strict regulation of advertising;
- Elimination of advertising directed to children under the age of twelve;
- Elimination of broadcast candidate advertising;
- Elimination or sharp reduction of the tax write-off of advertising as a business expense;
- Strict ownership limits on broadcast stations;
- Expansion of the nonprofit broadcast sector;
- Management of the electromagnetic spectrum as a public resource;
- Broadband availability to all for free as a basic right;
- Strict limits on copyright, returning to precorporate standards with expansion of the public domain and protection of fair use;
- Heavy regulation of digital "natural monopolies" or conversion of them to nonprofit services;
- Large expansion of funding to public, community, and student media;
- Steps to make cooperative and nonprofit media and journalism more practical;

- Large public investments in journalism, including citizenship news vouchers;
- Net neutrality: no censorship of or discrimination against legal digital activities;
- Strict online privacy regulations so that online activities are regarded in the same way as one's private correspondence in the mails;[1] and
- Strong legal barriers against militarization of the Internet and use of it for warrantless surveillance.

Enacting these measures would change America for the better and make it a much more democratic society. They would go a long way toward enabling us to address what seem like intractable social, economic, and environmental problems. Enactment might even make the capitalism of the catechism work much more effectively, producing a solid basis for free markets and competition in the context of a more democratic and humane society. Yet none of these policy reforms has a chance; only a few even have a hope of being debated in the corridors of power.

The reason is the corruption of the policy-making process. In really existing capitalism, the kind Americans actually experience, wealthy individuals and large corporations have immense political power that undermines the principles of democracy. Nowhere is this truer than in communication policy making. Most Americans have no idea that debates on policy could even exist or what the actual deliberations are, due to an effective news blackout on the topics, except on occasion in the business press.

This situation results not necessarily from a conspiracy, but rather from the quite visible, unabashed logic of capitalism itself. Capitalism is a system based on people trying to make endless profits by any means necessary. You can *never* have too much. Endless greed—behavior that is derided as insanity in all noncapitalist societies—is the value system of those atop the economy.[2] The ethos explicitly rejects any worries about social complications, or "externalities."

The fact that this basic problem is intrinsic to capitalism has been understood for a long time. It is called the Lauderdale paradox. James Maitland, the eighth Earl of Lauderdale (1759–1839), was the author of *An Inquiry into the Nature and Origin of Public Wealth and into the Means and Causes of Its Increase* (1804). Lauderdale argued that there is an inverse correlation between public and private wealth, such that an increase in the latter diminishes the former.[3]

Scarcity is necessary for something to have value in exchange and to augment private riches. "Scarcity," as Adam Smith said in *The Wealth of Nations*, "is degraded by abundance," and is a requirement for capitalist markets.[4] But this is not the case for public wealth, which encompasses all value in use and thus includes not only what is scarce but also what is abundant. This paradox led Lauderdale to argue that increases in the scarcity of necessary and normally abundant elements of life like air, water, and food would, if exchange values were attached to them, enhance individual private riches and indeed the riches of the country conceived of as "the sum-total of individual riches"—but only at the expense of the common wealth. For example, if one placed a fee on wells and thereby monopolized water that had previously been freely available, the measured riches of the nation would be increased at the expense of the growing thirst of the population.

Ecologists have embraced the Lauderdale paradox as providing a way to understand how growth in a nation's GDP and in its profitable investments may actually decrease the well-being of society. Capitalists are constantly locating new places to generate profits, and sometimes that entails taking what had been plentiful and making it scarce. So it is for the Internet. Information on it is virtually free, but commercial interests are working to make it scarce. To the extent they succeed, the GDP may grow, but society will be poorer.

Pause to consider how far the digital revolution has traveled from the halcyon days of the 1980s and early 1990s to where it is today. People thought that the Internet would provide instant free global access to all human knowledge. It would be a noncommercial zone, a genuine public sphere, leading to far greater public awareness, stronger communities, and greater political participation. It would sound the death knell for widespread inequality and political tyranny, as well as corporate monopolies. Work would become more efficient, engaging, cooperative, and humane. To the contrary, at what seems like every possible turn, the Internet has been commercialized, copyrighted, patented, privatized, data-inspected, and monopolized; scarcity has been created. One 2012 survey concludes that digital technologies, far from relieving workloads, have made it possible for the typical American worker to provide as much as a month and a half of unpaid overtime annually, just by using their smartphones and computers for work at all hours while outside the workplace: "Almost half feel they have no choice."[5] Precisely as

Lauderdale suggested, the economy is topped by gazillionaires who have succeeded in creating digital fiefdoms and adding to the GDP, but the public wealth is much less. Our wealth of information is increasingly accessible only by entering walled gardens of proprietary control feeding into monopolistic pricing systems. To make the Internet a capitalist gold mine, people have sacrificed not just their privacy—and to skeptics, their humanity—but much of the great promise that once seemed possible.

Don't get me wrong; the digital revolution, even in this context, still continues to amaze, astound, and engage. That only makes the paradox that much more striking.

Of course, capitalist societies—especially democratic ones—have mechanisms for popular pressure to prevent the total privatization of essential public services or the creation of artificial scarcity of abundant resources like water. Occasionally, especially when labor movements are strong, important reforms are won. Much of what is most humane about the United States—like what remains of progressive taxation, collective bargaining, public education, Social Security, unemployment insurance, consumer protection, environmental safeguards, and Medicare—is a result of such political organizing. But attaining and maintaining these benefits require difficult battles, and the playing field is tilted; today it seems the slope approaches 90 degrees. The electoral system and the judiciary are controlled by big money and dominated by people who live in gated communities, send their children to private schools, hang out with other millionaires (unless dealing with servants or sycophants), and divorce themselves from the reality most people live in. Traditional recourses for justice are increasingly ineffectual. Instead, all the previous victories are now in the crosshairs of big business. The fights now are mostly defensive, despite little popular enthusiasm for many of the rollbacks—a striking statement about the deterioration of self-government.

To win any of the Internet policy fights listed at the beginning of the chapter will require coalitions of people to form a common front and generate strength in numbers. This has been the principle behind Free Press, which works on several of these issues. But even getting copyright activists and independent journalists teamed up with community media activists and privacy advocates has not proven anywhere near sufficient. Some victories can be won, like passage of the 2011 Local Community Radio Act, which makes hundreds of new noncommercial radio stations possible. Some draconian measures can be delayed, as in the defeat of the Stop Online Piracy

Act in 2011–12. But the big stuff remains off the table. Success will require a broader political movement motivated by a general progressive agenda, not one specifically focused on the Internet or media. Only then will there be the enormous numbers possible to defeat the power of big money. As the legendary community organizer Saul Alinsky put it, the only thing that can beat organized money is organized people, lots of them.

Such a political movement will likely take flight only if it is designed to replace really existing capitalism. In "normal" times, such movements are mostly hypothetical in the United States. The political economy has been successful enough to prevent a groundswell of grassroots popular opposition. But these are not normal times, and we are getting further away from normal with every passing day. One need only look at the great protests of 2011—the likes of which we have not been seen for decades—against rampant inequality, corporate domination of the economy and politics, a deathlike embrace of austerity, endless warmaking, and a stagnant political economy that has no apparent use for young people, workers, or nature.

Nobel laureate economist Joseph Stiglitz captured the spirit of the protest movements in the United States and worldwide in 2012.

> Underlying most of the protests were old grievances that took on new forms and a new urgency. There was a widespread feeling that something is wrong with our economic system, and the political system as well, because rather than correcting our economic system, it reinforced the failures. The gap between what our economic and political system is supposed to do—what we were told that it did do—and what it actually does became too large to be ignored. . . . Universal values of freedom and fairness had been sacrificed to the greed of the few.[6]

Economist Jeffrey Sachs, who once was a leading architect of the promarket policies he now decries, notes that the U.S. and worldwide "protests have focused on four targets—extreme inequality of wealth and income, the impunity of the rich, the corruption of government, and the collapse of public services."[7]

In short, this is a critical juncture, and that fact changes everything. Stiglitz compares our moment to 1848 and 1968, two of the most tumultuous watershed years in modern history. People "all over the world seem to rise up, to say something is wrong, and to ask for change."[8] Capitalism is in the midst of its greatest crisis in eight decades, what Nobel laureate economist Paul Krugman argues is most definitely a depression of the 1930s type.[9] Growth rates that would have been considered subpar in the second half of the twentieth century would now be cause for jubilation. By 2012, only one in six young American high school graduates in the labor market—i.e., working-class young people—could secure full-time employment, and wages are stagnant or falling, with a massive oversupply of labor for available jobs.[10] A group of eighteen leading global environmental scientists came together in 2012 to report that humanity faces an "absolutely unprecedented emergency," and societies have "no choice but to take dramatic action to avert a collapse of civilization." In effect, the report rejected really existing capitalism in toto and called for a complete redesign of the economic system.[11]

Many of those in power or sympathetic to those in power understand that a crisis is at hand and new policies are necessary, as the status quo is unsustainable. David Brooks calls for a "structural revolution," while Edward Luce thoughtfully chronicles a nation in sharp decline, where the system is not working.[12] But there is little indication that those in power, unwilling to question the foundations of capitalism, have any idea how to return it to a state of strong growth and rising incomes, let alone address the environmental crisis that envelops the planet. Luce ends despondently, and if one is wedded to really existing capitalism, it is logical that one would tend toward depression, hopelessness, and depoliticization. But depoliticization eventually butts up against the reality of people's lives, their need to survive, and their desire for decent lives. A capitalist system "that no longer meets most people's needs," economist Richard Wolff writes, "has prompted social movements everywhere to arise, adjust, and coalesce in the active search for systemic alternatives."[13] This is the historical moment we seem to be entering now.

Those primarily concerned with Internet policies and hesitant to stick their toes into deeper political waters need to grasp the nature of our times. This isn't a business-as-usual period, when the system is ensconced and reformers need the benediction of those in power to win marginal reforms. The system is failing, conventional policies and institutions are increasingly discredited, and fundamental changes of one form or another are likely to come, for better or worse. One look at how different nations responded to the crises of the 1930s gives a sense of the broad range of possible outcomes.

Another question: can one reform the Internet and make it a public good in the manner suggested by the proposals at the top of the chapter,

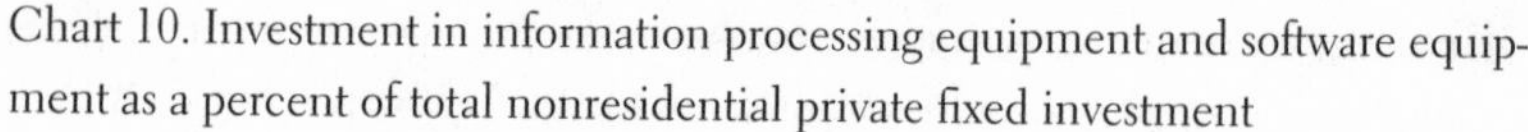

Chart 10. Investment in information processing equipment and software equipment as a percent of total nonresidential private fixed investment

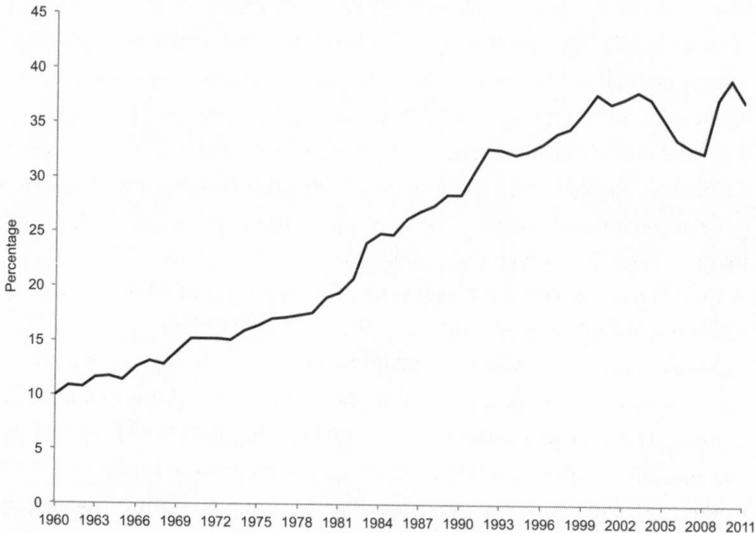

Source: Bureau of Economic Analysis (BEA), "Private Fixed Investment by Type," Table 5.3.5, bea.gov.

with capitalism still intact? As the chart below demonstrates, information technology accounts for some 40 percent of all nonresidential private investment in the United States, quadrupling the figure from fifty years ago.[14] In chapter 5 I discussed how Internet-related corporations now comprise nearly one half of the thirty largest firms in the United States in terms of market value. If one challenges the prerogatives of the Internet giants, odes to the catechism notwithstanding, one is challenging the dominant component of really existing capitalism.

This is an important question, too, for those who have paid little attention to Internet policies but are deeply concerned about injustice, poverty, inequality, and corruption. At times, one senses among such activists the celebrants' notion that digital technologies can create a new capitalist economy that is dramatically superior and that the existing Internet giants are allies, not adversaries, in creating this new friendly capitalism that will deliver the goods. The logic is sound: in the past, massive investments in railroads and automobiles (and related spin-off industries) propelled entire eras of capitalism to much higher growth rates and standards of living. When seeing the enormous investments in information technology, one wonders why can't it be that way again, and this time without all the environmental damage? The problem is simple: despite endless claims about the great new capitalism just around the bend thanks to digital technologies, there is little evidence to back them up.[15] In particular, the Internet giants comprise thirteen of the thirty most valuable U.S. firms, but only make up four of the thirty largest private employers.[16] There is clearly a lot of money for those at the top—who want to keep it that way—but little evidence that it is passing benefits down the food chain. Quite the contrary.

In my view, efforts to reform or replace capitalism but leave the Internet giants riding high will not reform or replace really existing capitalism. As chapters 4 and 5 document, the Internet giants are not a progressive force. Their massive profits are the result of monopoly privileges, network effects, commercialism, exploited labor, and a number of government policies and subsidies. The growth model for the Internet giants, as one leading business analyst put it, is "harvesting intellectual property," i.e., making scarce what should be abundant.[17] The entire range of Internet and media issues must be in the center of any credible popular democratic uprising. Given the extent to which the digital revolution permeates and defines nearly every aspect of our social lives, any other course would be absurd.

To some observers, like Peter H. Diamondis and Steven Kotler, there is no reason to worry: the digital revolution will solve capitalism's crisis and soon re-create the system better than ever. "Within a generation," they write, "we will be able to provide goods and services, once reserved for the wealthy few, to any and all who need them. Or desire them. Abundance for all is actually within our grasp."[18] Erik Brynjolfsson and Andrew McAfee make a more nuanced case that depends upon policy changes. Boiled down, though, the argument goes that while digital technologies may contribute to the current crisis of capitalism, they will also lead soon enough to a glorious future for capitalism, a "third industrial revolution."[19] They are correct that we have the technological and material capacity to do far better, both quantitatively and qualitatively, than we are currently doing.[20] However, the notion that such improvements can be accomplished under really existing capitalism is, to be polite, unconvincing.[21]

It is here that one of Karl Marx's greatest and most lasting insights moves to the fore. Though written 150 years before the Internet, that insight is relevant to this book. Marx and Engels argued that an inherent problem built into capitalism was the contradiction between its ever-increasing socialization and enhancement of production and its ongoing system of private appropriation of profit. In other words, society can produce more and more—it is capable of extraordinary material accomplishments—but because society's wealth is determined by what can generate maximum profit for the few who *control* society's wealth, we do far less than we could, and what we do is different from what would make sense for society.[22] "The central question is whether the prevailing relations of production promote or block, encourage or discourage the translation of these potentialities into practice," the economists Paul A. Baran and Paul M. Sweezy explained nearly fifty years ago. "The appearance and the widening of the gap between what is and what could be, demonstrate thus that the existing property relations and the economic, social and political institutions resting upon them have turned into an effective obstacle to the achievement of what has become possible."[23]

Now consider what this means for the United States. There has been a tremendous growth in worker productivity in American capitalism over the past forty years; far fewer workers are required to produce the same output. Yet to what extent has this enormous potential for the enhancement of human development been realized within the existing order? Stiglitz notes, for example, that when he recently returned to his hometown of Gary, Indiana, the output of one of the great steel mills was the same as it had been a generation earlier, but it now required only one sixth the number of workers. To varying degrees, this worker productivity growth is spread throughout the economy. By 2005, the average American worker produced what two workers could produce in 1970, and in manufacturing the increase was even more dramatic.[24]

In a sane world, this would be fabulous news. One might imagine that this tremendous increase in worker productivity would lead to higher incomes, shorter workweeks, earlier retirement ages, longer vacations, and a more pleasurable life. There would be quality employment for all—and less drudgery. Moreover, the United States would be a nation of such extraordinary wealth that it would provide quality health care, education, housing, and old-age pensions for all its citizens, clean up its own environment, and lead aggressive campaigns to address global economic, social, and ecological issues. The increase in productive capabilities would translate to a much higher standard of living. The ability to improve human life would accelerate almost beyond comprehension with the coming generation of robots, which will be able to do many of the most onerous labor tasks far more efficiently.[25] Those would be realistic expectations.

That hasn't happened and isn't going to happen on our present path because capitalism is not a sane political economy. Our economy is developed at the whim of those with capital. They invest society's wealth—the surplus all of the people have created—only if it can make them richer. Why not have the same number of workers produce six times as much steel in environmentally sound factories? Lord knows our deteriorating buildings and bridges could use the steel. But that won't happen, because if steel production increased sixfold, the handful of giant firms that dominate production would have to sell it at lower prices for less profit.

Instead of a flowering economy that makes the quality of life today vastly superior to that of forty or fifty years ago, millions go without work, much of our productive potential lies fallow, and our public sector is in squalor. People are working longer hours, with less vacation and later retirement, for stagnant or declining real wages, with less security, in an environment increasingly unable to sustain human civilization. Poverty has reached levels not seen for generations and found more commonly in the global South.[26] In 2012 U.S. businesses held $1.73 trillion in liquid assets—or cash, in shorthand—that they were not investing for apparent lack of profitable options. This was a 50 percent increase in the corporate cash reserves from 2007.[27] Is there any stronger evidence that the economic system is absurd? After commenting on the radical improvement in worker productivity, Stiglitz observed that "Gary looks like a ghost town."[28]

At every turn, the quality of life is under attack. The United States increasingly resembles a developing nation, not the nation with the greatest economic potential in history. It has seemingly privatized or outsourced almost anything on which money can be made. The catechism's notion of its most successful participants being honest businessmen competing to serve consumers and increase the quality and quantity of goods and services in the market can barely pass the giggle test; it has been replaced by the assumption that those at the top tend to "take wealth from others" through monopoly power and corruption rather than create wealth, as Stiglitz puts it.[29] In this climate, the real world of "corporate wrongdoing" has become a "routine occurrence," as the *New York Times* acknowledged in 2012, and rarely if ever punished. Cheating is increasingly the smart play for those atop the system.

As the *Times* concluded, a market system where the participants lose their trust in the integrity of dominant firms and players is a system in trouble.[30] Measures of human happiness place the contemporary United States well down the charts, below where it was fifty years ago. We now account for two thirds of the global market for antidepressant drugs.[31] To anyone not hypnotized by the catechism, our plight is absurd and indefensible.

The notion that capitalism has long outlived its usefulness is only confirmed when one considers the state of our infrastructure. As discussed in chapter 2, a great infrastructure is the foundation of any successful modern economy, capitalist or not. Financier Felix Rohatyn once told *New York Times* columnist Bob Herbert, "A modern economy needs a modern platform, and that's the infrastructure."[32] At midcentury, the United States had the most advanced infrastructure in the world by a wide margin; in the past three decades, it has fallen into collapse. The American Society of Civil Engineers estimates that the United States needs to spend $2.2 trillion over the next five years to get our infrastructure to the level of other economically advanced nations.[33] Politicians most closely associated with business interests evince almost no concern. In 2012 *The Economist* characterized America's neglect of its infrastructure "a foreseeable and utterly unnecessary disaster."[34] *Washington Post* columnist E.J. Dionne has written, "The American ruling class is failing us—and itself." He stated, in language unimaginable a few years ago, "America needs a better ruling class."[35] Another way to put it: *This is a system that no longer acts as though it has a future.* People at the top are just grabbing what they can while they can and letting the rest fend for themselves.

This is an issue that has perplexed many liberal reformers. How can the capitalists be so shortsighted, they wonder, as to oppose the use of government to build infrastructure, create jobs, and end stagnation, when other democratic governments have made capitalism operate far more efficiently and effectively? Economists Stiglitz and Robert Pollin each published books in 2012 with reasonable and thoughtful policy prescriptions for a full-employment, high-wage capitalism, but they command almost no support among the wealthy capitalists who subsidize American politicians.[36] Can't these business interests look at the historical record and see that capitalists have done far better and made more profits in the high-wage, high-growth, full-employment economies following the New Deal, arguably even in the social democratic nations of northern Europe? Why do they obsessively cling to the antiquated economic theories that were discredited in the 1930s and 1940s and have led present-day capitalism to crisis, stagnation, and decline? Economists like Krugman are almost apoplectic as they chronicle the absurdity and tragedy of this paradox.

In his 2012 book, *End This Depression Now!*, Krugman supplies an answer to this riddle. He cites a classic 1943 essay by the economist Michal Kalecki in which Kalecki argues that if the public realizes that the government has the resources to establish full employment, the realization would undermine the notion that the central duty of government is to create a climate in which business has confidence in the system and therefore eventually invests to create jobs. The "powerful indirect control over government policy" enjoyed by business would end, a prospect discomfiting to business leaders.[37] "This sounded a bit extreme to me the first time I read it," Krugman writes, "but it now seems all too plausible."[38] A successful state generating full employment might logically lead people to question why capitalists have so much economic power and what they provide that could not be better provided by more democratic means. In short, the wealthy and the corporations prefer a depressed and stagnant economy to a growing one led by state policies, if those in any way jeopardize their control over the government and their dominant position in society.[39]

Marx famously wrote that the main barrier to capitalism's growth and survival was capital itself, meaning that the logic of the economic system would invariably lead it to crisis. Contemporary evidence suggests that the main immediate problem of capitalism is capitalists. And if capitalists oppose reforms to make their own system functional, why exactly do we need them?

The digital revolution may have given a burst of life to capitalism as it provided new profit opportunities, but it also magnifies the tension Marx identified and that Baran and Sweezy discussed in detail. Indeed, digital technologies may bring to a head, once and for all, the discrepancy between what a society could produce and what it actually does produce under capitalism. The Internet is the ultimate public good and is ideally suited for broad social development. It obliterates scarcity and is profoundly disposed toward democracy. And it is more than that. The new technologies are in the process of truly revolutionizing manufacturing, for example, making far less expensive, more efficient, environmentally sound, decentralized production possible.[40] Under really existing capitalism, however, few of the prospective benefits may be developed—not to mention spread widely. The corporate system will try to limit the technology to what best serves its purposes. Given capitalism's track record and its corruption of the political system, we should not get our hopes up. Instead we need constantly to keep in mind Baran and Sweezy's emphasis on the "widening gap between what is and what could be" and how this demonstrates that "the existing property relations and the economic, social and political institutions resting upon them have turned into an effective obstacle to the achievement of what has become possible" for society.

For an increasing number of people, the logic suggests one thing: it is time to give serious consideration to the establishment of a new economy. "The capitalist system was able to thrive, on and off, during the eighteenth, nineteenth, and twentieth centuries," Jerry Mander wrote in 2012. "But it's now obsolete, nonmalleable, and increasingly destructive." Capitalism "had its day. If we care about the future well-being of humans and nature, it's time to move on." This is "radical" talk, but Mander, a former successful advertising executive, makes it clear that he is no socialist or Marxist. We are, in his view, at the point where we are dealing with an economy structured "to sustain the institutions and the people who sit at the top of the process." The "system is bound to fail."[41]

To return to a point from chapter 1, if we were assessing any noncapitalist society or a foreign capitalist society from bygone days, Mander's conclusions would not be especially controversial. But they elicit incredible fury in the contemporary United States. Capitalism has become what Mander terms "a kind of 'third rail' of politics—forbidden to touch." He acknowledges, "It remains okay to critique certain aspects of the system," but the capitalist system itself "occupies a virtually permanent existence, like a religion, a gift of God, infallible."[42] The reason is obvious: those in power do not wish the system that makes them powerful to be questioned. Keeping capitalism off-limits to critical review is essential for that system, because it generates demoralization, disengagement, and apathy. This is not a political economy that can withstand much engaged political participation. To question the performance and suitability of really existing capitalism at a time when the world is falling to pieces does not necessarily make one an anticapitalist in some universal sense. It means one recognizes that a system that promotes poverty, inequality, waste, and destruction—to the point of making the planet uninhabitable—deserves no free pass from democratic interrogation in the present, whatever its past achievements.

It is striking that, despite the universal reverence for it in the media and mainstream culture, capitalism is not especially popular with Americans. It's even more astonishing how popular socialism is, though one would be hard-pressed to find any favorable references to it in our mainstream culture. A global survey conducted by the BBC in 2009, even before the Occupy movement and the worldwide revolts of the last two years, found that some 15 percent of Americans agreed with the statement that free-market capitalism "is fatally flawed and a different economic system is needed." Another 50 percent of Americans thought capitalism had problems that required regulation and reform. A mere 25 percent thought that capitalism was doing a swell job and increased government regulation would be harmful.[43] Likewise, a survey conducted three years ago found that only 53 percent of Americans thought capitalism superior to socialism. Among Americans under the age of thirty, capitalism was preferred to socialism as the best system by a slim margin of 37 to 33 percent.[44] Today, three years later, people throughout the world, including the United States, are increasingly taking their protests against the system to the streets, recognizing that the pavement may be the last remaining realm of democracy.

It is only recently, as capitalism has floundered, that it has become almost mandatory to regard capitalism as permanent, irreplaceable, and benevolent. As recently as the 1960s and 1970s, when it produced golden-age results in America by today's standards, it was more common to have frank, no-holds-barred discussions of the system's merits and demerits. Going back further, many of the great economists, including John Stuart Mill and John Maynard Keynes, understood capitalism as a historically specific system, not as the eternal state of nature for humanity. Mill and Keynes saw capitalism as solving the "economic problem" and eventually making a world without scarcity—and therefore without capitalism—possible. Granted, Mill and Keynes saw that outcome as generations away and championed capitalism in their own times, but their historical perspective sharpened their critique and gave it tremendous lasting significance.[45]

During the depths of the Great Depression, Keynes wrote an extraordinary essay acknowledging that economists, as well as business and political leaders, had been woefully wrong about the economy and how to make it work for the bulk of the population. "The decadent international but individualistic capitalism, in the hands of which we found ourselves after the war," Keynes wrote in 1933, "is not a success. It is not intelligent, it is not beautiful, it is not just, it is not virtuous—and it doesn't deliver the goods." He argued that what was necessary was a wide-open period of debate and experimentation because the existing theories and policies had proven so disastrous and bankrupt. "When we wonder what to put in its place, we are extremely perplexed."[46] Although Keynes was an advocate of markets and the profit system, he said that there could be no sacred cows and that no honest observer could state with certainty that capitalism was not fatally flawed.

What Keynes proposed in the early 1930s is precisely the approach we need today. We need to be open-minded and to experiment. We have to escape the shackles of the current system and see what can work. We "need to imagine a different social order," Chris Hayes writes, "to conceive of what more egalitarian institutions would look like."[47] Certain values appear in most writing on the subject, especially from economists like Richard Wolff, Juliet Schor, and Gar Alperovitz:

- The wealth of a community has to be controlled by the people of that community.
- Decentralized and local community control should be emphasized, with the state reinforcing local planning.
- There must be a strong commitment to a variety of cooperatives and nonprofit organizations.
- Democratic control of enterprises by their workers is imperative.
- Planning for long-term goals must be generated from popular debates and deliberations.
- Environmentally sound production and distribution must be emphasized.[48]

In the American context, such words can make someone question an author's sanity; they seem so far removed from existing reality and conventional wisdom. But beneath the surface, there has been a rise in new kinds of economic ventures. In distressed communities, like Cleveland, they are a source of promise for the future. We are beginning to develop some experience about what a democratic, postcapitalist economy might look like and how it could function. There will be markets, there will be for-profit enterprises, but under the overarching logic of the system, the surplus will be mostly under nonprofit community control.

Absolutely central to building this new political economy will be constructing nonprofit and noncommercial operations to do journalism, produce culture, provide Internet access, and serve as bedrock local institutions. These can range from community radio and television stations and Internet media centers to cultural centers, sports leagues, and community ISPs.

Any such movement faces tremendous political and economic obstacles, and it cannot be successful while governments are doing the bidding of capital. Attempting to build this new world will put people in direct conflict with the current political system. The great political fights will be over whose interests the state will serve. But all the efforts cannot go into prodding or changing the state; work on building the next economy, the new cultural system, from the ground up has to begin in tandem. The new world must be born within the old. Until people can see and experience a different type of economy, they will be reluctant to support it or fight for it.

Ultimately the new economy cannot exist on the margins; it is in a fight for defining the overall logic of society. It is—dare I say it—a revolution. As such, it is about ultimately changing the culture and fostering a new type of human. Here again the vision tracks closely to that of celebrants like Yochai Benkler, with his argument that the Internet can encourage the more cooperative elements of human nature.[49]

In 2009 Michael Moore released his film on the financial crisis and economic collapse, *Capitalism: A Love Story*. Because of his prominence, Moore was able to secure interviews on cable TV networks, where for the first time, newscasters actually encountered criticism of the economic system they had simply taken for granted as quintessentially American and the embodiment of freedom. One particular CNN host was astounded by Moore's criticism of capitalism. He demanded of his guest, what would you replace capitalism with? After a pregnant pause, Moore replied, "Democracy." The host, like many Americans, was confused. Democracy, he said, was a political system while capitalism was an economic system. Moore was comparing apples and oranges.

But was he? Politics and economics are intimately connected. The crisis of our times is that capitalism undermines democracy. The choice we face is whether to expand democracy or let it continue to shrivel: Expanding it requires confronting really existing capitalism head-on. It is the defining issue of our times, the basis for the critical juncture in which we live.

The Internet is in the very middle of this critical juncture. It is central to the movement to build a more democratic society and extend self-government to the economy. Digital technologies make the new economy and self-management of decentralized units far more realistic. With enlightened public investments, the Internet can provide the greatest journalism and public sphere ever imagined. Digital technologies also are a crucial part of political movements to mobilize people effectively for social change. "In the age of social networks," as Jeffrey Sachs writes, "it will be possible to run effective campaigns on the energies of committed people, without vast sums."[50] "The Internet plays a huge role in allowing people to self-organize in non-hierarchical ways," Chris Hayes writes.[51] This point, one of the core arguments of the celebrants, is correct as far as it goes—but that is nowhere near far enough.

Left on their current course and driven by the needs of capital, digital technologies can be deployed in ways that are extraordinarily inimical to freedom, democracy, and anything remotely connected to the good life. Therefore battles over the Internet are of central importance for all those seeking to build a better society. When the dust clears on this critical juncture, if our societies have not been fundamentally transformed for the better, if democracy has not triumphed over capital, the digital revolution may prove to have been a revolution in name only, an ironic, tragic reminder of the growing gap between the potential and the reality of human society.

NOTES

1. What Is the Elephant in the Digital Room?

1. Discussed in David Weinberger, *Too Big to Know* (New York: Basic Books, 2011), 7.

2. Eli Pariser, *The Filter Bubble: What the Internet Is Hiding from You* (New York: Penguin, 2011), 11.

3. Rachel Botsman and Roo Rogers, *What's Mine Is Yours: The Rise of Collaborative Consumption* (New York: Harper Business, 2010), xiv; Peter H. Diamandis and Steven Kotler, *Abundance: The Future Is Better Than You Think* (New York: The Free Press, 2012), 282.

4. Nicholas Carr, *The Shallows: What the Internet Is Doing to Our Brains* (New York: W.W. Norton, 2010), 9–10, 87.

5. Cited in Jeffrey D. Sachs, *The Price of Civilization: Reawakening American Virtue and Prosperity* (New York: Random House, 2011), 154–55.

6. Elizabeth K. Englander, "Research Findings: MARC 2011 Survey Grades 3–12," *Research Reports*, paper 2, 2011, http://vc.bridgew.edu/marc_reports/2.

7. Lori Andrews, *I Know Who You Are and I Know What You Did: Social Networks and the Death of Privacy* (New York: The Free Press, 2011), 3.

8. Carr, *Shallows*, 9–10.

9. Diamandis and Kotler, *Abundance*, x, 9.

10. Cited in Pamela Lund, *Massively Networked: How the Convergence of Social Media and Technology Is Changing Your Life* (San Francisco: PLI Media, 2011), 3.

11. Rebecca J. Rosen, "A World With More Phones Than People," *The Atlantic*, July 19, 2012, theatlantic.com/technology/archive/2012/07/a-world-with-more-phones-than-people/260069/.

12. Michael Manges, "Overview," in *Maximizing Mobile* (Washington, DC: World Bank Group, 2012), 11.

13. E-mail to author from Ben Scott, Mar. 21, 2012.

14. Lund, *Massively Networked*, 3.

15. James Curran, "Reinterpreting the Internet," in James Curran, Natalie Fenton, and Des Freedman, *Misunderstanding the Internet* (Routledge, 2012), 3.

16. Robin Mansell, *Imagining the Internet: Communication, Innovation, and Governance* (Oxford: Oxford University Press, 2012), 1–2.

17. Clay Shirky, *Cognitive Surplus: Creativity and Generosity in a Connected Age* (New York: Penguin, 2010), 213, 27.

18. Henry Jenkins, *Convergence Culture: Where Old and New Media Collide* (New York: New York University Press, 2006), 4.

19. Michael Nielsen, *Reinventing Discovery: The New Era of Networked Science* (Princeton, NJ: Princeton University Press, 2012), 3, 6, 10, 41. See also "The Wow Factor," *The Economist*, Mar. 10, 2012, 92.

20. Yochai Benkler, *The Penguin and the Leviathan: How Cooperation Triumphs over Self-Interest* (New York: Crown Business, 2011), 3.

21. Cass R. Sunstein, *Republic.com* (Princeton, NJ: Princeton University Press, 2001).

22. Cass R. Sunstein, *Infotopia: How Many Minds Produce Knowledge* (New York: Oxford University Press, 2006), 8, 9.

23. Simon Mainwaring, *We First: How Brands and Consumers Use Social Media to Build a Better World* (New York: Palgrave Macmillan, 2011), 1.

24. Jeff Jarvis, *Public Parts: How Sharing in the Digital Age Improves the Way We Work and Live* (New York: Simon & Schuster, 2011), 11, 76.

25. Manuel Castells, *Communication Power* (New York: Oxford University Press, 2009), 346–62, 431–32. This point is discussed in Rebecca MacKinnon, *Consent of the Networked: The Worldwide Struggle for Internet Freedom* (New York: Basic Books, 2012), 13.

26. Diamandis and Kotler, *Abundance*, 25.

27. Lund, *Massively Networked*, 141.

28. Rory O'Connor, *Friends, Followers and the Future: How Social Media Are Changing Politics, Threatening Big Brands, and Killing Traditional Media* (San Francisco: City Lights Books, 2012), 20.

29. Jarvis, *Public Parts*, 11.

30. Shaheed Nick Mohammed, *The (Dis)information Age: The Persistence of Ignorance* (New York: Peter Lang, 2012), ii, 8.

31. Mark Bauerlein, *The Dumbest Generation: How the Digital Age Stupefies Young Americans and Jeopardizes Our Future* (New York: Tarcher/Penguin, 2008), inside flap, 13.

32. Jaron Lanier, *You Are Not a Gadget: A Manifesto* (New York: Knopf, 2010), 49–50.

33. Pariser, *Filter Bubble*, 89, 97. The historians of science that Pariser quotes are Aharon Kantorovich and Yuval Ne'eman.

34. Lanier, *You Are Not a Gadget*, 86.

35. MacKinnon, *Consent of the Networked*, especially chap. 3; Evgeny Morozov, *The Net Delusion: The Dark Side of Internet Freedom* (New York: PublicAffairs, 2011).

36. Michael Massing writes that those who have followed the Arab Spring uprisings on the ground in 2011 say the role of Facebook and social media has been greatly exaggerated in the West. "What caused the change in the Mideast," the *New York Times* Cairo bureau chief David Kirkpatrick said, "was people going into the streets." Indeed, Kirkpatrick said labeling the uprising a "Facebook revolution" was unpopular with many participants, who regarded it as "an attempt to put a 'Western brand name' on the event." See Michael Massing, "The Media's Internet Infatuation," *Columbia Journalism Review* online, August 15, 2012, cjr.org/the_kicker/internet_infatuation.php.

37. Virginia Eubanks, *Digital Dead End: Fighting for Social Justice in the Information Age* (Cambridge, MA: MIT Press, 2011), xv–xvi.

38. See the excellent collection: Saul Levmore and Martha Nussbaum, eds., *The Offensive Internet: Speech, Privacy, and Reputation* (Cambridge, MA: Harvard University Press, 2010).

39. Viktor Mayer-Schönberger, *Delete: The Virtue of Forgetting in the Digital Age* (Princeton, NJ: Princeton University Press, 2009).

40. Clifford Stoll, *High-Tech Heretic: Reflections of a Computer Contrarian* (New York: Anchor, 1999), 200–206.

41. Naomi Wolf has written about this for years. See Naomi Wolf, "Is Pornography Driving Men Crazy," June 20, 2011, globalpublicsquare.blogs.cnn.com/2011/06/30/is-pornography-driving-men-crazy. See also Peter Nowak, *Sex, Bombs and Burgers: How War, Pornography, and Fast Food Have Shaped Modern Technology* (Guilford, CT: Lyons Press, 2011), chap. 7.

42. Russell Banks, *Lost Memory of Skin* (New York: HarperLuxe, 2011). Banks referred to this point specifically in an interview with Amy Goodman on *Democracy Now!*, Dec. 28, 2011, democracynow.org/2011/12/28/author_russell_banks_on_writing_through. The quote is from the review of the book by Janet Maslin, "A Man Entrapped in a Host of Webs," *New York Times*, Sept. 25, 2011.

43. Stephen Marche, "Is Facebook Making Us Lonely?" *The Atlantic*, May 2012, 60–69.

44. Larry D. Rosen, *iDisorder: Understanding Our Obsession with Technology and Overcoming Its Hold on Us* (New York: Palgrave Macmillan, 2012).

45. Sherry Turkle, "The Flight from Conversation," *New York Times*, Apr. 22, 2012, Week in Review section, 1, 6.

46. For an article that develops Carr's concern that online reading is very different and more superficial than traditional reading, see Julie Bosman and Matt Richtel, "Finding Your Book Interrupted . . . by the Tablet You Read It On," *New York Times*, Mar. 5, 2012, A1, B2.

47. Carr, *Shallows*, 6, 11, 119, 125, 138, 180, 181.

48. Arianna Huffington, "Virality *Uber Alles*: What the Fetishization of Social Media Is Costing Us All," *Huffington Post*, Mar. 8, 2012, huffingtonpost.com/arianna-huffington/social-media_b_1333499.html.

49. John Naughton, Comments responding to Evgeny Morozov, Media, Power & Revolution conference, University of London, Apr. 2, 2012.

50. Mark Bauerlein edited a 2011 anthology with arguments "for and against" social media, including some of the writers cited in this chapter. Aside from the contributions of Douglas Rushkoff, capitalism can barely be found in the twenty-seven essays totaling 334 pages of text. See Mark Bauerlein, ed., *The Digital Divide: Arguments for and Against Facebook, Google, Texting, and the Age of Social Networking* (New York: Tarcher, 2011).

51. Robert A. Dahl, *Democracy and Its Critics* (New Haven: Yale University Press, 1989), 237. This is a common theme in the academic literature. For a nice recent discussion, see Gar Alperovitz, *America Beyond Capitalism: Reclaiming Our Wealth, Our Liberty, and Our Democracy*, 2d ed. (Boston: Democracy Collaborative Press, 2011), part 1.

52. See Larry M. Bartels, *Unequal Democracy: The Political Economy of the New Gilded Age* (New York: Russell Sage Foundation, 2008); Martin Gilens, "Inequality and Democratic Responsiveness," *Public Opinion Quarterly* 69, no. 5 (2005): 778–96. There is a superb discussion of this point, as well as a fine statistical summary of growing inequality in the United States over the past three decades in Jacob S.

Hacker and Paul Pierson, *Winner-Take-All Politics: How Washington Made the Rich Richer—and Turned Its Back on the Middle Class* (New York: Simon & Schuster, 2010).

53. This tension explains a gaping contradiction in U.S. foreign policy, one generally left unexplored in mainstream discourse because it upsets the conventional wisdom that capitalism equals democracy: why does the United States frequently support nations that are antidemocratic and lack elementary political freedom while occasionally opposing nations that are relatively democratic and have considerable popular support? A part of any credible answer has to do with whether these nations are comfortably situated within the existing global capitalist economic system in a manner the United States condones—social justice and human rights issues notwithstanding. Once one realizes that capitalism and democracy sometimes march to different beats and that capitalism tends to have a much louder drum, this is no longer much of a paradox.

54. Mainwaring, *We First*, 4, 1.

55. Benkler, *The Penguin and the Leviathan*, 23. He provides the basis for this argument in Yochai Benkler, *The Wealth of Networks: How Social Production Transforms Markets and Freedom* (New Haven, CT: Yale University Press, 2006).

56. Don Tapscott and Anthony D. Williams, *Wikinomics: How Mass Collaboration Changes Everything* (New York: Portfolio, 2006), 1, 3.

57. Jarvis, *Public Parts*, 6–7, 163–66.

58. Botsman and Rogers, *What's Mine Is Yours*, 224–25.

59. Mainwaring, *We First*, 231.

60. Cass R. Sunstein, *Infotopia: How Many Minds Produce Knowledge* (New York: Oxford University Press, 2006), 224.

61. Charles E. Lindblom, *The Market System* (New Haven, CT: Yale University Press, 2001), 3.

62. Ha-Joon Chang, *23 Things They Don't Tell You About Capitalism* (New York: Bloomsbury Press, 2010), vx.

63. Richard A. Posner, *A Failure of Capitalism: The Crisis of '08 and the Descent into Depression* (Cambridge, MA: Harvard University Press, 2009); and Richard A. Posner, *The Crisis of Capitalist Democracy* (Cambridge, MA: Harvard University Press, 2010).

64. This was never truer than in his final book. See John Kenneth Galbraith, *The Economics of Innocent Fraud: Truth for Our Time* (Boston: Houghton Mifflin, 2004).

65. See, for example, Dan Schiller, *How to Think About Information* (Urbana: University of Illinois Press, 2006); Luis Suarez-Villa, *Technocapitalism: A Critical Perspective on Technological Innovation and Corporatism* (Philadelphia: Temple University Press, 2009); and Vincent Mosco, *The Digital Sublime: Myth, Power, and Cyberspace* (Cambridge, MA: MIT Press, 2004). A couple of earlier works that have stood the test of time: Darin Barney, *Prometheus Wired: The Hope for Democracy in an Age of Network Technology* (Chicago: University of Chicago Press, 2004); and Kevin Robins and Frank Webster, *Times of the Technoculture: From the Information Society to the Virtual Life* (London: Routledge, 1999).

2. Does Capitalism Equal Democracy?

1. For a recent defense of capitalism along these lines, see Allan H. Metzger, *Why Capitalism?* (New York: Oxford University Press, 2012). There is another component to the upbeat free-market catechism that gets less attention but is arguably

the other side of the free-market coin. As comfortable as the free-market catechism is with a minimal government when it comes to interfering with the affairs of the wealthy on behalf of the general population, it is equally comfortable with a government that has considerable incarceration and policing powers over the general population. See Bernard E. Harcourt, *The Illusion of Free Markets* (Cambridge, MA: Harvard University Press, 2011).

2. Luigi Zingales makes a passionate defense of the catechism as the American way—and a criticism of many of the attributes of dominant "crony capitalism"—in *A Capitalism for the People: Recapturing the Lost Genius of American Prosperity* (New York: Basic Books, 2012).

3. I am obviously generalizing. For the classic explanation of this process, see Morton H. Fried, *The Evolution of Political Society: An Essay in Political Anthropology* (New York: McGraw-Hill, 1967).

4. Marcel Mazoyer and Laurence Roudart, *A History of World Agriculture: From the Neolithic Age to the Current Crisis* (New York: Monthly Review Press, 2006).

5. Jared Diamond, *Guns, Germs, and Steel: The Fate of Human Societies* (New York: W.W. Norton, 1997), 235.

6. See Ellen Meiksins Wood, *Liberty and Property: A Social History of Political Thought from Renaissance to Enlightenment* (London: Verso, 2012); Ellen Meiksins Wood, *The Origins of Capitalism: A Longer View* (New York: Verso, 2002).

7. Karl Marx and Friedrich Engels, *The Communist Manifesto* (New York: Monthly Review Press, 1964), 30.

8. David Wessel, "Rich-Poor Gap Widens—Class Mobility Stalls," *Wall Street Journal*, May 13, 2005.

9. Peter H. Diamandis and Steven Kotler, *Abundance: The Future Is Better Than You Think* (New York: The Free Press, 2012), 10.

10. Daisy Grewal, "How Wealth Reduces Compassion," *Scientific American*, Apr. 10, 2012.

11. Dacher Keltner, "Greed Prevents Good," Room for Debate section, NY Times.com, Mar. 16, 2012.

12. George Packer, "No Death, No Taxes: The Libertarian Futurism of a Silicon Valley Billionaire," *New Yorker*, Nov. 28, 2011.

13. The class basis of capitalism is nowhere to be found in the catechism because the emphasis is on merchants and customers coming together to voluntarily buy and sell goods and services in the market. In the case of labor, this is anything but a market where the two sides approach as equals.

14. For that reason I still remember a conversation I had nearly forty years ago when I was in college. I became friends with a happy-go-lucky guy from Long Island whose father had built up a rather sizable forklift business of some sort. A group of us began talking at a party and ruminating about our futures, as young people are wont to do. I will never forget what our Long Island friend said. "I plan to work for my father's business," he stated. The rest of us reacted like he just said he was planning to put himself in a forty-year coma; the business sounded so dreadfully dull. "Look," he responded, in a tone of voice we had never heard from him before. "This is how it works. You either work for someone else and make him rich or you get other people to work for you and make you rich."

15. I speak from personal experience on this point. I started and managed a successful rock magazine in the 1980s, and then I helped launch a fairly large nonprofit organization in the 2000s. As you might have guessed by now, I am pro-labor. I think the nation would be a much better place if we had the same unionization rates as

Scandinavia. But in both cases I had a visceral, unanticipated, and jarring negative reaction to the idea of workers organizing a union to negotiate their wages and conditions with me. I regarded it as unnecessary because I was so good to the workers and, more important, it would be an impediment to my ability to successfully manage the firms. I have spoken to or witnessed a few other people in similar situations who have had a similar response. For owners or managers who do not have my pro-labor background, the hostility to labor unions seems almost genetic.

16. Joseph E. Stiglitz, "Of the 1%, by the 1%, for the 1%," *Vanity Fair*, May 2011.

17. James K. Galbraith, *Inequality and Instability: A Study of the World Economy Just Before the Great Crisis* (New York: Oxford University Press, 2012).

18. For an illuminating discussion of this, see Charles H. Ferguson, *Predator Nation: Corporate Criminals, Political Corruption, and the Hijacking of America* (New York: Crown Business, 2012).

19. Jacob S. Hacker and Paul Pierson, *Winner-Take-All Politics: How Washington Made the Rich Richer—and Turned Its Back on the Middle Class* (New York: Simon & Schuster, 2010). Joseph Stiglitz agrees, writing "inequality is the result of political forces as much as economic ones." See Joseph E. Stiglitz, *The Price of Inequality: How Today's Divided Society Endangers Our Future* (New York: W.W. Norton, 2012), 30.

20. In Gar Alperovitz, *America Beyond Capitalism*, 2d ed. (Takoma Park, MD: Democracy Collaborative Press, 2011), x.

21. As the balance of power has shifted between labor and management, there has been increased employer militancy to eliminate unions and reduce wages and benefits. By 2012 employer lockouts had grown to become a record percentage of the nation's work stoppages. See Steven Greenhouse, "More Lockouts As Companies Battle Unions," *New York Times*, Jan. 23, 2012, A1, B2.

22. Bruce Western and Jake Rosenfeld, "Unions, Norms, and the Rise in U.S. Wage Inequality," *American Sociological Review* 76, no. 4 (2011): 513–37.

23. Bureau of Economic Analysis (BEA), "Value Added by Industry: Manufacturing," National Income and Product Accounts (NIPA); and St. Louis Federal Reserve (FRED) database, "Average Hourly Earnings of Production and Nonsupervisory Employees: Manufacturing (AHEMAN)" and "Production and Nonsupervisory Employees: Manufacturing (CES3000000006)," research.stlouisfed.org. Total annual compensation of production and nonsupervisory workers in manufacturing was calculated as follows: (AHEMAN*40[hours]*50[weeks])*CES3000000006.

24. Cited in Alperovitz, *America Beyond Capitalism*, xi.

25. See John Bellamy Foster and Robert W. McChesney, *The Endless Crisis: How Monopoly-Finance Capital Produces Stagnation and Upheaval from the USA to China* (New York: Monthly Review Press, 2012).

26. Paul Krugman, "Jobs, Jobs and Cars," *New York Times*, Jan. 27, 2012, A21. Krugman uses Apple's employment figure as 43,000 for the USA. It is placed at 60,000 in "An iPopping Phenomenon," *The Economist*, Mar. 24, 2012, 15.

27. Charles Duhigg and David Barboza, "In China, the Human Costs That Are Built into an iPad," *New York Times*, Jan. 26, 2012, A1, B10.

28. Robert Reich, "Bye Bye American Pie: The Challenge of the Productivity Revolution," *The Huffington Post*, Mar. 2, 2012, huffingtonpost.com/robert-reich/worker-productivity_b_1315814.html.

29. Steven Rattner, "The Rich Get Even Richer," *New York Times*, Mar. 26, 2012, A23.

30. David Hirschman, "On the Road to Riches: Those Under 35 With $100K Household Income," *Advertising Age*, May 22, 2011.

31. Ken Layne, "As American Middle Class Vanishes, Advertisers Focus Only on Richest 10%," *Wonkette*, June 2, 2011, wonkette.com/446740/as-middle-class-vanishes-advertisers-focus-only-on-richest-10.

32. Hope Yen, Associated Press, "Half Now Low-Income or Poor," *Wisconsin State Journal*, Dec. 15, 2011, A1, A10.

33. Matt Townsend, with Ashley Lutz and Christopher Palmeri, "A Star Customer Falls Back to Earth," *Bloomberg Businessweek*, Mar. 26–Apr. 1, 2012, 19–20.

34. Ryan Chittum, "Procter & Gamble and the Hollowing Out of the American Economy," *Columbia Journalism Review* online, Sept. 12, 2011, cjr.org/the_audit/procter_gamble_and_the_hollowi.php?page=all&print=true.

35. Timothy Noah, *The Great Divergence* (New York: Bloomsbury Press, 2012).

36. Drake Bennett, "Commentary: The Inequality Delusion," BloombergBusinessweek.com, Oct. 21, 2010; and Linda McQuaig and Neil Brooks, *Billionaires' Ball: Gluttony and Hubris in an Age of Epic Inequality* (Boston: Beacon Press, 2012), 214–15.

37. Richard Wilkinson and Kate Pickett, *The Spirit Level: Why Greater Equality Makes Societies Stronger* (New York: Bloomsbury Press, 2009).

38. Stiglitz, *Price of Inequality*, 43.

39. Thorstein Veblen, arguably the most original and greatest American economist of all time, was the first to grasp this fundamental change in capitalism, though many, of course, have followed in his wake. See Thorstein Veblen, *Absentee Ownership and Business Enterprise in Recent Times* (New York: Augustus M. Kelley, 1964). The book was originally published in 1923 and was Veblen's final work.

40. An industry is considered concentrated when the four largest companies account for at least 50 percent of its total shipment value. The Census Bureau adds or subtracts new industries each year. In 1987 and 1992, when the Standard Industrial Classification (SIC) system was in use, there were 457 and 458 industry categories, respectively. The SIC system was replaced by the North American Industrial Classification System (NAICS) in 1997. Since then the number of industries leveled off at approximately 472 (in 1997 and 2002, 473; in 2007, 471).

41. Simon Johnson, "The Bill Daley Problem," *Huffington Post*, Jan. 11, 2011, huffingtonpost.com/simon-johnson/bill-daley-obama-chief-of-staff_b_806341.html.

42. Stiglitz, *Price of Inequality*, 35.

43. Friedrich Hayek, *The Road to Serfdom* (Chicago: University of Chicago Press, 1944), 49.

44. Andrew Frye and Dakin Campbell, "Buffett Says Pricing Power More Important Than Good Management," Bloomberg, Feb. 18, 2011, bloomberg.com/news/2011-02-18/buffett-says-pricing-power-more-important-than-good-management.html.

45. I take up the manner in which mainstream economics has danced around the monopoly question in more detail with Duke Foster in Foster and McChesney, *Endless Crisis*.

46. Eric A. Schutz, *Markets and Power: The 21st-Century Command Economy* (Armonk, NY: M.E. Sharpe, 2001), 80–81.

47. Lawrence J. White, "Aggregate Concentration in the Global Economy: Issues and Evidence," Stern School of Business, New York University, Economic Working Papers, EC-03-13, Jan. 1, 2003, http://hdl.handle.net/2451/26166, pp. 3–4.

48. Today's giant corporations pursue two interrelated goals—maximum sales revenue and maximum profitability, which converge over the long run because larger market share provides the basis for higher monopoly profits, and higher profits are used to expand market share. See Peter Kenyon, "Pricing," in Alfred S. Eichner, ed., *A Guide to Post-Keynesian Economics* (White Plains, NY: M.E. Sharpe, 1979), 37–38.

49. Milton Friedman, *Capitalism and Freedom* (Chicago: University of Chicago Press, 2002).

50. "Surf's Up," *The Economist*, May 19, 2012, 83.

51. Luigi Zingales makes this point well. See Zingales, *Capitalism for the People*, 8–39.

52. David Brooks, "The Creative Monopoly," *New York Times*, Apr. 24, 2012, A23.

53. David Rothkopf, *Power, Inc.: The Epic Rivalry Between Big Business and Government—and the Reckoning That Lies Ahead* (New York: Farrar, Straus & Giroux, 2012), p. 266.

54. See Paul A. Baran and Paul M. Sweezy, "Some Theoretical Implications," *Monthly Review*, July–Aug. 2012, 40–41. This is a formerly unpublished essay that had been intended for their 1966 book, *Monopoly Capital* (Monthly Review Press), but was left out because Paul Baran died before they finished it.

55. I was told this story by a former advertising professional at Reeves's Ted Bates advertising agency. For somewhat different versions of the story, see Reed Hundt, chairman, Federal Communications Commission, "The Children's Emmy: An Award Worth Winning," speech to Children's Action Network, Los Angeles, Nov. 19, 1996, and Richard S. Tedlow, *The Watson Dynasty* (New York: HarperBusiness, 2003), 118.

56. William Greider, *Who Will Tell the People: The Betrayal of American Democracy* (New York: Simon & Schuster, 1992), 271.

57. Eli Pariser, *The Filter Bubble: What the Internet Is Hiding from You* (New York: Penguin Press, 2011), 159.

58. Darrell M. West, *Air Wars: Television Advertising in Election Campaigns, 1952–2008* (Washington, DC: CQ Press, 2010), 89. For a smart examination of the importance of visuals for TV news coverage of election campaigns, see Maria Elizabeth Grabe and Erik Page Bucy, *Image Bite Politics: News and the Visual Framing of Elections* (New York: Oxford University Press, 2010).

59. For a good short discussion of research on women's unhappiness and advertising, see Richard Layard, *Happiness: Lessons from a New Science* (New York: Penguin, 2005), 88–90.

60. Gary S. Becker and Kevin M. Murphy, "A Simple Theory of Advertising as a Good or Bad," *Quarterly Journal of Economics* 108, no. 4 (1993): 933.

61. Ibid., 934. For a nice discussion of the essential similarity of many heavily advertised products, see Juliet B. Schor, *The Overspent American* (New York: HarperCollins, 1999), 60–63.

62. For a fuller elaboration of these themes, see Hannah Holleman, Inger L. Stole, John Bellamy Foster, and Robert W. McChesney, "The Sales Effort and Monopoly Capital," *Monthly Review* 60, no. 11 (Apr. 2009).

63. Drew Weston, *The Political Brain: The Role of Emotion in Deciding the Fate of the Nation* (Cambridge, MA: Perseus, 2007).

64. James Rorty, *Our Master's Voice: Advertising* (New York: John Day, 1934).

65. "Most advertising, especially in expensive prime time, doesn't make claims

about product performance. It's all innuendos, associations, and images," former advertising copywriter Jerry Mander noted in 2012. "The problem with commercial advertising is not whether the ads are truthful or not; the problem is the image itself. Once it is ingested, it becomes our frame of reference. Over time, we begin to imitate the image. . . . We become what we see. And we share its values." See Jerry Mander, *The Capitalism Papers: Fatal Flaws of an Obsolete System* (Berkeley, CA: Counterpoint, 2012), 183.

66. This is from a personal conversation I had with Professor Miller around 1999 or 2000.

67. Wilhelm Ropke, *A Humane Capitalism: The Social Framework of the Free Market* (Wilmington, DE: ISI Books, 1960), 137.

68. James Livingston, *Against Thrift: Why Consumer Culture Is Good for the Economy, the Environment, and Your Soul* (New York: Basic Books, 2011), chap. 7.

69. Mara Einstein, *Compassion, Inc: How Corporate America Blurs the Line Between What We Buy, Who We Are, and Those We Help* (Berkeley: University of California Press, 2012).

70. Inger L. Stole, "Cause Marketing as Commercial Propaganda: Neoliberal Wolf in Sheep's Clothing?" in Gerald Sussman, ed., *The Propaganda Society: Public Persuasion in Liberal Democratic Regimes* (New York: Peter Lang, 2011), 130–44.

71. Michael J. Sandel, *What Money Can't Buy: The Moral Limits of Markets* (New York: Farrar, Straus & Giroux, 2012), chap. 3.

72. Robert E. Lane, *The Loss of Happiness in Market Democracies* (New Haven, CT: Yale University Press, 2000), 179. Paradoxically, advertising, by focusing obsessively on the individual, may also contribute to what has been termed the "narcissism epidemic" in the United States. The authors of a recent book on that subject attribute considerable importance to advertising's rampant "emphasis on uniqueness" in the individual. See Jean M. Twenge and W. Keith Campbell, *The Narcissism Epidemic* (New York: Free Press, 2009), 184–88. Here, too, the marriage of commercialism with new social media technologies is tight. Chris Hayes notes research that found only 12 percent of American teenagers in 1950 agreed that "I am an important person." In recent times that figure is over 80 percent. See Christopher Hayes, *Twilight of the Elites: America After Meritocracy* (New York: Crown, 2012), 162. In researching this book, I found no evidence that this self-obsession is producing happier people. As Twenge and Campbell argue, it tends to make people depressed and lonely.

73. Daryl Travis, *Emotional Branding: How Successful Brands Gain the Irrational Edge* (Roseville, CA: Orima Venture, 2000); and Marc Gobe, *Emotional Branding: The New Paradigm for Connecting Brands to People* (New York: Allworth Press, 2001).

74. Jeffrey D. Sachs, *The Price of Civilization: Reawakening American Virtue and Prosperity* (New York: Random House, 2011), 142, 144, 146–51.

75. John Maynard Keynes, *The General Theory of Employment, Interest, and Money* (New York: Harbinger, 1964; first published in 1936), chap. 1, 2.

76. Paul Krugman has a nice discussion of the importance of military spending to American macroeconomics. See Paul Krugman, *End This Depression Now!* (New York: W.W. Norton, 2012), 234–37.

77. John Bellamy Foster, Hannah Holleman, and Robert W. McChesney, "The U.S. Imperial Triangle and Military Spending," *Monthly Review*, Oct. 2008, 1–19.

78. "By 2004," James Galbraith writes, "it was clear that no modern war would have a major and sustained effect on domestic economic growth and job creation

at the level of the entire nation." James K. Galbraith, *Inequality and Instability: A Study of the World Economy Just Before the Great Crisis* (New York: Oxford University Press, 2012), 292.

79. There are differing explanations for why stagnation is the order of the day. John Bellamy Foster and I provide ours in *The Endless Crisis*.

80. Galbraith, *Inequality and Instability*, 291.

81. Paul Krugman, *End This Depression Now!*, 19.

82. Alfred D. Chandler Jr., *Scale and Scope: The Dynamics of Industrial Capitalism* (Cambridge, MA: Belknap Press of Harvard University Press, 1990).

83. The logical question then is: if this is the ideal family form, is it desirable to have an ethical system diametrically opposed to these values rule everywhere else in society? Ayn Rand, the hero and mentor for Alan Greenspan and Paul Ryan and countless other contemporary American free-market conservatives, was well aware of religion's and specifically Christianity's innate hostility to capitalist values. A confirmed atheist, Rand wrote that Christian values were "the best kindergarten of communism possible." See Jennifer Burns, "Atlas Spurned," *New York Times*, Aug. 15, 2012, A21.

84. It is worth noting that the externality of environmental damage has emerged as one of the central crises of the modern political economy. It truly threatens the continued existence of our species on the planet. One of the claims on behalf of the digital revolution was that it was ecofriendly. Digital communication, for example, did not require the reams of paper and barrels of ink used by its predecessor. New research by Toby Miller and Richard Maxwell debunks the ecofriendly claim. See Richard Maxwell and Toby Miller, *Greening the Media* (New York: Oxford University Press, 2012). They demonstrate that the production and disposal of the 22 billion or so Internet devices that will exist by 2020 will be doing tremendous environmental damage. This is a classic externality, as the cost is not borne by producer or consumer. Markets with large negative externalities require government regulation to lessen the damage, but getting the political muscle to enact such regulation is difficult.

85. For a good discussion of externalities and media, see Edward S. Herman, "The Externalities Effects of Commercial and Public Broadcasting," in Kaarle Nordenstreng and Herbert I. Schiller, eds., *Beyond National Sovereignty: International Communication in the 1990s* (Norwood, NJ: Ablex, 1993), 84–115.

86. The classic statement is Paul A. Samuelson, "The Pure Theory of Public Expenditure," *Review of Economics and Statistics* 36 (4) (1954): 387–389. Another classic work from that period is John Kenneth Galbraith, *The Affluent Society* (Boston: Houghton Mifflin, 1958), especially chapters 18–22.

87. Diane Ravitch, *The Death and Life of the Great American School System: How Testing and Choice Are Undermining Education* (New York: Basic Books, 2010).

88. The conclusion: "Public broadcasting was hailed by most respondents as a wonderful resource that avoided virtually all of the pitfalls of commercial media. Its news programs are viewed as objective and informative with no sensationalism, its commercial-free format is widely appreciated, and it offers quality educational content for children and adults alike. And yet, aside from a handful of passionate advocates, the vast majority acknowledged that they rarely, if ever, watch public broadcasting (except with their children) or tune in NPR, saying they simply do not think of it as an option on a daily basis and feel it is perhaps too dry. For all of their complaints about sensationalism, some grudgingly acknowledge they want to be entertained by their news." Gerstein-Agne Strategic Communications, "Media Reform

Focus Groups: Understanding Public Attitudes and Building Public Support for Media Reform," June 1, 2005, www.freepress.net/files/focus_groups.pdf.

89. Roper Public Opinion Poll on PBS, Jan. 2009, kpts.org/user/file/Roper2009 .pdf.

90. Aristotle, *Politics*, trans. Benjamin Jowett (Stilwell, KS: Digiereads, 2005), 60.

91. Gordon S. Wood, *The Idea of America* (New York: Penguin Press, 2011).

92. Cited in Thompson, *Politics of Inequality*, 57.

93. Abraham Lincoln, "1861 State of the Union Address," Dec. 3, 1861, presidentialrhetoric.com/historicspeeches/lincoln/stateoftheunion1861.html.

94. Jack Beatty, *Age of Betrayal: The Triumph of Money in America, 1865–1900* (New York: Knopf, 2007), xv.

95. Conversation with Paul Buhle, Feb. 2012.

96. "Justice Louis D. Brandeis," brandeis.edu/legacyfund/bio.html.

97. Cited in John Nichols, ed., *Against the Beast: A Documentary History of American Opposition to Empires* (New York: Nation Books, 2005), 14.

98. Ron Hayduk, *Democracy for All: Restoring Immigrant Voting Rights in the United States* (New York: Routledge, 2006), 3.

99. See Alexander Keyssar, *The Right to Vote: The Contested History of Democracy in the United States* (New York: Basic Books, 2000), 11, 15.

100. John Adams is reputed to have made the same statement. In fairness, Adams was no plutocrat. Although he was no democrat in the modern sense, he was also deeply concerned about the powerful having unchecked power. His correspondence with Jefferson at the end of their lives is illuminating in this regard. See Michael Perelman, *The Invisible Handcuffs of Capitalism* (New York: Monthly Review Press, 2011), 272.

101. Alex Carey, *Taking the Risk Out of Democracy* (Urbana: University of Illinois Press, 1996).

102. One of the celebrants' claims for the Internet was that it would undermine corporate PR efforts and give consumers greater leverage to force corporations to act in a more ethical manner. This claim reemerged with social media, with the idea that Facebook, Twitter, YouTube, and smartphones, along with Google search, could make consumers vastly more powerful against corporate adversaries. *Bloomberg Businessweek* observes that this has not become the rule, as corporations have become expert at applying their spin skills to social media and the Web. See Felix Gillette, "It's Getting Tougher to Bully Brands," *Bloomberg Businessweek*, Aug. 6–12, 2012, 20–22.

103. A recent PR campaign of tremendous success has been the work of the energy lobby to discredit the unanimous scientific work on climate change. See James Hoggan, *Climate Cover-Up: The Crusade to Deny Global Warming* (Vancouver: Greystone Books, 2009); and James Lawrence Powell, *The Inquisition of Climate Science* (New York: Columbia University Press, 2011).

104. Michel Crozier, Samuel P. Huntington, and Joji Watanuki, *The Crisis of Democracy: Report on the Governability of Democracies to the Trilateral Commission* (New York: New York University Press, 1975), 114.

105. Glenn W. Smith, "Republican Operative: 'I Don't Want Everyone to Vote,' " FireDogLake, Oct. 12, 2008. http://firedoglake.com/2008/10/12/republican-operative-i-dont-want-everyone-to-vote/

106. Richard L. Kaplan, *Politics and the American Press: The Rise of Objectivity, 1865–1920* (New York: Cambridge University Press, 2002), 24, 149.

107. V.O. Key Jr., *Politics, Parties, and Pressure Groups* (New York: Thomas Y. Crowell, 1955), chap. 19.

108. Walter Dean Burnham, "The Appearance and Disappearance of the American Voter," in Thomas Ferguson and Joel Rogers, eds., *The Political Economy: Readings in the Politics and Economics of American Public Policy* (Armonk, NY: M.E. Sharpe, 1984), 112–37.

109. See Hacker and Pierson, *Winner-Take-All Politics.*

110. Galbraith, *Inequality and Instability*, 164.

111. C.B. Macpherson. *The Life and Times of Liberal Democracy* (New York: Oxford University Press, 1977), 89–90. Erich Fromm made a similar argument around the same time. See Erich Fromm, *The Sane Society* (New York: Rinehart & Company, 1955), 184–91.

112. See Martin Gilens, *Affluence and Influence: Economic Inequality and Political Power in America* (Princeton, NJ: Princeton University Press, 2012); Kay Lehman Schlozman, Sidney Verba, and Henry E. Brady, *The Unheavenly Chorus: Unequal Political Voice and the Broken Promise of American Democracy* (Princeton, NJ: Princeton University Press, 2012).

113. Richard K. Matthews, *The Radical Politics of Thomas Jefferson: A Revisionist View* (Lawrence: University Press of Kansas, 1984), 83.

3. How Can the Political Economy of Communication Help Us Understand the Internet?

1. This is a somewhat idiosyncratic view of the political economy of communication, stylized both to my own tastes and to the purposes of this chapter and this book. For a more comprehensive yet also somewhat idiosyncratic perspective, I recommend Vincent Mosco, *The Political Economy of Communication*, 2d ed. (Thousand Oaks, CA: Sage, 2009).

2. I develop this notion of the problem of the media in a book with the same title. For a longer treatment, see Robert W. McChesney, *The Problem of the Media* (New York: Monthly Review Press, 2004).

3. Raymond Williams, *The Existing Alternatives in Communication* (London: Fabian Society, 1962).

4. Jürgen Habermas, *The Structural Transformation of the Public Sphere: An Inquiry into a Category of Bourgeois Society* (Cambridge, MA: MIT Press, 1989), first published in German in 1962).

5. This Manichaean framing of media options was a function of the Cold War and the nature of Soviet communism; it had nothing to do with Karl Marx or socialist theory. Indeed, for all the tension between liberal and radical thought in other areas, there is considerable confluence in matters of journalism and a free press. For a discussion of Marx's position on freedom of the press, see Robert W. McChesney, *Communication Revolution: Critical Junctures and the Future of Media* (New York: The New Press, 2007), chap. 2. Well into the twentieth century, radical socialists were among the foremost proponents of an independent, uncensored journalism. John Nichols argues persuasively that it was the socialists in the United States who "made" the First Amendment, by providing the basis for the seminal Supreme Court decisions in the years following World War I. See John Nichols, *The "S" Word: A Short History of an American Tradition . . . Socialism* (New York: Verso, 2011). Likewise, it has been the social democrats in Europe since the 1920s who have been most persistent in campaigning for extensive and independent public service

broadcasting. See, for example, Hakon Larsen, "Public Service Broadcasting as an Object for Cultural Policy in Norway and Sweden: A Policy Tool and End in Itself," *Nordicom Review* 32, no. 2 (Nov. 2011): 35–48. As the global democratic left moves forward in the coming years, it has a rich media tradition to embrace and develop. As the Hungarian socialist Gyula Hegyi put it in 2006, in a message to the successful left-wing governments in Latin America: "Believe me, compañeros, there is no democratic socialism without democracy—and the kind of socialism that exists without democracy could kill your dreams for the future." Gyula Hegyi, "Learn from Our Failures and Create a Socialist Democracy," *The Guardian*, Dec. 22, 2006.

6. See Ruth Berins Collier and David Collier, *Shaping the Political Arena: Critical Junctures, the Labor Movement, and Regime Dynamics in Latin America* (Princeton, NJ: Princeton University Press, 1991; South Bend, IN: Notre Dame University Press, 2002).

7. Giovanni Capoccia and R. Daniel Kelemen, "The Study of Critical Junctures: Theory, Narrative, and Counterfactuals in Historical Institutionalism," *World Politics* 59 (Apr. 2007): 368.

8. See Juan Gonzalez and Joseph Torres, *News for All the People: The Epic Story of Race and the American Media* (New York: Verso, 2011), chap. 16.

9. Michel Crozier, Samuel P. Huntington, and Joji Watanuki, *The Crisis of Democracy: Report on the Governability of Democracies to the Trilateral Commission* (New York: New York University Press, 1975). An excellent discussion of this point can be found in Noam Chomsky, *Necessary Illusions: Thought Control in Democratic Societies* (Boston: South End Press, 1989), 2–5.

10. Harold Innis, *Political Economy in the Modern State* (Toronto: Ryerson Press, 1946), *Empire and Communications* (Oxford: Clarendon Press, 1950), and *The Bias of Communication* (Toronto: University of Toronto Press, 1951).

11. See Eric McLuhan and Frank Zingrone, eds., *Essential McLuhan* (New York: Basic Books, 1995); Marshall McLuhan, *Understanding Media: The Extensions of Man* (1964; Cambridge: MIT Press, 1999, intro. Lewis H. Lapham); Marshall McLuhan and Quentin Fiore, *The Medium Is the Message: An Inventory of Effects* (New York: Bantam Books, 1967); and Marshall McLuhan, *The Gutenberg Galaxy: The Making of Typographic Man* (Toronto, University of Toronto Press, 1962). Another classic in this tradition is Jerry Mander, *Four Arguments for the Elimination of Television* (New York: Quill, 1978). Mander writes: "Without our gaining control over technology, all notions of democracy are a farce. . . . We are trapped in a state of passivity and impotence hardly to be distinguished from living under a dictator" (p. 352).

12. Neil Postman, *Amusing Ourselves to Death: Public Discourse in the Age of Show Business* (New York: Penguin, 1985).

13. Nicholas Carr, *The Shallows: What the Internet Is Doing to Our Brains* (New York: W.W. Norton, 2010), 45.

14. For a series of important essays on technological determinism, see Merritt Roe Smith and Leo Marx, eds., *Does Technology Drive History? The Dilemma of Technological Determinism* (Cambridge, MA: MIT Press, 1995).

15. Harold A. Innis, *Changing Concepts of Time* (Toronto: University of Toronto Press, 1952), 15.

16. Neil Postman, *Technopoly: The Surrender of Culture to Technology* (New York: Knopf, 1992), 170.

17. Carr, *Shallows*, 112, 156–57.

18. The "breakneck speed" at which technological change occurs—with minimal concern for consequences—is generally driven by commercial imperatives, a

point so often taken for granted that it disappears as a factor in the analysis. See, for example, Jim Taylor, *Raising Generation Tech* (Naperville, IL: Sourcebooks, 2012).

19. For examples of this overlap, see Sherry Turkle, *Alone Together: Why We Expect More from Technology and Less from Each Other* (New York: Basic Books, 2011); and Arlie Russell Hochschild, *The Outsourced Self: Intimate Life in Market Times* (New York: Metropolitan Books, 2012).

20. Steven Pinker, *The Language Instinct: How the Mind Creates Language* (New York: Morrow, 1994).

21. This point is discussed in Spencer Wells, *The Journey of Man: A Genetic Odyssey* (New York: Random House, 2003); and Jared Diamond, *The Third Chimpanzee: The Evolution and Future of the Human Animal* (New York: HarperCollins, 1992). See also Richard G. Klein and Blake Edgar, *The Dawn of Human Culture: A Bold New Theory on What Sparked the "Big Bang" of Human Consciousness* (New York: Wiley, 2002).

22. Marcel Mazoyer and Laurence Roudart, *A History of World Agriculture: From the Neolithic Age to the Current Crisis* (New York: Monthly Review Press, 2006).

23. Wayne M. Senner, ed., *The Origins of Writing* (Lincoln: University of Nebraska Press, 1989); and Stephen D. Houston, ed., *The First Writing: Script Invention as History and Process* (Cambridge, UK: Cambridge University Press, 2004).

24. Cited in Jared Diamond, *Guns, Germs, and Steel: The Fate of Human Societies* (New York: W.W. Norton, 1997), 235.

25. Carr, *Shallows*, 53.

26. The classic works are Elizabeth L. Eisenstein, *The Printing Press as an Agent of Change: Communications and Cultural Transformations in Early Modern Europe* (Cambridge, UK: Cambridge University Press, 1979), and *The Printing Revolution in Early Modern Europe* (Cambridge, UK: Cambridge University Press, 1983); Adrian Johns, *The Nature of the Book: Print and Knowledge in the Making* (Chicago: University of Chicago Press, 1998).

27. Carr, *Shallows*, 75.

28. Not surprisingly, the emergence of e-books is dramatically altering reading from "an intimate exchange between the reader and the words on the page" into "something measurable and quasi-public." Also not surprisingly, the impetus for this change is due as much to commercial imperatives as it is to the nature of the technology. See Alexandra Alter, "Your E-Book Is Reading You," *Wall Street Journal*, July 19, 2012.

29. Carr, *Shallows*, 116.

30. John Naughton, *What You Really Need to Know About the Internet: From Gutenberg to Zuckerberg* (London: Quercus, 2012).

31. The QWERTY keyboard was designed to slow down typists so early typewriters could function without the keys jamming. If a keyboard were to be designed for optimal efficiency, it would use a different layout.

32. Cited in Rebecca MacKinnon, *Consent of the Networked: The Worldwide Struggle for Internet Freedom* (New York: Basic Books, 2012), 53.

33. For a sophisticated history of the relationship of commercialism to popular music in the United States, see David Suisman, *Selling Sounds: The Commercial Revolution in American History* (Cambridge, MA: Harvard University Press, 2009).

34. Tim Wu succinctly and persuasively explains the economic value of media conglomeration for giant firms in Tim Wu, *The Master Switch: The Rise and Fall of Information Empires* (New York: Knopf, 2010), chap. 17.

35. Ibid.

36. Ibid., 228–29.

37. A classic study along these lines is Todd Gitlin, *Inside Prime Time*, 2d ed. (Berkeley: University of California Press, 2000).

38. This is a finding that predominates in the political economy of communication tradition. A classic example: Erik Barnouw, *The Sponsor: Notes on Modern Potentates* (New York: Oxford University Press, 1978).

39. See Robert W. McChesney, *The Problem of the Media: U.S. Communication Politics in the 21st Century* (New York: Monthly Review Press, 2004), chap. 4.

40. The dubious nature of this commercial education is examined in David George, *Preference Pollution: How Markets Create the Desires We Dislike* (Ann Arbor: University of Michigan Press, 2001).

41. For an elaboration of themes in these paragraphs, see Juliet Schor, *Born to Buy: The Commercialized Child and the New Consumer Culture* (New York: Scribner, 2004). See also McChesney, *Problem of the Media*, chap. 4.

42. See Martin Lindstrom, *Brandwashed* (New York: Crown Business, 2011), 17–21.

43. Susan Gregory Thomas, *Buy, Buy Baby: How Consumer Culture Manipulates Parents and Harms Young Minds* (Boston: Houghton Mifflin, 2007).

44. Cited in Joel Bakan, *Childhood Under Siege: How Big Business Targets Children* (New York: The Free Press, 2011), 51. See also Danielle Sacks, "Alex Bogusky Tells All: He Left the World's Hottest Agency to Find His Soul," *Fast Company*, Aug. 9, 2010.

45. Cited in Bakan, *Childhood Under Siege*, 6.

46. For this reason, some nations, such as Sweden, prohibit advertising to children under the age of twelve. The economist Richard Layard thinks it is a highly desirable policy for other nations to adopt. I agree. See Richard Layard, *Happiness: Lessons from a New Science* (New York: Penguin, 2005), 161.

47. This figure was created by the staff of former FCC commissioner Michael Copps in consultation with various experts and based upon evaluating the amounts raised during recent spectrum auctions. See "Remarks of Commissioner Michael J. Copps," National Conference on Media Reform, Memphis, TN, Jan. 12, 2007.

48. See McChesney, *Communication Revolution*, chap. 3.

49. Cited in Lewis Hyde, *Common as Air: Revolution, Art, and Ownership* (New York: Farrar, Straus & Giroux, 2010), 45.

50. To be accurate, the driving force behind copyright was not authors as much as publishers, whose business prospects hinged on getting government monopoly privileges.

51. Peter Decherney, *Hollywood's Copyright Wars: From Edison to the Internet* (New York: Columbia University Press, 2012), 3.

52. John Palphrey, *Intellectual Property Strategy* (Cambridge, MA: MIT Press, 2012), 144–45.

53. Wu, *Master Switch*, chap. 17. Wu demonstrates this brilliantly by dissecting the revenue sources of the contemporary conglomerate when it produces a motion picture.

54. See Lawrence Lessig, *Free Culture* (New York: Penguin, 2004); and Kembrew McLeod, *Freedom of Expression* (New York: Doubleday, 2005).

55. Milton Friedman, *Capitalism and Freedom* (Chicago: University of Chicago Press, 1962), chap. 8. Friedman filed a supporting brief for Lawrence Lessig in the Supreme Court's 2003 *Eldred v. Ashcroft* case over the constitutionality of Congress continually extending copyright terms for work that had already been done.

56. Lewis Hyde, *Common as Air: Revolution, Art, and Ownership* (New York: Farrar, Straus & Giroux, 2010), 199–206.

57. Don Clark, "Facing Early Losses, Some Web Publishers Begin to Pull the Plug," *Wall Street Journal*, Jan. 14, 1997, A8.

58. Cited in Joseph Turow, *The Daily You* (New Haven, CT: Yale University Press, 2011), 15.

59. J.D. Lasica, "John Perry Barlow: 'People Want to Bypass the Mass Media,' " May 24, 1996, www.jdlasica.com/1996/05/24/john-perry-barlow-people-want-to-bypass-the-mass-media.

60. Michael Mandiberg, introduction, in Michael Mandiberg, ed., *The Social Media Reader* (New York: New York University Press, 2012), 1.

61. See, for example, Clifford G. Christians, Theodore L. Glasser, Denis McQuail, Kaarle Nordenstreng, and Robert A. White, *Normative Theories of the Media: Journalism in Democratic Societies* (Urbana: University of Illinois Press, 2009).

62. See, for example, Mauro P. Porto, "Frame Diversity and Citizen Competence: Towards a Critical Approach to News Quality," *Critical Studies in Media Communication* 24, no. 4 (2007): 303–21; Minho Kim, "News Objectivity and Political Conversation: An Experimental Study of Mad Cow Disease and Candlelight Protest," *Development and Society* 41, no. 1 (June 2012): 55–75.

63. For hard data on newspaper markets in the late nineteenth and early twentieth centuries, see Robert W. McChesney and John Nichols, *The Death and Life of American Journalism: The Media Revolution That Will Begin the World Again* (New York: Nation Books, 2010), chap. 3.

64. Richard L. Kaplan, *Politics and the American Press: The Rise of Objectivity, 1865–1920* (New York: Cambridge University Press, 2002), 123–24.

65. For the classic treatment, see Upton Sinclair, *The Brass Check* (1919; Urbana: University of Illinois Press, 2003).

66. Robert M. La Follette, ed. Ellen Torelle, *The Political Philosophy of Robert M. La Follette* (Madison, WI: Robert M. La Follette Co., 1920).

67. Cited in Kaplan, *Politics and the American Press*, 166.

68. See Duane C.S. Stoltzfus, *Freedom from Advertising: E.W. Scripps's Chicago Experiment* (Urbana: University of Illinois Press, 2007).

69. William Neuman, "In 'Battle' with Media, a New Tactic in Ecuador," *New York Times*, Mar. 13, 2012, A10.

70. "The Media and the Mouth," *The Economist*, Mar. 3, 2012, 47.

71. Cited in Kaplan, *Politics and the American Press*, 126.

72. Ben Scott, "Labor's New Deal for Journalism: The Newspaper Guild in the 1930s," PhD dissertation, University of Illinois at Urbana-Champaign, 2009, chap. 7.

73. See Ronald K.L. Collins, *Dictating Content: How Advertising Pressure Can Corrupt a Free Press* (Washington, DC: Center for the Study of Commercialism, 1992).

74. The two classic works are: Walter Lippmann, *Liberty and the News* (Princeton, NJ: Princeton University Press, 2008); and Walter Lippmann and Charles Merz, "A Test of the News," *New Republic*, Aug. 4, 1920.

75. See John Nichols and Robert McChesney, "Bush's War on the Press," *The Nation*, Dec. 5, 2005.

76. Chris Hedges, *Empire of Illusion* (New York: Nation Books, 2009), 170.

77. For a variety of treatments of this issue, see Howard Friel and Richard A. Falk, *The Paper of Record: How the "New York Times" Misreports U.S. Foreign Policy* (New York: Verso, 2004); Edward S. Herman and Noam Chomsky, *Manufacturing*

Consent (New York: Pantheon, 1989); and Jonathan Mermin, *Debating War and Peace: Media Coverage of U.S. Intervention in the Post-Vietnam Era* (Princeton, NJ: Princeton University Press, 1999); and Matthew A. Baum and Tim J. Groeling, *War Stories: The Causes and Consequences of Public Views of War* (Princeton, NJ: Princeton University Press, 2010).

78. For a superb treatment of this issue, see W. Lance Bennett, Regina G. Lawrence, and Steven Livingston, *When the Press Fails: Political Power and the News Media from Iraq to Katrina* (New York: Cambridge University Press, 2007).

79. I.F. Stone, "What Few Know About the Tonkin Bay Incidents," *I.F. Stone's Weekly*, Aug. 4, 1964, also cited in Jeff Cohen, "Izzy Stone, Patron Saint of Bloggers," Common Dreams, June 16, 2008, commondreams.org/archive/2008/06/16/9646.

80. "The Press: The Newspaper Collector Samuel Newhouse," *Time*, July 27, 1962.

81. Michael Hastings, *The Operators: The Wild and Terrifying Inside Story of America's War in Afghanistan* (New York: Blue Rider Press, 2012), 90–91.

82. Glenn Greenwald, "What NPR Means by 'Reporting,' " Salon.com, Mar. 27, 2012.

83. Hastings, *Operators*, 329.

84. Ronald D. Smith, *Strategic Planning for Public Relations* (Mahwah, NJ: Routledge, 2004), 191; Norman Solomon, *Unreliable Sources: A Guide to Detecting Bias in News Media* (New York: Carol Publishing Group, 1992), 66; and Trevor Morris and Simon Goldsworthy, *PR—a Persuasive Industry? Spin, Public Relations, and the Shaping of the Modern Media* (Basingstoke, UK: Palgrave Macmillan, 2008). See also: Michael Turney, "Working with the Media," 2002, nku.edu/~turney/prclass/readings/media_rel.html.

85. Christopher Lasch, *The Revolt of the Elite and the Betrayal of Democracy* (New York: W.W. Norton, 1995), 162–63.

86. Lawrence Lessig, *Republic, Lost: How Money Corrupts Congress—and a Plan to Stop It* (New York: Twelve Books, 2011), 59.

87. See Amy Reynolds and Gary Hicks, *Prophets of the Fourth Estate: Broadsides by Press Critics of the Progressive Era* (Los Angeles: Litwin Books, 2012).

88. These incidents have received extensive treatment in the PEC literature. See Robert W. McChesney, *Telecommunications, Mass Media, and Democracy: The Battle for the Control of U.S. Broadcasting, 1928–1935* (New York: Oxford University Press, 1993); Victor Pickard, "The Battle over the FCC Blue Book: Determining the Role of Broadcast Media in a Democratic Society, 1945–1948," *Media, Culture & Society* 33, no. 2 (2011): 171–91; Victor Pickard, "Whether the Giants Should Be Slain or Persuaded to Be Good: Revisiting the Hutchins Commission and the Role of Media in a Democratic Society," *Critical Studies in Media Communication* 27, no. 4 (2010): 391–411; Inger L. Stole, *Advertising on Trial: Consumer Activism and Corporate Public Relations in the 1930s* (Urbana: University of Illinois Press, 2006); and Inger L. Stole, *Advertising at War: Business, Consumers, and Government in the 1940s* (Urbana: University of Illinois Press, 2012).

89. There is a nice discussion of this period in Juan Gonzalez and Joseph Torres, *News for All the People: The Epic Story of Race and the American Media* (New York: Verso, 2011), chap. 16.

90. I chronicle this history in McChesney, *Communication Revolution*, chap. 3.

91. For an example of the campaign, see " 'Glenn Beck': Net Neutrality Pits Free Speech Against Free Press," *Glenn Beck Show*, Fox News Channel, Apr. 5, 2010, foxnews.com/story/0,2933,590506,00.html#ixzz1pgCJQ4Lw.

92. Conversation between the author and the head of a public interest group in Washington, Mar. 2012.

93. Heather Brooke, *The Revolution Will Be Digitised: Dispatches from the Information War* (London: Heinemann, 2011), 15.

4. The Internet and Capitalism I: Where Dinosaurs Roam?

1. Transcript, "Special Event: George W. Bush Addresses Rally in Appleton, Wisconsin," Oct. 28, 2000, http://archives.cnn.com/TRANSCRIPTS/0010/28/se.02.html.

2. Tom Streeter notes that "it seems plausible that the 'Gore said he invented the Internet' quip did at least as much damage to Gore's final vote count as Ralph Nader." See Thomas Streeter, *The Net Effect: Romanticism, Capitalism, and the Internet* (New York: New York University Press, 2011), 114–15.

3. Transcript, "Vice President Gore on CNN's Late Edition," Mar. 9, 1999, www.cnn.com/ALLPOLITICS/stories/1999/03/09/president.2000/transcript.gore/index.html.

4. *Matrix News* 9, no. 4 (Apr. 1999), http://web.archive.org/web/20000125065813/http://www.mids.org/mn/904/vcerf.html.

5. Some conservatives are obsessed with discrediting or at least trivializing the idea that the government and the military played the foundational role in establishing the Internet, for explicitly political reasons. As former *Wall Street Journal* publisher Gordon Crovitz wrote on the *Journal*'s website, if people understand the government could create the Internet, it could be successfully "cited to justify big government." L. Gordon Crovitz, "Who Really Invented the Internet?" *Wall Street Journal* online, July 22, 2012, online.wsj.com/article/SB10000872396390444464304577539063008406518.html. The "argument" was immediately rebuffed for the ideological exercise it was by no less a free-market libertarian than economist Dan Mitchell. The government role in establishing the Internet is "well-established, easily discovered truth." Mitchell explained that this is "how innovation actually happens—sometimes: the government pours money and engineering talent into a research project, the results of which are then unleashed into the marketplace, where they are exploited and further developed by commercial interests." See Dan Mitchell, "Untruths at the Origins of the Internet," CNN Money, July 24, 2012, tech.fortune.cnn.com/2012/07/24/untruths-at-the-origins-of-the-internet.

6. Peter Nowak, *Sex, Bombs and Burgers: How War, Pornography, and Fast Food Have Shaped Modern Technology* (Guilford, CT: Lyons Press, 2011), 203.

7. Sascha D. Meinrath, James W. Losey, and Victor W. Pickard, "Digital Feudalism: Enclosures and Erasures from Digital Rights Management to the Digital Divide," *CommLaw Conspectus*, 19, no. 2 (2011): 459; and Tim Wu, *The Master Switch: The Rise and Fall of Information Empires* (New York: Knopf, 2010).

8. John Naughton, *What You Really Need to Know About the Internet: From Gutenberg to Zuckerberg* (London: Quercus, 2012), 45–46.

9. Susan Landau, *Surveillance or Security? The Risks Posed by New Wiretapping Technologies* (Cambridge, MA: MIT Press, 2010), 18.

10. Nathan Newman, *Net Loss: Internet Prophets, Private Profits, and the Costs to Community* (University Park, PA: Penn State University Press, 2002), 52–53.

11. James Curran, "Rethinking Internet History," in James Curran, Natalie Fenton, and Des Freedman, *Misunderstanding the Internet* (London: Routledge, 2012), 37.

12. Nowak, *Sex, Bombs and Burgers*, 9.

13. Newman, *Net Loss*, 51.

14. Joseph Stiglitz writes that when he was head of the Council of Economic Advisers, the CEA determined the "average social return on government R&D" to be "well in excess of 50 percent," far higher than returns on private sector R&D. See Joseph E. Stiglitz, *The Price of Inequality: How Today's Divided Society Endangers Our Future* (New York: W.W. Norton, 2012), 174.

15. Nowak, *Sex, Bombs and Burgers*, 11.

16. Newman, *Net Loss*, 26.

17. Linda McQuaig and Neil Brooks, *Billionaires' Ball: Gluttony and Hubris in an Age of Epic Inequality* (Boston: Beacon Press, 2012), 77, 83.

18. Newman, *Net Loss*, 21.

19. Nowak, *Sex, Bombs and Burgers*, 11, 12.

20. Chris Anderson, "Here Come the Drones," *Wired*, July 2012, 107.

21. E-mail from Sascha Meinrath to author, Jan. 6, 2011.

22. Newman, *Net Loss*, 57.

23. Kenneth David Nichols, *The Road to Trinity: A Personal Account of How America's Nuclear Policies Were Made* (New York: William Morrow, 1987), 34–35.

24. Wu, *Master Switch*, 276.

25. Eden Medina, *Cybernetic Revolutionaries: Technology and Politics in Allende's Chile* (Cambridge, MA: MIT Press, 2011).

26. Richard Adler, *Updating Rules of the Digital Road: Privacy, Security, Intellectual Property* (Washington, DC: Aspen Institute, 2012), 4.

27. Rebecca MacKinnon, *Consent of the Networked: The Worldwide Struggle for Internet Freedom* (New York: Basic Books, 2012), 18–19.

28. Heather Brooke, *The Revolution Will Be Digitised: Dispatches from the Information War* (London: Heinemann, 2011), 24. See also Johan Soderberg, *Hacking Capitalism: The Free and Open Source Software Movement* (New York: Routledge, 2008).

29. Naughton, *What You Really Need to Know About the Internet*, 82.

30. Joseph Turow, *The Daily You: How the New Advertising Industry Is Defining Your Identity and Your Worth* (New Haven, CT: Yale University Press, 2011), 38.

31. Ibid., 40.

32. Quotation from Eli Pariser, *The Filter Bubble: What the Internet Is Hiding from You* (New York: Penguin, 2011), 31.

33. Newman, *Net Loss*, 57.

34. Dan Schiller, *Telematics and Government* (Norwood, NJ: Ablex, 1982), 210–14.

35. Ryan Ellis, currently a Stanford postdoctoral fellow, is conducting historical research on this topic. See Ryan Ellis, "Binding the Nation Together? Postal Policy in the Era of Competition," International Communication Association Conference, San Francisco, May 2007, 57–65.

36. Nowak, *Sex, Bombs and Burgers*, 206.

37. Richard Adler, *Updating Rules of the Digital Road: Privacy, Security, Intellectual Property* (Washington, DC: Aspen Institute, 2012), 4.

38. Curran, "Rethinking Internet History," 45.

39. Tim Berners-Lee, *Weaving the Web* (New York: HarperCollins, 1999), 197–98.

40. Project Censored, http://www.projectcensored.org/top-stories/articles/category/top-stories/top-25-of-1996/page/3.

41. This story is brilliantly told in Fred Turner, *From Counterculture to Cyberculture* (Chicago: University of Chicago Press, 2006).

42. Siva Vaidhyanathan develops this point with the concept of "public failure." See Siva Vaidhyanathan, *The Googlization of Everything (and Why We Should Worry)* (Berkeley: University of California Press, 2011), 39–44.

43. See Ha-Joon Chang, *23 Things They Don't Tell You About Capitalism* (New York: Bloomsbury Press, 2010), for a superb debunking of this point and the other ideological ballast underlying neoliberal economics.

44. Matthew Crain, "The Revolution Will Be Commercialized: Finance, Public Policy, and the Construction of Internet Advertising in the 1990s," PhD dissertation, University of Illinois at Urbana-Champaign, 2013.

45. S. Derek Turner, "The Internet," in *Changing Media: Public Interest Policies for the Digital Age* (Washington, DC: Free Press, 2009), 12, www.freepress.net/files/changing_media.pdf.

46. Dan Schiller, *Digital Capitalism: Networking the Global Market System* (Cambridge, MA: MIT Press, 1999), 128.

47. The celebratory and largely fatuous coverage of the Internet continues in what remains of the news media to this day. In a 2012 report for the *Columbia Journalism Review,* Michael Massing noted that "reporters breathlessly chronicle the fortunes, mansions, and attire of the digerati." Yet the American press, "while writing endlessly about the Internet, has failed to examine some important questions about it." Specifically, "journalists tend to celebrate these moguls for their savvy and cool rather than examine the enormous wealth they've amassed and the political and economic ends to which they put it." I would add that the crucial policy debates that determine the direction of the Internet fare no better. Michael Massing, "The Media's Internet Infatuation," *Columbia Journalism Review* online, Aug. 15, 2012, cjr.org/the_kicker/internet_infatuation.php.

48. Jane Slaughter, "Interview with Henry Louis Gates Jr., Harvard Professor," *Progressive* 62, no. 1, Jan. 1998.

49. Yochai Benkler, *The Penguin and the Leviathan: How Cooperation Triumphs over Self-Interest* (New York: Crown Business, 2011), 212–23.

50. Naughton, *What You Really Need to Know About the Internet*, 89. See also Joseph Michael Reagle Jr., *Good Faith Collaboration: The Culture of Wikipedia* (Cambridge, MA: MIT Press, 2010).

51. Lawrence Lessig, *Republic, Lost* (New York: Twelve Books, 2011), 34.

52. See, for example, Charles M. Schweik and Robert C. English, *Internet Success: A Study of Open-Source Software Commons* (Cambridge, MA: MIT Press, 2012).

53. MacKinnon, *Consent of the Networked*, 20.

54. James Losey e-mail to author, May 31, 2012.

55. Vaidhyanathan, *Googlization of Everything*, 63. Tim Wu notes that *Wikipedia* entries consistently rank at the very top of Google searches, ahead of the official sites for the search term. See Wu, *Master Switch*, 287.

56. Somini Sengupta and Claire Cain Miller, "Zuckerberg's 'Social Mission' View vs. Financial Expectations of Wall St.," *New York Times*, Feb. 3, 2012, B1.

57. Wu, *Master Switch*, 244.

58. Much of the political fighting over the Telecommunications Act was between the long-distance companies, like MCI and Sprint, and the regional Baby Bells over the terms of deregulation.

59. Wu, *Master Switch*, 245–46.

60. In 2012 Mississippi passed a new law that, according to Brandon Presley, Northern District Commissioner for the State of Mississippi, "will allow" AT&T "to raise rates without any oversight at all." Presley noted that AT&T was the largest lobbying force in the state and got the bill they wrote. "We have a coin-operated government," Presley stated, adding, "That's wrong." See Phillip Dampier, "Mississippi Public Service Commissioner on Big Telecom $: 'We Have a Coin-Operated Government," Stop the Cap!, July 10, 2012, stopthecap.com/2012/07/10/mississippi-public-service-commissioner-on-big-telecom-we-have-a-coin-operated-government.

61. Wu, *Master Switch*, 247.

62. Thanks to Derek Turner of Free Press for his assistance with this section.

63. The FCC had only four members at the time, as Democrat Jonathan Adelstein was waiting to be confirmed for the open seat.

64. Meinrath, Losey, and Pickard, "Digital Feudalism," 434.

65. The information in this paragraph comes from *Connecting America: The National Broadcasting Plan* (Washington, DC: Federal Communications Commission, 2010), 37–38.

66. Ben Scott e-mail to author, June 14, 2012.

67. Sascha Meinrath e-mail to author, June 14, 2012.

68. Susan Crawford, " 'Survey: Mobile App Privacy Fears Continue to Escalate,' " scrawford.net/blog, July 17, 2012, scrawford.net/blog/survey-mobile-app-privacy-fears-continue-to-escalate/1627.

69. Michael Moyer, "Verizon and AT&T Accused of Being Threats to Democracy," *Scientific American*, Mar. 13, 2012.

70. Brian X. Chen, "A Squeeze on Smartphones," *New York Times*, Mar. 2, 2012, B1, B4.

71. Brian X. Chen, "A Data Plan That Devices Can Share," *New York Times*, June 13, 2012, B1.

72. Matt Stoller, "Corruption Is Responsible for 80% of Your Cell Phone Bill," *Republic Report*, Apr. 11, 2012. Stoller gets his data from the Organization for Economic Cooperation and Development (OECD), the FCC, and the former Cellular Telecommunications Industry Association, now known only by its acronym, CTIA.

73. Susan Crawford, "What's Good for Verizon and AT&T Is Terrible for American Consumers," Wired Business, July 26, 2012, wired.com/business/2012/07/whats-good-for-verizon-and-att-is-terrible-for-american-consumers. Harold Feld, the telecommunication policy expert for Public Knowledge, wrote that "when every single incentive to profit maximization relies on providing less service for more money and discouraging people from using your service, something is seriously messed up." Harold Feld, "The Wireless Market Is Seriously Messed Up When Every Incentive Is Anti-Consumer," *Wetmachine*, July 24, 2012, tales-of-the-sausage-factory.wetmachine.com/the-wireless-market-is-seriously-messed-up-when-every-incentive-is-anti-consumer.

74. "Fortune 500," CNN Money, http://money.cnn.com/magazines/fortune/fortune500/2011/full_list.

75. Harold Feld, "My Insanely Long Field Guide to the Verizon/SpectrumCo/Cox Deal," *Wetmachine*, Mar. 22, 2012, http://tales-of-the-sausage-factory.wetmachine.com.

76. Stacey Higginbotham, "Verizon to Buy Cox Spectrum to Remake Its Broadband Model," *Gigaom*, http://GigaOM.com, Dec. 16, 2011.

77. Christopher Mitchell, *Broadband at the Speed of Light: How Three*

Communities Built Next-Generation Networks (Washington, DC: Benton Foundation, Apr. 2012), 61.

78. Susan Crawford, "Water, Internet Access and Swagger: These Guys Are Good," Wired.com, Mar. 9, 2012.

79. Feld, "My Insanely Long Field Guide."

80. Hayley Tsukayama, "Justice Allows Verizon Deals with Cable Companies, with Conditions," *Washington Post* online, August 16, 2012, washingtonpost.com/blogs/post-tech/post/justice-approves-verizon-deal-with-cable-companies/2012/08/16/783aab14-e7a9-11e1-8487-64e4b2a7 9ba8_blog.html.

81. David Lazarus, "Why Is Verizon in Bed with Time Warner and Comcast?" *Los Angeles Times* online, July 26, 2012, latimes.com/business/la-fi-lazarus-20120727,0,2605145.column.

82. Matthew Lasar, "Do We Need a New National Broadband Plan?" *Ars Technica*, July 27, 2012, arstechnica.com/tech-policy/2012/07/do-we-need-a-new-national-broadband-plan.

83. Feld, "Wireless Market Is Seriously Messed Up."

84. Meinrath, Losey, and Pickard, "Digital Feudalism," 425.

85. For OECD data, see United Nations Organisation for Economic Co-operation and Development, Directorate for Science, Technology and Industry, OECD Broadband Portal, http://oecd.org. See also: James Losey and Chiehyu Li, *Price of the Pipe: Comparing the Price of Broadband Service Around the Globe* (Washington, DC: New America Foundation, 2010).

86. Cited in Benjamin Lennett, Darah J. Morris, and Greta Byrum, *Universities as Hubs for Next-Generation Networks* (Washington, DC: New America Foundation, Apr. 2012), 2. The authors of the report note that the U.S. rate lags behind peers even in densely populated areas, refuting the claim that the vast space of the United States accounts for its poor performance.

87. New America Foundation, *The Cost of Connectivity* (Washington, DC: New America Foundation 2010), 1.

88. Lasar, "Do We Need a New National Broadband Plan?"

89. Susan P. Crawford, "Team USA Deserves No Gold Medal for Internet Access," *Bloomberg View*, Aug. 5, 2012, bloomberg.com/news/2012-08-05/team-usa-deserves-no-gold-medals-for-internet-access.html.

90. Sascha Meinrath e-mail to author, Aug. 13, 2012.

91. Pickard and Meinrath demonstrate that there is a great deal of unused spectrum under government control that could be put into circulation without harming the government's needs. See Victor W. Pickard and Sascha D. Meinrath, "Revitalizing the Public Airwaves: Opportunistic Unlicensed Reuse of Government Spectrum," *International Journal of Communication* 3 (2009): 1052–84.

92. Nick Valery, "White-Space Puts Wi-Fi on Steroids," *The Economist*, Nov. 17, 2011, 48.

93. Richard Bennett, *Powering the Mobile Revolution: Principles of Spectrum Allocation* (Washington, DC: Information Technology and Innovation Foundation, 2012), 4, 5.

94. Meinrath e-mail to author, Aug. 13, 2012.

95. Feld, "My Insanely Long Field Guide."

96. Matt Wood e-mail to author, Aug. 22, 2012.

97. Karl Bode, "AT&T Wants FCC to Free More Spectrum—for Them to Squat On," *Broadband DSL Reports*, Jan. 14, 2011, http://dslreports.com.

98. For a superior examination of the spectrum issue, see Meinrath, Losey, and Pickard, "Digital Feudalism," 435, 437, 465, 466.

99. Peter Barnes, *Capitalism 3.0: A Guide to Reclaiming the Commons* (San Francisco: Berrett-Koehler, 2006), 127.

100. See Brian Chen, "Carriers Warn of Crisis in Mobile Spectrum," *New York Times*, Apr. 17, 2012. Chen quotes cell phone inventor Martin Cooper, who dismisses the claim as unfounded.

101. MacKinnon, *Consent of the Networked*, 120.

102. Bruce Upbin, "Complacent Telcos Deliver Americans Third Rate Service at High Prices," *Forbes* online, July 21, 2012, forbes.com/sites/bruceupbin/2012/07/21/americans-suffer-from-third-rate-broadband-at-high-prices.

103. Council of Economic Advisers, *The Economic Benefits of New Spectrum for Wireless Broadband* (Washington, DC: Executive Office of the President, Feb. 2012).

104. Brian X. Chen, "Sharing the Air," *New York Times*, June 7, 2012, B1; and Brian X. Chen, "On Sharing the Spectrum," *New York Times*, June 4, 2012, B5.

105. James Losey e-mail to author, Aug. 13, 2012.

106. Meinrath e-mail to author, Aug. 13, 2012.

107. Josh Smith, "FCC Chairman Lobbies Pentagon for More Spectrum," *National Journal* online, Aug. 3, 2012, techdailydose.nationaljournal.com/2012/08/fcc-chairman-lobbies-pentagon.php.

108. E-mail from S. Derek Turner, research director for Free Press, to the author, May 2, 2012.

109. Lynn Sweet, "Obama on Why He Is Not for Single Payer Health Insurance: New Mexico Town Hall Transcript," *Chicago Sun Times*, May 14, 2009, http://blogs.suntimes.com/sweet/2009/05/obama_on_why_he_is_not_for_sin.html.

110. Al Gore, "Networking the Future: We Need a National 'Superhighway' for Computer Information," *Washington Post*, July 15, 1990, B3.

111. See Streeter, *Net Effect*, 106–15.

112. Gerry Smith, "Without Internet, Urban Poor Fear Being Left Behind in Digital Age," *Huffington Post*, Mar. 1, 2012.

113. John Dunbar, "Poverty Stretches the Digital Divide," Investigative Reporting Workshop, American University School of Communication, Mar. 23, 2012.

114. In June 2012, the Obama administration announced plans to dramatically expand broadband access. See Carl Franzen, "White House Debuts Ambitious Plan to Remake the Web Using Broadband," TPM Idea Lab, June 13, 2012, idealab.talkingpointsmemo.com/2012/06/white-house-debuts-ambitious-plan-to-expand-broadband-again.php. After studying the measure, one policy expert told me it included wonderful buzzwords but few actual requirements on (or competitive challenges to) the cartel. "Like almost everything the Obama administration has announced in recent years, [it] seems to be a general whitewash for 'leave it to the private sector and everything will magically work out' policies."

115. Lennett, Morris, and Byrum, *Universities as Hubs*, 3.

116. Ibid.

117. The material in this paragraph comes from Mitchell, *Broadband at the Speed of Light*.

118. Denise Roth Barber, "Dialing Up the Dollars: Telecommunication Interests Donated Heavily to NC Lawmakers," National Institute on Money in State Politics, Mar. 20, 2012, followthemoney.org/press/ReportView.phtml?r=484.

119. "Municipal Broadband: Triumph of the Little Guys," *The Economist* online,

Aug. 10, 2012, economist.com/blogs/democracyinamerica/2012/08/municipal-broadband.

120. Masha Zager, "Santa Monica City Net: How to Grow a Network," *Broadband Communities*, May–June 2011, 44–47.

121. Higginbotham, "Verizon to Buy Cox Spectrum."

122. Wu, *Master Switch*, 285.

123. MacKinnon, *Consent of the Networked*, 121.

124. Erick Schonfeld, "Vint Cerf Wonders If We Need to Nationalize the Internet," *TechCrunch*, June 25, 2008, techcrunch.com/2008/06/25/vint-cerf-wonders-if-we-need-to-nationalize-the-internet.

125. Citation and link to video of Obama statement in: Timothy Karr, "Obama FCC Caves on Net Neutrality—Tuesday Betrayal Assured," *Huffington Post*, Dec. 20, 2010, huffingtonpost.com/timothy-carr/obama-fcc-caves-on-net-ne_b_799435.html.

126. Jeff Jarvis, *Public Parts: How Sharing in the Digital Age Improves the Way We Work and Live* (New York: Simon & Schuster, 2011), 208.

127. MacKinnon, *Consent of the Networked*, 122.

128. Jarvis, *Public Parts*, 208.

129. Charles Arthur, "Walled Gardens Look Rosy for Facebook, Apple—and Would-Be Censors," *The Guardian*, Apr. 17, 2012.

130. Ibid.

131. Eli M. Noam, *Media Ownership and Concentration in America* (New York: Oxford University Press, 2009), 365–69.

132. Barry C. Lynn, "Killing the Competition: How the New Monopolies Are Destroying the Competition," *Harper's*, Feb. 2012, 33.

133. Mergent Online, Moody's Investors Service, 2012, by subscription at http://mergentonline.com (accessed Apr. 24, 2012). I chronicle in detail the extent and nature of these media empires in the late 1990s in Robert W. McChesney, *Rich Media, Poor Democracy: Communication Politics in Dubious Times* (New York: The New Press, 2000), chap. 1.

134. I say "qualified" because although the Fortune list for 2000 technically did not include foreign-based media conglomerates with huge U.S.-based interests, like Sony, Vivendi, and Bertelsmann, I've included them for the sake of accuracy. This approach is meant to provide a rough idea of the increase in the number of media powerhouses, and not to be regarded as the final word on the matter. For a detailed statistical assessment, see Noam, *Media Ownership and Concentration*.

135. The classic work was Ben H. Badgikian, *The Media Monopoly* (Boston: Beacon Press, 1983), which has enjoyed many subsequent revised editions.

136. They also became conglomerates because media economics, as discussed in chapter 3, are rather unlike traditional markets for goods and services. Conglomeration is an especially effective way to reduce risk. An excellent discussion of this is in Wu, *Master Switch*, ch. 17.

137. Jaron Lanier, *You Are Not a Gadget: A Manifesto* (New York: Knopf, 2010), 87.

138. Steven Levy, "How the Propeller Heads Stole the Electronic Future," *New York Times Magazine*, Sept. 24, 1995, 58.

139. Lanier, *You Are Not a Gadget*, 87.

140. Adam Smith, *The Wealth of Nations* (1776; New York: Modern Library, 1937), 173.

141. This episode is chronicled in John Motavalli, *Bamboozled at the Revolution:*

How Big Media Lost Billions in the Battle for the Internet (New York: Viking, 2002). See also *Rich Media, Poor Democracy*, chap. 3.

142. One striking development is that media conglomerates are moving into education as a potential "cash cow" for textbooks and, especially, digital material. Rupert Murdoch's News Corporation hired former New York City schools chancellor Joel Klein to run Amplify, its for-profit education subsidiary. The entry of the conglomerates into education suggests an even greater opening toward commercialism and commercial values. It is an existing $7 billion market, a public trough for the giants to battle over. See Brooks Barnes and Amy Chozick, "The Classroom as a Cash Cow," *New York Times*, Aug. 20, 2012, B1, B8.

143. "Fortune 500," CNN Money, money.cnn.com/magazines/fortune/fortune500/2011/full_list.

144. MacKinnon, *Consent of the Networked*, 101.

145. See Tarleton Gillespie, *Wired Shut: Copyright and the Shape of Digital Culture* (Cambridge, MA: MIT Press, 2007).

146. Ian Katz, "Web Freedom Faces Greatest Threat Ever, Warns Google's Sergey Brin," *The Guardian*, Apr. 15, 2012.

147. David Kravets, "Analysis: Internet Blacklist Bill Is Roadmap to 'the End' of the Internet," *Wired*, Nov. 17, 2011.

148. See, for example, Brooke, *Revolution Will Be Digitised*, 47; and Dominic Rushe, "The Online Copyright War: The Day the Internet Hit Back at Big Media," *The Guardian*, Apr. 18, 2012.

149. Harold Feld, "Op-ed: MPAA/RIAA Lose Big as US Backs Copyright 'Limitations,'" Ars Technica, July 8, 2012, arstechnica.com/tech-policy/2012/07/op-ed-eus-rejection-of-acta-subtly-changed-trade-law-landscape.

150. Losey e-mail to author, Aug. 13, 2012.

151. Meinrath e-mail to author, Aug. 13, 2012.

152. MacKinnon, *Consent of the Networked*, 104–11.

153. Antoine Champagne, "Watching Over You: The Perils of Deep Packet Inspection," *CounterPunch*, Mar. 8, 2012.

154. Brendan Greeley, "Hollywood Tries to Wash the Web with SOPA," *Bloomberg Businessweek*, Dec. 19–25, 2011, 35–36. The conclusions were reached in a four-hundred-page report published by the Social Science Research Council in January 2011.

155. David D. Friedman, *Future Imperfect: Technology and Freedom in an Uncertain World* (New York: Cambridge University Press, 2008), 16.

156. Patricia Aufderheide and Peter Jaszi, *Reclaiming Fair Use: How to Put Balance Back in Copyright* (Chicago: University of Chicago Press, 2011); Benkler, *Penguin and the Leviathan*, 222–29; and Lawrence Lessig, *Remix: Making Art and Commerce Thrive in the Hybrid Economy* (New York: Penguin Press, 2008).

157. Rushe, "Online Copyright War."

158. Losey e-mail to author, Aug. 13, 2012. For a series of concerns about the prospective plan, see Douglas Rushkoff, "Will Your Internet Provider Be Spying on You?" CNN Opinion, July 6, 2012, cnn.com/2012/07/06/opinion/rushkoff-online-monitoring.

159. Amy Chozick, "Under Copyright Pressure, Google to Alter Search Results," *New York Times*, Aug. 11, 2012, B2.

160. Carl Franzen, "Google's Copyright Filtering Causes Concern," Talking Points Memo, Aug. 10, 2012.

161. Wood e-mail to author.

162. Greeley, "Hollywood Tries to Wash the Web," 36.

163. Adler, *Updating Rules of the Digital Road*, 2.

164. Steve Wasserman, "The Amazon Effect," *The Nation*, May 29, 2012. See also Julie Bosman, "Survey Details How E-Books Continue Strong Growth Trend," *New York Times*, July 19, 2012, B4.

165. Larry Downes perceptively notes that in this environment it is difficult for people to have any respect for copyright: "[Copyright] no longer holds any moral authority with most consumers. There's no longer an ethical imperative to obey it or even understand it. Self-enforcement is fading, and the rules are so severe and so frequently violated that effective legal enforcement has become nearly impossible. . . .

"Copyright is a law in name only—as obsolete and irrelevant as rules still on the books in some jurisdictions that regulate who can or must wear what kind of clothing." See Larry Downes, "How Copyright Extension Undermined Copyright: The Copyright of Parking (Part 1)," *Techdirt*, May 21, 2012, techdirt.com/articles/20120521/03153118987/how-copyright-extension-undermined-copyright-copyright-parking-part-i.shtml.

166. Lanier, *You Are Not a Gadget*, 89, 91.

167. Ben Sisario, "New Layer of Content Amid Chaos on YouTube," *New York Times*, Mar. 12, 2012, B1.

168. Evan Shapiro, "The 8 Most Important Things to Happen to TV in the Past 5 Years," *Huffington Post*, Mar. 8, 2012, huffingtonpost.com/even-shapiro/tvs-top-8_b_1328846.html.

169. "Charlie Rose Talks to Hulu CEO Jason Kilar," *Bloomberg Businessweek*, Mar. 5–11, 2012, 48.

170. RBC Capital Markets, "Brightcove, Inc.: Introducing the Video Cloud," Report for Subscribers, Mar. 28, 2012, 1.

171. Turow, *Daily You*, 161.

172. Bill Carter, "Where Have All the Viewers Gone?" *New York Times*, Apr. 23, 2012, B1, B3.

173. Kit Eaton, "The Future of TV Is Two Screens, One Held Firmly in Your Hands," *Fast Company* online, July 17, 2012, fastcompany.com/1842995/future-tv-two-screens-one-held-firmly-your-hands.

174. Brian Stelter, "New Internet TV Network to Feature Larry King," *New York Times*, Mar. 12, 2012, B5.

175. Nick Bilton, "In a Skirmish to Control the Screens," *New York Times*, June 4, 2012, B5.

176. Nick Bilton, "TV Makers Ignore Apps at Their Own Peril," *New York Times*, Mar. 12, 2012, B4; and Mike Hale, "Genres Stretch, for Better and Worse, as YouTube Takes On TV," *New York Times*, Apr. 25, 2012, A1, A3. For a thoughtful treatment of the dilemma the Internet has created for media firms and content production, see Robert Levine, *Free Ride: How Digital Parasites Are Destroying the Culture Business, and How the Culture Business Can Fight Back* (New York: Anchor, 2011).

5. The Internet and Capitalism II: Empire of the Senseless?

1. "Google," *Trefis*, Mar. 29, 2012, 2.

2. "Microsoft Corp.," *Standard & Poor's Stock Report*, Apr. 14, 2012.

3. Adam L. Penenberg, "The Evolution of Amazon," *Fast Company*, July 2009, 66–74.

4. "Apple, Inc.," *Standard & Poor's Stock Report*, Apr. 14, 2012.

5. Claire Cain Miller, "Motorola Set for Big Cuts as Google Reinvents It," *New York Times*, Aug. 13, 2012, B1.

6. Barry C. Lynn, "Killing the Competition: How the New Monopolies Are Destroying the Competition," *Harper's*, Feb. 2012, 33.

7. Linda McQuaig and Neil Brooks, *Billionaires' Ball: Gluttony and Hubris in an Age of Epic Inequality* (Boston: Beacon Press, 2012), 38.

8. "U.S. Commerce—Stock Market Capitalization of the 50 Largest American Companies," Weblists, iweblists.com/us/commerce/MarketCapitalization.html (accessed June 14, 2012). Many of these firms, especially after the top ten, frequently move up and down a slot or two due to variations in the share price of their stock. On the date I checked, banks occupied numbers 31 and 32, so it is possible the big banks would occupy as many as four of the top thirty slots on a random day.

9. John A. Byrne, "The 12 Greatest Entrepreneurs of Our Time," *Fortune*, Apr. 2012, 68–86.

10. Chris Anderson, "The Web Is Dead; Long Live the Internet: Who's to Blame: Us," *Wired* 18 (Sept. 2010): 164. This requires the full panoply of what Joseph Schumpeter called "monopolistic practices" (or "the editing of competition") to bring it about. See Joseph A. Schumpeter, *Capitalism, Socialism and Democracy* (New York: Harper & Row, 1950), 90, and *Essays* (Cambridge, MA: Addison-Wesley Press, 1951), 56.

11. Carl Shapiro and Hal R. Varian, *Information Rules* (Boston: Harvard Business School Press, 1999), 173.

12. Anderson, "Web Is Dead," 122–27, 164.

13. Metcalfe's law is discussed in Eli Pariser, *The Filter Bubble: What the Internet Is Hiding from You* (New York: Penguin, 2011), 41.

14. "A Fistful of Dollars," *The Economist*, Feb. 4, 2012, 11.

15. Somini Sengupta and Nick Bilton, "Facebook Plays Offense and Defense in a Single Deal," *New York Times*, Apr. 11, 2012, B4.

16. For a discussion of this point, see Rahul Tongia and Ernest J. Wilson III, "The Flip Side of Metcalfe's Law: Multiple and Growing Costs of Network Exclusion," *International Journal of Communication* 5 (2011): 665–81.

17. Peter Martin, "Big Guy Embraces the Net," *Financial Times*, June 13, 1996, 10.

18. Hal R. Varian, Joseph Farrell, and Carl Shapiro, *The Economics of Information Technology* (Cambridge, UK: Cambridge University Press, 2004), 37, 49, 71–72; and Richard Gilbert and Michael L. Katz, "An Economists's Guide to US v. Microsoft," *Journal of Economic Perspectives* 15, no. 2 (2001): 30.

19. Sascha D. Meinrath, James W. Losey, and Victor W. Pickard, "Digital Feudalism: Enclosures and Erasures from Digital Rights Management to the Digital Divide," *Comm Law Conspectus* 19, no. 2 (2011): 458–59.

20. Ibid., 476–77. Joseph Stiglitz has a useful discussion of economic rents and their relationship to monopoly power and inequality in Joseph E. Stiglitz, *The Price of Inequality: How Today's Divided Society Endangers Our Future* (New York: W.W. Norton, 2012), chap. 2.

21. Eduardo Porter, "Tech Suits Endanger Innovation," *New York Times*, May 30, 2012, B2.

22. For a fascinating history of how patent law and intellectual property were used by business to appropriate workers' knowledge of and innovation in production, see Catherine L. Fisk, *Working Knowledge: Employee Innovation and the Rise of*

Corporate Intellectual Property, 1800–1930 (Chapel Hill: University of North Carolina Press, 2009).

23. Paul M. Barrett, "Apple's Jihad," *Bloomberg Businessweek*, April 2–8, 2012, 59; Ashlee Vance, "Hiring a Mercenary for the New Patent War," *Bloomberg Businessweek*, Aug. 13–26, 2012, 41.

24. "Opening Remarks," *Bloomberg Businessweek*, April 9–15, 2012, 14; and Peter Burrows, "Google's Bid to Be Everything to Everyone," *Bloomberg Businessweek*, Feb. 20–26, 2012, 37.

25. Elizabeth Wasserman and Michelle Quinn, "Tech Firms Behaving Badly," *Politico*, Apr. 23, 2012, politico.com/news/stories/0412/75498.html. In August 2012 Apple won the greatest patents case of the Internet era in its battle with Samsung over smartphone patents. As the *New York Times* noted: "It could shape the balance of power in the growing smartphone and tablet computer business. It could also give Apple a tool it can use to more aggressively protect its innovations from a fleet of rivals flooding the market with competing services." See Nick Wingfield, "Jury Gives Apple Decisive Victory in a Patents Case," *New York Times*, Aug. 25, 2012, A1.

26. Some argue Craigslist has been able to maintain its monopoly because it uses the threat of breaches of patent law to prevent any new competition, despite providing what many regard as a substandard service. See Nick Bilton, "Innovations Snuffed Out by Craigslist," *New York Times*, July 30, 2012, B1, B6. Jodie Griffin of Public Knowledge argues that the government-approved deal carving up the ISP market by the phone and cable giants discussed in chapter 4 will make it possible for them to pool patents and have a "monopoly over foundational technologies for the next generation of internet access services." See Jodie Griffin, "Verizon, Comcast, and the Patent Wars," Public Knowledge, July 27, 2012, publicknowledge.org/blog/verizon-comcast-and-patent-wars.

27. Porter, "Tech Suits Endanger Innovation." As Porter points out, there is now an entire industry of "patent trolls," whose only business is to buy patents and sue for royalties. See also Vance, "Hiring a Mercenary."

28. Tim Wu, *The Master Switch: The Rise and Fall of Information Empires* (New York: Knopf, 2010), 290–91.

29. Peter Decherney, *Hollywood's Copyright Wars: From Edison to the Internet* (New York: Columbia University Press, 2012), 215.

30. Wu, *Master Switch*, 292.

31. John Naughton, *What You Really Need to Know About the Internet: From Gutenberg to Zuckerberg* (London: Quercus, 2012), 279, 285.

32. Discussion of this, with Johnson's quote, is in Decherney, *Hollywood's Copyright Wars*, 220.

33. Charles Arthur, "Walled Gardens Look Rosy for Facebook, Apple—and Would-Be Censors," *The Guardian*, Apr. 17, 2012.

34. Ian Katz, "Web Freedom Faces Greatest Threat Ever, Warns Google's Sergey Brin," *The Guardian*, Apr. 15, 2012.

35. Peter Lunenfeld, *The Secret War Between Downloading and Uploading* (Cambridge, MA: MIT Press, 2011), 177.

36. Cisco caused a stir in 2012 when it reconfigured its large cloud service so the service agreement allowed Cisco the formal right to spy on its customers' Internet use and sell the findings. Cisco backed down from elements of the plan when the changes were publicized, but reserved the right to implement the policy in the future. See Cory Doctorow, "Cisco Locks Customers Out of Their Own Routers, Only Lets Them Back In if They Agree to Being Spied Upon and Monetized,"

Boing Boing, July 3, 2012, boingboing.net/2012/07/03/cisco-locks-customers-out-of-t.html.

37. Matthew Hindman, *The Myth of Digital Democracy* (Princeton, NJ: Princeton University Press, 2009), 84–86. Hindman does a superb job of demonstrating the immense capital expenses Google incurs to assure its dominance, which all but guarantee that no other firm can or will challenge it in the search-engine market.

38. Siva Vaidhyanathan, *The Googlization of Everything (and Why We Should Worry)* (Berkeley: University of California Press, 2011), 54.

39. Naughton, *What You Really Need to Know About the Internet*, 201–2. These enormous data centers also have significant negative effects on the environment. See James Glanz, "Power, Pollution and the Internet," *New York Times*, Sept. 23, 2012, 1, 20.

40. Peter F. Cowhey and Jonathan D. Aronson, *Transforming Global Information and Communication Markets* (Cambridge, MA: MIT Press, 2009), 44.

41. David Streitfeld and Edward Wyatt, "U.S. Is Escalating Inquiry Studying Google's Power," *New York Times*, Apr. 27, 2012, A16.

42. Steve Wasserman, "The Amazon Effect," *The Nation*, May 29, 2012. The investigative report by Spencer Soper, "Inside Amazon's Warehouse," appeared in the local newspaper, the *Morning Call*, on September 18, 2011.

43. Courteney Palis, "What Apple Looks Like in Numbers," *Huffington Post*, May 9, 2012, huffingtonpost.com/2012/05/09/what-apple-looks-like-in-_n_1503017.html.; and Todd Bishop, "Charts: Apple Has More Cash Than Google and Microsoft Combined," *GeekWire*, Feb. 23, 2012, geekwire.com/2012/charts-putting-apples-growing-cash-pile-perspective.

44. Jenna Wortham, "At Facebook, Its Targets May Hint at Its Future," *New York Times*, May 14, 2012, B1, B2.

45. Jenna Wortham, "Facebook to Buy Mobile Start-up for $1 Billion," *New York Times*, Apr. 10, 2012, A1.

46. Yahoo!'s annual sales fell from $7.2 billion in 2008 to $5 billion in 2011, while all the other empires saw massive revenue growth. "Yahoo! Inc.," *Standard & Poor's Stock Report*, Apr. 14, 2012. See also, Nicole Perlroth, "Revamping at Yahoo to Focus on Its Media Properties and Customer Data," *New York Times*, Apr. 11, 2012, B4; and Michael J. de la Merced, "New Cast Atop Yahoo Faces Stubborn Problems," *New York Times*, May 15, 2012, B3.

47. Evelyn Rusli and Nick Bilton, "Apple Officials Said to Consider Stake in Twitter," *New York Times*, July 28, 2012, A1, B6.

48. So it was that Microsoft sold a number of important patents to Facebook for $550 million to help Facebook compete with their mutual foe, Google. See Nick Wingfield, "$550 million Patent Pact for Facebook and Microsoft," *New York Times*, Apr. 24, 2012, B1.

49. Wasserman and Quinn, "Tech Firms Behaving Badly."

50. When Facebook completed its IPO, the *New York Times* published an article outlining Facebook's rivalries with many of the other giants, including Google, Apple, Twitter, and the cartel. See Brian X. Chen, "As Facebook Moves On from Its I.P.O., the Challengers Draw Battle Lines," *New York Times*, May 21, 2012, B8.

51. For a comprehensive and astounding review of Google's empire and the markets it now dominates, see Vaidhyanathan, *Googlization of Everything*.

52. Steven Johnson, "Can Anything Take Down the Facebook Juggernaut?" *Wired*, June 2012.

53. "Making It Click," *The Economist*, Feb. 25, 2012, 75.

54. "Amazon.com Inc.," *Standard & Poor's Stock Report*, Apr. 14, 2012.

55. See Steve Pearlstein, "Pick Your Monopoly: Apple or Amazon," *Washington Post*, Mar. 10, 2012; David Welch, "Why Wal-Mart Is Worried About Amazon," *Bloomberg Businessweek*, April 2–8, 2012, 25–26; "The Walmart of the Web," *The Economist*, Oct. 1, 2011, 65–66; and David Carr, "For E-Book, Navigating a Tightrope by Amazon," *New York Times*, Apr. 30, 2012, B1, B3.

56. Stephanie Clifford, "Amazon Is Taking a Leap into the High End of the Fashion Pool," *New York Times*, May 8, 2012, A1, A3.

57. Interview quoted in Lynn, "Killing the Competition," 33.

58. Joseph E. Stiglitz, *The Price of Inequality: How Today's Divided Society Endangers Our Future* (New York: W.W. Norton, 2012), pp. 45–46.

59. Bill Keller, "Wising Up to Facebook," *New York Times*, June 11, 2012, A19.

60. "Internet Weekly," *Deutsche Bank Markets Research*, Apr. 2, 2012, 4.

61. "A Fistful of Dollars," *The Economist*, Feb. 4, 2012, 11. According to annual filings data compiled by Compustat, between 2000 and 2011, the net value of acquisitions by Amazon, Apple, AT&T, Comcast, eBay, Google, IBM, Intel, Microsoft, and Yahoo! came to over $121 billion. Other respected sources place the total value of acquisitions closer to $200 billion over the same time. Any way one slices it, this sector has been the overwhelming leader in acquisitions in the American economy since 2000, accounting for around 20 percent of all deals and nearly doubling the deal making of the entire financial sector ($66 billion). Compustat North America, Fundamentals Annual, Wharton Research Data Services, University of Pennsylvania (retrieved June 4, 2012).

62. Jenna Wortham and Nicole Perlroth, "When to Believe the Buzz," *New York Times*, May 7, 2012, B1, B2.

63. Nick Wingfield, "Battle Nears for Office Apps," *New York Times*, June 11, 2012, B7; Brian X. Chen and Nick Wingfield, "Apple Updates Laptops and Mobile Software," *New York Times*, June 12, 2012, B3; and Nick Wingfield, "Microsoft Is Expected to Introduce a Tablet," *New York Times*, June 16, 2012, pp. B1, B3.

64. "Joyn Them or Join Them, *The Economist*, Aug. 11, 2012, 60.

65. Matt Wood e-mail to author, Aug. 22, 2012.

66. Susan P. Crawford, "Is Google a Monopoly? Wrong Question," Bloomberg View, July 8, 2012, bloomberg.com/news/2012-07-08/is-google-a-monopoly-wrong-question.htm l; Stacey Higginbotham, "The Economics of Google Fiber and What It Means for U.S. Broadband," GigaOM, July 26, 2012, gigaom.com/2012/07/26/the-economics-of-google-fiber-and-what-it-means-for-u-s-broadband; Marcus Wohlsen, "Google Attacks Cable and Telcos with New TV Service," Wired Business, July 26, 2012, wired.com/business/2012/07/cable-companies-shouldnt-fear-googles-networkyet.

67. Burrows, "Google's Bid to Be Everything to Everyone," 37–38.

68. David Streitfeld, "Seeking the Captive Consumer," *New York Times*, Feb. 13, 2012, B1. The business press in 2012 was teeming with articles on how all the Internet giants are plotting to move into nearly every major area of digital activity. See, for example, Claire Cain Miller, "Back to the Drawing Board for Nexus Q," *New York Times*, Aug. 9, 2012, B1, B2; "Social Whirl," *The Economist*, June 23, 2012, 65–66; Ashlee Vance, "Dear PC Makers: It's Our Turn, Now," *Bloomberg Businessweek*, June 25–July 1, 2012, 38–41; Nick Wingfield and Nick Bilton, "The Race in Tablets Heats Up," *New York Times*, July 16, 2012, B1, B6.

69. Burrows, "Google's Bid to Be Everything to Everyone," 37.

70. Streitfeld, "Seeking the Captive Consumer," B7.

71. Anderson, "The Web Is Dead," 127; and Varian, Farrell, and Shapiro, *Economics of Information Technology*, 14.

72. Streitfeld, "Seeking the Captive Consumer," B7.

73. Ruben Rodrigues, "Privacy on Social Networks: Norms, Markets, and Natural Monopoly," in Saul Levmore and Martha C. Nussbaum, eds., *The Offensive Internet* (Cambridge, MA: Harvard University Press, 2010), chap. 13.

74. Schumpeter, *Capitalism, Socialism and Democracy* (New York: Harper and Row, 1942), 90; and Paul A. Baran and Paul M. Sweezy, *Monopoly Capital* (New York: Monthly Review Press, 1966), 73–74.

75. Anderson, "The Web Is Dead," 126.

76. See David Brooks, "The Creative Moment," *New York Times*, Apr. 23, 2012.

77. Lori Andrews, *I Know Who You Are and I Saw What You Did: Social Networks and the Death of Privacy* (New York: The Free Press, 2011), 9.

78. Liam Murphy and Thomas Nagel, *The Myth of Ownership: Taxes and Justice* (Oxford, UK: Oxford University Press, 2002), cited in McQuaig and Brooks, *Billionaires' Ball*, 34.

79. When the Justice Department investigated Comcast for anticompetitive practices toward nascent online video competitors in 2012, a media analyst for Sanford C. Bernstein & Company said it was "reasonable to assume that Netflix is a principal mover" of the investigation. See Brian Stelter and Edward Wyatt, "Cable TV's Data Curbs Get Scrutiny," *New York Times*, June 14, 2012, B1.

80. David Streitfeld and Edward Wyatt, "U.S. Is Escalating Inquiry Studying Google's Power," *New York Times*, Apr. 27, 2012, A1. See also: Wasserman and Quinn, "Tech Firms Behaving Badly."

81. Gar Alperovitz quotes the work of University of Chicago prewar economist Henry C. Simons, a mentor of Milton Friedman. Simons argued that "few of our gigantic corporations can be defended on the ground that their present size is necessary to reasonably full exploitation of production economies." Simons was skeptical of the ability of the government to regulate giant firms, given that the regulatory process would invariably be "captured" by the firm. This was also the position of later Chicago economists such as Friedman and George Stigler. To Simons, the evidence led in one direction: "Every industry should be effectively competitive or socialized." That meant the state should actually take over, own, and manage directly "industries in which it is effectively impossible to maintain effectively competitive conditions." See Gar Alperovitz, "Wall Street Is Too Big to Regulate," *New York Times*, July 23, 2012, A19.

82. André Schiffrin, *Words and Money* (London: Verso, 2011).

83. Evgeny Morozov, *The Net Delusion: The Dark Side of Internet Freedom*, paperback edition (New York: PublicAffairs, 2011), 323.

84. For recent examples of how regulators condone what in economic theory would be regarded as highly concentrated markets, see James Kanter, "Microsoft Faces a New Antitrust Action and Fines in Europe," *New York Times*, July 18, 2012, B3; Jeff John Roberts, "Justice Department Slams Apple, Refuses to Modify E-book Settlement," paidContent, July 23, 2012, paidcontent.org/2012/07/23/justice-department-slams-apple-refuses-to-modify-e-book-settlement.

85. "Over to You, and Hurry," *The Economist*, May 26, 2012, 65–66. See also Charles Arthur, "Google Faces Mobile Services Pressure in Antitrust Case," *The Guardian*, July 20, 2012.

86. James Kanter and David Streitfeld, "Europe Weighs Antitrust Case Against Google," *New York Times*, May 22, 2012, A1, A3.

87. Wasserman and Quinn, "Tech Firms Behaving Badly."

88. For an excellent general discussion of the issue, see Des Freedman, "Outsourcing Internet Regulation," in James Curran, Natalie Fenton, and Des Freedman, *Misunderstanding the Internet* (London: Routledge, 2012), 95–120.

89. Michael del Castillo, "Google Spends Big in Washington," Portfolio.com, Apr. 24, 2012, portfolio.com/companies-executives/2012/04/24/google-lobbying-expenses-surpass-major-competitors.

90. MacKinnon, *Consent of the Networked*, 7.

91. David Saleh Rauf, "Tech Group Executives Making Big Money," *Politico*, July 9, 2012, politico.com/news/stories/0712/78306.html.

92. Andrews, *I Know Who You Are*, 1.

93. MacKinnon, *Consent of the Networked*, 165.

94. Because to do justice to the matter would require more space than I can justify in this chapter, I leave aside the issue of the Internet sales tax moratorium, whereby e-commerce businesses do not pay state sales taxes on deals with out-of-state customers. It costs state governments, conservatively, $12 billion annually in lost revenues. See Declan McCullagh, "Politicians, Retailers Push for New Internet Sales Taxes," CNET, Apr. 17, 2012; and Deborah Swann, "Weekly Round-up: Another State Strikes a Deal with Amazon," BNA.com, June 1, 2012.

95. Nicholas Shaxson, *Treasure Islands: Uncovering the Damage of Offshore Banking and Tax Havens* (New York: Palgrave Macmillan, 2011), 14–15.

96. See Charles Duhigg and David Kocieniewski, "How Apple Sidesteps Billions in Taxes," *New York Times*, Apr. 29, 2012, A1, A20, A21.

97. Ibid.

98. Meinrath, Losey, and Pickard, "Digital Feudalism," 426.

99. Robert W. McChesney, *Rich Media, Poor Democracy: Communication Politics in Dubious Times* (New York: The New Press, 2000), 237.

100. Inger L. Stole, *Advertising on Trial: Consumer Activism and Corporate Public Relations in the 1930s* (Urbana: University of Illinois Press, 2006), and *Advertising at War: Business, Consumers, and Government in the 1940s* (Urbana: University of Illinois Press, 2012).

101. James Rorty, *Our Master's Voice: Advertising* (New York: John Day, 1934). See also James Rorty, *Order on the Air!* (New York: John Day, 1934).

102. Joseph Turow, *The Daily You: How the New Advertising Industry Is Defining Your Identity and Your Worth* (New Haven, CT: Yale University Press, 2011), 40–41. For a superior discussion of the entire debate over commercializing the Internet in the 1990s, see Dan Schiller, *Digital Capitalism: Networking the Global Market System* (Cambridge, MA: MIT Press, 1999).

103. Turow, *Daily You*, 49.

104. Ibid., 57–63.

105. See Lauar J. Gurak, *Cyberliteracy: Navigating the Internet with Awareness* (New Haven, CT: Yale University Press, 2001); and Reg Whitaker, *The End of Privacy: How Total Surveillance Is Becoming a Reality* (New York: The New Press, 1999).

106. Turow, *Daily You*, 57–63.

107. Alexis Madrigal, "I'm Being Followed: How Google—and 104 Other Companies—Are Tracking Me on the Web," *The Atlantic*, Feb. 2012.

108. Pariser, *Filter Bubble*, 6.

109. "US Internet Advertising to Surpass Print in 2012," eMarketer.com, Jan. 19, 2012, www.emarketer.com/PressRelease.aspx?R=1008788.

110. Olga Kharif, "Taking the Pulse of Neighborhood News," *Bloomberg Businessweek*, Mar. 12–18, 2012, 39. Bank of America Merrill Lynch predicts the mobile advertising market will surge to $18.3 billion in 2015. See Sarah Frier, "Big Brands Move to Little Screens," *Bloomberg Businessweek*, July 9–15, 2012, 33.

111. Brian Wieser, "Internet Advertising: Content Passes the Crown," *Pivotal Research Group Report*, Feb. 24, 2012, 1.

112. "Mad Men Are Watching You," *The Economist*, May 17, 2011, 67; and Lori Andrews, "Facebook Is Using You," *New York Times*, Feb. 5, 2012, Week in Review section, 7.

113. The line is from Andrew Lewis, cited in Pariser, *Filter Bubble*, 21.

114. Somini Sengupta, "Trust: Ill-Advised in a Digital Age," *New York Times*, Aug. 12, 2012, 5.

115. Somini Sengupta and Evelyn M. Rusli, "Personal Data's Value? Facebook Set to Find Out," *New York Times*, Feb. 1, 2012, A1.

116. Somini Sengupta, "Facebook Test: How to Please the New Faces," *New York Times*, May 15, 2012, B2; and Stephen Marche, "Is Facebook Making Us Lonely?" *The Atlantic*, May 2012, 62, 69.

117. Peter Eavis and Evelyn M. Rusli, "Investors Get the Chance to Assess Facebook's Potential," *New York Times*, Feb. 2, 2012, B1.

118. Stephanie Clifford, "Social Media as a Guide for Marketers," *New York Times*, July 31, 2012, A1.

119. Andrews, *I Know Who You Are*, 5.

120. Turow, *Daily You*, 75.

121. Ibid., 1.

122. Aleks Krotoski, "Big Data Age Puts Privacy in Question as Information Becomes Currency," *The Guardian*, Apr. 22, 2012.

123. Joshua Brustein, "Start-ups Aim to Help Us Put a Price on Their Personal Data," *New York Times*, Feb. 13, 2012, B3.

124. Turow, *Daily You*, 2.

125. The leading database marketing firm is Acxiom, with 23,000 computer servers collecting data on 500 million consumers worldwide. Acxiom has 1,500 data points per person. It sells its data to corporate clients. Acxiom combines extensive offline data with online data. See Natasha Singer, "A Data Giant Is Mapping, and Sharing, the Consumer Genome," *New York Times*, Sunday Business Section, June 17, 2012, 1, 8. How comprehensive is their data set? In *The Filter Bubble*, 42–43, Pariser writes about how the Bush White House discovered that Acxiom had more data on eleven of the nineteen 9-11 hijackers than the entire U.S. government did.

126. Pariser, *Filter Bubble*, 7. See also Noam Cohen, "It's Tracking Your Every Move and You May Not Even Know It," *New York Times*, Mar. 26, 2011, A1, A3.

127. Peter Maass and Megha Rajagopalan, "That's No Phone, That's My Tracker," *New York Times*, July 13, 2012.

128. Scott Thurm and Yukari Iwatani Kane, "Your Apps Are Watching You," *Wall Street Journal*, Dec. 17, 2010.

129. Emily Steel and Julie Angwin, "The Web's Cutting Edge: Anonymity in Name Only," *Wall Street Journal*, Aug. 3, 2010.

130. Cited in Heather Brooke, *The Revolution Will Be Digitised: Dispatches from the Information War* (London: Heinemann, 2011), 133.

131. Madrigal, "I'm Being Followed."

132. Ryan Gallagher, "Skype Won't Say Whether It Can Eavesdrop on Your

Conversations," *Slate*, July 20, 2012, slate.com/blogs/future_tense/2012/07/20/skype_won_t_comment_on_whether_it_can_now_eavesdrop_on_conversations_.html.

133. Quoted in Pariser, *Filter Bubble*, 147.

134. Sengupta, "Trust." For elaboration, see Bruce Schneier, *Liars and Outliers: Enabling the Trust That Society Needs to Thrive* (Indianapolis: John Wiley & Sons, 2012).

135. David Rosen, "America's Spy State: How the Telecoms Sell Out Your Privacy," AlterNet, May 29, 2012.

136. Quotation of Alexander Howard in Krotoski, "Big Data Age Puts Privacy in Question."

137. Jaron Lanier, *You Are Not a Gadget: A Manifesto* (New York: Knopf, 2010), 55.

138. Bill Keller, "Wising Up to Facebook," *New York Times*, June 11, 2012, A19.

139. Turow, *Daily You*, 171.

140. Lori Andrews, "Facebook Is Using You," *New York Times*, Feb. 5, 2012, Week in Review section, 7.

141. Jason Ankeny, "Survey: Mobile App Privacy Fears Continue to Escalate," FierceMobileContent, July 16, 2012, fiercemobilecontent.com/story/survey-mobile-app-privacy-fears-continue-escalate/2012-07-16. The survey was conducted by Harris Interactive for TRUSTe, a privacy management firm.

142. Turow, *Daily You*, 184–89.

143. Quotation by Paul Ohm, cited in Kate Murphy, "How to Muddy Your Tracks on the Internet," *New York Times*, May 3, 2012, B9.

144. It is interesting how public opinion works in American governance. When there are such dramatic majorities in favor of something that benefits powerful interests, leaders shout from the mountaintops about the necessity of respecting the will of the people in their infinite wisdom. When there is a conflict between public opinion and the needs of very powerful interests, the mountaintops are vacant, and barely a peep can be heard. For a discussion of this point, see W. Lance Bennett, "Toward a Theory of Press-State Relations in the U.S.," *Journal of Communication* 40 (Spring 1990): 103–25; W. Lance Bennett, "Marginalizing the Majority: Conditioning Public Opinion to Accept Managerial Democracy," in Michael Margolis and Gary Mauser, eds., *Manipulating Public Opinion: Essays on Public Opinion as a Dependent Variable* (Pacific Grove, CA: Brooks/Cole, 1989).

145. Turow, *Daily You*, 185–87.

146. Kevin J. O'Brien, "Facebook, Eye on Privacy Laws, Offers More Disclosure to Users," *New York Times*, Apr. 13, 2002, B4.

147. James Ball, "Me and My Data: How Much Do the Internet Giants Really Know?" *The Guardian*, Apr. 22, 2012.

148. Tanzina Vega, "Opt-Out Provision Would Halt Some, But Not All, Web Tracking," *New York Times*, Feb. 27, 2012, B1.

149. Cited in Richard Adler, *Updating Rules of the Digital Road: Privacy, Security, Intellectual Property* (Washington, DC: Aspen Institute, 2012), 10.

150. Murphy, "How to Muddy Your Tracks."

151. The one area that would be most likely to motivate Americans into action is online data collection and advertising to children. Perhaps the one great legislative victory in the public interest was 1998's Children's Online Privacy Protection Act (COPPA). The law, which is enforced by the FTC, makes it illegal for companies to collect personally identifiable information from children under age thirteen without

parental consent. Facebook does not permit under-thirteens to enroll, but kids can lie about their age, and by most counts nearly 6 million preteen Americans have done just that. Facebook was working in 2012 to establish a formal program for preteens with stricter privacy rules to quash this public relations nightmare. At the same time, Facebook has definite incentive to "get young kids hooked early." See "Let the Nippers Network," *The Economist*, June 9, 2012, 18; and "Kid Gloves," *The Economist*, June 9, 2012, 70. For a nice discussion of COPPA, see James P. Steyer, *Talking Back to Facebook* (New York: Scribner, 2012), chap. 1. Reports of websites violating COPPA and collecting data on children continue to proliferate. See Natasha Singer, "Web Sites Accused of Collecting Data on Children," *New York Times*, Aug. 22, 2012, B1, B7. In August 2012 the FTC announced plans to tighten its rules on websites' data collection on children. See Edward Wyatt, "F.T.C. Seeks Tighter Rules on Web Sites for Children," *New York Times*, Aug. 2, 2012, B3; Carl Franzen, "FTC Seeks More Nuanced Rules for Child Data Collection Online," TPM Idea Lab, Aug. 2, 2012, idealab.talkingpointsmemo.com/2012/08/ftc-child-data-collection-online-web.php.

152. Federal Trade Commission, *Protecting Consumer Privacy in an Era of Rapid Change: Recommendations for Businesses and Policymakers* (Washington, DC: FTC, Mar. 2012), ftc.gov/os2012/03/120326privacyreport.pdf.

153. "Sorry, Friends," *The Economist*, Dec. 3, 2011, 79.

154. Claire Cain Miller, "Google, Accused of Skirting Privacy Provision, Is to Pay $22.5 Million to Settle Charges," *New York Times*, Aug. 10, 2012, B2; Ryan Singel, "FTC's $22M Privacy Settlement with Google Is Just Puppet Waving," Wired Threat Level, July 10, 2012, wired.com/threatlevel/2012/07/ftc-google-fine.

155. Will Oremus, "For Violating Users' Privacy, Google Pays FTC Fine of Approximately 0 percent of Revenues," *Slate*, Aug. 9, 2012, slate.com/blogs/future_tense/2012/08/09/google_ftc_privacy_settlement_22_5_million_fine_or_about_0_percent_of_ revenues.html. Oremus notes that the fine would be the equivalent to a $25 fine for a person with an annual income of $50,000, or less than a parking ticket.

156. Karen Weise, "Who Does Google Think You Are?" *Bloomberg Businessweek*, Feb. 6–12, 2012, 39; Tony Romm, "Google Privacy Changes: Tech Giant Bucks Scrutiny," *Politico*, Mar. 1, 2012, www.politico.com/news/stories/0312/73495.html; and Eric Pfanner, "France Says Google Plan Violates Law," *New York Times*, Feb. 29, 2012, B9.

157. Brad Stone, "Idiot Proof," *Bloomberg Businessweek*, Mar. 5–11, 2012, 64–65.

158. Brian Wieser, "Internet Advertising: Content Passes the Crown," *Pivotal Research Group Report*, Feb. 24, 2012, 1.

159. "Mad Men Are Watching You."

160. Edward Wyatt, "White House, Consumers in Mind, Offers Online Privacy Guide," *New York Times*, Feb. 23, 2012, B1.

161. Federal Trade Commission, *Protecting Consumer Privacy*, 72.

162. Quentin Hardy, "Big Data Era and Privacy," *New York Times*, June 11, 2012, B7.

163. "Change of Track," *The Economist*, June 9, 2012, 70.

164. Madrigal, "I'm Being Followed."

165. Wyatt, "White House . . . Offers Online Privacy Guide."

166. "Attack of the Covert Commercials," *The Economist*, July 7, 2012, 60.

167. Mark Milian, "Technology," *Bloomberg Businessweek*, July 2–8, 2012, 29.

168. Pariser, *Filter Bubble*, chap. 8; and Jarvis, *Public Parts*, 210–17.

169. Jarvis, *Public Parts*, 5, 120.

170. Madrigal, "I'm Being Followed."

171. Turow, *Daily You*, 113.

172. For a classic treatise on this matter by a longtime executive at the Newspaper Advertising Bureau, see Leo Bogart, *Commercial Culture: The Media System and the Public Interest* (New York: Oxford University Press, 1995).

173. Stuart Elliott, "This Time the Co-Brand Makes It into the Title," *New York Times*, Feb. 29, 2012, B3.

174. Turow, *Daily You*, 111.

175. Andrew Adam Newman, "Boundaries Expand When Marketing Links Drama of TV and the Web," *New York Times*, May 24, 2012, B3.

176. Elliott, "This Time the Co-Brand Makes It into the Title."

177. Turow, *Daily You*, 8.

178. Ibid., 112.

179. Wieser, "Internet Advertising," 1.

180. "Mad Men Are Watching You."

181. Madrigal, "I'm Being Followed."

182. Turow, *Daily You*, 69, 118–22.

183. Madrigal, "I'm Being Followed."

184. Pariser, *Filter Bubble*, 49.

185. Alan D. Mutter, "Retailers Are Routing Around the Media," *Reflections of a Newsosaur*, Mar. 13, 2012, newsosaur.blogspot.com/2012/03/retailers-are-routing-around-media.html.

186. "Mad Men Are Watching You."

187. Turow, *Daily You*, 159.

188. Pariser, *Filter Bubble*, 120–21.

189. "The All-Telling Eye," *The Economist*, Oct. 22, 2011, 100–101.

190. Pariser, *Filter Bubble*, 120–21.

191. Alan D. Mutter, "Newspaper Digital Ad Share Hits All-Time Low," *Reflections of a Newsosaur*, Apr. 23, 2012, newsosaur.blogspot.com/2012/04/newspaper-digital-ad-share-hits-all.html.

192. For the way BuzzFeed is working with the corporate sector on this matter, see Felix Gillette, "I Can Haz Click Crack," *Bloomberg Businessweek*, Mar. 26–Apr. 1, 2012, 72–75.

193. Turow, *Daily You*, 94. Facebook got bad publicity for this advertising technique: Sending ads to a Facebook user's friends with the Facebook user's endorsement of the product in the ad. Buried in its four-thousand-word terms-of-service agreement, Facebook has the right to take its customers' favorable comments about products and use them in ads for that product aimed at other Facebook users. The practice gained publicity when a Facebook user made a joking comment about a fifty-five-gallon barrel of personal lubricant, only to find himself promoting the product to all his Facebook friends. See Somini Sengupta, "So Much for Sharing His 'Like,' " *New York Times*, June 1, 2012, A1, B4.

194. Alan D. Mutter, "Publishers Need to Focus on Facebook," *Reflections of a Newsosaur*, newsosaur.blogspot.com, Nov. 8, 2011.

195. ComScore, "Changing How the World Sees Digital Advertising," vCE Charter Report, Mar. 2012.

196. Pariser, *Filter Bubble*, 204.

197. Turow, *Daily You*, 158.

198. Lanier, *You Are Not a Gadget*, 14.

199. Pariser, *Filter Bubble*, 215.

200. Turow, *Daily You*, 17.

201. Bliven quote cited in "Gleanings from Varied Sources," *Education by Radio*, Apr. 18, 1935, 20.

202. For a superb treatment of this subject, see Andrew J. Bacevich, *Washington Rules: America's Path to Permanent War* (New York: Metropolitan Books, 2010).

203. John Bellamy Foster, Hannah Holleman, and Robert W. McChesney, "The U.S. Imperial Triangle and Military Spending." *Monthly Review*, Oct. 2008, 1–19.

204. Rachel Maddow, *Drift: The Unmooring of American Military Power* (New York: Crown, 2012), 247.

205. See, for example, R. Jeffrey Smith, "Public Overwhelmingly Supports Large Defense Spending Cuts," Center for Public Integrity, May 10, 2012, publicintegrity .org/2012/05/10/8856/public-overwhelmingly-supports-large-defense-spending-cuts. This article has a link to the actual questionnaire that was used in the survey.

206. See Tom Engelhardt, *The United States of Fear* (Chicago: Haymarket Books, 2011).

207. Maddow, *Drift*, 7.

208. Tom Engelhardt, "That Makes No Sense! Your Security's a Joke (And You're the Butt of It)," TomDispatch.com, July 19, 2012, www.tomdispatch.com/ archive/175570.

209. Fareed Zakaria, "Fareed's Take: U.S. Has Made War on Terror a War Without End," CNN.com, May 6, 2012, globalpublicsquare.blogs.cnn.com/2012/05/06/ national-security-state.

210. The best treatment is Dana Priest and William M. Arkin, *Top Secret America: The Rise of the New American Security State* (New York: Little, Brown, 2011).

211. Maddow, *Drift*, 6–7.

212. Naughton, *What You Really Need to Know About the Internet*, 261.

213. Nick Hopkins, "Militarisation of Cyberspace: How the Global Power Struggle Moved Online," *The Guardian*, Apr. 16, 2012.

214. James Bamford, "The Black Box," *Wired*, Apr. 2012, 80–81.

215. Bill Quigley, "Thirteen Ways the Government Tracks Us," Common Dreams, Apr. 10, 2012, commondreams.org/view/2012/04/09-14.

216. Susan Landau, *Surveillance or Security? The Risks Posed by New Wiretapping Technologies* (Cambridge, MA: MIT Press, 2010), xii.

217. Naughton, *What You Really Need to Know About the Internet*, 288.

218. Zakaria, "Fareed's Take: U.S. Has Made War on Terror a War Without End."

219. David Rosen, "America's Spy State: How the Telecoms Sell Out Your Privacy," AlterNet, May 29, 2012, alternet.org/story/155628/america's_spy_state%3A _how_the_telecoms_sell_out_your_privacy.

220. Brooke, *Revolution Will Be Digitised*, 151.

221. Nick Hopkins, "Militarisation of Cyberspace."

222. Morozov, *Net Delusion*, 324.

223. MacKinnon, *Consent of the Networked*, 50. It is MacKinnon's emphasis in the quoted passage.

224. Rory Carroll, "Google Illicit Networks Summit Calls for Unity Between Activists and Technology," *The Guardian*, July 18, 2012.

225. Glenn Greenwald, *With Liberty and Justice for Some: How the Law Is Used to Destroy Equality and Protect the Powerful* (New York: Metropolitan Books, 2011), 75–76. All of chapter 2 is devoted to this scandal, and it is by far the most thorough treatment in print.

226. The extent of the lawlessness is underlined when one realizes that getting approval for surveillance under the FISA is not at all difficult. There is a secret FISA court that handles all applications from security and law enforcement agencies; it rejected a "grand total of 11 applications" out of more than 30,000 between 1979 and 2011. "Little Peepers Everywhere," *The Economist*, July 21, 2012, 24.

227. Ibid., 79.

228. Dana Priest and William M. Arkin, "A Hidden World, Growing Beyond Control," *Washington Post*, July 19, 2010.

229. Pariser, *Filter Bubble*, 145.

230. Brooke, *Revolution Will Be Digitised*, 223.

231. I base this upon a confidential interview I had with a State Department official who was closely involved with the WikiLeaks affair as it unfolded.

232. MacKinnon, *Consent of the Networked*, 85–86.

233. Eric Lichtblau, "Wireless Carriers Who Aid Police Are Asked for Data," *New York Times*, May 3, 2012, A22; and Josh Smith, "ACLU: Most Police Departments Track Cell Phones Without Warrants," *National Journal*, Apr. 10, 2012.

234. Charlie Savage, "Hearing Held on Program Monitoring Social Media," *New York Times*, Feb. 23, 2012, A17.

235. Andrews, "Facebook Is Using You."

236. Eric Lichtblau, "Cell Carriers Called on More in Surveillance," *New York Times*, July 9, 2012, A1.

237. Jasmin Melvin, "Cell Phone Companies See Spike in Surveillance Requests," Reuters, July 10, 2012.

238. "The End of Privacy?" *New York Times*, July 14, 2012. In September 2012 the ACLU released documents it got from the Justice Department after months of litigation demonstrating that warrantless electronic surveillance of Americans had spiked between 2009 and 2011 to levels far greater than in the past without "sufficient oversight, or meaningful accountability." See American Civil Liberties Union, "New Justice Department Documents Show Huge Increase in Warrantless Electronic Surveillance," Sept. 27, 2012, aclu.org/blog/national-security-technology-and-liberty/new-justice-department-documents-show-huge-increase.

239. Rosen, "America's Spy State."

240. Katz, "Web Freedom Faces Greatest Threat Ever."

241. "Little Peepers Everywhere."

242. Jennifer Valentino-Devries, "Covert FBI Power to Obtain Phone Data Faces Rare Test," *Wall Street Journal*, July 18, 2012, A1.

243. Declan McCullagh, "How CISPA Would Affect You (FAQ)," CNET, Apr. 27, 2012, news.cnet.com/8301-31921_3-57422693-281/how-cispa-would-affect-you-faq.

244. Sascha Meinrath e-mail to author, May 7, 2012.

245. Barack Obama, "Taking the Cyberattack Threat Seriously," *Wall Street Journal*, July 19, 2012.

246. Carl Franzen, "Cybersecurity Bill Backed by Obama Won't Protect U.S., Experts Agree," TPM Idea Lab, July 21, 2012, idealab.talkingpointsmemo.com/2012/07/president-obamas-warning-on-cyber-attacks-divides-experts.php; Ed O'Keefe, "Cybersecurity Bill Fails in Senate," *Washington Post* online, Aug. 2, 2012, washingtonpost.com/blogs/2chambers/post/cybersecurity-bill-fails-in-the-senate/2012/08/02/gJQABofxRX_blog.html.

247. Sascha Meinrath e-mail to author, Aug. 22, 2012.

248. Sascha Meinrath e-mail to author, May 7, 2012.

249. Ari Melber, "Obama Sides with Civil Libertarians on Cyberwar

Policy," TheNation.com, May 3, 2012, thenation.com/blog/167706/obama-sides-civil-libertarians-cyberwar-policy.

250. Tim Karr e-mail to author, May 7, 2012.

251. "Declaration of Internet Freedom," internetdeclaration.org/freedom.

252. Daniel J. Solove, *Nothing to Hide: The False Tradeoff Between Privacy and Security* (New Haven, CT: Yale University Press, 2011), 207.

253. Zakaria, "Fareed's Take: U.S. Has Made War on Terror a War Without End."

254. Cited in John Nichols, ed., *Against the Beast: A Documentary History of American Opposition to Empires* (New York: Nation Books, 2005), 14.

255. Vaidhyanathan, *Googlization of Everything*, 97.

256. Landau, *Surveillance or Security?*, 256.

257. MacKinnon, *Consent of the Networked*, 279.

258. Sanford J. Ungar, "Unnecessary Secrets," *Columbia Journalism Review*, Mar.–Apr. 2011, 35, 37.

259. Michael Hastings, *The Operators: The Wild and Terrifying Inside Story of America's War in Afghanistan* (New York: Blue Rider Press, 2012), 156–57.

260. Christopher Hayes, *Twilight of the Elites: America After Meritocracy* (New York: Crown, 2012), 127.

261. Michael Hastings, "Exclusive: Homeland Security Kept Tabs on Occupy Wall Street," RollingStone.com, Feb. 28, 2012 rollingstone.com/politics/blogs/national-affairs/exclusive-homeland-security-kept-tabs-on-occupy-wall-street-20120228; and Dave Lindorff, "White House & Dems Back Banks over Protests: Newly Discovered Homeland Security Files Show Feds Central to Occupy Crackdown," Nation Of Change, May 15, 2012, nationofchange.org/white-house-dems-back-banks-over-protests-newly-discovered-homeland-security-files-show-feds-central.

262. See Bertram Gross, *Friendly Fascism: The New Face of Power in America* (Boston: South End Press, 1980), for a prescient take on the matter.

6. Journalism Is Dead! Long Live Journalism?

1. Data from the Newspaper Association of America, naa.org/Trends-and-Numbers/Advertising-Expenditures/Annual-All-Categories.aspx.

2. Jeff Sonderman, "The One Chart That Should Scare the Hell out of Print Media," Poynter, May 30, 2012, poynter.org/latest-news/mediawire/175619.

3. For a discussion of this, see Bruce A. Williams and Michael X. Delli Carpini, *After Broadcast News* (New York: Cambridge University Press, 2011), 7–10.

4. Alan D. Mutter, "Publishers Are Flubbing the iPad," *Reflections of a Newsosaur*, Feb. 7, 2012, newsosaur.blogspot.com/2012/02/publishers-are-flubbing-ipad.html.

5. Tom Rosenstiel and Amy Mitchell, "Survey: Mobile News and Paying Online," in *The State of the News Media 2011: An Annual Report on American Journalism* (Washington, DC: Pew Research Center, Project for Excellence in Journalism, 2011).

6. See Alex S. Jones, *Losing the News: The Future of the News That Feeds Democracy* (New York: Oxford University Press, 2009), 4.

7. There has been an extensive debate within the journalism community on these claims. See, for example, Dean Starkman, "Confidence Game: The Limited Vision of the News Gurus," *Columbia Journalism Review*, Nov.–Dec. 2011, cjr.org/essay/confidence_game.php?page=all.

8. Jeff Jarvis, foreword to Elliott King, *Free for All: The Internet's Transformation of Journalism* (Evanston, IL: Northwestern University Press, 2010), x.

9. Clay Shirky, "Newspapers and Thinking the Unthinkable," in Robert W. McChesney and Victor Pickard, eds., *Will the Last Reporter Please Turn Out the Lights: The Collapse of Journalism and What Can Be Done to Fix It* (New York: The New Press, 2011), 38–44.

10. Yochai Benkler. "A New Era of Corruption?" *New Republic*, Mar. 4, 2009, tnr.com/story_print.html?id=c84d2eda-0e95-42fe-99a2-5400e7dd8eab.

11. Clay Shirky, Richard S. Salant Lecture on Freedom of the Press, Joan Shorenstein Center on Press and Politics, John F. Kennedy School of Government, Cambridge, MA, Oct. 14, 2011.

12. Scott Gant, *We're All Journalists Now: The Transformation of the Press and the Reshaping of the Law in the Internet Age* (New York: The Free Press, 2007).

13. Rory O'Connor, *Friends, Followers and the Future: How Social Media Are Changing Politics, Threatening Big Brands, and Killing Traditional Media* (San Francisco: City Lights Books, 2012), 271.

14. Peter H. Diamandis and Steven Kotler, *Abundance: The Future Is Better Than You Think* (New York: The Free Press, 2012), 147.

15. Alan D. Mutter, "Newspaper Job Cuts Surged 30% in 2011," *Reflections of a Newsosaur*, newsosaur.blogspot.com, Dec. 18, 2011, newsosaur.blogspot.com/2011/12/newspaper-job-cuts-surged-30-in-2011.html.

16. The editors, "The Future of News," *New York Observer*, Mar. 21, 2012.

17. Jessica Sieff, "It Could Be Worse—You Could Be a Lumberjack," *Niles* (MI) *Daily Star*, Apr. 18, 2012.

18. Alan D. Mutter, "Philly Papers Sold at 10% of 2006 Value," *Reflections of a Newsosaur*, April 2, 2012, newsosaur.blogspot.com/2012/04/philly-papers-sold-at-10-of-2006-value .html.

19. "The State of the News Media 2006," Project for Excellence in Journalism. This material comes from the introduction to the report, online at stateofthemedia.org/2006/overview.

20. Steve Myers, "What the Future of News Looks Like in Alabama After Advance Cuts Staff by 400," Poynter, June 14, 2012, poynter.org/latest-news/top-stories/177191.

21. "Union and Peoria Take on Wall Street—Can the PSJ be saved?" Peoria Story.typepad.com, Apr. 9, 2012.

22. Jim Romenesko, "Newspaper Executives' 2011 Compensation," Jim Romenesko.com, Apr. 19, 2012, jimromenesko.-com/-2012/-04/-19/-newspaper—executives—2011—compensation/-.

23. Quoted in Michael R. Fancher, "Seattle: A New Media Case Study," in *The State of the News Media 2011: An Annual Report on American Journalism*, Pew Research Center, Project for Excellence in Journalism, 2011, stateofthemedia.org/2011/mobile-survey/seattle-a-new-media-case-study.

24. David Carr, "Fissures Are Growing for Papers," *New York Times*, July 9, 2012, B6.

25. See James O'Shea, *The Deal from Hell: How Moguls and Wall Street Plundered Great American Newspapers* (New York: PublicAffairs, 2011). After chronicling the ongoing drastic cuts in journalism, Eric Alterman put the matter bluntly: "It's a fair question to ask how long we can pretend that profit-minded business executives are going to invest in the money-losing enterprise of investigative reporting, particularly given how many enemies it tends to make when it goes after people in power." See Eric Alterman, "Think Again: Bad News About the News," Center for American Progress, July 26, 2012, americanprogress.org/issues/media/news/2012/07/26/11943/think-again-bad-news-about-the-news.

26. Steven Waldman and the Working Group on Information Needs of Communities, *The Information Needs of Communities: The Changing Media Landscape in a Broadband Age* (Washington, DC: Federal Communications Commission, June 2011), 5.

27. David Carr, "Newspaper as Business Pulpit," *New York Times*, June 11, 2012, B1.

28. David Sirota, "The Only Game in Town," *Harper's Magazine*, September 2012, 49.

29. Comment by Dan Rather on *Real Time with Bill Maher*, HBO network, May 18, 2012. See also Dan Rather, *Rather Outspoken: My Life in News* (New York: Grand Central, 2012), 287–88.

30. All quotations and statistics mentioned are from "The Study of the News Ecosystem of One American City," Pew Research Center, Project for Excellence in Journalism, Jan. 11, 2010, journalism.org/analysis_report/how_news_happens.

31. David Carr, "Newspaper Barons Resurface," *New York Times*, Apr. 9, 2012, B1.

32. Amy Chozick, "Tax Benefit in Asset Sale Lifts Profit at Times Co.," *New York Times*, Apr. 20, 2012, B3.

33. The *Washington Post*, for example, which has fared better than all but a few papers, has reduced its editorial staff by a third and has closed its Los Angeles, New York, and Chicago bureaus. See Jeremy W. Peters, "A Newspaper, and a Legacy, Reordered," *New York Times*, Business section, Feb. 12, 2012, 1, 5.

34. Daniel R. Schwarz, *Endtimes? Crises and Turmoil at the New York Times, 1999–2009* (Albany: State University of New York Press, 2012), inside front cover.

35. Comment by Dan Rather on *Real Time with Bill Maher*. See also Rather, *Rather Outspoken*, 287–88.

36. For chilling detail, see Waldman, *Information Needs of Communities*, 44–45.

37. Dean Starkman argues that this leads to the "hamster wheel" for working reporters, which he describes as "volume without thought. It is news panic, a lack of discipline, an inability to say no. It is copy produced to meet arbitrary productivity metrics." See Dean Starkman, "The Hamster Wheel," *Columbia Journalism Review*, Sept.–Oct. 2010.

38. Brian Stelter, "You Can Change the Channel, but Local News Is the Same," *New York Times*, May 29, 2012, A1, A3.

39. Waldman, *Information Needs of Communities*, 23.

40. Josh Stearns, "Hindsight Journalism," WordPress.com, May 16, 2012.

41. This point is developed by Gavin Sheppard in "How Citizen Journalism Is Setting the Local Agenda," *The Guardian*, Mar. 9, 2012.

42. Christine Haughney, "The Undoing of the Daily," *New York Times*, June 4, 2012, B1, B8.

43. Waldman, *Information Needs of Communities*, 12, 46, 52, 90.

44. "Total and Minority Newsroom Employment Declines in 2011 but Loss Continues to Stabilize," American Society of News Editors, April 4, 2012, asne.org/Article_View/ArticleId/2499.

45. "Study of the News Ecosystem of One American City." As Lance Bennett demonstrates, this is also a fertile environment for conjecture, gossip, and half-baked stories to get into the news. See W. Lance Bennett, "Press-Government Relations in a Changing Media Environment," in Kate Kenski and Kathleen Hall Jamieson, eds., *The Oxford Handbook of Political Communication* (New York: Oxford University Press, forthcoming).

46. Robert W. McChesney and John Nichols, *The Death and Life of American*

Journalism: The Media Revolution That Will Begin the World Again (New York: Nation Books, 2011). See the preface to the paperback edition and appendix 3.

47. This is a fruitful scenario for those who wish to have their press releases published as "news." The head of an environmental organization in Wisconsin told me in 2012 that his group has never had as much success getting what remains of newspapers in his state to carry their unadulterated press releases. His group gets little coverage otherwise. It is even better for those who can afford slick, high-quality press releases with video material for television and websites.

48. David Coates, Rebecca Bredholt, Julie Holley, Kyle Johnson, and Katrina M. Mendolera, *State of the Media Report 2011: Adapting, Surviving, and Reviving* (Beltsville, MD: Vocus Cloud-Based Marketing and PR software, 2011), 2, 3, 8.

49. Lymari Morales, "Americans' Confidence in Television News Drops to New Low," Gallup, July 10, 2012, gallup.com/poll/155585/americans-confidence-television-news-drops-new-low.aspx.

50. *Information Needs of Communities*, 226.

51. For an account of the seeming glory days of professional journalism, see Jones, *Losing the News*.

52. David Simon, the former *Baltimore Sun* journalist who created television's *The Wire*, explained to the Senate in May 2009, "When locally based family-owned newspapers like the *Sun* were consolidated into publicly owned newspaper chains, an essential dynamic, an essential trust between journalism and the community served by that journalism was betrayed. Economically, the disconnect is now obvious. What do newspaper executives in Los Angeles or Chicago care whether readers in Baltimore have a better newspaper, especially when you can make more money putting out a mediocre paper than a worthy one? Where family ownership might have been content with ten or 15 percent profit, the chains demanded double that and more. And the cutting began, long before the threat of new technology was ever sensed." See *Hearing on the Future of Journalism, Senate Committee on Commerce, Science, and Transportation, Subcommittee on Communications, Technology, and the Internet*, 111th Cong. (May 6, 2009, testimony of David Simon).

53. John H. McManus, *Market-Driven Journalism: Let the Citizen Beware?* (Thousand Oaks, CA: Sage, 1994); Penn Kimball, *Downsizing the News: Network Cutbacks in the Nation's Capital* (Washington, DC: Woodrow Wilson International Center for Scholars, 1994); James D. Squires, *Read All About It! The Corporate Takeover of America's Newspapers* (New York: Random House, 1995); and Doug Underwood, *When MBAs Rule the Newsroom: How Marketers and Managers Are Reshaping Today's Media* (New York: Columbia University Press, 1993).

54. David Weaver et al., *The American Journalist in the 21st Century* (Mahwah, NJ: Lawrence Erlbaum Associates, 2007), 3.

55. Paula Constable, "Demise of the Foreign Correspondent," *Washington Post*, Feb. 18, 2007, B1, washingtonpost.com/wp-dyn/content/article/2007/02/16/AR2007021601713_pf.html; and Tom Fenton, *Bad News: The Decline of Reporting, the Business of News, and the Danger to Us All* (New York: HarperCollins, 2005).

56. See, for example, Gene Roberts, ed., *Leaving Readers Behind: The Age of Corporate Newspapering* (Fayetteville: University of Arkansas Press, 2001); William Serrin, ed., *The Business of Journalism: Ten Leading Reporters and Editors on the Perils and Pitfalls of the Press* (New York: The New Press, 2000); and Davis Merritt, *Knight Ridder and How the Erosion of Newspaper Journalism Is Putting Democracy at Risk* (New York: Amacom, 2005).

57. Gilbert Cranberg, Randall Bezanson, and John Soloski, *Taking Stock:*

Journalism and the Publicly Traded Company (Ames: Iowa State University Press, 2001).

58. It was a short step from 2001 to 2011–12, when newspaper and broadcast news media provided the Kardashian family forty times more coverage than it did striking developments in ocean acidification, one of the major impacts of fossil fuel–fired climate disruption. David Helvarg, "The Corporate Media Cares Way More About the Kardashians Than Climate Change," *The Progressive* online, July 11, 2012, progressive.org/corporate_media_climate_change.html.

59. Tom Rosenstiel, Mark Jurkowitz, and Hong Ji, "How Newspapers Are Faring Trying to Build Digital Revenue," Journalism.org, Mar. 5, 2012, journalism.org/analysis_report/search_new_business_model.

60. Alan D. Mutter, "Banner Ads Flop in Consumer-Trust Poll," *Reflections of a Newsosaur*, Apr. 16, 2012, newsosaur.blogspot.com/2012/04/banner-ads-flop-in-consumer-trust-poll .html.

61. Rosenstiel, Jurkowitz, and Ji, "How Newspapers Are Faring."

62. Rick Edmonds, Emily Guskin, and Tom Rosenstiel, "Newspapers: Missed the 2010 Media Rally," in *The State of the News Media 2011: An Annual Report on American Journalism* (Washington, DC: Pew Research Center, Project for Excellence in Journalism, 2011), stateofthemedia.org/2011/newspapers-essay.

63. From Rodney Benson, "American Journalism Between a Rock and a Hard Place: Are Foundations the Solution?" PowerPoint presentation, University of London, Apr. 2, 2012. Benson presented preliminary findings from his forthcoming book, *How Media Ownership Matters* (Oxford, UK: Oxford University Press).

64. The editors, "The Future of News," *New York Observer*, Mar. 21, 2012.

65. There is considerable debate about how much value hedge funds and private equity firms actually produce, and whether they are more parasites than productive players in the economy. One 2012 review of the research concluded: "The truth is that the record of private equity managers is long on cost cutting, amassing debt, and destroying jobs as they enrich themselves, and short on creating jobs, fostering innovation for over the long haul, and paying taxes on the millions they accumulate." See John Miller, "Private Equity Moguls and the Common Good," *Dollars & Sense*, July–Aug. 2012, 10.

66. "Major Trends," in *The State of the News Media 2011: An Annual Report on American Journalism* (Washington, DC: Pew Research Center, Project for Excellence in Journalism, 2011), stateofthemedia.org/2011/overview-2/major-trends.

67. Carr, "Fissures Are Growing."

68. Mutter, "Philly Papers Sold at 10% of 2006 Value."

69. Tanzina Vega, "Study Finds News Sites Fail to Aim Ads at Users," *New York Times*, Feb. 13, 2012, B3.

70. Joseph Turow, *The Daily You: How the New Advertising Industry Is Defining Your Identity and Your Worth* (New Haven, CT: Yale University Press, 2011), 78.

71. Alan D. Mutter, "Four Ways Newspapers Are Failing at Digital," *Reflections of a Newsosaur*, Apr. 11, 2012, newsosaur.blogspot.com/2012/04/four-ways-newspapers-are-failing-at.html.

72. Edmonds, Guskin and Rosenstiel, "Newspapers: Missed the 2010 Media Rally."

73. Russell Adams, "Papers Put Faith in Paywalls," *Wall Street Journal*, Mar. 4, 2012.

74. Matthew Ingram, "Why the Washington Post Will Never Have a Paywall," GigaOM, July 18, 2012, gigaom.com/2012/07/18/why-the-washington-post-will-never-have-a-paywall.

75. "Major Trends," in *State of the News Media 2011*.

76. Jeff Sonderman, "Gannett Says Paywalls Are Generating Strong Revenue, Despite Circulation Declines," Poynter, June 29, 2012, poynter.org/latest-news/mediawire/178778; Steve Myers, "Paywalls Now Affect One-Third of Daily Newspaper Readers," Poynter, July 9, 2012, poynter.org/latest-news/mediawire/180323.

77. Ken Doctor, "The Newsonomics of Paywalls All Over the World," Nieman Journalism Lab, Mar. 8, 2012, niemanlab.org/2012/03/the-newsonomics-of-pay walls-all-over-the-world; and William F. Baker, "A National Paywall That Works: Lessons from Slovakia," *Columbia Journalism Review* online, Feb. 14, 2012, cjr.org/the_news_frontier/a_national_paywall_that_works.php.

78. Staci D. Kramer, "Murdoch's Daily Adds iPhone App; Lower Price, Some Free Stories," paidContent, May 3, 2012, paidcontent.org/2012/05/03/murdochs-daily-adds-iphone-app-lower-price-some-free-stories.

79. "The Daily Lays Off 50 Staffers, Announces Content and Design Changes," *Huffington Post*, July 31, 2012, huffingtonpost.com/2012/07/31/the-daily-lays-off-50-staffers_n_1725334.html; Tom Rosenstiel and Amy Mitchell, "Survey: Mobile News and Paying Online," in *The State of the News Media 2011: An Annual Report on American Journalism* (Washington, DC: Pew Research Center, Project for Excellence in Journalism, 2011).

80. Jeremy W. Peters, "A Newspaper, and a Legacy, Reordered," *New York Times*, Business section, Feb. 12, 2012, 5.

81. Turow, *Daily You*, 87, 89, 127–30, 133.

82. Greg Mitchell e-mail to author, May 21, 2009.

83. Turow, *Daily You*, 135.

84. Ira Boudway, "A Content Farm That Grows Books," *Bloomberg Businessweek*, Oct. 31–Nov. 6, 2011, 45–46.

85. Turow, *Daily You*, 6–7.

86. Olga Kharif, "Taking the Pulse of Neighborhood News," *Bloomberg Businessweek*, Mar. 12–18, 2012, 38–39.

87. Carl Franzen, "Social News Apps Vie for News Readers' Attention," TPM Idea Lab, June 4, 2012, idealab.talkingpointsmemo.com/2012/06/social-news-apps-vie-for-news-readers-attentions.php.

88. Carr, "Fissures Are Growing."

89. Sean Roach, "The Constant Gardener," *Columbia Journalism Review*, Mar.–Apr. 2012, 24–29.

90. Rodney Benson, "Arianna Huffington Meets Citizen Kane," *Le Monde Diplomatique*, May 2011.

91. Tim Rutten, "AOL Hearts HuffPo: The Loser? Journalism," *Los Angeles Times*, Feb. 9, 2011, latimes.com/news/opinion/commentary/la-oe-rutten-column-huffington-aol-20110209,0,7406565.column.

92. Coates et al., *Vocus State of the Media Report 2011* (Vocus), 2, 3, 8.

93. "Obstacles to Change: The Culture Wars," in *The Search for a New Business Model* (Washington, DC: Pew Research Center, Project for Excellence in Journalism, 2012).

94. Michael Wolff, "The Web Is Dead; Long Live the Internet: Who's to Blame? Them," *Wired*, Sept. 2010, 122–27, 166.

95. I am indebted to Hindman for letting me see the prospectus for his forthcoming book, tentatively titled *The Elephant and the Butterfly*. That is where the quotation is from.

96. John Naughton, *What You Really Need to Know About the Internet: From Gutenberg to Zuckerberg* (London: Quercus, 2012), 268–69.

97. Matthew Hindman, *The Myth of Digital Democracy* (Princeton, NJ: Princeton University Press, 2009), 51–54.

98. "News of the World," *The Economist*, Mar. 17, 2012, 73.

99. Rutten, "AOL Hearts HuffPo."

100. Ibid.

101. David Watts Barton, "What I Saw at the Hyperlocal Revolution," *Columbia Journalism Review* online, Nov. 17, 2011, cjr.org/the_news_frontier/what_i_saw_at_the_hyperlocal_revolution.php. There is a crucial problem with all-volunteer-based journalism: volunteers will cover only what they want to cover, and they are accountable to no one. One exchange in particular captured this. When I visited a prominent Midwest university in 2010, a journalism professor disputed my claim that the Internet was not providing a sufficient basis for a new era of journalism. He explained that he and several friends who had been laid off by the local daily newspaper had begun a website where they covered movies, music, restaurants, ballgames, and the art scene in their city. He claimed the coverage was as good as what had been produced by the old media, even at its peak. It was largely a volunteer operation, with revenues from donations and a few micro-ads. I asked this professor how good a job his website did covering the county board meetings, where every now and then crucial zoning issues were decided. "The county board?" he replied. "We don't cover stuff like that. You'd have to pay me." Precisely.

102. The material on Journatic is drawn also from the following pieces: Ryan Smith, "My Adventures in Journatic's New Media Landscape of Outsourced Hyperlocal News," *The Guardian*, July 6, 2012; Michael Miner, "The Burbs' First Look at Journatic," *Chicago Reader* online, Apr. 27, 2012, chicagoreader.com/Bleader/archives/2012/04/27/the-burbs-first-look-at-journatic; Hazel Sheffield, "Journatic Busted for Using Fake Bylines," *Columbia Journalism Review* online, July 6, 2012, cjr.org/behind_the_news/media_start-up_journatic_buste.php; Robert Channick, "Tribune Newsroom Staffers Petition Editor over Use of Journatic," *Chicago Tribune*, July 26, 2012; Anna Tarkov, "Journatic Worker Takes 'This American Life' Inside Outsourced Journalism," Poynter, June 30, 2012, poynter.org/latest-news/top-stories/179555.

103. Hazel Sheffield, "Pasadena Publisher Launches a System for Outsourcing Local News," *Columbia Journalism Review* online, Aug. 27, 2012, cjr.org/behind_the_news/pasadena_publisher_launches_a.php.

104. Buster Brown, "Robo-Journos Put Jobs in Jeopardy," *Huffington Post*, July 19, 2012, huffingtonpost.com/buster-brown/robo-journalism_b_1683564.html. The *Hartford Courant* already runs its entire site through Google Translate to produce its Spanish-language edition. Former *Courant* columnist Bessy Reyna compiled some of the more egregious errors in translation and said, "It would take hours to fix the many problems found in each piece." See Andrew Beaujon, "Hartford Courant's Spanish Site is Google Translate," Poynter, Aug. 17, 2012, poynter.org/latest-news/mediawire/184645.

105. *Information Needs of Communities*, 16.

106. For an account of the approach of a newspaper publisher that would have been regarded as draconian a few years ago but is now hailed as visionary in the move from print to digital, see David Carr, "Newspapers' Digital Apostle," *New York Times*, Nov. 14, 2011, B1, B6.

107. This point is made carefully and convincingly in Diane Ravitch, *The Death and Life of the Great American School System: How Testing and Choice Are Undermining Education* (New York: Basic Books, 2010).

108. For an excellent discussion, see Floyd Norris, "Colleges for Profit Are Growing, With U.S. Aid," *New York Times*, May 25, 2012, B1, B7.

109. These inquiries are covered in McChesney and Nichols, *Death and Life of American Journalism*, especially in the afterword to the paperback edition.

110. Tom Stites, "Layoffs and Cutbacks Lead to a New World of News Deserts," Nieman Journalism Lab, Dec. 8, 2011, niemanlab.org/2011/12/tom-stites-layoffs-and-cutbacks-lead-to-a-new-world-of-news-deserts.

111. John Nichols, *Uprising: How Wisconsin Renewed the Politics of Protest, from Madison to Wall Street* (New York: Nation Books, 2012), 115.

112. For variations on this theme, see Charlie Beckett and James Ball, *WikiLeaks: News in the Networked Era* (Malden, MA: Polity, 2012); and Micah L. Sifry, *WikiLeaks and the Age of Transparency* (Berkeley, CA: Counterpoint, 2011).

113. Heather Brooke, *The Revolution Will Be Digitised: Dispatches from the Information War* (London: Heinemann, 2011), 77–78.

114. Glenn Greenwald, "How the US Government Strikes Fear in Its Own Citizens and People Around the World," speech to the Lannan Foundation, Mar. 8, 2011, published on AlterNet.org, Mar. 21, 2011.

115. See Jane Mayer, "The Secret Sharer: Is Thomas Drake an Enemy of the State?" *New Yorker*, May 23, 2011. See also Patrick B. Pexton, "Leaks Bill: Bad for Journalism, Bad for the Public," *Washington Post*, Aug. 3, 2012.

116. Jay Rosen, "The People Formerly Known as the Audience," in Michael Mandeberg, ed., *The Social Media Reader* (New York. New York University Press, 2012), 13.

117. Hindman, *Myth of Digital Democracy*, 51–54.

118. Rodney Benson, "American Journalism Between a Rock and a Hard Place: Are Foundations the Solution?" PowerPoint presentation, University of London, Apr. 2, 2012. Benson presented preliminary findings from his forthcoming book, *How Media Ownership Matters* (Oxford University Press).

119. It would help matters if the government would do whatever it could to encourage nonprofit news operations. Instead, the Internal Revenue Service regards journalism as a commercial undertaking, and has dragged its heels granting nonprofit status to numerous legitimate start-ups. That makes fundraising far more difficult. Free Press has made this a major organizing campaign. See Ryan Chittum, "Nonprofit News and the Tax Man," *Columbia Journalism Review*, CJR.org, Nov. 17, 2011.

120. Charles Lewis, Brittney Butts, and Kaye Musselwhite, "A Second Look: The New Journalism Ecosystem," Investigative Reporting Workshop, Nov. 30, 2011, investigativereportingworkshop.org/ilab/story/ecosystem.

121. "IRS Policy and the Future of Nonprofit News," Free Press, Apr. 16, 2012, freepress.net/irs.

122. Josh Stearns e-mail to author, May 23, 2012.

123. Eric Newton e-mail to author, May 23, 2012.

124. Eric Newton e-mail to author, May 7, 2012.

125. Carroll Bogert, "Old Hands, New Voice," *Columbia Journalism Review*, Mar.–Apr. 2009, 29–31.

126. Eric Newton e-mail to author, May 23, 2012.

127. The *New York Times* eventually followed up on the CMD's trailblazing ALEC work. See Mike McIntire, "A Conservative Charity's Role as Stealth Business Lobbyist," *New York Times*, Apr. 22, 2012, A1, A18.

128. Christine Haughney, "The Undoing of the Daily," *New York Times*, June 4, 2012, B8.

129. David H. Weaver and G. Cleveland Wilhoit, *The American Journalist in the 1990s: U.S. News People at the End of an Era* (Mahwah, NJ: Lawrence Erlbaum Associates, 1996).

130. Mayur Patel and Michele McLellan, *Getting Local: How Nonprofit News Ventures Seek Sustainability* (Miami: Knight Foundation, October 18, 2011), 6.

131. "Public Broadcasting Revenue Reports," Corporation for Public Broadcasting, cpb.org/stations/reports/revenue.

132. Benson, "American Journalism Between a Rock and a Hard Place." As Benson told me, the *SF Press* also produces a print edition.

133. Charles Lewis, "The Non-Profit Road," *Columbia Journalism Review*, Sept.–Oct. 2007; and Vince Stehle, "It's Time for Newspapers to Become Nonprofit Organizations," *The Chronicle of Philanthropy*, Mar. 18, 2009.

134. "Reporters Without Orders," *The Economist*, June 9, 2012, 64.

135. Ibid., 65.

136. Josh Stearns e-mail to author, May 23, 2012.

137. "Reporters Without Orders," 64.

138. Benson, "American Journalism Between a Rock and a Hard Place."

139. Cited in Michele McLellan, "Emerging Economics of Community Media," in *The State of the News Media 2011: An Annual Report on American Journalism* (Washington, DC: Pew Research Center, Project for Excellence in Journalism, 2011).

140. Eric Newton e-mail to author, May 7, 2012.

141. Cited in McLellan, "Emerging Economics of Community Media."

142. Eric Newton e-mail to author, May 23, 2012.

143. It was striking that in 2012 the Ford Foundation elected to make $1.5 million in donations to the *Los Angeles Times* and the *Washington Post* to support their reporting. It was both an acknowledgment of the immediate crisis commercial journalism faces and the failure of the nonprofit sector to generate suitable replacements. See Andrew Beaujon, "Ford Foundation Gives Washington Post $500,000 Grant for Government-Accountability Reporting," Poynter, July 30, 2012, poynter.org/latest-news/mediawire/183327. One critic wrote, "Ford should focus more on long-term remedies than on plugging short-term gaps in reporting at established newspapers whose publishers should foot the bill for good journalism." See Pablo Eisenberg, "Ford Needs a Smarter Approach to Newspaper Grants," *Chronicle of Philanthropy* online, Aug. 14, 2012, philanthropy.com/article/Ford-Needs-a-Smarter-Approach/133629.

144. Eric Newton e-mail to author, May 7, 2012.

145. Tim de Lisle, "Good Times, Bad Times," *More Intelligent Life*, July–Aug. 2012, 102–11.

146. *Papers of Thomas Jefferson*, vol. 11: 48–49, press-pubs.uchicago.edu/founders/print_documents/amendI_speechs8.html.

147. This issue is dealt with at length in John Nichols and Robert W. McChesney, *Tragedy and Farce: How the American Media Sell Wars, Spin Elections, and Destroy Democracy* (New York: The New Press, 2005).

148. Fittingly, Jefferson and Madison proposed in 1791 that President George Washington name as the first postmaster general the most daring and controversial of our country's pamphleteers, Thomas Paine. It was a radical notion, too radical for Washington, who was ill at ease with Paine's challenges to organized religion, consolidated wealth, and authority in general. This history is covered in detail in McChesney and Nichols, *Death and Life of American Journalism*.

149. Potter Stewart, "Or of the Press," *Yale Law Report* 21, no. 2 (Winter 1974–75): 9–11.

150. Cited in Donald R. Simon, "Big Media: Its Effect on the Marketplace of Ideas and How to Slow the Urge to Merge," *The John Marshall Journal of Computer and Information Law* 20, no. 2 (Winter 2002): 273.

151. Alexis de Tocqueville, *Democracy in America* (1840; New York: Signet Classics, 2001), 93.

152. Richard John e-mail to author, June 2009.

153. Michael Hastings, *The Operators: The Wild and Terrifying Inside Story of America's War in Afghanistan* (New York: Blue Rider Press, 2012), 28.

154. Rodney Benson and Matthew Powers, *Public Media Around the World: International Models for Funding and Protecting Independent Journalism* (Washington, DC: Free Press, 2011), 61.

155. Ibid., 34, 49–53. The French government provides roughly 13 percent of the revenues of the French newspaper industry. The total revenues of the U.S. newspaper industry in 2008 were approximately $48 billion. See data of the Newspaper Association of America, naa.org/TrendsandNumbers.aspx. My estimate does not include the emergency three-year $950 million subsidy the French government made to address the crisis facing French newspapers. On a per capita basis, that would be like the U.S. government making a three-year $5 billion additional subsidy.

156. "Democracy Index 2011: Democracy Under Stress," *The Economist*, Intelligence Unit, pages.eiu.com/rs/eiu2/images/EIU_Democracy_Index_Dec2011.pdf.

157. *Freedom of the Press 2010* (Washington, DC: Freedom House, 2010), freedomhouse.org/report/freedom-press/freedom-press-2010.

158. Two researchers, Edson Tandoc Jr. and Bruno Takahashi, compared the Freedom House data with 2010 Gallup data on countries' happiness and determined that the existence of a vibrant free press system is a reliable indicator of a country's happiness. Tandoc credited it to the watchdog function, "which helps expose corruption at all levels in a community." See Andrew Beaujon, "Study: Happiest Countries Have Press Freedom," Poynter, Aug. 6, 2012, poynter.org/latest-news/mediawire/184146.

159. Between 2009 and 2012, there were sharp cutbacks in support for public broadcasting at the state level, primarily in states where Republicans controlled the government. See Josh Stearns and Mike Soha, *On the Chopping Block: State Budget Battles and the Future of Public Media* (Washington, DC: Free Press, Nov. 2011).

160. Rodney Benson e-mail to author, June 4, 2012.

161. Benson and Powers, *Public Media Around the World*, 9.

162. Rodney Benson e-mail to author, June 4, 2012.

163. Josh Stearns, "Public Television: We're #1," SaveTheNews.com, Feb. 28, 2012. Stearns chronicles the polling data that repeatedly demonstrates that Americans rank public media among the two or three most popular uses of federal funds.

164. Reporters Without Borders, *2011–2012 World Press Freedom Index*, Jan. 25, 2012, en.rsf.org/IMG/CLASSEMENT_2012/C_GENERAL_ANG.pdf.

165. James Curran, Shanto Iyengar, Anker Brink Lund, and Inka Salovaara-Moring, "Media System, Public Knowledge, and Democracy: A Comparative Study," *European Journal of Communication* 24, no. 1 (2009): 5–26.

166. Stephen Cushion, *The Democratic Value of News: Why Public Service Media Matters* (forthcoming in 2013).

167. Benson and Powers, *Public Media Around the World*, 34, 49–53.

168. Rodney Benson, "Public Funding and Journalistic Independence: What

Does the Research Tell Us?" in McChesney and Pickard, eds., *Will the Last Reporter Please Turn Out the Lights*, 314–19.

169. Peter Preston in Britain's *The Observer* notes that commercial journalism is "draining away," and that without "those 19,000 reporters, writers and photographers" in our print news media, "news provision would shrink drastically." He continues, "Suddenly the derided licence fee [for the BBC] doesn't look on its last legs at all, more the only means of keeping a key news resource in being." See Peter Preston, "Without Print's News Gatherers, Plurality Becomes Academic," *The Observer*, July 8, 2012, 44.

170. See, for example, Nick Davies, *Flat Earth News* (London: Vintage, 2008); and Jay G. Blumler and Stephen Coleman, "Political Communication in Freefall: The British Case—and Others?" *International Journal of Press/Politics* 15, no. 2 (2010): 139–54. See also Miguel-Anxo Murado, "Spain's Cowardly Purge of the Journalists Who Ask Difficult Questions," *The Guardian*, Aug. 7, 2012, guardian.co.uk/commentisfree/2012/aug/07/spain-purge-journalists-government-votes.

171. James Carey, "American Journalism on, Before, and After September 11," in Barbie Zelizer and Stuart Allan, eds., *Journalism After September 11* (New York: Routledge, 2002), 89.

172. Bruce Ackerman has developed his own voucher proposal. See Bruce Ackerman, "One Click Away: The Case for the Internet News Voucher," in McChesney and Pickard, eds., *Will the Last Reporter Please Turn Out the Lights*, chap. 28.

173. Bill Grueskin, Ava Seaves, and Lucas Graves, *The Story So Far: What We Know About the Business of Digital Journalism* (New York: Columbia Journalism School, 2011).

174. Todd Gitlin, "A Surfeit of Crises: Circulation, Revenue, Attention, Authority, and Deference," in McChesney and Pickard, eds., *Will the Last Reporter Please Turn Out the Lights*, 101.

7. Revolution in the Digital Revolution?

1. This point was made elegantly in a *New York Times* editorial. See "The End of Privacy?" *New York Times*, July 14, 2012.

2. This point was developed brilliantly in Robert Heilbroner, *The Nature and Logic of Capitalism* (New York: W.W. Norton, 1985).

3. This section draws on John Bellamy Foster, Brett Clark, and Richard York, *The Ecological Rift* (New York: Monthly Review Press, 2010), 53–72.

4. Adam Smith, *The Wealth of Nations* (1776; New York: Modern Library, 1937), 173.

5. The findings come from a 2012 survey commissioned by Good Technology and conducted by OnePoll in May 2012. "Good Technology Survey Reveals Americans Are Working More, But on Their Own Schedule," July 2, 2012, good.com/news/press-releases/current-press-releases/161009045.html. See also Ina Fried, "Mobile Technology Frees Workers to Work Any 20 Hours a Day They Choose," *AllThingsD*, July 2, 2012, allthingsd.com/20120702/mobile-technology-frees-workers-to-work-any-20-hours-a-day-they-choose.

6. Joseph E. Stiglitz, "Introduction: The World Wakes," in Anya Schiffrin and Eamon Kircher-Allen, eds., *From Cairo to Wall Street: Voices from the Global Spring* (New York: The New Press, 2012), 2.

7. Jeffrey D. Sachs, foreword, Schiffrin and Kircher-Allen, eds., *From Cairo to Wall Street*, xvi.

8. Stiglitz, "Introduction: The World Wakes," in Schiffrin and Kircher-Allen, eds., *From Cairo to Wall Street*, 1. See also Immanuel Wallerstein, "Structural Crisis in the World-System," *Monthly Review*, Mar. 2011, 13–39.

9. Paul Krugman, *End This Depression Now!* (New York: W.W. Norton, 2012).

10. Catherine Rampell, "More Young Americans out of High School Are Also out of Work," *New York Times*, June 6, 2012, B1.

11. John Vidal, "Civilisation Faces 'Perfect Storm of Ecological and Social Problems,' " *The Guardian*, Feb. 20, 2012. The evidence keeps pouring in that the ecological crisis is more severe than even many scientists had thought. See Justin Gillis, "Study Finds More of Earth Is Hotter and Says Global Warming Is at Work," *New York Times*, Aug. 7, 2012, A13. Tragically, due to the massive public relations campaign to discredit concerns about climate change, fewer Americans in 2012 appreciate the dimensions of the problem compared to a decade earlier. See James Lawrence Powell, *The Inquisition of Climate Science* (New York: Columbia University Press, 2011).

12. David Brooks, "The Structural Revolution," *New York Times*, May 8, 2012, A23; and Edward Luce, *Time to Start Thinking: America in the Age of Descent* (New York: Atlantic Monthly Press, 2012).

13. Richard Wolff, *Democracy at Work: A Cure for Capitalism* (Chicago: Haymarket, 2012), introduction.

14. See Charles H. Ferguson, *Predator Nation: Corporate Criminals, Political Corruption, and the Hijacking of America* (New York: Crown Business, 2012).

15. The best research to date on the effect of the digital revolution and information technology on economic growth, compared to the role of major technologies in earlier eras, concludes that information technology is nowhere near as powerful a source for growth as the automobile or earlier major technological innovations. The technological impetus to investment and prosperity, which is a significant factor in economic growth in the history of industrial capitalism, has petered out. Therefore, the prospects for achieving the sort of economic growth traditionally associated with a healthy capitalist economy appear unlikely going forward. See Robert J. Gordon, "Is U.S. Economic Growth Over? Faltering Innovation Confronts the Six Headwinds," Working Paper #18315, National Bureau of Economic Research, Aug. 2012, nber.org/papers/w18315.

16. Compustat North America, Fundamentals Annual; Wharton Research Data Services (WRDS), University of Pennsylvania (retrieved June 4, 2012).

17. Andrew J. Sherman, *Harvesting Intangible Assets* (New York: Amacom, 2012), xi.

18. Peter H. Diamandis and Steven Kotler, *Abundance: The Future Is Better Than You Think* (New York: The Free Press, 2012), 9.

19. Erik Brynjolfsson and Andrew McAfee, *Race Against the Machine* (Lexington, MA: Digital Frontier Press, 2011), 76.

20. Jeremy Rifkin was on to this at the beginning of the digital era. See Jeremy Rifkin, *The End of Work: The Decline of the Global Labor Force and the Dawn of the Post-Market Era* (New York: G.P. Putnam's Sons, 1995). A recent book that takes a hard look at the revolutionary potential of technology for manufacturing is Peter Marsh, *The New Industrial Revolution: Consumers, Globalization and the End of Mass Production* (New Haven, CT: Yale University Press, 2012).

21. There are others who make a similar argument, from a variety of political perspectives. See, for example, Moulier Boutang, *Cognitive Capitalism*, trans. Ed Emery (Malden, MA: Polity, 2011), first published in French in 2008. For a critical

take on the matter, see Luis Suarez-Villa, *Technocapitalism* (Philadelphia: Temple University Press, 2009).

22. Karl Marx and Friedrich Engels, *The Communist Manifesto* (1848; New York: Monthly Review Press, 1964), 10–11.

23. Paul A. Baran and Paul M. Sweezy, "Some Theoretical Implications," *Monthly Review*, July–Aug. 2012, 26–27. This essay was unpublished until 2012; it was originally written for inclusion in their book *Monopoly Capital* (New York: Monthly Review Press, 1966) but was not approved by both authors before Baran's untimely death in 1964.

24. The United States produces nearly 25 percent greater output than it did in 1999 with the same number of workers, but real wages have been stagnant or declined. See David J. Lynch, "Did That Robot Take My Job?" *Bloomberg Businessweek*, Jan. 9–15, 2012, 15.

25. See John Markoff, "Skilled Work, Without the Worker," *New York Times*, Aug. 19, 2012, A1.

26. For a moving account of the deterioration of American life and specifically the growth of poverty among the working class, see Chris Hedges and Joe Sacco, *Days of Destruction, Days of Revolt* (New York: Nation Books, 2012).

27. Moira Herbst, "Where Are the US Jobs? Ask the Corporate Cash Hoarders," *The Guardian*, Aug. 5, 2012.

28. Stiglitz, "Introduction: The World Wakes," in Schiffrin and Kircher-Allen, eds., *From Cairo to Wall Street*, 16.

29. Joseph E. Stiglitz, *The Price of Inequality: How Today's Divided Society Endangers Our Future* (New York: W.W. Norton, 2012), 32.

30. Eduardo Porter, "The Spreading Scourge of Corporate Corruption," *New York Times*, July 11, 2012, B1, B5. Glenn Greenwald assesses the sharp decline of the rule of law in the United States in Glenn Greenwald, *With Liberty and Justice for Some: How the Law Is Used to Destroy Equality and Protect the Powerful* (New York: Metropolitan Books, 2011). The point was underlined by the release of a 2012 report conducted by the former chief economist at McKinsey that found the global elite had stashed $21 trillion in foreign bank accounts to avoid taxation in their home countries. The United States was well represented. It can only make those who play by the rules feel like chumps. See Heather Stewart, "£13tn Hoard Hidden from Taxman by Global Elite," *The Guardian*, July 21, 2012.

31. For a discussion of this issue, see Morris Berman, *Why America Failed: The Roots of Imperial Decline* (Hoboken, NJ: Wiley, 2012), 59–62.

32. Bob Herbert, "Risking the Future," *New York Times*, Feb. 2, 2009.

33. American Society of Civil Engineers, Infrastructure Report Card, infrastructurereportcard.org.

34. "A Patch on the Road," *The Economist*, July 7, 2012, 34.

35. E.J. Dionne, "America Needs a Better Ruling Class," *Washington Herald News*, Apr. 17, 2011. heraldnews.com/opinions/columnists/x1225326175/E-J-DIONNE-America-needs-a-better-ruling-class.

36. Stiglitz, *Price of Inequality*, chap. 12; Robert Pollin, *Back to Full Employment* (Cambridge, MA: MIT Press, 2012).

37. Michal Kalecki, "Political Aspects of Full Employment," in *Selected Essays on the Dynamics of the Capitalist Economy* (Cambridge, UK: Cambridge University Press, 1970), 139.

38. Krugman, *End This Depression Now!*, 94–95.

39. The great irony for those economists (and activists) who believe capitalism

can be reformed and want to reform it along New Deal or social democratic lines is that by swearing a loyalty oath to capitalism, they encourage their own irrelevance. Societies that have enacted sweeping progressive reforms of capitalism—from the modest New Deal in the United States to the more sweeping changes in northern Europe—did so because those in power were scared that unless they enacted reforms, far worse could happen. Even if one's goal is simply to reform capitalism, it is politically valuable to support radical criticism of capitalism, and support anticapitalist movements, to get the attention of those in power.

40. "A Third Industrial Revolution," *The Economist*, Apr. 21, 2012. For a particularly nice discussion of this, see Juliet B. Schor, *Plenitude: The New Economics of True Wealth* (New York: Penguin Press, 2010), chap. 4.

41. Jerry Mander, *The Capitalist Papers: Fatal Flaws of an Obsolete System* (Berkeley, CA: Counterpoint, 2012), 3, 4.

42. Ibid., 11.

43. James Robbin, "Free Market Flawed, Says Survey," *BBC News*, Nov. 9, 2009, news.bbc.co.uk/2/hi/8347409.stm.

44. "New Poll: Socialism Is Gaining Popularity in America," *Cleveland Leader*, Apr. 9, 2009, clevelandleader.com/node/9655.

45. See John Maynard Keynes, "Economic Possibilities for Our Grandchildren," in *Essays in Persuasion* (New York: W.W. Norton, 1963), 358–73. The essay was first published in 1930.

46. John Maynard Keynes, "National Self-Sufficiency," *Yale Review* 22 (1933): 761.

47. Christopher Hayes, *Twilight of the Elites: America After Meritocracy* (New York: Crown, 2012), 239.

48. Schor, *Plenitude*; Wolff, *Democracy at Work*; Gar Alperovitz, *America Beyond Capitalism: Reclaiming Our Wealth, Our Liberty, and Our Democracy*, 2d ed. (Boston: Democracy Collaborative Press, 2011); Richard Wolff in conversation with David Barsamian, *Occupy the Economy: Challenging Capitalism* (San Francisco: City Lights Books, 2012). Perhaps the best treatment of the subject is found in Wolff, *Democracy at Work*.

49. Yochai Benkler, *The Penguin and the Leviathan: How Cooperation Triumphs over Self-Interest* (New York: Crown Business, 2011).

50. Jeffrey D. Sachs, foreword, in Schiffrin and Kircher-Allen, eds., *From Cairo to Wall Street*, xvii.

51. Hayes, *Twilight of the Elites*, 238.

INDEX

Celebrating Independent Publishing

Thank you for reading this book published by The New Press. The New Press is a nonprofit, public interest publisher. New Press books and authors play a crucial role in sparking conversations about the key political and social issues of our day.

We hope you enjoyed this book and that you will stay in touch with The New Press. Here are a few ways to stay up to date with our books, events, and the issues we cover:

- Sign up at www.thenewpress.com/subscribe to receive updates on New Press authors and issues and to be notified about local events
- Like us on Facebook: www.facebook.com/newpressbooks
- Follow us on Twitter: www.twitter.com/thenewpress

Please consider buying New Press books for yourself; for friends and family; or to donate to schools, libraries, community centers, prison libraries, and other organizations involved with the issues our authors write about.

The New Press is a 501(c)(3) nonprofit organization. You can also support our work with a tax-deductible gift by visiting www.thenewpress.com/donate.